LIFFE: A Market and its Makers

LIFFE: A Market and its Makers

David Kynaston

GRANTA EDITIONS

© London International Financial Futures and Options Exchange, 1997
Cannon Bridge, London EC4R 3XX, United Kingdom

Published by Granta Editions
25–27 High Street, Chesterton, Cambridge CB4 1ND,
United Kingdom.

*Granta Editions is a wholly owned imprint
of Book Production Consultants plc*

First published in 1997

A CIP catalogue record for this book is available from the British Library.

ISBN 1 85757 056 1

Frontispiece: Bill Jacklin's depiction of the LIFFE trading floor in 1988,
now hanging in the Bank of England.

Designed by Mary Luckhurst
Design, editorial and production in association with
Book Production Consultants plc, 25–27 High Street, Chesterton,
Cambridge CB4 1ND, United Kingdom
Reprographics in Great Britain by Jade Reprographics, Braintree, Essex
Printed in Great Britain by Butler & Tanner Ltd, Frome and London.

Contents

Preface

I WAS INTRIGUED as well as pleased to be asked to write LIFFE's history. I was aware that it had been one of the City of London's great success stories since its start in 1982, but otherwise knew very little about it – an ignorance, I soon discovered, shared by many others. In the course of a summer's research, two things shaped my thinking about this book. One was the welcome discovery that LIFFE's culture is essentially open, outward-looking and, for want of a better word, non-neurotic. The other was a series of strokes of good fortune, as I came across wholly unsuspected archival resources for the 1980s. Together, these two developments meant that I felt I had the opportunity to write 'real' history, even for such a recent period. It is an opportunity that I have attempted to take, with the full backing of LIFFE's current Chairman, Jack Wigglesworth. Contemporary history has its pitfalls, and I am sure I have fallen into many of them, but I have tried my best to write a full and honest account of the story of a remarkable market.

David Kynaston

DAVID KYNASTON
London
30 September 1996

Foreword

by Jack Wigglesworth

THIS IS A remarkable book. But of course, it is a remarkable story. Looking back the relatively short time to the late 1970s, it is difficult to believe how different the City of London and the UK's financial services sector then were. At the personal level it is seen in the change from bowler hats, stiff collars and furled umbrellas – a rigid uniform for the previous half century – to the casual dress of the highly paid young experts, now including many more women, in exotic options and structured products. These were instruments unheard of before the explosive growth of derivatives from the mid-1980s onwards; and of course, modern City dress is epitomised by the coloured jackets of LIFFE traders at Cannon Bridge and Commodity Quay.

At the institutional level there has been the radical change from the strict demarcation of the services that could be offered by companies and firms in the many, narrowly defined professions. Just as with ethics in general in societies, where there are long-term cyclical swings from one extreme to the other, as a result of events earlier in the century you were only allowed to use banks to borrow or deposit money, insurance companies for insurance, stockbrokers to buy or sell securities, and so on. Stockbroking firms were not allowed to have the conflict of interest of owning securities themselves. This was the market-making role of jobbers, who were not allowed to deal with the public. There were also building societies, money brokers, discount houses, commodity brokers, merchant banks – each category prevented from offering the services of, or owning, the others.

Three main pressures lay behind the breakdown of these rigid divisions: technological developments, particularly in global communications; the turmoil of floating exchange rates following the demise in the early 1970s of the Bretton Woods fixed exchange rate regime; and the competitive threat to the London securities industry that ensued from the deregulation of the US securities markets. Globalisation had to come. The predominantly Germanic names of London merchant banks are evidence of a previous age of deregulation; and, significantly, the recent recapitalisation of that sector has come from German and Dutch sources. All these different services can now be had under one roof in the vast international conglomerate investment banking groups.

LIFFE itself was a major catalyst in the deregulation of the City, remembered most vividly by Big Bang in 1986. Participation in the new financial futures market was invited from all the functionally separated businesses. There was no rule to stop them all joining the new exchange. LIFFE is the symbol of the new age in the City.

It seems so easy now. LIFFE has left its European competition behind and is challenging the mighty Chicago exchanges for world leadership. In London, LIFFE proudly takes its place as one of the two great securities exchanges and one of the institutions that underpins London as the pre-eminent international centre for trading commodity and financial instruments.

It did not always look so easy. It certainly did not always seem so obvious that LIFFE could succeed so spectacularly.

Those of us who were there are only too aware of this. As one of the members of the first working party, I know how true David Kynaston's description of the early difficulties is. The questions to be answered could have seemed intractable. What contracts to launch? What clearing arrangements? What relationship with the Stock Exchange? How to convince a cautious Bank? What specification for the gilt contract? Could we ever launch at all?

I am proud to have been one of those pushing forwards, sometimes it seemed against a strong and resistant tide. Like all of us who were part of the first team, I know what we owed to the drive and determination of our captain, John Barkshire. As is clearly chronicled in this book, his vision and commitment did not waver. We at LIFFE owe a lot to him.

The story of how bright young people, free from restrictive practices, could make a success of exchange-traded futures and options in London has been captured in this book. LIFFE was designed by its founding fathers very deliberately to be totally transparent in terms of price formation and dealings, truly international in terms of its products and members; to be run by a highly qualified team of executives, backed by a board and committees made up mainly of young executives running the businesses of the member firms; and to take advantage of the robust system encompassing instruments which are highly liquid proxies for whole markets, inexpensive to deal in, marked to market and cleared every day by a clearing house whose integrity is beyond question. Attention to detail in the products, procedures, surveillance, audit trails and other world-beating computer systems has been the key to this success. Like marriage, the governance of an exchange, owned by hundreds of members, has to be worked at, to prevent any clique of powerful, privileged members from dominating and beginning to obfuscate the inner workings in order to gain advantages over other members.

After our launch the next fifteen years were not always an untroubled sequence of successes. The book is direct and honest about our mistakes. Some may, indeed, be shocked by the access that David Kynaston has had to LIFFE's archives – quoting Board meeting minutes right up to 1996.

I have always been clear about this. LIFFE is a highly transparent market. Subjecting practices to direct sunlight is the best way of keeping a well-regulated market. Our tradition is openness. Our attitudes to our history must be the same.

The result is not always comfortable. The reader will discover that not everyone supported our successful decisions. Not even the launch of the German Government Bond was universally endorsed. Yet this proved a critical milestone in LIFFE's history. At the time suffering a pause in its growth, and threatened by its French competitor MATIF, LIFFE took a giant decision. In the following years it left behind the European league of derivatives exchanges and played in the world league. This league had previously contained only Chicago-based exchanges. Now LIFFE is the only non-Chicago player in it.

Our owners are predominantly Continental European, British, United States and Japanese businesses turning over £165 thousand million a day in the money market, bond, equity index and traded options, agricultural and soft commodity products of seven major currencies, some of which instruments will settle against Euro interest rates if EMU goes ahead. Our links with exchanges in other time zones mean that we can offer instruments for our global members and their international customers in the three major currency blocs, as well as having our own European currency instruments trade in other time zones.

What may come as a surprise to many readers is the real economic value created by LIFFE. This book explains what the market is for. It provides financial security. It enables banks and financial institutions to provide that to their customers. A corporate treasurer does not want to find that an investment programme funded by borrowing becomes unprofitable if interest rates rise. Nor does he or she want to employ an economics intelligence unit to forecast the movements of interest rates or asset prices. Instead, this treasurer seeks security – perhaps from a bank, perhaps by trading financial futures directly on LIFFE. This way interest rates can be fixed, investment programmes protected and jobs made secure. Indeed, there are more investments and more jobs as a result.

The same principles apply to small businesses, whose owners wish to escape from overdraft finance and use fixed-rate finance instead. Individuals like to fix their mortgage rates. Banks and other financial institutions can offer their customers these services by offsetting their own risks on LIFFE. The risks are taken on by speculators – who take long or short term views and trade on them.

For savers, as well as borrowers, LIFFE provides opportunities. Pension funds can protect their portfolios. Even individuals can insure against falls in individual stocks. Financial institutions have used LIFFE as the basis for new savings vehicles.

This is the real story of LIFFE. The colour of the trading floor is unique. The action that is very visible and the fierce personalised trading is fascinating. It is, nevertheless, just part of the picture. Underlying the frenzied activity are individuals. Those individuals are buying their homes, seeking security in their jobs, building small businesses and saving for their pensions. They can be more secure in their jobs, richer in retirement and more hopeful of their futures because of LIFFE.

We have been very fortunate to secure the services of David Kynaston to tell our story. David is a professional historian who has established a reputation for writing the history of City institutions. As the last member of the working party which created LIFFE still to be involved in the governance of the Exchange, I am keen to have the story recorded, warts and all. In particular I am determined that the indispensable role of John Barkshire, without whose enthusiasm and drive LIFFE would not have got off the ground, should be properly acknowledged.

JACK WIGGLESWORTH
Chairman of LIFFE
February 1997

Abbreviations

AFBD	Association of Futures Brokers and Dealers	LIFFE	London International Financial Futures Exchange; from March 1992 the London International Financial Futures and Options Exchange
AIBD	Association of International Bond Dealers		
APT	Automated Pit Trading	LIT	London Investment Trust
APT+	APT Options Trading System	LME	London Metal Exchange
BNP	Banque Nationale de Paris	LOTS	LIFFE Order Transit System
BOTCC	Board of Trade Clearing Corporation	LTOM	London Traded Options Market
BTP	Buoni del Tesoro Poliennali	MATIF	Marché à Terme Instruments Financières (The French Financial Futures Market); latterly Marché à Terme Internationale de France
CBOE	Chicago Board Options Exchange		
CBOT	Chicago Board of Trade		
CD	Certificate of Deposit		
CFTC	Commodity Futures Trading Commission	MEFF	Meff Renta Fija (The Spanish Financial Futures Market) and Meff Renta Variable (The Spanish Equity Derivatives Market)
CMAC	Corporate Merger Advisory Committee		
CMC	Clearing Member Committee		
CME	Chicago Mercantile Exchange (the Merc)	MIF	Mercado Italiano Futures (The Italian Financial Futures Market)
CPS	Clearing Processing System	MMs	Market Makers
CSFB	Credit Suisse First Boston	NAPF	National Association of Pension Funds
DTB	Deutsche Terminbörse (Goffex)		
EASy	Exchange Access System	NYFE	New York Futures Exchange
EOE	European Options Exchange	OM	Stockholm Options Market
EPT	Ex-pit Transaction	OMLX	London Securities and Derivatives Exchange
ERM	Exchange Rate Mechanism		
FBA	Futures Brokers' Association	OTC	Over the Counter
FOW	*Futures and Options World*	PHLX	Philadelphia Stock Exchange
FRS	Futures Reporting System	SBC	Swiss Bank Corporation
FSA	Financial Services Act	SEAQ	Stock Exchange Automated Quotation System
FSE	Frankfurt Stock Exchange		
FX	Foreign Exchange	SEC	Securities and Exchange Commission
GGB	German Government Bond		
GLOBEX	Global Exchange	SFA	Securities and Futures Authority
GNI	Gerrard & National Intercommodities	SFE	Sydney Futures Exchange
		SIB	Securities and Investments Board
GOFFEX	German Options and Financial Futures Exchange	SIMEX	Singapore International Monetary Exchange
GRE	Guardian Royal Exchange	SOFFEX	Swiss Options and Financial Futures Exchange
ICCH	International Commodities Clearing House		
		SPAN	Standard Portfolio Analysis of Risk
IDB	Inter-Dealer Broker		
IFR	*International Financing Review*	SROs	Self-regulatory Organisations
IMM	International Monetary Market	T-Bill	Treasury Bill
JEC	Joint Exchanges Committee	T-Bond	Treasury Bond
JGB	Japanese Government Bond	TIFFE	Tokyo International Financial Futures Exchange
LCE	London Commodity Exchange		
LCH	London Clearing House	TRS	Trade Registration System
LDE	London Derivatives Exchange	TSA	The Securities Association
LFOM	London Futures and Options Market	TSE	Tokyo Stock Exchange
		UBS	Union Bank of Switzerland
LIBOR	London Inter-Bank Offered Rate	UDT	United Dominions Trust

Prologue

The Chicago Model

L IFFE, FOR ALL its youthfulness, has antecedents going back to the middle
of the nineteenth century. In 1848, the year after the electric telegraph had
been invented, the Chicago Board of Trade [CBOT] was established. It
quickly became the premier grain market in the United States and
indeed the world. It was a market that made increasingly sophisticated use of
telegraphic communication (far faster than anything the world had previously
seen); it developed a standard grading system that made redundant the need for
grain dealers to send and inspect samples of particular shipments; and during the
Civil War it responded to the enormous speculation in oats and pork (the staples
of the Union Army) by instituting in 1865 recognisably modern futures contracts.
Within ten years Chicago's cash grain business, in other words for grain physically
present in Chicago, was running at some $200 million a year; but its trade in
futures – that is, in contracts for the *future* delivery of grain – at some $2 billion.
By the 1880s the differential between the two markets was even greater. Put
another way, the Chicago grain market had become no longer a market in grain
itself but instead a market in the *price* of grain. The grain itself might not yet exist,
but buyers and sellers could secure a price, and speculators could try to guess
correctly whether that price would rise or fall.

The CBOT may or may not have pioneered commodity futures – the
Liverpool Cotton Brokers' Association and the New York Cotton Market each
have plausible claims – but the crucial point is that by the last quarter of the
nineteenth century these markets existed, offering not only a new form of risk
management (as pursued by the hedgers in the market) but also rich speculative
possibilities. Of course, commodity merchants and others had practised *forward*
trading through the ages, seeking to mitigate the uncertainties of weather, harvests
and so on, but futures trading in commodities was fundamentally different – in
two crucial respects. Firstly, whereas forward trading had involved individually
negotiated contracts, futures trading was based on *standardised* contracts.
Secondly, the existence in futures trading of an acceptable third party – the clearing
house – which not only settled contracts but also assumed counterparty risk meant
that, unlike in forward trading, there was no need for mutual familiarity between
the two parties doing the actual trading. In short, futures trading took place on
organised exchanges backed by a clearing house, thereby largely removing credit
risk; and (in the words of David Courtney, in his historical survey of commodity
trading) these new-fangled markets were 'claimed to be "perfect" by many
economists', being places in which 'buyers and sellers are brought together in an
environment where everyone present is simultaneously aware of prevailing prices
and is free to trade there'. Hedgers could hedge, speculators could speculate, and

apart from the occasional disagreeable attempted corner, usually by a syndicate, all was apparently for the best – not least for farmers, who at last could achieve certainty in prices without government control.

With its somewhat conservative streak, however, the City of London took a certain amount of convincing. Was dealing in commodity futures an incitement to rash speculation? Or was it merely a sensible way of hedging one's bets in what was often a fluctuating market? The London Metal Exchange was established in 1882, but six years later the debate took a sharp turn in the context of a proposed clearing house in London for coffee and sugar – a proposal from which some of Mincing Lane's leading broking and merchanting firms withdrew their initial support. However, the new venture had the support of several merchant banks, while from Mincing Lane itself the deputy chairman was the leading sugar broker-cum-merchant, Julius Caesar Czarnikow, who was largely responsible for recruiting staff from Hamburg and knew the ways of that city's produce clearing

Sketches of the London Commercial Sale Rooms in Mincing Lane in the nineteenth century.

house. Operations began on 1 May 1888, and in its first year the London Produce Clearing House (direct forerunner of the modern London Clearing House) cleared transactions in 2.26m bags of coffee and 1.27m bags of sugar. Those remained the staples, but in ensuing years it introduced contracts for futures dealing and settlement in a host of other soft commodities, including pepper, raw silk, indigo and tea.

Over the next three-quarters of a century or so, London's futures markets enjoyed a chequered record. The two world wars were hugely damaging (involving government controls, loss of markets, and destruction of human as well as physical capital), but from the 1950s something of a revival was staged. Some markets disappointed, such as cotton, wheat and wool, but others largely flourished, such as copper and the metals markets generally, under the continuing umbrella of the London Metal Exchange. By the mid-1970s, partly fuelled by the boom in commodity prices, London's futures transactions were contributing some £100–200m annually to UK invisible earnings. Even so, if anyone had been asked at the time, or indeed during much of the twentieth century, where the most powerful, high-volume commodity futures markets resided, the answer could only have been one place: Chicago.

In that windy city the two great futures exchanges – the CBOT and the Chicago Mercantile Exchange – battled it out. The latter, known now as the Merc or CME, had been founded in 1898 as the Butter and Egg Board before being renamed in 1919. Grain and oilseed remained for a long time the CBOT's staples, while the CME traded contracts that eventually would include cheese, lumber and potatoes as well as butter and eggs. Whereas the London futures markets were almost entirely professional, discouraging retail business and organised around firms rather than individual traders, the Chicago approach was very different. Traders largely traded for themselves and the American public – that legendary dentist in Iowa – was more than welcome to trade also. By the beginning of the 1960s both exchanges seemed to be running out of steam; but a range of new contracts through the decade, including in live cattle, frozen pork bellies and plywood, resulted in volume increasing more than threefold, up by 1970 to 13.6 million contracts, with the term referring in this sense to the standard unit of trading in futures markets. 'Trading in live beef futures conjured up romantic images of Old West cattle drives and cowboys,' a CME vice president would recall, adding that 'people who bought cattle futures felt just like the cattle barons'; while according to a trader who in 1967 left the more staid CBOT in order to trade pork bellies down the road, 'the Merc's reputation was green eye shades and sleeve garters'. A Chicago myth, already potent, was becoming irresistible – albeit some outsiders, unhappy about the continuing existence of trading cliques and price manipulation despite the Commodity Exchange Act that from 1936 had made manipulation a felony, preferred to describe the Merc as 'the Whorehouse of the Loop'.

Two crucial things happened in the early 1970s. Both were directly attributable to Leo Melamed, chairman of the CME from 1969 and one of those rare financial figures who have managed to combine the instincts of a visionary with those of a born trader. Firstly, he took determined steps to clean up the marketplace, in particular ensuring that corners became almost a thing of the past. Secondly, and of still greater significance, he pioneered a futures market in currencies, following the collapse of the post-war Bretton Woods system of fixed exchange rates that had tied the whole world to the US dollar, redeemable at the rate of $35 to one ounce of gold. The palpable break-up, after years of increasing strain now intensified by the impact of the Vietnam War on the American economy, began in the summer of 1971: such was the flight of international funds out of the dollar that several currencies were revalued or (in the case of the deutschmark) floated; and in August the US left the gold standard. Seizing the moment, Melamed asked the already legendary Chicago economist Milton Friedman to write a paper assessing the desirability of a market that would enable the hedging of currency fluctuation risk. Friedman, with his strong free market sympathies, gladly agreed, for a fee of $5000.

On 13 December the world's finance ministers tried to put together a new system of fixed exchange rates but, even with an expanded leeway permitted for other currencies to fluctuate against the dollar, it was soon clear that world-wide fixed exchange rates were no longer appropriate for a world of rapid economic shocks. On the 20th, a week after the Smithsonian Agreement, the CME announced that it would be setting up a new exchange, to be called the International Monetary Market [IMM], that would trade seven contracts against the US dollar: British pounds, Canadian dollars, German marks, Italian lira, Japanese yen, Mexican pesos and Swiss francs. Quotations from Friedman's 11-page paper – unequivocally called 'The Need for Futures Markets in Currencies' – were freely sprinkled in the accompanying press release. 'Its development here,' Friedman wrote about the putative exchange, 'will encourage the growth of other financial activities in this country, providing both additional income from export of services and easing the problem of executing monetary policy.' Or as he would recall a decade and a half later, what made a financial futures market possible was 'the shift from a commodity [i.e. gold] to a paper-money standard; the fact that there was no longer an anchor for foreign exchange. And without an anchor we shortly had inflation and price

Opposite: The floor of the Chicago Mercantile Exchange in 1921.

Leo Melamed in action in 1969.

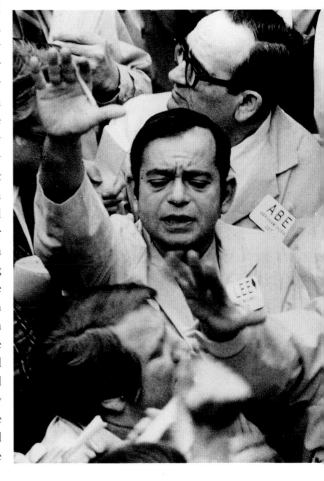

uncertainty.' The purpose of a futures market is to control uncertainty as well as to profit from it, and Chicago in 1971 appreciated before anywhere else that much of the world's uncertainty was now going to be specifically financial.

The prospective new market received invaluable support from the four major Chicago banks, but when Melamed went to court Wall Street the responses of the leading bankers there varied from incomprehension to outright hostility. One reputedly asked him if he had escaped from a mental institution. Nor were Europe's bankers any more enthusiastic. 'The extension of a futures market in certain foreign currencies could no doubt be of interest to small individual investors,' Edmund de Rothschild of the London house conceded to Melamed, before going on to state politely but flatly that 'as you are aware, there is a very highly sophisticated international market for foreign exchange operations in which the major banks of the world participate' and 'banks are, therefore, able to offer their customers all the requisite services for futures trading in the major currencies'. On these grounds he declined to attend a conference being organised by the IMM in February. There was also little help from the press. 'The New Currency Market: Strictly for Crapshooters' was the headline of a piece in *Business Week* that was published in April, shortly before the exchange was due to open on 16 May 1972; and it took the unfriendly line that 'if you fancy yourself an international money speculator but lack the resources ... your day has come'. On opening day itself a less than amiable story on the front page of the *Wall Street Journal*, headlined 'New Game in Town', quoted a New York foreign exchange dealer: 'I'm amazed that a bunch of crapshooters in pork bellies have the temerity to think that they can beat some of the world's most sophisticated traders at their own game.'

Inevitably there was a strong element of turf wars involved, but Melamed in his memoirs almost a quarter of a century later valuably recalled the larger social context:

Long before the major devaluation by the Bank of England in the late 1960s, it had become common in government circles to blame major currency changes on pressures caused by speculators. Speculators in general never have had much of a favorable image in the world of finance, and the genre money speculators were considered the worst of the breed. The speculator was pictured as those sleazy-looking characters who lurked about the financial centers of London, Zurich and Frankfurt selling a pound here and a dollar there, buying a yen or a deutschmark, going short Swissy when it pleased them and so on. These utterly despicable characters then gleefully laughed up their collective sleeves when they earned a profit at the expense of the central banks. Money speculators – unpatriotic, greedy, irresponsible, no-good louts – became the rallying symbol of the central bankers who, in turn, were the good guys – patriotic, responsible, respectable, fighting bravely for law, order, and values for their currencies.

The International Monetary Market in 1972.

But there was, Melamed knew, one fundamental flaw to this perspective: the speculators (who anyway are 'often corporate treasurers of multinational firms, bankers, sovereign nations, or highly regarded financiers') often tell the truth about currency values, when governments and central bankers are seeking to mask or distort it.

Trading on the IMM started respectably and grew steadily: an average of over a thousand contracts a day during the first month; a total of over 144,000 by the end of 1972; and volume rising threefold in the course of 1973. The disintegration of the Bretton Woods system continued apace. When Melamed and his colleagues paid a largely fruitless visit to London and other European financial centres in June 1972, he suggested to the governor of the Bank of England, Sir Leslie O'Brien, that if the Bank really wanted to help the new market it would kindly float the pound. A strained smile greeted the wisecrack – and the next day the newspaper headlines announced that this was what the British authorities had indeed decided to do, though for different reasons. In February 1973 the yen was floated, soon afterwards the dollar was further devalued, and on 19 March the major central banks formally abandoned their commitment to maintaining their exchange rates within a predetermined band in relation to the dollar.

Later that year there began to unfold an alarming sequence of events – the Arab–Israeli War, the oil embargo, and dramatic hikes in the oil price – that made 1973 such a watershed date in modern history. Interest rates skyrocketed, including American interest rates, and at the CBOT the recently recruited economist Richard ('Doc') Sandor saw the opportunity to develop a new type of financial futures product, this time an interest rate contract not a currency contract. The interest rate volatility, which was a recent experience and yet which seemed likely to continue, provided two opportunities. Firstly, it created a new demand, amongst borrowers and savers, for a means to achieve certainty in the interest rates they were to pay or receive. Secondly, there was more scope for the growing band of

Chicago traders to speculate. In this case the legal and regulatory process took an inordinate amount of time and difficulty; but at last on 20 October 1975 trading began on the CBOT in mortgage-backed futures contracts. Each trade, *Business Week* noted, 'represents a contract for delivery of a Government National Mortgage Assn. (Ginnie Mae) 8% certificate worth $100,000 – and 808 contracts were traded', the report adding that 'the market is likely to take some time to reach the substantial volume its backers hope for'. That might be true, but Chicago now had two futures markets diversifying into financial products, making it that much harder for enemies of the fledgling industry.

Sandor at the time expressed the hope that Treasury Bill futures would be the CBOT's next contract, but in the event the IMM got there first, launching a 90-day US Treasury Bill contract in January 1976. Friedman rang the bell, Melamed and others vigorously propagated the idea of T-bill futures as a hedge against rate volatility, and the new contract proved an almost instant success. The CBOT responded in August 1977 with a 30-year Treasury Bond futures contract, and it was soon apparent that the two exchanges would play complementary roles in interest rate futures, with the CME/IMM dominating the short end of the yield curve and the CBOT the long end.

In September 1977 the *Financial Times* published a survey on US Commodity Markets, largely written by John Edwards. Noting that Ginnie Maes had 'proved to be a tremendous attraction clocking up regular increases in turnover activity', he indulged in some prediction:

Richard Sandor.

> *Many companies believe that the growth in the industry will mainly appear in the long term from the new financial markets which have got off to a very good start so far. They are attracting increasing support month by month, while turnover in the traditional commodity futures market is tending to wax and wane according to supply and demand. The trend will be for the commodities tag to be dropped when describing the futures trading industry – already a rather more accurate description.*

Edwards also contributed a piece, called 'Speculators are made welcome', about the army of professional speculators in Chicago who traded on their own account in the futures markets there and provided up to 60% of total turnover. 'It is the "locals",' he wrote, 'operating exclusively for themselves, who make the U.S. market so different from London, where all the business [i.e. in London's commodity markets] is channelled through member companies of the exchange.' The gauntlet was not exactly thrown down, but five years after the birth of financial futures it was becoming high time that London looked west, if only to contrast and compare.

Chapter One

A City Initiative

ondon financial future
arket 'by 1982'

AVID MARSH

NCIAL futures market
n forward contracts in
s and interest rate
nts may be set up in
n late 1981 or early
cording to proposals
yesterday by a group
titutions.

ket would allow busi-
d investors to take
cover to minimise
n volatile foreign
credit markets.
rkshire, chairman
ers Mercantile
and head of the
that has put
conceded
rket would
re" of

vinced that the market satisfies
a genuine need and that speculative activity can be kept to a
reasonable level.

Under a financial futures
contract, a market participant
agrees to buy or sell a standard
quantity of a set type of financial instrument or currency at
a pre-determined date in the
future. The full price of the
contract is not paid until it
matures.

The profit or loss accrues
from the difference between the
market price of the contract
when it matures and the price
which the participant originally
agrees. This difference depends
on the movement of interest

The capital costs of
exchange work would
through the sale of
members, which were
to cost less than £10,000

The futures
planned to deal in
dollar interest rate
through sterling
dollar certificates
U.S. financial
trades in Euro
Barkshire felt th
particular inter
national inve
tions.

Forward
dollars
Deutsch
franc

THE FIRST PUBLICLY recorded sighting of a specifically City interest occurred in the *Investors Chronicle* on 13 January 1978. 'Money is a raw material of business, but a material at whose cost British business can now only guess,' wrote Christopher Fildes, before going on: 'That should change, with plans now afoot to give London a new financial market – a futures market in money.' After contrasting the extreme volatility in London money rates over the past eighteen months with the possibilities offered in Chicago of hedging against a rise or fall in the price of money, he explained what he meant by 'afoot':

> *Of late, observers from the London money market have been quietly packing their silk hats and catching the plane to Chicago for a closer look. They have found that the International Commodities Clearing House [ICCH] was there before them. This is the body which registers all futures contracts in the principal London markets in 'soft' commodities, handles all payments, and guarantees that all contracts will be performed. The thriving Chicago money markets set ICCH wondering who might make one in London, and how it might work. The discount houses, London's 'official' money market, would be ICCH's natural partners; and though some have reservations, this is where the plans are being made.*

The current proposal, Fildes explained, was for a London market in Treasury bills at four different delivery dates, three months apart, with the Treasury bill as the 'obvious instrument for such a market' granted that it was 'the key money-market rate in the unique sense of determining the Bank of England's Minimum Lending Rate'. Would such a market work? Fildes had his doubts, but was broadly positive:

Investors Chronicle,
13 January 1978.

110   **INVESTORS CHRONICLE 13 JANUARY 1978**

FINANCE

CITY NOTEBOOK

Riding the interest-rate switchback with a futures market in money

Money is a raw material of business, but a material at whose cost British business can now only guess. That should change, with plans now afoot to give London a new financial market—a futures market in money.

Certainly no price now seems more volatile. In the last eighteen months, London money rates, have, first, almost doubled: then fallen by two-thirds: then risen by one-third—and now have set off down again. By comparison, the price of copper looks stable, and the market in cocoa a hive of inactivity. A business which has to buy copper or cocoa can guard against fluctuations in the price by using the London commodity markets.

which registers all futures contracts in the principal London markets in "soft" commodities, handles all payments, and guarantees that all contracts will be performed. ICCH, too, has its eyes open for new business—it will handle the London market in traded stock options, another idea originating in Chicago. The thriving Chicago money markets set ICCH wondering who might make one in London, and how it might work. The discount houses, London's "official" money market, would be ICCH's natural partners; and though some have reservations, this is where the plans are being made.

The proposal now is for a London market in Treasury bills at four different

CHRISTOPHER FILDES

running out of control five and six years ago. The forward commitments which the

Chicago operates these markets on the principle of 'open outcry': that is, all business is done on the trading floor... Members, brokers, staff mill frenziedly about in their distinctive jackets – one member, to be quickly noticeable, sports a dashing confection of a harlequin patchwork decorated with purple stars – and the noise is deafening. It would be fun to have a London money market like that, but it seems not quite Lombard Street's, or the Bank of England's style. A worry not of style but of substance is that the new market might lead to manipulation or even cornering of the Treasury bills themselves. Supervision is part of the answer: control over margins, another part: the size and marketability of the Treasury issue, another. And Chicago experience suggests that only a small proportion of contracts remain open through to maturity.

The piece ended with a speculative, optimistic paragraph:

An effective London market in Treasury bill futures would point the way to others. Thus, one of the biggest American broking firms [almost certainly Merrill Lynch] has been looking for a way to introduce futures trading to the international money market. Here the monetary instrument would be the Eurodollar Certificate of Deposit. And one futures market for which the demand must be ready-made would be along the lines of the Chicago market in currencies... Exchange control has so far ruled such a market out for London: will it for ever? Where there is demand and supply, there tends, one way or another, to be a market.

Exchange controls had been in operation since the start of the Second World War, and by now the City was pushing hard for their abolition. However, as long as a Labour government stayed in office, that remained outside the realm of practical politics.

Almost certainly one of the Chicago-bound silk hats belonged to Tommy Fellowes of Gerrard & National. Earlier in the 1970s Gerrards had been market makers in what was for a time a hugely active forward market in sterling certificates of deposit [CDs]. However, partly because of the absence of a clearing house, it all ended in tears when a rescue party, including the Bank of England and the clearing banks, had to bail out the Scottish Co-op to the tune of £29m following some ill-judged forward commitments. At some point in 1977, following a visit of its own to Chicago in February, ICCH approached Gerrards (by now, like some other discount houses, becoming active in T-bill futures) with a view to doing some exploratory work together on financial futures; and so began what would soon become a City tradition of fieldwork trips to Chicago. ICCH itself (the former London Produce Clearing House) had become increasingly aware by this time that it needed to diversify, and that through developing a general concept of central clearing for a variety of products it could shed its historical dependence on commodity volatility. Already it was involved in the traded equity options market that was about to start in London; and it cleared for the Sydney Futures Exchange, which in October 1979 would launch a contract on 90-day bank-accepted bills, the first financial futures product outside the United States.

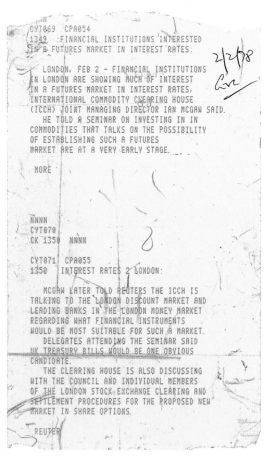

On 2 February 1978, soon after the article by Fildes, ICCH's joint managing director, Ian McGaw, told a seminar on investing in commodities that talks with discount houses and leading banks in the London money market about the possibility of establishing a financial futures market in London were still 'at a very early stage'. The question was discussed of what instruments would be most suitable for such a market, and delegates agreed that UK Treasury bills would be an obvious candidate. A few days later 'Lex' in the *FT* touched on the possibility but with no great enthusiasm, noting that 'apart from all the technical obstacles that need to be overcome, any such market would automatically need the Bank of England's blessing and as yet it has not even addressed itself to the possibility'. Soon afterwards, on 14 February, the *FT* ran a story from New York headed 'Row over regulation of U.S. securities futures', a row that in part reflected the unease of the Securities and Exchange Commission [SEC] about the way in which financial futures were expanding into areas 'affecting the nation's financial and capital raising systems', as an SEC memorandum put it to Congress. 'This looks like the end of another of my ideas!!' scribbled Fellowes on top of the cutting.

Reuters take up the story, 2 February 1978.

In fact, thanks largely to ICCH, the concept of a financial futures market in London still breathed. On 22 June, in an internal memo, Fellowes recorded the latest state of play: 'I talked to Neil Matthewson of ICCH yesterday. They have hired an expert from Chicago to come over to London and make a detailed study of the whole question of interest rate futures in London. Matthewson said would either Fellowes or Williamson [Brian Williamson, also of Gerrards] attend an informal meeting for a general discussion on interest rate futures when the chap arrived. I said that we certainly would.' The expert from Chicago was John Harding, an English economist working for Richard Sandor at Conti Financial. An able man, he came with Sandor's recommendation and was well chosen by

ICCH. By the autumn of 1978 he was hard at work, and in December the *FT* reported that he was 'expected to put forward a strongly positive recommendation'.

Harding's enthusiasm reflected continuing growth in the American financial futures markets by the late 1970s, especially with the big wire houses and the New York broker houses now starting to use them and become active members of the exchanges. Volume on the CBOT rose from 1.53m financial futures contracts traded in 1978 to 3.56m in 1979, and on the Merc from 2.33m to 4.17m; while between 1977 and 1980 as many as six other exchanges in North America introduced financial futures contracts, though seldom with the impact enjoyed by the founding fathers in Chicago. Regulators and others continued to worry about the wider economic impact of these instruments, but in May 1979 a study of the financial futures markets, jointly undertaken by the Treasury and the Fed, declared that 'empirical studies of both agricultural and financial markets have not been able to prove that there is greater price variability in spot markets during periods in which the good or security in question was traded on a futures market'. The arguments did not go away, but it was an important assessment at the time. Later, once LIFFE had become established, an assessment published by the Bank of England agreed with other academic studies that futures markets *reduced* rather than increased volatility in the underlying markets.

Meanwhile, back in London, Harding's report was submitted in June to ICCH; whereupon Matthewson informally showed it to a number of City institutions, including Gerrards, which was more enthusiastic than most. There it was increasingly Williamson rather than Fellowes who had got the financial futures bit between the teeth, and he told Matthewson that what was now needed was an assessment written from a British academic point of view to complement Harding's more American commercial perspective. Williamson knew the ways of the City, including the Bank of England, well enough to appreciate the importance of respectability. He also had someone in mind – Robert Miller, a full-time researcher at the Institute of Economic Affairs who had recently co-written a paper called 'Exchange Control For Ever?', with the hopeful answer decidedly in the negative. Matthewson was persuaded, and ICCH agreed to fund an additional report.

The Bank of England also now moved. Pen Kent, a rising star, was on secondment to the IMF, and the Bank asked him to devote part of the summer to finding out about the policy issues involved in financial futures. Kent spent three weeks talking to a wide range of key figures, and the outcome was a substantial report on US financial futures markets presented in September to his colleagues at the Bank. Although conceding that 'there are those who believe that all the Chicago futures markets are run by a bunch of wide boys, whose taint could impair the reputation of the government debt markets,' Kent himself could find 'no overriding evidence of damage caused to Government debt markets, perhaps even some evidence of benefits,' and argued that therefore 'there seems no reason why futures markets should impair the attainment of monetary policy goals'. He added that 'familiarity with them has tended to allay rather than increase suspicion of them'. Kent then turned to nearer home:

> *Could a London market be set up on dealing boards like the foreign exchange or interbank markets, or would it have to follow the commodity model with a pit (ring) where the participants physically meet? Surely it would have to start on a dealing floor somewhere – either in the Stock Exchange or the Commodity markets where both the physical infrastructure and the market skills are present. The key to a successful market would be liquidity – i.e. an adequate supply of market makers. In the US these are at present provided by the locals. It is not obvious to me who would be the London counterpart of these. London commodity traders may be more conservative than US ones and less willing to treat financial futures as just another commodity – particularly when the single regulatory authority, the Bank of England, has such powers to influence the markets at all points of entry, in a way impossible in the US, and so alter the behaviour of those markets from day to day. Could they be the Discount Houses? If they got into trouble as a result of overeagerness to make a market, could or would the Bank isolate that position from other calls on the Discount House's position which would normally be met by recourse to the Bank? Would the Bank find itself intervening as a consequence in the futures markets as it does in the forward foreign exchange market?*

Perhaps most importantly, Kent insisted that the whole question of London as an international financial centre needed to be borne in mind:

> *The financial institutions of the US are trying many ploys to bring more of the international money and capital markets to America. Their proposals include offshore banking facilities in New York, the removal of withholding tax on interest and dividend payments to non-residents, reserve requirements on euro-currency deposits – and perhaps even understandings on minimum capital requirements for international banks. It is alleged by the Swiss (according to American sources) that the world gold price is now determined by the US gold futures markets. We have also lost other markets to foreign competition. Most of the US proposals will fail, and anyway it would be wrong to argue that any business is good business. Obviously the safest answer to a request to start financial futures markets in London would be 'not yet', but maybe the question of the wider competitiveness of London and not only the needs of one segment of it would be worth considering.*

Finally, could this projected new market be adequately regulated? Kent was clear: 'If the will were present to overcome the other difficulties and objections, prudential and regulatory problems should be capable of solution given that they would all be in the hands of a single regulatory authority, the Bank of England.' In sum, although 'there must be doubts whether the ingredients for success – i.e. market makers providing liquidity, a physical dealing ring where the commodity and banking community would be prepared to mix their cultures – are present in London', Kent stated that he had been 'impressed enough by exposure to these markets in the US to believe that we should not oppose them out of hand'. There were no immediate consequences as a result of Kent's paper, but it helped to persuade people at the Bank to think more clearly about financial futures.

Pending the publication of the Miller/Harding study, there were three other important developments in the early autumn of 1979. Firstly, the chairman of the rapidly expanding London-based financial group Mercantile House recommended to his board serious involvement in financial futures. This was John Barkshire, who had been paying a series of visits to Chicago since December 1978 and now expected the emphasis of the American financial futures scene to switch away from individual to institutional members of the exchanges, many of whom were Mercantile customers. Barkshire had also been visiting New York, where he expected financial futures to move out of the embryo stage, and in addition he anticipated that non-American markets (and not just Sydney) would start to emerge. In a typically thorough, 120-page study of 'Financial Futures' that he presented to the Mercantile board on 1 October, he explained his prediction that, within a few years, they would be achieving a higher turnover than that in the cash markets:

The principal reason for this is that futures enable investment managers in banks, financial institutions and industry to hedge, or reduce, their exposure in the markets. In the 1960s and early 1970s the desire of investment managers was to maximise their profit and many did this successfully but the last decade has seen a dramatic increase in the volatility of the money markets and attendant rates and this has resulted in some spectacular losses, often by corporations whose main business did not lie in the securities industry. It was assumed that provided research was done thoroughly it was possible to forecast the future with reasonable accuracy and make investment decisions based on a long term view: events have proved this to be incorrect and costly. Investment managers are therefore looking for ways of minimising risks and in the US they are turning to futures and options in order to do this.

Barkshire's immediate recommendations for Mercantile were focused on the American markets, but he also looked further ahead: 'Investigate possibility of futures market in London being developed by us in conjunction with others,' he wrote.

The second development, five days later, was the so-called 'Saturday Night Massacre' of 6 October 1979, when the Fed announced that in order to curb inflation and bolster the dollar it would henceforth focus on the growth of the money supply rather than short-term interest rates – in effect, letting the market decide where interest rates went. The immediate upshot was a collapse in stock and bond prices, given added resonance by the fact which shortly emerged that Salomons, one of the lead underwriters in a recently flopped huge IBM issue, had managed to offset its heavy losses from unloading that issue by hedging in the Chicago financial futures market. Interest rate risk – potentially devastating – now affected all investors as a result of the extreme volatility and historic highness in rates created by the Fed's new policy, and the importance of hedging started to be more widely appreciated than it had been earlier in the decade.

Thirdly, and perhaps most importantly, there took place what was arguably the seminal moment of Thatcherism, less than five months after the Conservative election victory. This was the abolition of exchange controls, which announcement was received by a generally pleased, slightly alarmed, almost entirely surprised City on 23 October. Few at the time fully appreciated the possibilities, that the City was now being given the chance to revert to something like its pre-1914 role, when at the very zenith of its powers it stood at the centre of an international network trading in free flows of money, capital and goods. The evolution of a successful, internationally oriented financial futures market would have been barely conceivable without this fundamental change of policy. 'It is hardly possible to overstate the critical importance of our decision,' Nigel Lawson would modestly write in his memoirs: as usual he had a point.

A month later, in late November, ICCH released 'Financial Futures in London?'. In their independent, well-argued papers, both Miller and Harding asserted that London was suited to establish a successful market in financial futures, granted the existence of a wide array of standardised debt instruments, the Bank of England's central control over any would-be City market, and the generally extensive international use of London's markets as a whole. The Bank, Miller in particular argued, was the crux, noting that 'the power of the Bank of England to stop banks trading in the financial futures markets would give it an authority to deal with difficulties which American agencies might envy but could not match'.

Both agreed that all sorts of contracts were possible – British government debt of over one year maturity, sterling certificates, sterling CDs, foreign currency futures, the British retail price index, Eurobonds, stock indices, Eurodollar CDs, US Treasury obligations – but Miller was more sceptical than Harding about UK Treasury bills on the grounds of possible shortages in deliverable supply. As for the appropriate trading mechanism, Harding had no doubts: 'US experience has shown almost conclusively that in order to be successful a futures market must be by physical open outcry with substantial "local" participation to provide a market making function… The suggestion that the London market use a remote trading system with traders linked by video screens, while possibly technically feasible, would be a new and unproven development.'

The papers were buttressed by some impressive appendices, and in the event two quite bulky volumes were distributed to some 250 City firms and other institutions. In its introduction ICCH, after observing that the likeliest contracts were for short and long gilts, sterling CDs and possibly Eurodollar CDs, made it clear that somebody else now needed to pick up the ball:

ICCH cannot, of course, of itself create a market. This requires detailed and full participation from those involved in the financial markets in order to set up an exchange, organise floor trading, elect members, determine the terms of the futures contracts, etc. While ICCH has received a considerable amount of advice and help from certain City financial institutions, if markets are to be brought into existence, a determined effort from a group of participants is required.

In ICCH's view the participation should include all sections of the City who are exposed to interest rate risk or who have clients with a similar exposure. Participants should include, for example, discount houses, moneybrokers, merchant banks, stockjobbers, stockbrokers, clearing banks and commodity brokers.

While ICCH is confident that corporate and institutional customers will in due course come to use the market to hedge their risks, this will not happen until the market has been formed and its liquidity demonstrated. The onus therefore rests upon the professional money market participants in the City to provide this facility.

The suggested wide range of participants challenges some traditional City practices such as restrictions on exchange membership to certain categories of organisation and limitations on the ability of some types of firm to deal with others. To achieve success ICCH believes that the widest possible participation is essential…

The welcome suspension of Exchange controls provides an additional challenge to the London markets. There is conceptually no reason why a market in sterling interest rates should not be formed and function effectively in other parts of Europe or the United States. In addition the relaxation opens the additional possibility of currency futures in London or elsewhere.

To progress investigation and planning further a working group should be formed, comprising representatives from potential market participants.

A clarion call one might have thought, but at this stage only one person was willing to take up the challenge: John Barkshire of Mercantile House.

Aged forty-four, the man who would be the single most important figure in the history of LIFFE possessed formidable energy and resource, as a farmer of 300 acres in Sussex as well as an increasingly heavyweight presence in the City. His career there had not lacked controversy. Joint managing director from 1963 of the discount house Cater Ryder, he became increasingly aware that the cosy, cartelised world of the London discount market was no longer adequate to meet the challenges of international money broking; and eventually, in 1972, when the Bank of England ordered discount houses to divest themselves of money broking activities, he felt compelled to lead what was in effect a management buy-out of the money broking operation at Caters. It was not a move that endeared him to the City establishment, but Barkshire himself was enough of a City insider – and classic City gentleman, always impeccably turned out – to take the storm in his stride. After all, his father had been private secretary to a governor (Kim Cobbold) of the Bank of England and then secretary to the Committee of London Clearing Bankers; while Barkshire himself since 1955 had given Territorial Army service in the Honourable Artillery Company, becoming CO in 1970 and Regimental Colonel two years later. In short he did not frighten the horses, above all the rather slow-moving, conservative beast that was the Bank of England. He would later reflect on the relationship in highly characteristic tones:

I've always kept very close to the Bank of England. I've always told them exactly what I was doing, and to this day I still do. And whenever I was proposing to make any commercial move of any sort at all I would always go and see them and talk to them and explain what I was doing and why. And indeed ask their advice. But the great thing I always felt with the Bank of England was, never surprise them. They don't like being surprised. Tell them.

Yet Barkshire could also see the bigger picture, as he had shown first at Cater Ryder and more recently at his own creation, Mercantile House, seeking to diversify and internationalise following its successful flotation in July 1979. By this time, even before the abolition of exchange controls, he was convinced that almost all the barriers were about to be demolished between the world's different financial markets and between the functions that different financial institutions traditionally carried out. His goal for Mercantile was no less than that of becoming (in the words of its historian, George Bull) 'one of the world's select, multinational, multiservice institutions'. The creation of a financial futures market in London was entirely compatible with that vision, and Barkshire was soon giving a significant part of his time and talents to ensuring the reality. 'A shortish, slightly rubicund man who talks precisely and briskly,' a profile in *The Times* would observe, 'he carries around the air of someone who is accustomed to things going right because he has prepared the ground.' Now in the closing weeks of 1979 he picked up the ball that ICCH had put into play and, with ICCH's help, began to gather together a working party.

He later recalled the process:

I really just rang up some friends, and I thought that we ought to have representation from the different elements who might make up the market. And so I felt we needed Stock Exchange representation, and in those days with single capacity we therefore needed a broker and a jobber, and so I rang up Pip Greenwell of Greenwells, and David LeRoy-Lewis at Akroyd & Smithers, as being the two broadest-minded brokers and jobbers that I reckoned I knew, and said how about it, and went round and saw them and talked to them about it. I then thought of a merchant bank, and so I rang David Scholey of Warburgs; I thought of a discount house so I rang Roger Gibbs at Gerrard & National; it seemed sensible to have a clearing house involved, so ICCH... I asked them to get somebody from the commodity markets, as plainly we needed somebody with expertise in commodities, and so they came up with Woodhouse, Drake & Carey. And that was the little team that we set up.

John Barkshire.

In its initial form the London Financial Futures Working Party was seven-strong in addition to Barkshire himself and its secretary, Tony de Guingand, supplied by ICCH: David Burton of Warburgs; Neil Matthewson of ICCH; John Morris of Woodhouse, Drake & Carey; Stephen Raven of Akroyd & Smithers, one of the two leading gilts jobbers and at this stage, under LeRoy-Lewis's auspices, a lot more enthusiastic about financial futures than Wedd Durlacher was; Jess Tigar of the merchant bank Guinness Peat, which had fairly recently acquired a significant presence in commodities; Jack Wigglesworth of the stockbrokers Greenwell, thanks to Gordon Pepper at the height of its powers in the gilt-edged market; and Brian Williamson of Gerrards. None of the working party was a passenger, but quite quickly the 'gang of four' would emerge as Barkshire, Williamson, Burton and Wigglesworth. Each of the last three was half a generation younger than Barkshire, each had a career to make, and in large part financial futures would be that career.

The Bank of England, meanwhile, was predictably circumspect. 'Fears that speculation in the futures market will have a destabilising effect on spot prices seem overstated,' a paper dated 17 January 1980 by M.J. Pratt of the Bank's economic intelligence department conceded. However:

Whether or not there is a strong demand for financial futures trading in London is arguable. The prospects are perhaps less favourable than in the US,

where speculation in commodity futures is more significant. The lack of success in the Traded Options market [i.e. in London] is evidence of the lack of demand for relatively risky forms of investment. Rather markets in the UK are more dominated by institutional investors who will probably approach financial futures markets with caution.

This was the Bank's first, private assessment of the Miller/Harding study. 'No official opinion has yet been sought from the Bank,' the *FT* noted on 1 February, adding accurately that 'officials have shown no great enthusiasm,' though 'so far it has received only preliminary and very informal discussion'.

Barkshire's networking continued, and on 12 February he telephoned Warburgs in order to sign up Burton. He told the bank's Oscar Lewisohn that the working party would not be meeting under ICCH's

Jack Wigglesworth.

auspices, though it would provide secretarial services and a meeting room, but as 'an independent group of City professionals'; and added that it was his intention to have 'relatively few committee meetings', instead expecting that 'each "specialist" will be asked to help on the specific aspects on which he is able to contribute'. Two days later Barkshire went public over his involvement, telling the press that the question of a financial futures market for London was coming up 'more and more frequently' over City lunch tables and expressing the hope that 'by the spring or early summer a group of people will have emerged and someone will say "I am going to make this thing go forward"'. With a nod back to the City's revival from the late 1950s, he also forecast that it could be 'the single most important development in London since the advent of the Eurodollar market'.

Where would this market actually be situated? 'It is to be hoped that one of the existing exchanges would assist by providing space, expertise and ancillary facilities,' the ICCH had written in its introduction to the Miller/Harding report. Now, on 22 February, Douglas Dawkins of the Bank of England noted: 'I had a talk with Peter Wills [deputy chairman of the Stock Exchange] this morning about the interest of the Stock Exchange in a financial futures market… They had no ambitions to establish a futures market themselves, in gilts or in anything else…' Conceivably, though, this did not preclude a future role as host to the market. Dawkins himself had previously been in charge of exchange control, and at about this time he picked up the financial futures baton from Kent and over the next few years became the key Bank figure – and an almost entirely helpful and positive one – as far as financial futures in London were concerned. Preparations continued, meanwhile, for the first meeting of the working party, scheduled for 25 March. Just over a week before, David Scholey of Warburgs sent Burton a note that might have been written by the great Sir Siegmund himself: 'In about 3/6 months I suggest that you and Lewisohn should consider whether the working party is doing any useful work, because I certainly would not wish to tie up your valuable time in a talking shop. Indeed, if the working party's work is not completed within 6 months, I would doubt its effectiveness.'

David Burton.

The working party gathered at 2.30 pm on Tuesday, 25 March 1980 in the attic at Roman Wall House, 1/2 Crutched Friars, the home of ICCH. Eight City men, still learning, then listened for half an hour to a talk, complete with flip-charts, by a young American woman, Kimberly Albright. Harvard-educated, she had recently helped to start up the London office of the IMM ('a missionary on the shores of darkest Africa', she would recall), and Barkshire knew her through his trips to Chicago. On this occasion, given a free hand by Barkshire, she concentrated mainly on how a clearing house works in a futures market and the crucial importance of its guarantee function.

The meeting proper began with the unanimous election of Barkshire as chairman of the working party. He reported on the background that had led to the working party's formation and 'expressed the hope that a role would be found for a Financial Futures Market in London which would help maintain London's place as one of the world's leading financial centres', adding that the Bank of England had formed its own working party, headed by Dawkins, to 'review the impact of financial futures in London'. The meeting agreed to appoint Coward Chance (traditional specialists in futures) as legal advisers and Price Waterhouse as financial advisers. Barkshire then reported that the Bank of England had indicated that it would like to express its views 'at an early stage in the discussions

```
Kim Albright (920.0722 - until 6.30 pm)

The following headings are what she intends to talk about
to ICCH meeting  tomorrow - are they OK, or do you want her
to go in another direction because they might already have
heard it!??


1.  Functions of a Financial Futures Market
2.  Kind of participants:   Hedgers
                            Speculators
                            Arbitragers
3.  Who are they?
        1)  Participants off the trading floor -
            names of several kinds of companies

        2)  Participants on the trading floor -
            locals and arbitragers
4.  How financial futures trading is different from
    other markets.
        Open Outcry
        No date system
        Clearing House strength
        Clearing Member organisation
        Exchange policing power

5.  Question time.




Please ring her either this evening before 6.30 or tomorrow
morning.
-----------
Alex McCullom CME - here on WEdnesday, 26th, at 10 a.m.
```

London Financial Futures Working Party

AGENDA for the First Meeting of the Working Party to be held
on Tuesday, 25th March 1980 at Roman Wall House at 3.00 p.m.

The Meeting is to be preceded by a thirty minute presentation
on Financial Futures to be given by Miss K. Albright of the
International Monetary Market of Chicago, starting at 2.30 p.m.

```
1.   Appointment of Chairman
2.   Appointment of Secretary
3.   Statement by Chairman
4.   Discussion and Questions
     -----------
5.   Composition of Working Party (see attached)
6.   Role of ICCH
7.   Appointment of legal and financial advisors
8.   Brief
9.   Consideration of paper "Principle Decisions and Problems" (see
     attached)
10.  Timetable and method of operating.  Allocation of further
     responsibilities
11.  Consideration of:

           Paper on possible contracts (attached)

           Coward Chance letter of 21st February 1980 (attached)

           Price Waterhouse letter

           VAT implications (attached)

12.  Appointment of Consultants
13.  Agreement of list of Associations whose views should be solicited
     (attached)
14.  Agreement of Press release (attached)
15.  Any other business
16.  Next Meeting

     To be held on Thursday, 24th April 1980 at Roman Wall House at
     2.30 p.m.
```

The first meeting of the Working Party, 25 March 1980.
Left: Kim Albright's notes.
Right: The Agenda.

on the clearing and guarantee systems', but that it 'would not envisage a system of statutory controls over the market'. He also said that 'any decision on whether the market should be opened as part of an existing Exchange or be formed as an independent Exchange should wait until decisions on what contracts were to be traded had been taken'. Individual members of the party were assigned to investigate possible contracts, and Barkshire remarked that 'the right choice of contract and the right specifications for the contract were the key to the success of the market'. That only left the schedule, and Barkshire suggested that 'a relatively tight, but realistic, timetable should be set' – namely, completion by the end of June of a feasibility study, to go to the Bank of England, and the opening of the market some fifteen months later, on 1 October 1981. As he rather breezily put it to the press soon afterwards: 'Assuming there are no hiccups and we can arrange such mundane things as telephones I would be aiming at the autumn of next year for a start.'

By mid-April the working party had a new member: Michael Mayo, treasurer of Barclays Bank International and the nominee of the Committee of

London Clearing Bankers, whose request to have a representative was a major fillip. Following an intensive round of small meetings on specific questions, the working party as a whole met again on 24 April. The merits and demerits of individual contracts were discussed; Barkshire informed the meeting that the Bank of England was 'looking for stringent regulations with regard to the market, both of an external and an internal nature'; and it was agreed that 'the open outcry method of trading should be adopted for the market'. One part was especially interesting:

> Mr Morris informed the Meeting that the Administration Committee [i.e. of the working party] had decided, after reviewing the various options available, that using ICCH would probably be the best method of clearing and guaranteeing the market. The Chairman said that the Bank of England had strongly indicated that they expected the market to be subject to an independent guarantee rather than any form of mutual guarantee. Mr Raven asked what other clearing organisations were available of an independent nature to guarantee the market. It was agreed that there were no other existing independent Clearing Houses of sufficient capability in London to guarantee the market. However, the Committee were requested to produce arguments for and against the setting up of another independent Clearing House as against using ICCH.

The Bank's insistence on an *independent* guarantee was in contrast to the usual American practice, where the guarantee was mutual – in other words, the clearing members picked up the tab in the event of a default. An independent guarantee would of course require remuneration. Undoubtedly, however, it would add to the new market's strength, enabling all those in it – ranging from the largest member to the smallest independent trader – to trade confidently with each other, in the knowledge that there existed a single, independent, well-capitalised counterparty: the clearing house. Nor would they need to undertake the expensive and time-consuming task of keeping track of all the different bilateral negotiations taking place in the market. Anyone could trade easily with anyone else, thereby bringing together in the trading pit the forces of supply and demand to make a perfect market.

Overall the mood remained optimistic. Those responsible for investigating individual contracts (Tigar for currencies, Raven and Wigglesworth for gilts, Williamson and Burton for UK Treasury bills and CDs, and Williamson and Tigar for Eurodollar CDs) had started talking to some of those likely to be involved, and Burton on the 30th reported to Warburgs that he had 'made initial approaches to various members of the money market, both discount houses, merchant banks and clearing banks, and have received positive responses from most potential market participants'. There was, of course, one other crucial matter. Before the

working party's second meeting, Matthewson and de Guingand of ICCH suggested
some possible names for the proposed exchange:

London Financial Futures Market/Exchange
European Financial Futures Market/Exchange
International Financial Futures Market/Exchange
Financial Futures Market/Exchange of London/Europe

They added that 'of the above combinations it is suggested that the name
"European Financial Futures Exchange" (E.F.F.E.) be adopted'. The acronym had
interesting oral possibilities, but at the working party's meeting Barkshire agreed
to discuss the proposed name with the Bank of England, and the meeting's
consensus was that 'the word "London" should be incorporated into the name'.

Early in May half the working party – Raven, Wigglesworth, Williamson and
Burton, accompanied by Trevor Slade of ICCH – took off for a few days in Chicago
and New York. The visit was characterised by much help from the American
futures exchanges. Watching futures trading in action made a deep impression on
those who had not seen it before. Burton's reaction was probably typical: a
meaningless din and chaos for the first ten minutes, but then starting to get the
hang of the various hand-signals and who was doing what in the pits, and soon
wanting to get down there himself and start trading. On his return he was at pains
to reassure Warburgs: 'It is doubtful whether the open outcry system as seen on
the CBOT will be allowed to develop in London but I would envisage a more
orderly operation with far fewer individual traders.'

On the important, potentially vexed question of an independent clearing
house, this had been left – perhaps surprisingly on the face of it – to Matthewson
of ICCH to make an assessment of the relative advantages and disadvantages of
attempting to set one up. 'I have tried to approach the subject without bias,' he
told Morris on 9 May, but perhaps inevitably his strong preference was for the
would-be new market to stick to ICCH, on the combined grounds of avoiding
major set-up costs, obviating the need for founder-members to put up substantial
capital resources for a market that might be unsuccessful, reassuring prospective
members coming from the soft commodity markets that already used ICCH, and
maintaining the confidence of the Bank, in that 'while ICCH is well known to the
Bank of England, who fully understand ICCH procedures, the same would not be
true of a new independent clearing house'.

Uncertainty – even defensiveness – was in the air as well as optimism. On 21
May, the eve of the third meeting, Williamson wrote an important letter to Barkshire:

*I think it would be useful for all of us on the Working Party to have a clearer
idea of the way in which the Bank of England is approaching Futures and its*

attitude to (and expectations of) the Working Party. There are some important decisions we as a group ought to make, such as whether we could really justify the markets for users outside the financial system, and these would be easier to make if we had a better feel of the Bank's thinking.

Peter Wills has just been in New York and appears to be following our tracks around in Chicago. Stephen Raven spoke to him and I gather Peter Wills would like him and Jack Wigglesworth to go on to a Stock Exchange committee. This obviously raises an important point of principle. My own view is that any involvement by the Stock Exchange is liable to add two years or more to the start date for any exchange. It seems to me important that the money markets and the futures contracts based on them would be better served by a separate exchange. This argument is of course weakened if we started with a gilts contract, but looking ahead one can see that any London futures exchange would in the main be dealing with contracts outside the Stock Exchange and based instead on the money and foreign exchange markets.

What do you envisage the role of the Working Party to be after our report has been submitted to the Bank of England? I am slightly apprehensive that there is a danger we shall be seen as a private club for getting an exchange going for our own benefit, and this might prejudice the general enthusiasm we want to stimulate in the City. Some of these fears of course would be removed if we have all done a successful job in persuading other people of the benefits, but I suspect it may be necessary as time goes by for us to reconstitute the Working Party.

Brian Williamson.

At Crutched Friars the next day, Raven with his somewhat iconoclastic streak 'queried whether the various committees were studying the contracts in too great a detail and that the organisational structure, institutional reactions and details of who was to establish the market were subjects that should be addressed more closely'. To which Barkshire replied that the emphasis was unavoidable, granted that the submission to the Bank 'would have to show that potential contracts were workable and had a commercial use'. As for the Bank itself, Barkshire was able to give the meeting a resumé of the current thoughts of the working party there under Dawkins. It would be 'interested' in who would be members of the new exchange; it accepted that these would include overseas members; it 'would have to give a Treasury Bill contract a great deal of thought', but otherwise there was 'no objection in principle to any other contract'; any gilts contract 'should be discussed with the Stock Exchange'; 'contracts should be larger rather than small, to deter excessive speculation, unless there are sound commercial reasons otherwise'; the Bank 'would retain the right to override Exchange rules in extreme situations'; regulation 'would be Supervisory rather than Statutory, but the Bank would maintain a very close liaison'; and the Bank wished to see the letter that was being submitted to the Department of Trade applying for recognition of the members of the proposed exchange as an association of dealers in securities under the 1958 Prevention of Fraud Act.

There was also the question of clearing and guarantee. The Bank, Dawkins had told Barkshire, 'would exclude many City institutions from any mutual body' and was thus 'in favour of a market guaranteed by an independent City body'. The meeting discussed this last point and agreed that 'to set up an independent company to perform the clearing and guaranteeing functions would take much time and money', that 'ICCH already had the necessary expertise', that 'there were benefits to be gained from having one clearing house for all markets', and that 'there was no other body in London who had the expertise or who had expressed an interest in doing the work'. In sum, 'provided there was a substantial change in the ownership of ICCH it would be a logical choice as the clearing and guaranteeing body to the market'. In Barkshire's eyes, as he privately remarked to Dawkins at about this time, the ideal owners of ICCH would be a consortium comprising the clearing banks and the Bank of England, a change of ownership that among other advantages would give it far stronger financial backing. But quite apart from that question, 'the Meeting agreed that the degree of interest shown by the Bank in Financial Futures was most encouraging'.

This meeting did not consider the issue of the Stock Exchange's involvement, but as Williamson's letter had indicated it loomed large in the background. Some weeks previously, on 1 April, David Steen of the jobbers Pinchin Denny had submitted a report to Wills, in turn passed on to Dawkins, on 'Financial Futures Markets'. Taking the Miller/Harding report as 'a starting point', and referring to the Chicago floor traders as 'quaintly described as "the locals"', Steen was in no doubt that 'the widest interest would certainly lie in gilt-edged futures' and that 'if financial futures were to be introduced in London, it is inconceivable that they would not be made available on gilts'. He then argued that though 'a market in futures on certain gilt-edged securities could be established on the Stock Exchange trading floor, and it might even enjoy some degree of success,' this 'would almost certainly be the wrong solution'. Instead, Steen advocated 'the creation of a new monetary futures exchange', with membership 'open to all securities houses in London, to Clearing Banks, Merchant Banks, Discount Houses, Money Brokers and similar entities', as well as 'individual memberships for sole traders... In this way, the broadest possible trading interest would be drawn into the market to deal in futures on Bonds, Currencies, CDs and whatever other instruments might be introduced. The idea would be novel. Like all new ideas, it would arouse fears, most of them probably groundless.'

It was a remarkable assessment, and came from someone who through his intimate involvement in the Stock Exchange's faltering traded options market well understood the problems faced by a subordinate market within a larger exchange; but probably what it did was less to convince Wills of the general merits of allowing a free-standing, independent exchange in financial futures to be established, rather to alert him to the possible folly of letting financial futures slip the Stock Exchange's orbit without at least giving the matter some more serious consideration than it had so far received. Whatever the cause and effect, Wills added a financial futures dimension to his already planned trip to the States. On 28 May, following a conversation, Dawkins noted that 'it is in Wills' mind that, if the financial futures market is established in London, it should be located in the Stock Exchange Building and be subject to Stock Exchange rules'. Accordingly, Dawkins added, 'this means that the Stock Exchange would have to be some sort of partner in the venture'. At this stage, despite the Stock Exchange's reputation as an overly conservative body, clogged up by committees and presiding over a stagnant, almost entirely domestic market-place that was missing almost all the big opportunities in international equity dealing, it is doubtful if Barkshire and his colleagues would have felt able to resist a firm approach from the Stock Exchange to become 'some sort of partner' in the new market.

In practice, in a paper written on 6 June for the Stock Exchange Council, Wills ruled out the possibility of a dominant degree of involvement. He addressed explicitly the question of whether the Stock Exchange should establish, manage and control the new market:

A number of factors must be taken into account:

(A) Instruments: The suggested instruments which would be traded include only one (Gilt-Edged Futures) which are of interest to more than a handful of Member Firms.

(B) Participation: Soundings among the Gilt Edged Jobbers demonstrate that the majority are unlikely to participate actively, though they might wish to hedge their own positions through dealing in the Market.

(C) Dealers: The vibrant atmosphere of U.S. markets, particularly those in Chicago, can weave a deceptive spell. It must be remembered that The Stock Exchange is no training ground for dealers in an Auction Market, and under its present dealing systems is unlikely to become one. It is also less than sympathetic to the concept of the individual market maker, a species which abounds in the U.S.A.

(D) Regulation: In its self-regulatory role, the Council is disinclined to countenance risk-taking except within parameters of proven antiquity. It is thus

likely to approach a new market with suspicion rather than enthusiasm, and to devote its best endeavours to the prevention of failure. In a new market, such endeavours should more properly be directed to the promotion of success, commensurate of course with reasonably prudent safeguards.

(E) Membership: It is unlikely that The Stock Exchange could provide enough members to run the market on its own, indeed it seems unlikely that more than a handful of firms would wish, or have the expertise, to participate at all. The members of The Market would therefore largely have to be drawn from outsiders if it is to have any chance of success.

In summary, The Stock Exchange appears unlikely to produce the membership, the expertise, the dealers, or the business in the new Market.

Therefore, Wills concluded, 'it would not appear that The Stock Exchange should attempt to set the Market up itself, and arguably could be more profitably occupied in making the Traded Options Market viable'. Nevertheless, he added, 'the Council might consider co-operating with the founders of the new Market by offering space for the market place in The Stock Exchange building (though not, of course, on the Floor)'. At the next Council meeting, on 17 June, Wills' analysis seems to have been broadly accepted.

The working party's individual committees continued to beaver away during June, closely watched over by Barkshire, whose mastery of the detail was formidable; and on 8 July a feasibility study (61 pages long) into financial futures was presented to the Bank. It referred to the need for a financial futures market in London (essentially the minimising of risk in an era of volatility in both exchange rates and interest rates), declared the working party to be 'unanimous in their preliminary conclusions that a financial futures market should be formed in London and enthusiastic in their wish to progress to the next stage', and announced that the proposed name was the London Financial Futures Exchange. Hindsight gives added interest to some other particular proposals. The paper declared that 'the day to day administration of the Exchange will be carried out by the clearing house', with no mention of a full-time executive. Trading hours for the proposed contracts would begin respectively at 8.30 (currencies), 8.45 (Eurodollar CD), 9.00 (sterling CD) and 10.00 (gilt). A system of price limits would be used 'which provides for the market to be closed for one hour once the limit has been reached and that the market, when it re-opens, will have no price limits for the remainder of that trading day'. And autumn 1981 was still given as the provisional date for the market's opening.

The meat of the study concerned the individual contracts, prefaced by the riders that 'contracts in gold, precious metals and stock market indices were considered to be of less immediate relevance to a financial market' and that 'it was also felt that proliferation of contracts was undesirable in the initial stages'. Seven contracts were proposed: a gilt contract with 20 years to maturity; a sterling CD contract with 90 days to maturity; a Eurodollar CD contract with 90 days to maturity; and currency contracts in sterling, deutschmarks, Swiss francs and Japanese yen. A long gilt contract was put forward as appropriate partly because it made available a wider choice of stocks for delivery, partly because there would be significant demand for short hedging of long-term interest rates; and it was anticipated that, in terms of 'economic justification' for the contract, corporate treasurers would protect their companies from an anticipated rise in interest rates through the sale of long gilt futures contracts, that institutions involved in underwriting long-term debt issues could similarly cover themselves against a rise in yields, that jobbers making a market in long-term debt instruments would use gilt futures to hedge and thereby reduce the risks to their open positions from unanticipated changes in rates, and that institutional investment managers (insurance companies, pension funds and so on) would find a futures market in long-term bonds helpful to secure a current high interest rate if they anticipated a fall in yields before cash funds were available. Similarly convincing end-user arguments were put forward for the other six contracts.

How would the package as a whole play inside the great white building in Threadneedle Street? 'The working party has expressed the hope', wrote 'Lex' on 14 July, 'that the Bank might respond within a few months, opening the way to a start of operations before, say, the end of 1981. But the Bank has declined to commit itself to any timetable, and it will take whatever time it thinks necessary'.

There followed a period of silence, though on 7 August the *FT* ran a major feature on financial futures. The occasion was the start of trading that day on the New York Futures Exchange, a subsidiary of the New York Stock Exchange, with Alan Friedman providing a London perspective on the subject. He outlined the progress that had been made since ICCH's November 1979 report and described the three months taken by the working party to produce its study as 'a rapid pace for the City'. But though the idea of financial futures in London had its keen proponents, he also noted that 'others in the City are wary of a new and untested market', indeed that 'many are unconvinced of the need and even suggest that such trade could have a destabilising effect on the underlying markets'. Meanwhile, he added, the working party was getting on with producing a document which it hoped to be able to circulate during the autumn and would deal not only with contracts but also criteria for participation in the market and a set of standards for operating.

More immediately, also in August, the economist Gordon Gemmill, of City University Business School in London, sent the Bank of England a draft paper headed 'Financial Futures in London: Rational Market or New Casino?' In it he broadly supported the creation of a new market and very much played down the casino aspect, though at the same time argued that 'the gain in terms of hedging of risks would seem to be rather small'. Equally, however, 'the potentially damaging effects of the new markets, in terms of distorted prices due to corners/squeezes, ill-informed waves of speculation or difficulty in pursuing monetary policy, seem to be very small'. A thoroughly sober assessment, with little sense of an exciting new financial market in the potential offing, it probably played a significant part in allaying Bank of England fears.

At the next meeting of the working party, on 2 September, Barkshire began by noting that the Bank had not yet given its reaction to the feasibility study and then gave a summary of his recent meeting with Wills:

> *Mr Barkshire expressed his own views to Mr Wills that the Financial Futures Exchange would have to be an independent Exchange with its own rules and that it would not be subject to existing Stock Exchange rules. However, within those limitations there is considerable scope for co-operation and possibly some form of sponsorship… Mr Barkshire had suggested that if the Stock Exchange had considerable objection to the introduction of a gilt futures contract then this could be removed from the list of proposed contracts and we would also be glad to consider an offer of floor space. Mr Wills agreed that this would be well received…*
>
> *The Meeting agreed with the views expressed by Mr Barkshire.*

Over the ensuing winter there remained a possibility that the Stock Exchange would lease some space, but by the end of 1980 the working assumption was that it would not.

How worrying was the Bank's silence? 'Governor [Gordon Richardson] has not yet made his mind up,' scribbled Burton on his agenda for the 2 September 1980 meeting. 'Douglas Dawkins in favour (+ committee).' It was a reaction that he glossed further in his report to Warburgs:

> *Barkshire feels, however, that the Bank of England will agree to the establishment of a Financial Futures Market if the City of London feel that there is a genuine need. It is up to the members of the Working Party to convince the Bank that there is a need for such a market and it has been suggested that a series of seminars should be held during November with a view to attracting opinion from the City, both on an official and unofficial basis. At the end of that time, these views would be incorporated in a further report to be presented to the Bank of England in the form of a Green Paper. It is proposed that four seminars will be held…*

Burton added that there was to be a press conference on 29 September, at which it would be stressed that individual members of the working party 'do not represent views of their own organisations but collectively subscribe to the views presented to the Bank of England'.

The first formal official reaction to the feasibility study came on 8 September, when Mayo submitted the comments of the clearing banks. None 'had any particular comment to make at this stage on the desirability or otherwise of establishing a Financial Futures Market in London', but there were several specific criticisms of the feasibility study: the proposed discussion period (October/November 1980) was 'insufficient' for the consultations that would be required within the City; the concept of contracts in currency futures was flawed, in that 'the Forward Foreign Exchange Market [in which the clearers were major players] provides all that is required for hedging', so that 'arguably' the only benefit they supplied was 'support for speculation'; also in those contracts, 'the concept of the same price for all participants regardless of standing for any given contract is questionable'; and an 8.30 start time was necessary for all contracts, 'if the intention is for the London market to attract the business of Europe and Middle East'.

Three days later the working party (now starting to meet at Mercantile House's offices at 66 Cannon Street) was told by Raven that the board of Akroyd & Smithers 'would have to consider whether they wished him to remain on the Working Party if it was proposed not to trade gilts', before Barkshire reported on his meeting with Dawkins. It transpired that Dawkins' committee studying the feasibility study had a number of specific comments – mostly involving margins and the protection of clients – but the crucial fact was that, in the reported words of Barkshire, it 'had written a memorandum to the Governor saying that the proposals contain no technical problems and that if City opinion was in favour of the market, then the Bank of England should not stand in its way'.

It was, from the working party's point of view, a hugely comforting response, though in the discussion paper to be published at the end of the month Dawkins would only allow it to be stated that 'the Bank of England has been kept informed of the Working Party's discussions but it is not, at this stage, committed to supporting the establishment of a financial futures market in London, nor is it committed to any of the detailed proposals in the discussion paper'. Some 10,000 copies of the discussion paper were printed, with a distribution list to City institutions and so on of 6,500, and an accompanying press conference held in the Drawing Room at Ironmongers' Hall. The paper covered much of the same ground as the feasibility study, though in addition to giving details of the autumn seminars it stated, following a steer from the Bank, that 'the financial requirements of members will depend on which function they intend to perform and their financial worth will also limit the number of open positions that they are allowed at any one time'. Furthermore, 'any applicant for membership must enjoy, and have for a reasonable time enjoyed, a high reputation and standing in the financial community'. One way and another the requirements would be, as Barkshire emphasised at the press conference, 'tough enough to exclude the gambler'.

Press reaction was broadly supportive. *The Times* thought that the market in currency futures would 'probably bring with it cheaper prices than the inter-bank market and in some cases more flexibility for unwinding contracts quickly'. The *Daily Telegraph* argued that 'properly set up and regulated' the new market would 'provide further grist to the City's mill' – with the slightly ominous proviso 'so long as it is not handicapped from birth, like, for instance, the traded options market which has struggled through infancy with defects (mostly fiscal) that should have been sorted out long before'. 'Lex' in the *FT* was rather more sceptical: 'The two fundamental questions are whether London needs a market like this to enhance its position as a financial centre, and whether the necessary volume of trade can be found to make it feasible. The thrust for setting up a market has so far come from commission earners rather than end users. There is nothing wrong with this, but genuine potential traders are now required to make their voices heard.' The *FT* also published a letter from Mr G.D. Ranald, writing from his club at 54 Pall Mall. 'Although bringing with it a whiff of Chicago, Middle West and gun smoke', the new market, he argued, 'must be welcomed for the simple reason that any extension of a market place must eventually produce a more efficient system for future price evaluation'. What troubled him, however, was the fact that the German, Swiss and Japanese currency contracts were to be traded in US dollars as opposed to the pound sterling, when similar trading in dollars was already available in Chicago. 'Why should the City seek to reinforce the U.S. dollar as the reserve currency by duplicating that which is already provided?'

The seminars would be vital, for as the working party agreed on 20 October, 'it was believed that the Governor currently had no firm opinion about the desirability of a market and would be swayed by "City opinion"'. In the event six one-day public seminars were held between late October and early December at the Institute of Marine Engineers in Mark Lane: gratifyingly over-subscribed, they were attended by 900 people. In addition, private presentations were given in the same period to another 1,200 people, including tailor-made sessions for the

Financial Times,
30 September 1980.

David Marsh looks at plans for the new London financial market

Just no future for the gambler

THE financial requirements of the proposed London futures market will be " tough enough to exclude the gambler," says Mr. John Barkshire, chairman of money brokers Mercantile House and head of a City working party which yesterday unveiled its plans for the new financial market.

Mr. Barkshire and his working party colleagues, drawn from a range of City institutions, are keen to underline

Market users might range from building societies to insurance brokers, from local authority treasurers to multinational corporations, the working party suggests.

A financial futures contract is an agreement to buy or sell a standard quantity of a set type of financial instrument or currency at a pre-determined date in the future.

Interest rates

contract and hope to buy a matching one more cheaply when it matures. Thus, he would make a profit which would compensate for the higher interest rate on the loan he then decides to raise.

If all goes well, the London market could get under way by the end of 1981 or early 1982, Mr. Barkshire says. But, a number of hurdles have still to be cleared.

The working party still has to

fil a genuine need, and whether it might increase the short-term volatility of the spot market in debt instruments and foreign currencies, have not been discussed.

Interest rate contracts to be traded on the proposed exchange comprise a short-term sterling interest rate based on sterling certificates of deposit, and Eurodollar interest rates based on Eurodollar

Committee of London Clearing Bankers and the London Discount Market Association. The seminars and private presentations were attended by 187 banks, 13 discount houses, 232 industrial and commercial companies, 18 pension funds and insurance companies, and a wide variety of other institutions. At the one-day seminars, Barkshire gave an introductory speech and was then followed by Tigar on currency contracts, Williamson on dollar interest rate contracts, Burton on sterling interest rate contracts, and Matthewson on the operation of the market. After tea there was an hour for informal discussions in four groups. The seminars improved as they went on – giving more practical examples of the use of financial futures, using visual aids to better effect, and getting more adept at promoting informal discussion – and at the end of the process were rightly judged to have been a considerable success.

Barkshire ten years later recalled the City's reaction:

To say that we had a majority in favour of what we were proposing would be an exaggeration. But there were very, very few who were against it, very few. There were a minority who were utterly opposed to it. It was new, it came from America, it knocked down the City barriers, it potentially threatened their closed shop, were generally the reasons that they were against it, which they would have put together under the heading of saying that this wasn't good for the City of London and anyway it wouldn't last. So, there was some very strong opposition, but it was very much in the minority.

Two important elements of the City were, for the most part, particularly unenthusiastic. One was the discount market. 'Despite the excellence of your presentation the members of the Market did not feel that they were sufficiently informed yet to give an authoritative response,' Richard Petherbridge, chairman of the London Discount Market Association, wrote to Barkshire on 15 December. 'I was therefore asked to write to you saying that it was premature for us to express an opinion and that we were still looking into the matter.' Someone who attended that presentation, in the basement of Union Discount, would remember it as a painful meeting in which most of the leading figures in the discount market, their 'top hats metaphorically on their heads', failed to grasp all the underlying concepts involved. The other main negative attitudes came from the Stock Exchange's membership: most stockbrokers, still protected by minimum commission, found the likely commission rates unattractively low; there was the larger question of the new market's probable incompatibility with single capacity, which the Stock Exchange looked likely to have to defend to the Restrictive Practices Court; and, living a generally comfortable, ring-fenced life, the natural tendency of many if not most firms was not to exercise the grey matter unnecessarily.

The crux, however, remained the Old Lady. Barkshire caused anxiety by telling the working party on 27 November 1980 that 'there was concern at the Bank about endorsing the market in case something untoward occurred in which case the Bank could be held responsible'. The firm view of the meeting, however, was that 'some reaction was necessary from the Bank, even if it was neutral, if wide participation in the establishment of the market was to be obtained'; and it was accordingly agreed that the summary paper to the Bank, recording the City's response to the seminars and due by the end of the year, 'should specifically request a response'. A week later, at a buffet lunch at Phillips & Drew, Burton bumped into Eddie George and they had, as Burton reported to the rest of the working party, a profitable chat:

> George has particular responsibility for the gilt department and I gained the impression that he would in fact be in favour of a long gilt contract. In our next report that is due to be submitted to the Bank, he feels it would be useful if we could show that the introduction of a long gilt contract would perhaps encourage the re-establishment of the corporate debenture market. This move would produce substantial benefit to the monetary aggregates. George indicated that it would also be useful if we could examine the possibility of a contract in long gilts actually assisting the funding programme of the Government.
>
> As a general comment, the Bank are concerned at the expected influence of a futures market on the cash markets and, although I mentioned the study last year in America by the Fed. which had not been able to substantiate any adverse movement in the cash markets, George felt that this report was in fact inconclusive. The Bank also feel that there may be too many hedgers in the early days and not enough speculators with the result that this could create a liquidity shortage in the futures market. I outlined at length our hopes on this subject and confirmed the views of the Working Party that sufficient liquidity would be created by the major operators in the money market i.e. banks, discount houses and so on.
>
> As a general pointer to our discussion, I was heartened by the positive views expressed by George.

The working party's submission to the Bank was duly sent on New Year's Eve, and it made much of the City's positive response and the benefits to London that would accrue from the new market. Indeed, there was a direct competitive factor involved, for with Amsterdam, Zurich and Paris all by this time 'showing an interest in forming financial futures markets', the submission argued that 'there is probably only room for one such international market in Europe and the first centre to take the initiative would effectively prevent the others from having a viable market'. With Bank reservations in mind, the submission went out of its way to emphasise the importance of the clearing members:

It is only they who have a relationship with the clearing house and the clearing house's guarantee extends only to them: the clearing members are financially responsible for all those who clear through them whether they be outside customers or other members. It is therefore essential that the total number of open positions a clearing member is allowed is strictly related to his own capital resources and that this is carefully monitored by the clearing house.

Accordingly, the financial requirements demanded from would-be members would vary according to the role the member was proposing to play in the market. Another, related passage equally sought to reassure:

At the centre of the financial integrity of the market is the clearing house guarantee to clearing members which is provided as part of the process of substitution by which the clearing house becomes a party to every trade. The clearing house is able to provide this guarantee because its position is always totally matched as it is party to both the buyer and seller in each deal and it is fully margined by both parties. Furthermore the system of price limits, daily examination of members' positions and the general supervision of the markets completes the interrelated package which safeguards the system, and there is the additional safeguard of the capital of every clearing member backing its position with the clearing house. Behind all of this is the clearing house's own capital and reserves.

Never for one moment taking their eyes off the fundamental need to persuade the Bank to allow their project to go ahead, and quickly and sensibly incorporating all the suggestions (often implicit or even coded) that one way or another emanated from the Bank, Barkshire and his men had done all they could. 'The Working Party feels that no further progress can be made until consent for the formation of a market is received from the Bank of England,' it was now agreed. From the perspective of the mid-1990s, when the era of the governor controlling the City merely by raising his eyebrows is little more than a folk memory, it might seem that the market's founding fathers were unduly deferential. But to the men of 1980 there was – even after the abolition of exchange controls and thereby the removal of a whole raft of the Bank's authority – realistically no other way of playing it.

American financial futures, meanwhile, maintained their remarkable growth. The *FT* on 16 January recorded that in the first eleven months of 1980 the volume of Treasury bond contracts traded on the CBOT amounted to 5.5m, more than three times the volume in the comparable period of 1979; while on the IMM the volume of Treasury bill contracts in the same period was up from 1.7m to 2.9m, and in foreign currency futures up from 2.0m to 3.8m. Melamed's recent claim that financial futures would be the 'leading edge of international finance for the balance of this century and beyond' did not seem entirely fanciful. On the other hand, as one senior Wall Street figure was quoted in the same *FT* survey, the undeniable fact remained that 'there is a mystique and fear surrounding financial futures which it could take a generation to get rid of'. That would remain equally true in London, though soon afterwards the *National Westminster Bank Review* did its bit by publishing Gemmill's largely sanguine assessment of the likely impact of 'Financial Futures in London'.

For Barkshire, waiting on the Bank's response, the main concern had become the ICCH situation, following the announcement of an offer by the Trustee Savings Banks for United Dominions Trust. He wrote on 9 February to UDT's chairman, Leonard Mather, formerly the Midland's chief general manager and a much respected figure:

> If ICCH become owned by a single commercial entity, whether that be the Trustee Savings Banks, Lloyds & Scottish, or some other company, we would have considerable doubts as to whether such single ownership would be appropriate for clearing financial futures and we would have to explore the possibility of making alternative arrangements for the provision of our clearing and guarantee facilities. We would very much hope therefore that it will be possible for ICCH to end up by being owned by a consortium of clearing banks, or clearing and other banks, and we believe that such ownership would considerably enhance the reputation of the London markets to the benefit of the whole City of London.

Mather's reply was friendly as well as reassuring:

> Whilst I obviously cannot be specific at this stage in the midst of takeover prospects, I am confident that ICCH will be 'appropriately owned' long before you are ready to open your new market, and their expertise and long experience will be readily available to you to ensure successful operation...
>
> Let me seize this opportunity to congratulate you most warmly upon the outstanding way in which you have led your team in the Working Party and presented your views so clearly to all concerned. I have naturally studied all your submissions and particularly enjoyed your recommendations to the Bank of England. Your enthusiasm and drive has made it all possible.

The working party met for what would be the last time on 17 February 1981. Barkshire, confident of the Bank's eventual pronouncement, outlined how the existing organisation would broaden into a steering committee representative of the City as a whole. He reported that, following a wistful glance at St Paul's,

Richard Saunders & Partners had identified three possible locations for the market: the Royal Exchange, Bucklersbury House and Cunard House. 'It was recognised that the provision of telephones, particularly direct lines, would be a major problem.' Three fundamental decisions were taken with regard to membership: membership would be of one class only; the number of seats sold would be in the range of 150 to 350; and the purchase of a seat would entitle the owner to only one trader on the floor at any one time, but this trader could trade in any pit. Finally, 'it was agreed that the financing prior to opening should be raised by an initial sale of seats at a price below the main sale price'.

On 26 February the Bank spoke. J.B. Page, an executive director in charge of banking and supervision, wrote to Barkshire:

The Bank has no objection to the establishment of a financial futures market in London if further work shows that this can be achieved. The Bank wishes to be consulted as further work proceeds and to be satisfied with the design of the market, the means by which its financial integrity is to be ensured and the contracts to be traded. To this end, the Bank will provide an observer on whatever body carries out this work.

If a market is established, its authorities would have the prime responsibility for ensuring its continuing integrity. However, the Bank would expect the market authorities to accept on behalf of all participants its surveillance and to respond fully to such requests, including the provision of information, as the Bank may reasonably make.

The Bank would have no objection in principle to the development of a long gilt contract although this could be done only in close consultation with the Stock Exchange.

Page's letter was sent to Barkshire by Dawkins, who added: 'I am glad you will be consulting us about the composition of the Steering Committee. Had you not offered, we would have asked!'

To the untrained eye, Page's letter may not have seemed wildly enthusiastic, but Barkshire was well versed in the nuances of Bankspeak, and on releasing it to the press he provided a suitable gloss: 'The whole letter was a surprise. I didn't expect it to be quite so positive or favourable. The Bank could have said it wouldn't stand in our way. That would have been damning.' He added that the appointment of an official observer from the Bank 'indicated more commitment to the idea than I would have expected at this stage'. Williamson was even more bullish. 'The Bank roared ahead of the expectations of most of the City,' he told *American Banker*. 'And the really big news is its no objection in principle to a futures contract in British long bonds.' *The Times* in its reaction to the Bank's statement took the high ground: 'Whatever doubts the Bank may have entertained, it has in effect given

BANK OF ENGLAND
Threadneedle Street
London
EC2R 8AH

26 February 1981

R R StJ Barkshire Esq

Dear Mr Barkshire,

The Bank has now considered the proposals of the London Financial
Futures Working Party.

The Bank has no objection to the establishment of a financial futures
market in London if further work shows that this can be achieved.
The Bank wishes to be consulted as further work proceeds and to be
satisfied with the design of the market, the means by which its
financial integrity is to be ensured and the contracts to be traded.
To this end, the Bank will provide an observer on whatever body
carries out this work.

If a market is established, its authorities would have the prime
responsibility for ensuring its continuing integrity. However, the
Bank would expect the market authorities to accept on behalf of all
participants its surveillance and to respond fully to such requests,
including the provision of information, as the Bank may reasonably
make.

The Bank would have no objection in principle to the development of a
long gilt contract although this could be done only in close
consultation with the Stock Exchange.

Yours sincerely,

JB Page

permission to a wide range of new markets which could be the biggest single financial development in years... In so far as the City will be exposed to well established foreign competition it is a decisive step.' The *FT*'s 'Lex' emphasised the practical problems of installing a communications system for the new market: 'British Telecommunications, in its own way, presents just as formidable a hurdle as the Bank.'

The equivalent of a green light inevitably occasioned a sense of euphoria, telephone wires notwithstanding, but there were those who reflected that it had all taken a terribly long time to reach this point. 'The significant fact about a London futures exchange is not that a new marketplace will appear out of thin air, but that the idea is several years overdue,' observed *Euromoney* in March:

Opposite: The Bank's permission.

Trading in financial futures – futures based on interest rate movements – has been successful for at least five years. There is enormous commercial demand for a mechanism that would protect all kinds of market participants from swings in LIBOR [the London Inter-Bank Offered Rate]. London is the natural marketplace for a futures exchange; futures markets in commodities are an established feature in the City, which is also the most important Eurobanking centre. Yet London has, until now, let the initiative slip to Chicago...

Why had it taken so long? The Bank's relative sluggishness in making up its mind was one reason, but not the only one. Arguably more important was the City's failure, *before* the ICCH/Barkshire initiative, to seize the opportunity. Should a senior City figure – maybe a merchant banker – have had the vision sometime in the mid-1970s? Should the Stock Exchange have positively reached out for a new, related form of business? Perhaps they should; but bearing in mind how financial futures began and grew in Chicago there is surely a defensible case for pointing the finger mainly at the London commodity markets. No Melamed-type figure emerged, and leading a fairly easy, protected, profitable life there was little apparent incentive to expand into this new, alien area, apparently the preserve of individual speculators, even though following the break-up of Bretton Woods the need to hedge against currency instability was clearly becoming a major component in commodity dealing.

Yet all that said, one needs to remember the environment in which the City was operating in the mid to late 1970s. The secondary banking crisis and severe stock market slump were still fresh in everyone's minds, the political party in office was at best lukewarm towards financial markets, and – crucially – exchange controls remained in place. Moreover, to concentrate unduly on how long it took London to establish a financial futures market is to risk ignoring what a remarkable achievement it was to create one at all, granted how sectional and fragmented the City still was. Above all it was Barkshire's achievement, providing the drive and the focus, both before and after the Bank's endorsement knocking heads together in his unremitting pursuit of the bigger goal. 'I believe that the establishment of a financial futures market will be one of the most important things to happen in the City of London for a very long time,' he told the press at the start of March 1981. Not everyone was convinced, but in his own mind – one that took few prisoners – he was certain.

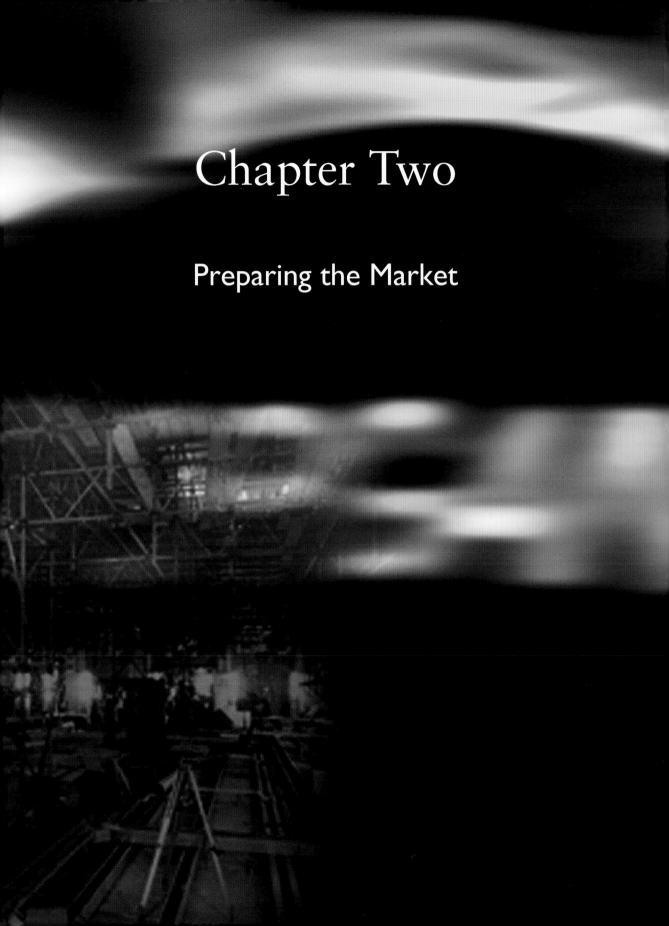

Chapter Two

Preparing the Market

BARKSHIRE EXPRESSED THE hope, in the wake of the Bank of England's letter, that the new market would be in action by early 1982, but in the event it did not open until 30 September 1982. During the year and a half prior to opening, decision-making was vested initially in the steering committee and then an elected board of directors. The steering committee was 22-strong and included, in addition to members of the working party, representatives of most of the potentially relevant City organisations. An executive committee, buttressed by a handful of sub-committees on specific questions, dealt with practical and technical matters on a day-to-day basis, but the steering committee had overall authority. That phase ended in May 1982 with the election of a board, of whom over half came from the original working party. Barkshire throughout was chairman, whether of the steering committee or the board. He ran the meetings with a firm hand. 'Is that agreed?' he would ask, and at that point few were inclined to raise their voices.

Michael Jenkins.

By spring 1981 the original notion that ICCH would run the market had been dropped, and soon afterwards the head-hunters Spencer Stuart were asked to find suitable candidates for the position of chief executive. The man who came through was Michael Jenkins. 'We had a short list of people,' Barkshire would recall of the executive committee's selection meeting, 'all of whom understood the futures market except for Michael, and he said, "You don't want somebody who understands the futures markets, you want somebody who is an organiser, a manager, and who will run the project for you." And we scratched our heads and thought about that, and said, "Well we thought we wanted somebody who knew about futures, but actually we think you're right," and hired him.' Jenkins had been intimately involved in the late 1970s in helping to set up and develop the European Options Exchange, based in Amsterdam, so he can hardly have been altogether innocent of futures; on the other hand, he presumably did know less about the subject than his main rival for the job, Neil Matthewson of ICCH. At the time, recommending the appointment to the steering committee, Barkshire noted that Jenkins 'is very much a project manager and is particularly interested in setting up the Exchange and in its formative stage', indeed that 'he recognises that he may not be the right person to manage the Exchange on a long term continuing basis'. Greenwells and Akroyd & Smithers expressed reservations about the appointment, on the grounds that Jenkins had been asked to leave an earlier position with the Stock Exchange, but the steering committee ratified it on 8 June.

Jenkins's Stock Exchange past was in fact highly pertinent. From 1971 to 1977 he had been technical director there, responsible against considerable resistance for defining requirements for the new computer-based settlement system – TALISMAN – and then forming a team to design and build it. At that point, with the Stock Exchange Council unwilling to make any further technological decisions, he had fallen out with the chief executive and taken on the Amsterdam job. For Barkshire for one, this background was almost certainly a positive recommendation. It proved a hugely successful appointment, and Jenkins stayed on for much longer than he had anticipated. Over the years he exercised a sure touch in overseeing the exchange's

John Foyle.

increasingly complicated systems development; maintained an admirably flat management structure; and for all his charm, and a more refined literary taste than most City men, showed himself to be a highly pragmatic operator, capable of bargaining toughly and riding out criticism, usually external rather than internal. During his early years he built up a high-quality management team that stayed together for a long time and felt considerable loyalty to him as well as to the institution. 'He hopes that people will work hard and are conscientious,' one remarked in 1991, 'but he wants to make sure people have fun. The respect for Michael within the exchange is enormous.' A former chairman observed at the same time that Jenkins had 'managed to sustain the interest and enthusiasm of the full-timers at the exchange' and 'goes out of his way to create an atmosphere that produces ideas'. It was entirely appropriate praise for a figure second only to Barkshire in LIFFE's history.

Jenkins made two particularly important appointments in his early days as chief executive. One was John Foyle to be market secretary, responsible for all legal,

Gerry Rodgers.

accountancy and taxation matters. The position was originally offered to Tony de Guingand, but at the last moment he decided to stay with ICCH. An accountant by profession and still in his early thirties, Foyle had been seconded by Price Waterhouse from 1976 to 1978 to the Inflation Accounting Steering Group, where as secretary he was responsible for developing the UK's accounting

Above: Patricia Duncan.
Middle: Juliette Proudlove.
Below: Bernard Reed.

standard on current cost accounting. Meticulous but with a creative streak, and capable of wrestling with apparently intractable problems until they cried for mercy, he soon became LIFFE's administrative linchpin. The other key appointment was that of Gerry Rodgers to be communications and systems manager. A qualified engineer, he had been for the past two years the project manager and operations consultant for the automation and relocation of the Winnipeg Commodity Market. An engaging, somewhat maverick Devonian, he needed his own space and time to perform, but Jenkins trusted him and wisely gave him those valuable commodities. Managing all the physical aspects of setting up the exchange was an enormous task, but Rodgers proved wonderfully equipped for it.

Other staff members, appointed in the course of 1981/2, would also make major contributions. Patricia Duncan, who had worked for Jenkins at the Stock Exchange, was his first appointment to the new management team, and in this pioneering phase she undertook, with good humour and pertinacity, a great variety of different, often difficult tasks. Juliette Proudlove had worked for a long time in the City Offices Company before coming to LIFFE, and over the years her outgoing, determined personality meant that she was given special responsibility for the exchange's membership. Bernard Reed, possessing a broad range of financial and industrial experience, was brought in as marketing and education manager. Ken Heymer was appointed floor manager, having performed a similar role at first the London Commodity Exchange and then the recently established International Petroleum Exchange, the latter experience giving Heymer the taste for developing the operational side of a brand new exchange. He worked closely and effectively with Rodgers, and the two became known as 'Rodgers & Heymerstein'.

Until shortly before the market opened, the staff worked, in increasingly crowded conditions, in Mercantile House's offices at 66 Cannon Street, having been allocated three rooms plus the board room on the ground floor. Two of the unsung heroines were Audrey Witham and Lucinda Young, secretaries to Barkshire and Foyle respectively. The prevailing mood was hard work, dedication, camaraderie, a sense of fun, and that wonderful feeling of creating from scratch something entirely new. There were few rules to follow and plenty of scope for improvisation. Money was quite tight, even after the initial sale of seats; Barkshire and the other 'inner' members of the old working party were strong characters, not always easy to work for; but none of those centrally involved would later deny that it was a thoroughly rewarding experience.

A more general – and crucial – principle was also being established in these early, defining years. Barkshire, Jenkins and Wigglesworth were, from their different vantage points, familiar with the Stock Exchange model of corporate governance (though that term was still barely in use) and were absolutely determined that their new market would be run on more flexible lines. In their eyes there were three main flaws to the Stock Exchange model: firstly, its governing body, the Council, invariably included a significant number of members who in business terms were regarded by their firms as semi-passengers and could therefore easily be spared, a view that hardly added to the Council's authority; secondly, there had grown up over the years an appalling proliferation of committees, with the result that decision-making had become an extremely cumbersome process; and thirdly, the existence of all these members' committees meant that little leeway and initiative was given to staff, with inevitable consequences on morale and quality. In explicit contrast, Barkshire and his colleagues were determined that LIFFE's board should be lean and have a substantial proportion of openly elected heavyweight practitioners, that committees should be kept to a minimum, and that as far as reasonably possible the executive should be left to get on with the job. It is an incalculable blessing, of course, to start from scratch with no historical baggage, but the founding fathers had the sense to learn from the past. Corporate governance alone can never be decisive, but it is very difficult to succeed if one gets it wrong. LIFFE got it right.

Ken Heymer.

An exchange needs a name. At the first meeting of the steering committee (its meetings were held at 10 Lombard Street, on the invitation of the Committee of London Clearing Bankers) 'it was agreed that the market will be known as The London International Financial Futures Exchange (LIFFE)'. The question of how to pronounce the acronym was a tricky one, but three months later the steering committee took the advice of Christopher Morgan, whose firm of the same name had recently been appointed to look after the exchange's public relations, that it 'should be pronounced as in "life" rather than as in "Liffey"'. It was a good and striking decision, though over the years would be the cause of too many tired sub-editors writing too many predictable headlines.

As for membership of this market, the basic thinking was that (in the words of an executive committee paper submitted to the steering committee in April 1981) 'a small restricted number of members, while entirely suitable for single produce commodity exchanges with a more limited general interest, would not be the most appropriate solution for a financial futures market which would be likely to attract active participation from a wide range of financial and commercial institutions'. Moreover, restricting the numbers to, say, 25–40 'would create impossible tasks of selection and would concentrate too much power and potential profit into too few hands'. Instead, it was decided to make an initial offer of up to 200 seats, each available at £20,000. Inevitably that figure was the subject of keen debate, but it was felt to be high enough to generate adequate, much-needed revenue to finance setting up the exchange, but low enough not to debar too many smaller firms. Invitations to be part of the first tranche of seat-holders (with a subsequent second tranche of a further 200 seats envisaged) were sent out in mid-May, and applicants were informed that, whether they be a company, a partnership or an individual, they would 'be required to satisfy the board that they are of suitable financial and business standing to be members of the Exchange'. Barkshire told the press that members were likely to be drawn mainly from banks, stockbrokers, discount houses, commodity traders and bond dealers from the City and abroad; and that last word was a reminder of how different LIFFE was likely to be from the Stock Exchange of the early 1980s.

The emerging structure did not please everyone. The Bank of England had recently received a letter of protest, written on 24 April by Derek Whiting of the Comfin Group to Anthony Rucker of the London Commodity Exchange. Based in Paris (Sucres et Denrees Ltd) and New York (Westway Trading Corp) as well as London, where it was a floor member of various commodity exchanges, Comfin had wide trading interests in insurance and banking as well as, *inter alia*, in meat, dairy products and molasses. If the commodity markets had somewhat failed to punch their weight on the working party, Whiting now attempted to make up for lost time:

LONDON INTERNATIONAL FINANCIAL FUTURES EXCHANGE

Invitation to apply for membership

Applications for membership of the Exchange are now invited by the Steering Committee. There will be one class of membership, which will carry with it the right to trade on the floor of the Exchange itself, in all contracts.

Up to 200 memberships will be allocated in this initial offering at a price of £20,000 (plus VAT) for each membership, of which £10,000 (plus VAT) will be payable on application. This offering will close on 29th June, 1981. The proceeds from this offering will be used to finance the establishment of the Exchange and the construction and preparation of the trading floor.

A further and final offering of memberships (up to a likely total maximum of 400) will take place prior to the opening of the Exchange. It is proposed that the second offering of seats will be at a substantially higher price than this first offering.

Application forms and full details of the offer and terms of membership are obtainable from the Chairman of the Steering Committee at 66, Cannon Street, London EC4N 6AE. Please mark your envelope LIFFE.

Financial Times, 14 May 1981.

> *In our opinion, the new market should follow as closely as possible the policies and practices of the established markets in London, together with the functions performed by the International Commodities Clearing House. It is accepted that there will be differences of procedure but the reservoir of expertise represented by the London soft and hard commodity markets, and acquired over many years of practical experience, should not be disregarded. The system is readily understood by those operating futures markets and will provide a firm base from which the new market could develop.*

It is important in our view that the membership of the market should be restrained and kept to as small a number as possible. A multiplicity of traders would make for chaos, lack of control and would be more difficult to police. The success of the London commodity markets is, in large part, due to the practice of the major users and suppliers standing aside and leaving the market trading to appropriately designated trade houses and brokers. To achieve this in an FX [Foreign Exchange] futures market, banks should be excluded from full membership and membership confined to numbers similar to those appropriate in the other markets, say 50 members. This can, perhaps, be achieved by setting a substantial membership fee, say £250/500,000, together with some qualification such as futures trading or foreign exchange dealing experience.

LIFFE had already invited applications for membership when, on 19 May, Dawkins went to Comfin for lunch. Whiting reiterated his views about the desirability of a restricted membership of brokers only, but Dawkins could do little more in response than say it was rather late in the day to be airing them. In due course Whiting would become a director of LIFFE and a good friend of the exchange; but for rather too long he and other leading figures in the commodity markets had tended to assume that this new market in financial futures was not really going to happen, until it was too late to control it.

Closing date for applications for membership was 29 June, and they were processed and vetted by LIFFE but with a list shown to the Bank of England. Indeed, early in the month Dawkins told Barkshire that the Bank was concerned that 'applications for seats from small houses would be rejected in favour of the large institutions', and Dawkins said he thought 'the market would be more soundly based if there were an appropriate spread of membership between small and large'. Barkshire agreed to take the point on board. In the event the first tranche of 200 seats was oversubscribed, with 223 applications being received for 366 seats. After a lengthy process, 172 members were accepted and 215 seats allotted. No accepted applicant was allotted more than two seats, but 43 – mainly commodity brokers, who had indicated a strong commitment to trade and who, it was hoped, might also act as principals in the market – were each allowed two seats. In some cases different applicants were companies belonging to the same group but performing quite separate operations, and in these cases up to four seats were allocated to one group. Indeed, one such group was the chairman's, Mercantile House Holdings, whose recently acquired subsidiary, the old-established commodity broking firm R.J. Rouse & Co, was allocated two seats in addition to Mercantile House's two.

The successful applicants were a gratifyingly diverse spread: 47 UK commodity brokers; 28 UK banks, including Rothschilds, Lazards, Morgan Grenfell and Schroders as well as all the main clearers; 25 overseas banks, including familiar names like Citicorp and First National Bank of Chicago and less familiar names like Havana International Bank and Hungarian International Bank; 22 members of the Stock Exchange (at this stage against the wishes of its Council, which wanted first to see the new market's rules), including the three main jobbers as well as a reasonable range of stockbrokers, of whom Messels and Phillips & Drew each received two seats; 13 US and overseas commodity and futures brokers; 10 money brokers, of whom several (including Tullett & Riley) received two seats each; nine US investment banks, including the ambitious Drexel Burnham Lambert; nine trading companies and individuals; five discount houses (Allen Harvey & Ross, Cater Ryder, Gerrard & National, Jessel Toynbee, Union Discount); three investment companies; and one insurance broker, C.E. Heath & Co, whose founder had long ago broken down barriers at Lloyd's. Non-applicants included Barings, Warburgs and Cazenove's.

Overall, the presence in the membership of so many major banks was crucial to the prestige of the new market, giving it a credibility that it would have found very difficult to acquire by any other means. As for the substantial American interest, this owed something to a positive report on financial futures recently published by the Fed. Fifty-one applicants were rejected, mainly a mixture of commodity brokers and various individuals. Determined to let in as few rotten apples as possible, Barkshire and his colleagues largely succeeded, though some unsuccessful applicants no doubt had a legitimate grievance.

What exactly would be the initial financial requirements for members? Reporting at this time, the financial supervision sub-committee concluded that the net worth for clearing members should be at least £1 million, reduced to £500,000 for clearing members trading only for their own account; and that the minimum net worth for non-clearing members would be set at £100,000, excluding the principal place of residence of individual members. Some members of the steering committee, however, felt that £100,000 was too steep a requirement for non-clearing members, being much higher than Chicago's requirements and likely to discourage individuals from seeking to become members; and it was suggested that, for members operating through a clearing member, an appropriate guarantee should be accepted as a substitute for net worth.

It was a theme that Jenkins took up, submitting a discussion paper on 22 July. He argued that though the outcome of the first offering of seats had been 'very encouraging', it was unlikely that LIFFE had yet attracted 'a sufficient number of professional traders, i.e. well-capitalised speculators, that it will need to provide liquidity – particularly at the outset'. He therefore suggested that, for the next offering, capital requirements should be set at 'a relatively low level for traders', who would be backed by a few well-capitalised clearing members 'experienced in monitoring such traders'. He also thought the exchange should 'promote the idea of forming partnerships/companies bringing together experienced traders and

FINANCIAL FUTURES

London squares up to Chicago

By David Marsh

HOW THE CHICAGO FUTURES EXCHANGES HAVE GROWN

MERCANTILE EXCHANGE

BOARD OF TRADE

A TRANS-ATLANTIC tussle is shaping up over the world's most frenetic and fastest growing money market.

The spectacularly successful financial futures show—trading in forward contracts in interest rates and currencies—makes its debut in London next year after a record-breaking opening run in Chicago.

Financial futures markets strip money down to the status of a commodity that can be freely traded for future dates as well as in the present.

Financial futures can be used to make—and lose—large sums of money for profit-hungry banks and speculators. But they also have the solidly no-nonsense function of allowing companies and investors to "hedge" or insure against risks on volatile foreign exchange and credit markets.

The backers of the London futures exchange—planned to start next spring or summer—believe they have a box-office hit on their hands. Unlike other commercial ventures, financial futures thrive on instability and uncertainty—and there is no shortage of either at present.

The London market's first offer of 200 membership places has just been drastically over-subscribed.

The City has the initial low-key aim of complementing rather than challenging the Chicago exchanges, the Board of Trade and the Mercantile Exchange. The Big Two pioneered financial futures during the 1970s, and after a slow start, have been raking in the receipts ever since.

In the longer run, however, the opening of the London market may herald the start of drawn into competition—the silky-voiced bankers of the City and the grizzled commodity market barons of the American mid-West.

One London financial manager who has followed developments on both sides of the Atlantic sums it up thus: "The Chicago people think they've seen off the stumblebums in New York and now it's the turn of the City. In London, on the other hand, we say: 'Who are these hicks in Chicago?—They don't know what these markets are all lay. a speculator or hedger can invest in a large volume of financial instruments.

In view of sharp rises in interest rates, this feature of "putting in a little and getting a lot"—as one Chicago dealer puts it—has attracted a lot of people into financial futures in recent years. It also heightens the risks.

Turbulence on the currency markets and—more recently—unprecedented volatility of U.S. interest rates have provided a powerful engine for growth of the first five months this year rose 35 per cent compared with the same 1980 period.

On the Board of Trade, the older of the two exchanges (it started in 1848), the increase in business has been even bigger. The Board trades only interest rate futures (mainly Treasury bonds)—and it is here, rather than in currencies, that the largest growth rates have been registered this year.

Interest rate futures volume at the Board has risen more than 100-fold since 1976—and volume so far this year is run exchanges. Many dealers tend to move from pork belly trading to Treasury bills when they realise where the growth and the money are.

As well as responding to volatility, futures markets are widely suspected of contributing to it too. Both the West German Bundesbank and the New York Federal Reserve Bank believe that trading on the International Monetary Market can add to currency fluctuations.

With the sterling/dollar the most widely traded currency

HOW TO USE FINANCIAL FUTURES

THE TWO essential elements in the financial futures equation are (a) the price agreed in advance on the futures contract and (b) the price of the contract when it reaches maturity, which depends on subsequent movements of the spot price of currencies or interest rate instruments on financial markets.

The difference between (a) and (b) is the profit or loss accruing to the trader. One example of where futures trading can be used to reduce risks is when a U.S. pension fund forecasts a fall in interest rates but does not have an outright deposit. Instead, it buys a futures contract in three month U.S. Treasury bills.

If interest rates do indeed fall, the price of the contract would rise. The pension fund can sell for a profit after three months—gaining compensation for the loss it would otherwise have suffered because of the lack of cash to make the outright investment.

Many banks and investment institutions buying new issues of U.S. Treasury bonds these days automatically hedge their positions by selling forward on the futures market.

If interest rates rise, the capital value of the newly-purchased bonds would fall. But banks would be compensated for this loss by an equivalent fall in the value of futures contracts. This would allow them to make a profit by buying back an equivalent Treasury bond contract at below the originally agreed selling price.

Companies hedging forward export and import contracts can use the financial futures markets as an alternative to the forward rates quoted by banks.

professional dealers — and straightforward gamblers—who have supplied liquidity to the Chicago exchange for generations. Without this element, commercial orders have simply dried up. The same fate could await the London market.

NYFE hopes for a shot in the arm when new contracts—certificates of deposit (CDs) in both domestic and Euro-dollars—are introduced on all three U.S. exchanges.

The New York exchange is due this week to start futures trading in domestic CDs, following the green light from the

Financial Times, 6 July 1981.

firms/individuals willing to put up risk capital'. In sum, over this liquidity problem, he wanted the exchange to take the initiative, knowing well from personal experience that the majority of members 'are content to sit back and wait until the last minute and assume all will be well on the opening date'. For the moment Jenkins made little headway, the general assumption remaining that institutional members by themselves would provide adequate liquidity.

The second offering was made in January 1982. Minimum net worth was laid down as £100,000, with a higher net worth to be required in respect of clearing members. For this tranche a further 185 seats were offered at £30,000 each, a raised price that was presumably one of the reasons for the offer being slightly undersubscribed. In the event 69 new corporate and individual members came in by late February, and together with old members they were allocated a further 158 seats. Largely thanks to the influence of Yuji Shirakawa of Nikko, over one-third of the new members were Japanese, mainly banks, bringing an important potential dimension to the market; this time round Warburgs came in; but from the Stock Exchange there were only five new members, including Mullens, the Government brokers. A significant minority of applications continued to be rejected.

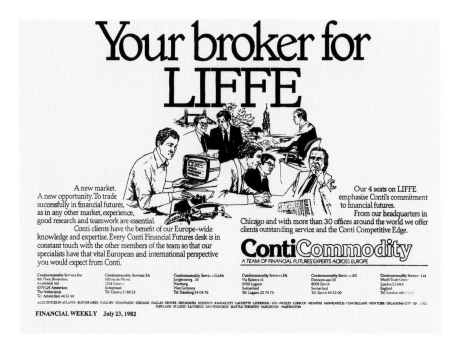

Jenkins, meanwhile, continued to worry about liquidity. With an eye now particularly on the leasing of seats, about to become permissible, he asked the membership and rules sub-committee on 22 March 'to give consideration to whether LIFFE should revise its net worth requirement to £25,000 for a member or tenant who is trading solely for his own account', which 'would exclude anyone who traded on behalf of another member or who wished to do business with a non-member'. He also pointed out that in Chicago the net capital requirement was only $25,000. This time there was a more sympathetic response, and Jenkins at once pressed home his suggestion to the executive committee. 'I am concerned,' he wrote on the 24th, 'that we take every reasonable step open to us to encourage liquidity. I am not yet convinced that this will not be a problem when we open in September.'

He had his way, and in due course the net worth requirement for members and tenants was reduced to £25,000. Those with net worth between £25,000 and £100,000 were not permitted to act on behalf of non-member clients, but could make transactions on their own account and offer an execution service to other members or tenants as a pit broker or floor broker. 'It should be noted,' added a circular to members in June, 'that this reduction in net worth will not weaken the financial integrity of the Exchange as a whole since member/tenants with net worth of between £25,000 and £100,000 will be required, like other non-clearing members, to make clearing arrangements with a clearing member who will guarantee that all transactions made by such non-clearing members, or by tenants, will be duly registered and margined with the Clearing House.' It would be a while yet before liquidity-enhancing, Chicago-style locals were attracted in any numbers to the London market, but at least the theoretical possibility now began to exist. Perhaps Barkshire should have moved further and earlier in this direction, but he was deeply conscious not only of the City's institutional character but also of the need not to put off the British banks, keen though some of them were to deal in gilt futures in particular.

A similar need to combine respectability with market values underlay the complicated task of writing a rule book *ab initio*. The banks needed a strong regulatory structure in order to feel comfortable with other elements in the membership, above all the commodity brokers. West of Gracechurch Street the perception was, fairly or unfairly, that there was a lot of fast practice in the commodity markets. It was not an easy task. Not only was there no legislative framework for financial futures, but LIFFE would be unable to monitor what members – indeed, banks especially – were doing in other parts of their business. Moreover, to ask a merchant bank to submit a financial return disclosing its inner reserves was likely to produce a dusty response. Notwithstanding all of which, draft rules were drawn up by late 1981, with written comments invited from members.

NatWest focused on the question of a daily price limit, arguing that while it was understandable that members from London's soft commodity markets wished to continue in the new market their usual practice of not having a daily price limit, this was not advisable. Unlike in the commodity markets, where the number of participants in each market was relatively limited, on LIFFE the 'number of prospective users is enormous' and 'they are likely to come from widely disparate financial backgrounds'. The integrity of the market thus required the introduction of a daily limit, 'with no trades permitted in excess of this figure on the same day'. Other members supported a limit, but with a shorter suspension period, and in the end a system of price limits was introduced, though rarely exercised and later abandoned. As for hours of trading, the eight members who commented were unanimous in preferring a continuous trading period to splitting the day into two trading periods. Several banks, predictably, objected to the notion of access to their records by LIFFE's supervision department. Several were also explicitly unhappy about the proposed requirement for quarterly returns, though mainly on the grounds of having to pay substantial audit fees. In terms of trading rules, there was little dissent about the need specifically to prohibit pre-arranged trades; while as for trading ahead of client orders, the point made forcibly by Continental Bank that 'in the execution of orders it is imperative that we are allowed to treat our internal dealing units as outside customers and let them make independent trading decisions' prompted Foyle to concede, in his written comments on members' responses, that 'if members cannot treat their internal dealing units as ordinary clients it will become extremely complex for a member to trade on his own behalf as well as for clients'. Writing a rule book is comparable to painting the Forth Bridge, but Foyle relished the prospect.

On one of the more intractable questions, David Walker at the Bank of England received a visit in May 1982 from Gordon Pepper of Greenwells, inquiring about LIFFE's current proposal that members were not required to segregate clients' assets from their own assets. After the visit, L.G. Lloyd of the Bank informed Walker that LIFFE had been 'initially very reluctant to be seen to be trying to force on its very heterogeneous membership a requirement which is alien to the ways most of them operate' – a reference to non-segregation as common practice in both commodity firms and banks. He added, however, that it was now having to rethink its position in the context of not only 'comments from the Bank', but also 'general press comment and Gowerish thinking', an allusion not to the elegant left-hander but to the professor, sponsored by the Department of Trade, whose interim report on investor protection had recently appeared. Lloyd added that 'the opinion of the staff is that they will probably have to move towards across the board segregation of clients' accounts', even though 'this will be difficult for them as it will mean that all their prospective members will have to have new accounting procedures in place and working before the start-up date in September'. A few days later Dawkins told Walker that he had spoken to Pepper: 'He thinks segregation is desirable and is concerned lest it be rejected by LIFFE for the wrong reasons (i.e. that members do not want to see it transferred to cash markets). He merely wished to have an informal word in confidence with the Bank about it – he does not wish Greenwells to be accused of being the member which brought segregation down on everybody's head, so to speak.' For the moment segregation continued to be resisted, but it remained a live issue.

Pepper's tactful intervention was another reminder of the underlying tensions between LIFFE and the Stock Exchange. Nevertheless, when a few months earlier, in January 1982, a special committee on financial futures that was chaired by Wills presented its report to the Stock Exchange Council, its tone was notably positive. 'Participation by Member Firms is not only in the interests of The Stock Exchange, but is also necessary to the success of LIFFE,' the report concluded. 'It believes, therefore, that Member Firms should participate in LIFFE...' And furthermore: 'The Committee would commend to the Council its view that The Stock Exchange should assist LIFFE wherever possible, and that its attitude should be one of encouragement.' How would that translate for member firms that wished to operate in both exchanges? A fortnight later Wills informed the executive committee that the Stock Exchange Council was determined to uphold the principle of single capacity, and that therefore as far as LIFFE was concerned jobbers would not be permitted to act as agents, nor brokers as jobbers. The executive committee 'noted that these restrictions may make membership of LIFFE less attractive to Stock Exchange members', and indeed few applied for the second round of seats. This determination to keep member firms to a single capacity role in the new exchange was made clear in a letter, made public early in February, from the Council to senior partners. 'SE turns frosty on financial futures market,' was the *Daily Telegraph*'s headline; and Wills was quoted as saying that 'the first duty of our members is to their clients and other Stock Exchange firms' and that 'anything else must fit in with that primary duty'.

That September, shortly before the market opened, a strongly worded article by Maggie Urry in the *Investors Chronicle* ('LIFFE spells death for Stock Exchange sacred cows') had a prophetic ring:

Single capacity is the jargon phrase for the rigid Stock Exchange jobber/broker distinction. A broker cannot act as a principal; a jobber cannot act as an agent. Minimum commissions are fixed scales of dealing charges. The Stock Exchange insists on both: LIFFE on neither. All LIFFE deals will be on negotiated commission. And LIFFE members will be free to act as both principal and agent.

Fine. But what about the 26 Stock Exchange members – brokers and jobbers – who are also members of LIFFE? The Stock Exchange has ruled that its members must stick to single capacity even when dealing in LIFFE. But that would leave the Stock Exchange firms at a significant disadvantage to all other LIFFE members. And some members of both exchanges are saying privately that they expect this rule to be disobeyed virtually from day one. Even the Stock Exchange has been realistic enough not to try and impose minimum LIFFE commissions on its members.

But if single capacity and minimum commissions do not obtain in the futures market how long can they survive in the cash market? Dual capacity will creep from LIFFE from the backdoor into the Stock Exchange, and it will bring negotiated commissions with it…

The Stock Exchange's problem is at its worst in LIFFE's long gilt contract. Arbitrage between the cash and futures market will form an important source of business. A jobber (who had abandoned single capacity in LIFFE) would be able to deal for a client in the futures market but not in the cash market. A broker could deal for itself in the futures market but would have to employ a jobber in the cash market. Half the deal would be subject to Stock Exchange rates of commission: commission on the other half could be negotiated. That is absurd.

Add this to the other, mounting pressures on the Stock Exchange's single capacity/minimum commissions system, and there is little chance of the Restrictive Practices case against the Stock Exchange ever coming to court.

The Stock Exchange Council has only itself to blame. It has set its face against the winds of change which have been blowing through the City in recent years, and its features have frozen. It nearly killed its own traded options market by failing to spend enough on publicity. It could have been more involved in LIFFE if it hadn't adopted an 'ignore it and it might go away' attitude. It could have brought gilt futures under its own jurisdiction if it had been more flexible and forward-looking…

The City in 1982 was on the verge of extraordinary change, and LIFFE was not only on the cutting-edge but was helping – by accident as well as by design – to hasten the revolution.

There was, quite apart from locating and equipping the actual physical exchange, an enormous amount of difficult, technical work to be done before the market could open. Much of it, between spring 1981 and summer 1982, involved contracts and relations with the clearing house.

By far the most straightforward to design of the seven initial contracts were the four currency contracts. Burton (chairman of the contracts sub-committee) told the steering committee in September 1981 that it was important 'to accommodate the needs of smaller users and to provide flexibility'. A few months later Graham Croft-Smith of Rouse Woodstock (part of the Mercantile House empire) expressed his concern that there was 'a serious risk of insufficient liquidity to make these contracts viable'. Burton in reply, in March 1982, could do little more than take the party line: 'I think one appreciates that the London market will not develop on the same lines as Chicago, primarily because the number of "locals" will be much smaller. We believe that, with the number of banks and financial institutions in London and elsewhere, there will be sufficient liquidity…' It was presumably a reflection of some anxiety that in June the size of the currency contracts was halved to £25,000, DM125,000, Sw Fr125,000 and Yen 12,500,000. The question remained of whether the European (i.e. Forex) or North American (i.e. IMM) method of quotation should be used. The board decided in July that all four currency contracts would be quoted in US dollars, with a minimum price movement (known as the tick value) of $12.50. 'During the deliberations over the method of quotation,' the circular noted, 'a number of members advocated a "jumbo" currency contract with face value of $1,000,000. The board recognise that a requirement for this size of contract may develop once the market has started.' It added that once the currency contracts had started actively trading the possible need for a smaller tick value would also be reviewed.

The design of the long-term sterling interest rate contract, based on a long gilt and generally referred to as the gilt contract, was largely Wigglesworth's responsibility, and at an early stage he co-opted John Lewis of Phillips & Drew to add his technical input. The Stock Exchange at the outset expressed its fears – including the possible fragmentation of the market in Government securities, the erosion of traditional jobbing principles and the danger that clients dealing direct on the floor of LIFFE would encourage 'off the floor trading' on a direct basis – and throughout the process a conscious attempt was made to keep the Stock Exchange onside as much as possible. During one early discussion it was felt that the minimum price movement was too large at ¹⁄₁₆%, and it was decided to move into line with the other contracts by adopting a minimum price movement of .01; however, the draft contract that was sent out in autumn 1981 to banks and stockbrokers for their comments had reverted to ¹⁄₁₆%, possibly in deference to Stock Exchange sensitivities. Comments were generally positive, including Pepper's: 'I am satisfied with the general terms of the contract, i.e. the £50,000 nominal unit of trading in a notional 20-year bond, with a 12% coupon, against which delivery may be made of any gilt-edged stock having 15 or more years to maturity and a coupon within the range of 10–14%.'

Soon afterwards, in March 1982, there was a small but illuminating episode. At a meeting of the steering committee, Wills declared that the Stock Exchange was 'concerned' about LIFFE's proposal to open its gilt contract before the Stock Exchange's gilt market opened at 10 am. Burton's internal note following the meeting nicely conveys the prevailing atmosphere of Young Turks at work:

This is nonsense, and once again underlines the 'head in the sand' attitude currently being propounded by the Stock Exchange. When we discuss the gilt contract with their internal LIFFE people, I feel we should resist this proposal quite strongly as I do not believe that the futures market in any way depends on the cash market being open at the same time and vice versa. What we may wish to recommend is that the Stock Exchange, and therefore the Bank of England, consider advancing their opening times to bring these more in line with 1982 business thinking!

There was no immediate resolution of this undeniably symbolic matter. In July the board decided to push for 9.15 as opening time for trading in the gilts contract, but it soon emerged that the Bank of England's preference was for the contract to open at the same time as the cash market opened. In response to which, at the board on 13 August, 'it was agreed that the opening of trading could be delayed until 9.30 am but that it would not be satisfactory if it was later than this time'.

The contracts that really caused all the headaches were the short-term Eurodollar and sterling interest rate contracts. By early 1982, after a year of intensive and often necessarily arcane discussions and consultations, the working party's original proposal that the contracts should be based on certificates of deposit had been ruled out, on the grounds of a potential lack of deliverable stock, even leading to a corner if such a shortage coincided with delivery. Instead, a preference emerged for, in both cases, a time deposit contract with a cash settlement option. The question was whether such a contract, without a provision for delivery, would fall within Section 18 of the Gaming Act of 1845 and as a result be void in law as being in essence a wager. Accordingly, Counsel advised that LIFFE should gather evidence of commercial users' support for cash-settled short interest rate contracts, and that spring a good response was epitomised by the reply from National Westminster: 'As long as arbitrage and efficient sampling for establishment of final settlement prices are present, we should have good hedging vehicles whose ultimate delivery is irrelevant to commercial purpose.'

Jenkins, Foyle and the Sterling Contract sub-committee, chaired by Burton, were almost there but not quite. Further consultations with Counsel followed in May and June. 'Counsel reiterated their previously expressed view that there is an overwhelming need to show that the market (when in existence) has commercial purpose,' a summarising note recorded. 'A contract providing for delivery is more apt to show bona fide commercial intentions of the parties than is a contract which does not provide for delivery... It is the idea of a "legitimate commercial transaction" which lies at the root of Counsel's argument.' Clearly it would be very difficult to demonstrate a new contract's hedging and other commercial purposes right at the start of its active life, yet it might be that at the start a challenge to that contract's enforceability was made. Over the next few weeks, a complicated but convincing solution was devised, through which the settlement rate was LIBOR minus not ⅛% but ¼% (i.e. 25 ticks), enabling the arranger of the deposit an opportunity to obtain a market rate of interest which was readily achievable; a time deposit was optional; and a delivery mechanism was included, albeit at the buyer's option. The details were not included in the joint written opinion submitted – and in due course available to members – by Counsel on 21 July, but from the point of view of market users this piece of technical legerdemain was an important bulwark to Counsel's 'clear conclusion that a genuine commercial need for the cash settlement contract does exist and can be proved, if necessary, to the satisfaction of the Courts, and that on the proper application of the legal principles established by the decided cases such a contract is not a wager in law'. Over the next month further discussions and minor modifications were required, to ensure first that ICCH was willing to clear the contracts and then that the clearing banks as major members of LIFFE would support them, but well before the market opened there was assurance for the membership as a whole that the danger of a legal challenge to these contracts was virtually nil.

ICCH itself by this time was under new ownership. In spring 1981 the steering committee had agreed to appoint it as the independent clearing house 'provided its capital backing and ownership were ultimately acceptable to the Exchange', as seemed likely granted that the chairman of the Trustee Savings Bank had publicly indicated that the TSB intended to divest itself of the majority of its holding of ICCH. Significantly, the steering committee had 'felt that the Exchange should retain the option to set up its own clearing house and that the contract with ICCH should initially be limited to two or three years and should afterwards be subject to annual renewal'. It was known that the Bank of England wanted the ownership of ICCH to be transferred to the clearing banks, in order to guarantee ICCH's financial solidity for its role as effective underwriter of the contracts to be traded on LIFFE. However, all went quiet until in November 1981 the *FT* ran a story that the banks were jibbing at the price tag of £80m, twice as much as they believed ICCH, with its post-tax profits of around £4.5m, to be worth. At the steering committee on 14 December, it was agreed that if the question of ownership had not been resolved by the end of January, then LIFFE would need to establish its own clearing house in time for the opening of the market. Barkshire 'advised that he would ensure that all of the interested parties were aware of the need for a final decision to be taken not later than 31st January'. At last the banks bowed to the Bank of England – a classic, very late example of the old City in action – and agreed to pay what amounted to almost £56m. The consortium comprised Barclays (20%), Lloyds (20%), Midland (20%), National Westminster (20%), Standard Chartered (10%) and Williams and Glyn's (10%). 'A bargain buy for the Big Five' was the *Guardian*'s somewhat inaccurate headline.

Serious negotiations could now begin over the financial relationship between exchange and clearing house. After several weeks of suggestions and counter-suggestions flying between Cannon Street and Crutched Friars, agreement was reached in the spring over a charging package for LIFFE's clearing members. No interest to be received on initial credit margins (payable in order to hold a position on a futures contract) would subsidise, as far as ICCH was concerned, daily payment of profits and a flat registration fee of 25p per contract. It was further agreed to review the package six months after the opening of the exchange. At the same board meeting that accepted this compromise, Barkshire read out a letter from ICCH in which it 'set out a number of reasons why the Board of ICCH was strongly of the view that the contract between the Exchange and ICCH should be for a period of 5 years'. With explicit reluctance LIFFE's board agreed, while noting that 'the contract will not entail any financial commitment to ICCH'.

Then and subsequently, LIFFE tended to be impatient of what it saw as a ponderous, inflexible organisation, apparently intent on treating it as just another market; while for its part ICCH felt misunderstood and under-appreciated – not only having given an enormous amount of unpaid help in setting up the market but also making available, at LIFFE's insistence, an independent guarantee into which its shareholders had bought expensively. A letter in May 1982 from Jenkins to Matthewson conveys, from one side anyway, something of the flavour that, unfortunately, would persist for a long time:

> *Whilst there are obvious advantages in having procedures that are common to all London markets using ICCH services, I do not think this is being realistic; the differences between the exchanges are too great. LIFFE is structured quite differently to other exchanges, and its approach to a range of issues as well as its*

rules which have been hammered out over the past few months significantly different. In sum, LIFFE is sui generis *in much the same way as the traded options market and to try to create one common system is likely to be fraught with dissension and to be unfruitful. I believe that ICCH as a service organisation should provide the service that individual exchanges require...*

A subject of keen interest in the City at large was where the new market would be located. Even before the steering committee met for the first time, the enclosed and covered courtyard of the Royal Exchange had been identified as a possible location; and by spring 1981 it was conclusively clear that the Stock Exchange was not willing to give some space to the new market and thus lend it an initial respectability, with Raven and Wigglesworth being memorably told that 'we don't want anything to do with russet-baking potatoes', a reference to an American futures contract, though hardly a financial future. That summer, under the expert guidance of David Bell, senior partner of the chartered surveyors Richard Saunders, the Royal Exchange emerged as very much the front-runner. It satisfied the crucial requirements: over 6,000 square feet in size, at least 25 feet high; a further 4,000 square feet of single-height space; and plumb in the heart of the City. For all its historical resonance, going back to Sir Thomas Gresham and the establishment of the first Royal Exchange in 1570, the area had barely been used for active trading in the last century. Indeed, by 1972 the whole fabric was starting to decay so badly that the Lord Mayor was quoted as saying that 'when a building is just a hollow shell like the Royal Exchange sitting on a site worth £20 million, it is an absurd waste of assets'. Seven years later, with the roof unsafe, the building had to be closed to the public; and almost the only activity left was the selling of charity Christmas cards, leaving the pigeons undisturbed for the rest of the year. It could hardly, in other words, have been a bolder, more imaginative choice as a site for the new market.

It was a choice in which the hand of Barkshire was writ large, but of course turning it into even theoretical reality was a tricky, time-consuming business. By October 1981 permission had been given both by the Common Council of the City of London and the Secretary of State for the Environment; while a timely telephone call by Christopher Morgan had managed to secure Sir John Betjeman's support for the project and thereby allay the fears of the Victorian Society. Then, in February 1982, a lease was signed with the Joint Grand Gresham Committee, representing the Royal Exchange's freeholders, the City Corporation and the Worshipful Company of Mercers; the Joint Grand Gresham was happy to have someone else restore the Royal Exchange to a state of respectability without itself losing ultimate control. The rent would be peppercorn until Christmas 1982, then £125,000 per annum until Christmas 1986, and thereafter to be reviewed until

Signing the lease for the
Royal Exchange, 12 February
1982. From left:
G.M.M. Wakeford,
D.N. Vermont,
Sir Christopher Leaver
(the Lord Mayor),
G.E.I. Clements,
R.R.St.J. Barkshire.

the lease expired in 1998. A complicating factor was the offices of Guardian Royal Exchange [GRE] above what would be the trading floor. GRE was, from the first, notably unenthusiastic about the prospect, partly because it had had different ideas for the use of the Royal Exchange (apparently having a sophisticated shopping centre in mind) and partly on the understandable grounds of likely noise. LIFFE's architects, the Whinney Mackay-Lewis Partnership, proposed a false ceiling above the trading floor, more certain to combat noise than the original idea of hanging sound-absorbent flags from the roof, which would have made the Royal Exchange resemble St George's Chapel in Windsor; and the steering committee reluctantly agreed to what would be a considerable additional expense, fearing – perhaps unrealistically – that GRE would otherwise apply for an injunction to prevent the market operating.

Almost any sacrifice was worth making in order to pull off what was, potentially anyway, a wonderful coup. 'There is no place in the town which I so much love to frequent as the Royal Exchange,' Joseph Addison had written in *The Spectator* in 1711. 'It gives me a secret satisfaction, and in some measure gratifies my vanity, as I am an Englishman, to see so rich an assembly of countrymen and foreigners consulting together upon the private business of mankind, and making this metropolis a kind of emporium for the whole earth.' That was the vision – culminating in the early nineteenth century, when Nathan Rothschild made his reputation and that of his house by trading in the Royal Exchange – that the new market now sought to recreate.

Even before the formal permissions were given, it was clear that the fundamental stipulation facing LIFFE was that no damage was to be done to the

Overleaf: The courtyard of
the Royal Exchange before
work began.

Two views of construction work at the Royal Exchange.

existing structure of the Royal Exchange, built in 1844 by William Tite after the second Royal Exchange had, like the first one, burnt down. Whinney Mackay-Lewis' solution, in tandem with the structural engineers Ove Arup, was to construct a building within a building – in effect, a 'shoebox' or 'envelope' within which the trading floor and also the offices (to be located, at Jenkins' insistence, inside the Royal Exchange, on a mezzanine floor) would be built. It was constructed round a freestanding structural steel frame, which in turn meant that large sections of the LIFFE building could be pre-fabricated off-site, and altogether proved a brilliant solution. 'When the time does come for LIFFE to move on,' *The Times* noted on the day of the market's opening, 'the envelope will simply be unbolted and removed and the false floor laid to protect the historic York stone paving of the courtyard will be taken up.' The building operation (a £3m contract) was carried out to an extremely tight schedule, with Chris Cotton and Cliff Lovering of Whinney Mackay-Lewis providing much of the driving force.

Similarly intensive was the technological aspect, with some 330 members' booths having to be installed with a dense array of telephones, visual display units and paging equipment. This project alone cost some £1.5m and, confounding the doubters, was successfully completed ahead of schedule by British Telecom, which fortunately was at the time keen to undertake a high-profile job in the City in order to rehabilitate its reputation there. It was not uncommon to have to wait for over a year for only one new phone line, and the great breakthrough came when Jenkins persuaded BT to appoint a project manager, breaking all its rules. Involving at least

55 miles of cabling, a Monarch and Herald call-connect system, a Cheetah telex, 25 racks of control and signalling equipment, over 300 dealer boards, 650 exchange lines, more than 800 private circuits, a 30-line Datel 600 network for computer data communications, 60 Ambassador telephones, and several public cardphones daringly using plastic cards instead of money, this was the largest single telecommunications project of its kind yet handled by BT. And in general, equipping Tite's venerable building was, for all concerned, a memorably exciting, high-pressure experience involving an almost daily application of ingenuity – as when, for example, tents had to be installed round the dealer boards, dust having first been vacuumed out, in order to enable the phones to be fitted in a suitably pristine setting. Even so, just before opening, a storm led to serious flooding of floor and booths, causing the frantic application of hair-driers rather than the scheduled final testing.

Nevertheless, if the architects and engineers justifiably took much of the public credit, there was also an equally important, equally nuts-and-bolts matter being decided and implemented in the months leading up to the exchange's opening. In early August a circular to members, some of whom had been getting increasingly impatient for elucidation, explained all: 'The major issue has been whether the Exchange should adopt the single-slip system used generally in LCE [London Commodity Exchange] markets where one party (e.g. the seller) completes the slip and the buyer initials it, or a two-slip system where each party completes a clearing slip and the exchange or clearing house checks that the key information on the two slips matches.' It went on: 'There has been considerable

The Royal Exchange.

discussion between the members of the Floor Committee, LIFFE staff and ICCH staff as to which method is the more suitable for LIFFE. It has been decided to adopt the two-slip system, together with a continuous matching operation.' There had indeed been 'considerable discussion'. ICCH was naturally reluctant to go down the two-slip road, running counter as it did to existing practice in the London commodity markets; but Rodgers in particular, on the basis of his Winnipeg experience, was convinced that there was no alternative. Roger Barton was brought in from Price Waterhouse Management Consultants to specify the matching system, and he stayed on to implement it. Above all, it was the real-time approach – virtually on-line clearing, with a card collection every quarter of an hour – that gave LIFFE a significant competitive advantage, even over Chicago; and it represented the start of what would become a tradition of extremely high standards in all matters technological.

During the first half of 1982 a programme of education gathered pace under the very professional direction of Bernard Reed. At first it was aimed almost entirely at the membership, without whose active involvement it was unlikely that the exchange would generate adequate liquidity to attract non-members to use it. 'Many of the members likely to be early users of the exchange will be traders rather than hedgers,' noted Reed in a progress report in April, 'and we are therefore giving due emphasis to trading in our education programme.' The key word was 'trading', with Reed careful throughout to avoid the term 'speculation', always a problematic word this side of the Atlantic. His tools to educate the membership in these pre-opening months included an introductory slide kit, in-depth courses in administration and accounting, and a simulated trading course (developed in liaison with Jacques Pézier of Investment Intelligence Systems Corporation) to provide members with a method of testing LIFFE's products. This course included publication via Reuter screens of realistic prices for LIFFE contracts, telephone dealing facilities and daily preparation of transaction summaries and position statements, for all of which members paid a charge of £920 in order to take part. Operating with a limited budget, Reed was determined that LIFFE's educational products should not be under-valued. There was also available (at £553 per participant) an intensive five-day course in hedging and trading techniques. Here a major input came from the City University Business School in the persons of Desmond Fitzgerald, Gordon Gemmill and Roy Batchelor, the three having received expert tuition from Nancy Rothstein of First National Bank of Chicago.

It was a propaganda campaign as well as an education, and much else was involved. The exchange's leading figures gave a series of lectures and seminars, Barkshire for example telling representatives of Jersey's financial community that 'I believe the 1980s will be the decade of financial futures as the 1960s and 70s were for the Eurodollar market' and that £80m had been committed by members to the new market; members themselves (such as the money brokers Fulton Packshaw, run by Robin Packshaw, a member of the steering committee) contributed helpful articles to specialist magazines; and well-disposed academic economists were enlisted, including Fitzgerald, who wrote a lengthy piece for the April issue of the *Banker* on 'Using the financial futures market', positive but not denying that it 'does not provide the ability to hedge perfectly all financial instrument transactions and may also involve an institution in commitments over and above the underlying transaction'. End-users as well as members started to be incorporated into the formal educative process by the second half of the summer, though on the eve of opening one member (quite possibly American) said to the man from the *FT* that 'everybody on the London exchange has been trying to sell themselves to each other rather than the likes of IBM'. That critic may have had a point, but he underestimated the innate tendency of most people not to believe in something new until they see it working.

Certainly a careful reading of the press cuttings would have suggested that conclusion. 'The first thing that hits you is that the question of speculators keeps

'A Day in the LIFFE'. Terry Quirk's impression of the floor before the market opened.

popping up,' Gerry Leahy of Unilever told the *FT* as early as July 1981. 'If there's one thing that makes a company board reach for the aspirin, it's mention of speculation.' Barkshire the following February addressed a meeting of corporate treasurers in London, and *Euromoney* quoted one of those present: 'There was a large degree of scepticism, quite honestly, especially on the foreign currency futures. I got the impression that interest rate futures were a fairly novel concept for many.' Another corporate treasurer, Daniel Hodson of Unigate, was less conceptually challenged but not immediately bullish when he talked in June to the *Sunday Telegraph*: 'I am sure that, in the fullness of time, treasurers will use the futures markets, primarily for hedging interest rate risk. But I doubt whether we will see much volume in the first year.' As for other potential institutional end-users, two pension fund managers quoted by *Pensions* in May were probably typical. George Dennis, of the Post Office Staff Superannuation Fund, observed that 'pension funds are generally conservative', in that 'as a fund one has to carry the trustees with you and some funds might have problems'. The other, John McLachlan of the British Rail Pension Fund, remarked that 'the reaction of a typical pension fund trustee to any new investment departure is to ask for the names of six other funds that are already doing it', adding that in his own case 'we will not be in the vanguard of pension funds using LIFFE'.

Inevitably there was much discussion, amongst professionals, about which contracts would flourish and which would wither on the vine. 'What you hear on the cocktail circuit depends on who you talk to,' one London-based American banker told *Euromoney* early in 1982. 'The Stock Exchange people are looking to the gilt contract. The international banking set pick the Eurocontract. But you never talk to anyone who says the currency futures will make it.' Another American banker was even franker about the four currency contracts: 'A waste of time. God knows who's going to use them. They should have been Eurocurrency deposits contracts instead.' Or as an American broker put it, mindful that Chicago had already been trading a Eurodollar futures contract since late 1981 but that London was the major Eurodollar cash market, 'as the Eurocontract goes, LIFFE may go'. A few months later, in June, *Financial Weekly* took soundings that confirmed the low expectations felt about the currency contracts. 'Until someone demonstrates to us the advantages of the currency contracts over normal forward exchange rates,' stated Ron Porter of National Westminster's international treasurer's department, 'we will remain unimpressed'. He cited the fixed size of the currency contracts and the relatively high costs of hedging in currencies on the futures market, and Richard Golding, head of Grieveson Grant's futures team, agreed: 'The futures market for currencies will just ride on the coat tails of the forward exchange market. If you want to trade in currency futures, you can do it already in the strong London forward market.' Both board and membership seem to have been split about 50–50 over the wisdom of introducing these currency contracts. The banks had no interest in them, indeed arguably wanted them killed; and the main users were likely to be smallish companies wanting to hedge currency exposures up to £1 million. Barkshire, however, saw them as a convenience – the embryonic idea of LIFFE as a one-stop supermarket – and his voice was probably decisive.

On 7 July, LIFFE's business development committee discussed which two contracts should be traded on opening day, the decision having already been reached that the initial seven contracts should be phased in over the market's first few weeks. Important information was that, in response to a recent questionnaire, 76 members had indicated their willingness to trade actively from the start on their own account in the short sterling and Eurodollar interest rate contracts, compared to 58 making that commitment for the currency contracts and 55 for the gilt contract. One choice was fairly obvious, the committee noting that the Eurodollar contract 'seems likely to be eventually the most successful contract of the seven we have initially designed'. The other choice was more problematic. The gilt contract was ruled out, partly because the Department of Trade had not yet recognised LIFFE as an association of licensed dealers (though it was rightly expected that it would), and there was therefore a possibility that half the membership would have to apply for a principal's licence in order to execute transactions in the gilt contract. Since it was felt that the short sterling interest rate contract was too similar to the Eurodollar contract to be its running mate, there was no alternative but to choose one of the currency contracts. The committee identified potential arbitrage opportunities with Chicago as a significant factor; yet even though the IMM's volume in the currency contracts ranged between 4,000 per day for sterling to 10,000 for the deutschmark, the vote went to the sterling currency contract. Presumably, albeit unstated, there were also considerations of sentiment.

Not surprisingly, the mood and expectations of the membership varied greatly during the nine months or so before the market opened. 'I have sensed that a number of brokers who have committed themselves to a presence in the market are becoming uneasy about the costs involved relative to the likely business,' Michael Foot of the Bank of England's gilt-edged division noted in April. 'The most frequent question I get over lunch is "What are other people doing?"' One of those brokers concerned about costs but not wanting to lose any influence in gilts in general was Greenwells, which in July announced a joint venture with the Chicago-based futures firm Hennessy & Associates through which Greenwells would supply the business, especially in the gilt contract, and Hennessy the know-how in execution on the trading floor. Expertise was clearly at a premium: earlier in the year, in March, London Investment Trust [LIT], which already controlled the old London commodity firm E. Bailey, acquired the leading Chicago clearing firm and broker Shatkin Trading, thereby enabling LIT to provide a full service in London; and soon afterwards, in May, London's second biggest discount house, Gerrard & National, announced that it was buying a 10 per cent stake in the successful commodity broking company Inter Commodities in order to cement an already formed joint venture – to be called GNI – that would seek to play a major role on LIFFE.

London's two leading jobbers saw things very differently. Whereas Akroyd & Smithers had been positive throughout, recruiting Sandor as a consultant and building up a team of around thirty, Wedd Durlacher was a highly reluctant entrant to the market. Indeed, alarmed by the threat to the long-standing monopoly enjoyed by the gilt jobbers of being allowed to go short on gilts, Wedd's senior partner, John Robertson, even made an informal appeal to Wigglesworth, as a fellow-member of the Stock Exchange, to attempt to stop the new market. Wedd's motive for participating was essentially defensive (as almost certainly it was with many other members), and the task of setting up a fairly modest operation was assigned to Nicholas Durlacher, a young partner. 'At the time,' he would recall, 'I was sure it would prove to be the biggest disaster of my life.' Durlacher had been to Chicago in 1979 and come away impressed but at the same time convinced that financial futures would not work in London. The third biggest jobbers, Smith Brothers, were late but hungry converts. 'We have changed our view on the market,' the firm's Philip Barnett explained in June to the *Sunday Times*. 'It seems there is a very considerable commitment being given to the new market amidst the current volatility of interest rates and currencies.'

By this time seats were available for transfer as well as leasing (C.E. Heath, for example, sold its to Commarco and ceased to be a member), and Smiths was soon active in the transfer market, acquiring seats from the individual P.J. Watling and the stockbroking firm Henry Cooke, Lumsden & Co, both ceasing to be members. Hungarian International Bank also dropped out shortly before the market opened, selling its seat to Grindlays Futures. On 15 September, though the figures were constantly changing, 261 members were in possession of the 373 seats, with a seat now fetching about £27,000. Just under a hundred of the members were overseas-based, giving the market an international character right from the start. UK commodity brokers held 97 seats (softs outnumbering hards by about three to one), followed by overseas banks (63), UK banks (55) and Stock Exchange firms (35). Would the City's West End or East End take the ultimate spoils? Those coming from the financial world presumably understood the rationale for the products, but much less so the vehicle to trade them; while for commodity people, accustomed to futures and the world of open outcry, it was the other way round as they learned about money. Predictably in retrospect, but by no means forecast in 1982, product knowledge proved the key, if in some cases involving a waiting game.

All that lay ahead in the summer of 1982, a hectic time of recruiting floor traders. The personnel manager of Credit Suisse First Boston [CSFB] told the *FT* that 'the job needs somebody who knows the numbers business, who's willing to stand up and make a price, but has the sense and maturity to get out fast if it's wrong'. He added that salary, bonus and perks could add up to £50,000 for a top trader already experienced in financial futures, and to £30,000-plus for someone requiring conversion. CSFB, however, may have been unusually generous, for soon afterwards *Financial Weekly* reported that 'the basic salaries offered are at a premium to those on the soft commodity futures markets and average between £11,000 for a number two floor dealer to £23,000 for a senior dealer'. Inevitably the majority came from the commodity markets, but they like almost everyone else would have to adjust to an environment firmly based on the Chicago model rather than, say, the cocoa or coffee markets in London. This model had three prime characteristics: pits (not rings), with steep steps; open, low booths (not boxes that allowed private conversation); and a big display board, in LIFFE's case acquired from Ferranti Packard for $300,000, involving a successful hedge on the IMM that itself was used as part of the education programme.

Those already familiar with this milieu were the ten or a dozen traders who were natives of Chicago, several of them recruited (including Mark Stanton as floor manager) to man the Smith Brothers' operation. 'It's hard to be humble when you're from Chicago,' boasted the badge, but most of the Chicago traders were open, engaging people happy to share their knowledge. Even they, however, had to take part in the practice trading sessions, and sit what were then less than stringent exams, that took place in the second half of the summer in an office in Old Jewry. There was an array of hand signals to be learned, complementing open outcry, but not everyone treated these training procedures as seriously as no doubt they should have.

What would the traders wear? The Chicago model dictated the coloured jacket, and though not compulsory it soon became LIFFE's hallmark, never before seen in the City. Certain colours were keenly competed for by member firms, as Christopher Fildes' fictional character Herbie (of Last National Bank of Boot Hill, Moorgate) reported back home in *Euromoney*:

> But, mom, here at Moorgate we get lucky, it all begins with the newest game in town, called Lifejackets, only spelt LIFFE which is Chicago money futures with a British accent, £30,000 get you to play and you wear a coloured jacket and the game is to get the smartest colour, I go for Buck's Fizz, which is champagne and orange half and half, and trying this on at the tailor's run into a guy from Barclays looking radiant in turquoise.
>
> So I tell him On you it looks good, and he grins like a catful of cream and says Yes, Herbie, but the real beauty is Amex want turquoise too, and they think they get in first with LIFFE, but we get in first with the makers, we land a world corner in turquoise cloth and Amex are reduced to stripes, and maybe this is a good omen…

Composition of Membership at the end of July 1982.

Breakdown of members into category and number of seats held in each category

	No of Members	No of Seats
Total No of Members as at end - July 1982		261
Total No of Seats Held		373
Banks (overseas)	56	64
Banks (UK)	32	54
Commodity brokers (overseas)	6	7
Commodity brokers (UK)	53	95
Discount houses	4	6
Investment companies	5	5
Moneybrokers	11	22
Securities companies (overseas)	4	4
Stock Exchange	27	35
Trading companies and individuals	30	32
US and overseas investment banks	15	25
US and overseas commodity futures brokers	17	23
Insurance brokers	1	1
	261	373

All together shout!
The scene during a LIFFE
rehearsal. *Financial Weekly*,
1 October 1982.

Turquoise would do nicely, but there were plenty of other colours to choose from. LIFFE had to approve the choice of members' trading jackets, and almost the only one rejected was a design made out of Union Jack material: the worry was that it would be seen on television selling the pound down the river.

LIFFE's staff moved over the weekend of 11/12 September 1982 from 66 Cannon Street to the mezzanine floor at the Royal Exchange, and the following Thursday mock trading sessions began on the floor itself. 'The scene could be from an act devised by French mime artist Marcel Marceau,' declared the *Evening Standard*, featuring a large photograph in which women traders were prominent – another defining characteristic of the new market, both on and off the floor, as it further challenged the assumptions of the old City. The practice sessions went well in the first few days, but with one exception. This was that, as Jenkins informed members in a circular on the 22nd, 'floor traders and staff have not been completing clearing slips accurately and promptly', which in turn 'has had a serious effect on the exchange's ability to match transactions and therefore to report them to ICCH for clearing'. Jenkins attributed this partly to 'the general lack of discipline amongst floor traders', there being 'a suggestion that as they are dummy trades there is no need to bother with completing clearing slips'. Accordingly, he called upon members to impose the necessary discipline over their traders.

However, the fact was that they *were* dummy trades, and this soon led to another, much more serious problem. Seeking to keep themselves amused, the traders simply could not resist trading enormous, utterly unrealistic volumes – up to 200,000 lots a day, when the matching system was specified to handle only up to 10,000 lots – and as a result the system crashed on four consecutive days. Raven, as chairman of the floor committee, felt unable to recommend going live on the 30th; but Barkshire, with all the formalities in train for that opening date and feeling that the credibility of the exchange was at stake, would brook no postponement, receiving strong support at the vital board meeting from Williamson and de Guingand, the latter emphatic that the matching system would work. The original notion had been to ask the Queen to perform the opening ceremony, but in the event it was the governor of the Bank of England who was asked to do so and who willingly agreed. Gordon Richardson was not someone to look kindly on a failure to meet the most fundamental of targets.

Already on the 16th, a fortnight before his engagement, he had given the Court of the Bank of England his assessment:

Tony de Guingand.

> *The design of successful futures markets is notoriously difficult and no one has any real idea whether LIFFE will be a roaring success or a just fade quietly into the background. We are confident that the preparation has been as thorough as it has been energetic and that the market authorities are fully conscious of the heavy burden of self-regulation which they bear. However, whether, in the long term, it flourishes or withers away, the opening of this new market is a very important event in the City calendar.*

Over that next fortnight the general tone of the press was friendly enough; and on the opening morning itself, *The Times* published a survey on financial futures ('The ultimate commodity in capitalism's heartland', the headline ran), while the *FT* in its main leader put the new exchange in the broader context of the argument that 'if the City is to retain its reputation as an international financial centre it must be ready to innovate and experiment'.

The Times,
30 September 1982.

The London International Financial Futures Exchange opens today, bringing an American-style market to Europe. Providing facilities for dealing in interest rates and currencies it makes a significant break with traditional ways of trading

The ultimate commodity in capitalism's heartland

Opposite: The founder and his creation: John Barkshire a few days before the opening of the exchange.

Nevertheless, goodwill apart, there continued to persist in these final weeks before opening a mood of caution shading into scepticism about the prospects for the new market. On 14/15 September the *FT* held a two-day conference on financial futures, with Melamed as the star speaker. Saying that 'we understand your anxieties only too well', he argued that from the point of view of financial futures as a whole 'today's global environment makes LIFFE's creation mandatory'. During his London stay he was also interviewed by the *Investors Chronicle* (as part of its 30-page special report on financial futures) and gave a fairly sober assessment: 'We don't know if there will be enough liquidity… Speculators are not so big in London markets or as open as they are in the US. That will have to be developed in an educational context. The money is here, but the markets are fraught with danger… In Chicago it took our financial community a long time to learn how it should apply commercial needs to the market.' The *Economist* tended to agree: 'It is no coincidence that Chicagoans invented these instruments and so far have been the only ones to make them work well,' it wrote on the 25th. 'New Yorkers, by contrast, and possibly Londoners are temperamentally inclined to view the futures markets as an investment medium or a safety net, rather than a casino. If they all want to hedge and none to speculate, a financial futures market is on a one-way ticket to the mortuary.' Similarly, two days later, the *FT*'s 'Lex' worried about the lack of interest – even understanding – shown to date by the market's end-users. 'Hands up who knows what a fill or kill contract is?' it asked any corporate treasurer who might be reading, and concluded with typical acuity:

> *It is inevitable that LIFFE will have teething problems and that technicians will be busy reprogramming the market's many computers. It is even likely that some of the seven initial contracts will fail and be withdrawn. But the real success or failure of LIFFE will probably be determined by the willingness of commercial and institutional companies to make use of it. A futures market needs technical operators in order to function efficiently. But their activity cannot of itself sustain a living market.*

On the 28th, as if to buttress this somewhat sombre analysis, the American research firm Money Market Services published the results of a telephone survey conducted with over a hundred of LIFFE's leading members. It reported 'considerable scepticism regarding hedging business emerging until liquidity is proved and far-out months begin trading'; too many firms would be chasing business, likely to lead to a major reduction in broking capacity during the first year of operation; and ICCH was widely criticised for attempting to cover its fixed costs too quickly, with the probable consequence that LIFFE would be a more expensive market to trade in than Chicago and fail to draw from there sufficient volume of business in the Eurodollar contract, as well as inhibiting the

Opposite: Toasting the future at the Guildhall, 29 September 1982.

development of the currency contracts. Indeed, on the ICCH question, 'several respondents regarded an exchange-owned clearing house as far preferable to a commercial clearing house, not simply because of the profit motive of the ICCH but also because accountability for the clearing house's action would then rest with the exchange members rather than the clearing house shareholders'. Estimates of size of business in the first year varied greatly, but worked out at a daily average of some 5,000 contracts. Jenkins, in his comments on the survey's findings, was characteristically robust: 'This kind of volume does not imply a failure! Indeed, it is consistent with my expectations of the long-term growth of the exchange.' And he added that if a shake-out resulted in the emergence of some 25–30 dominant brokers, plus specialists in the gilt sector, then this would be perfectly acceptable. As for brokers' complaints about ICCH, his skilful reply necessarily left much unsaid: 'Margin concessions will come over time… We felt the ICCH wouldn't be able to cope with the implementation of concessions as of day one. It's no good trying to complicate the market too much!'

All these issues seemed rather parochial on Wednesday the 29th when a message for Barkshire arrived from the Prime Minister, Margaret Thatcher:

Best wishes to the new Financial Futures Exchange. Its establishment puts London at the forefront of the financial futures market in Europe. It will enhance London's already formidable reputation as a financial and commercial centre. It creates a new source of earnings and jobs for Britain. A lot of hard work and hard cash has been invested. I hope and trust that your faith will be rewarded in the years to come.

LIFFE would not have happened without the macro-economic changes of the 1970s; but nor would it without the Thatcherite revolution that followed, so this was an appropriate blessing. That evening there took place a well-attended reception (in theory invitation only, tickets priced at £12.50) at the Guildhall. Barkshire and Jenkins shook well over a thousand pairs of hands; people were already well oiled, and the acoustics were poor, when Barkshire and the Lord Mayor (Sir Christopher Leaver) made their barely audible speeches; and at one point in the proceedings there was an additional wave of noise and activity, prompting Robert Miller to think that this must be because the sugar market had arrived and that therefore the new market in the Royal Exchange was going to be a success.

Chapter Three

On 'Change

A FEW MINUTES before 10 o'clock, on the morning of the long-awaited Thursday 30 September, Richardson made a few appropriately gubernatorial remarks prior to declaring the market open. After noting the fittingness of the Royal Exchange as its site, and offering a brief historical survey of futures markets, he went on:

Cutting the tape.

A futures market aims to afford an opportunity of transforming risk to certainty. To the extent that LIFFE, through the development of an effective market, increases possibilities for hedging, a means of coping with financial risk will have become more readily available. This can bring gains in efficiency. By reducing the uncertainty against which companies and others have to take decisions a better allocation of resources becomes possible.

It will not have escaped your notice that, by locating itself in the Royal Exchange, LIFFE has placed itself under the direct gaze of the Bank of England. It will not find this a new experience. We have observed the progress of discussion and planning – from the very beginning. Our concern with the need for financial integrity, careful regulation and proper conduct in a market such as LIFFE has met its counterpart in a like concern on the part of all those involved in its design and establishment...

We are about to see the opening of a new market, owing no doubt much in inspiration to the vigorous markets in Chicago, but already bearing the distinctive stamp of the City of London and ready to fit into the structure of the existing City markets, just as this new trading floor accommodates itself so splendidly within this building.

Time alone can show success to crown their efforts. If good wishes can ensure that, there can be no doubt about the result. Let us hope then that today we shall have seen the birth of a market which will come to take its place among the major markets of the City and will bring credit to its progenitors, its members and to the City in which it has its existence.

Opposite: Gordon Richardson (left) arrives with John Barkshire to open LIFFE.

A white ribbon was hanging just in front of the pulpit, and Richardson now cut it. The countdown then began – 'ten, nine, eight, seven, six, five, four, three, two...' chanted the multi-coloured throng on the trading floor around the pulpit

Watching the opening
ceremony.
Above: From left:
Bernard Reed; Roy Gamble;
Michael Mayo; John Morris;
Jack Wigglesworth;
Gerry Rodgers.
Below: From left: Stephen
Raven; David Burt (back);
Brian Williamson; Chris
Carter; Jack Cunningham;
David Burton.

Opposite: 23 seconds after
the opening of trading.

– and on the stroke of 10 o'clock Gerry Rodgers rang the bell as, amidst a mighty roar, trading began. The bell (found by Rodgers's brother, Brian, who was working at LIFFE as a mechanical engineer) had been an original doorbell of the Royal Exchange, for its eastern entrance, after its rebuilding in the 1840s, and the ringing of it was a nice touch of continuity.

There were many claimants – then and later – to the accolade of having done the first trade, but what is reasonably clear is that an initial flurry of excitement for twenty minutes or so gave way to quieter trading for the rest of the day, apart from a pick-up in the early afternoon through arbitrage with Chicago when the IMM's Eurodollar contract opened. A total of 4,265 contracts were traded, almost equally divided between the two contracts. 'A thoroughly sensible day's trading,' was Barkshire's verdict; while Jenkins deemed the volume 'reasonable', adding that he preferred moderate first-day volume rather than an extremely high figure to be followed by a gradual decline, as was proving the case with London's recently established gold futures market.

Importantly, the event as a whole attracted plenty of attention, in the foreign as well as domestic press. 'NEW L.I.F.F.E. AT ROYAL EXCHANGE – PICTURES' proclaimed the *Standard*'s placard, and the next morning's papers included plenty of 'colour' pieces. The *FT* described 'a gum-chewing lady trader with a voice like a klaxon making her presence felt in the currency pit among her vividly dressed colleagues'; the *Daily Telegraph* spotted someone on the floor with the motto 'LIFFE is the pits' on his T-shirt; *The Times* wrote of how 'they came in orange, red and blue jackets, trying for attention and recognition in and around the pit at London's newest, biggest and most complicated commodity market'; the *Daily Mail* stressed the pandemonium of several hundred traders at work ('"Nine for two," shrilled a Cockney voice. "Nine bid for two." Every arm around seemed to fly towards the ceiling, accompanied by a deafening unanimous cry of "Yes!"'); and the *Daily Express* quoted a 21-year-old dealer, Julian Rogers-Coltman, presumably not with a Cockney inflection: 'I know it looks hectic but it works. It is certainly a young man's game. In fact, it is an ideal opportunity for a young man without commitments to make money provided he's ready to work hard.'

Even more important than the adequate volume and not unfriendly publicity was the fact that the systems worked. In particular there was, as Rodgers and

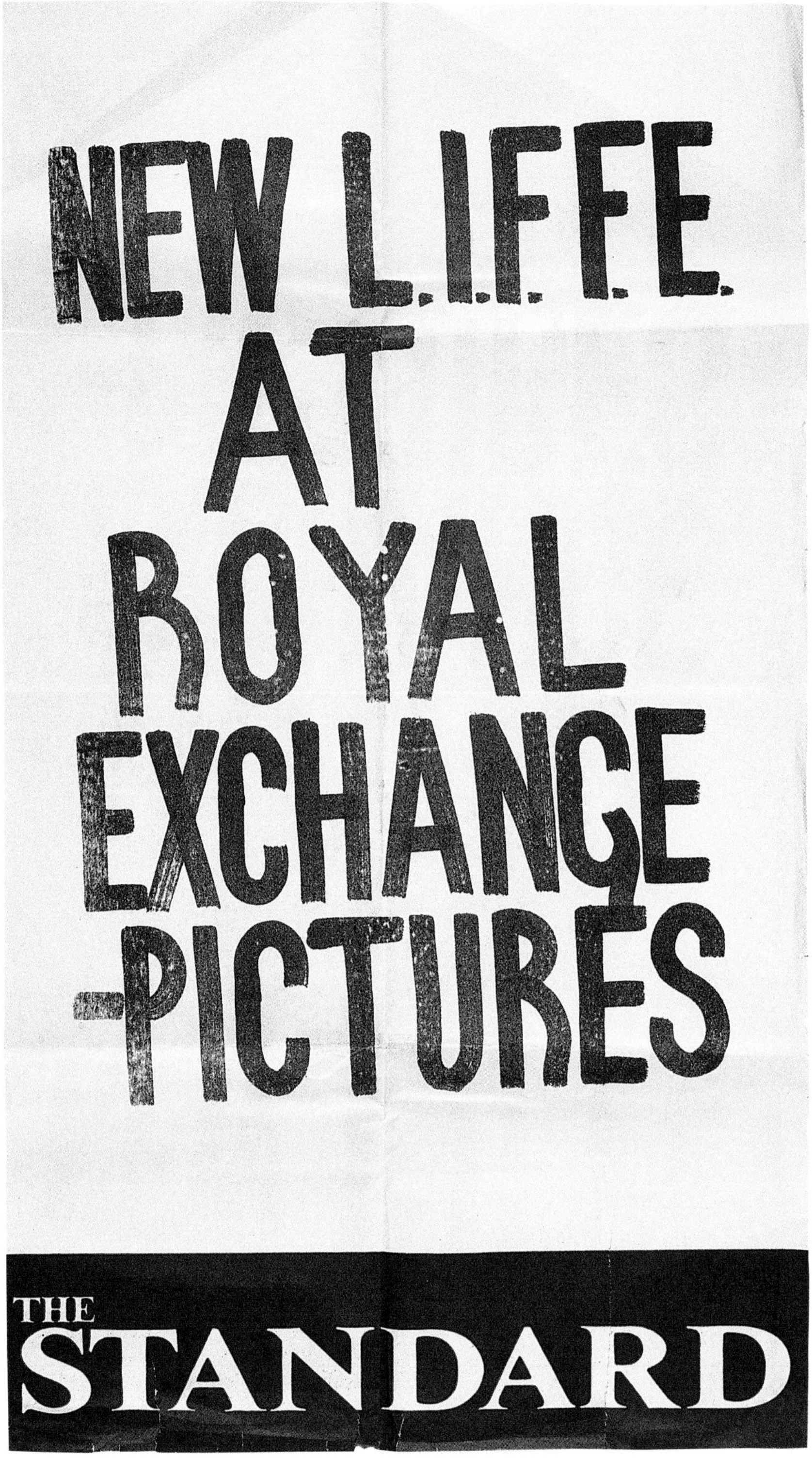
NEW L.I.F.F.E.
AT
ROYAL
EXCHANGE
-PICTURES
THE
STANDARD

Barton had confidently predicted, no problem over matchings. The British press more or less ignored this aspect, but the Americans knew how important it was. 'LIFFE Avoids Serious Mishaps' was the realistic headline of the *Journal of Commerce*, though Sandor (who had made one of the earliest trades on the floor) suggested to that paper that problems could develop if volume were to increase substantially.

What did the Americans make of it all? One trader from Chicago was rumoured to have given up by lunchtime and taken the first plane back to the windy city, but Reed on behalf of LIFFE naturally preferred to draw press attention to the busy pit activity on the part of several Chicago locals, including Norman Seltzer, Ron Goodman and Jerry Manne. The *FT* quoted an American trader on the first-day floor: 'I am not too impressed so far with this on-line clearing where all the cards have to go in every 15 minutes to reconcile the trades. You will never be able to handle the volume if the volume gets busy.' While as for the dealing itself: 'I have made $75, trading 28 or 30 contracts. We're looking for a few dollars here, a few dollars there – scalping. It will take time for these fellows. They are all young... Right now this market's dominated by the big commercial interests. It is very difficult for the guy on the floor, the local trader, to speculate. You can do it, but it is tough.'

The American traders' patron saint, Melamed, was by this time back at his Chicago desk, where Richard Lambert interviewed him (also for the *FT*) on LIFFE's prospects. His eyes flickering restlessly over the screens as he spoke, and once breaking off in mid-sentence to snap a large order down the phone, he stated that the London exchange had chosen the right contracts in which to trade ('they've used IMM blueprints to a tee'), but remained doubtful if it would be able to develop enough local speculative interest to turn it into a truly liquid and broadly based institution, insisting that at best this would take several years to happen. 'If the backers of LIFFE expect to show instant results, they are in for a disappointment,' he warned.

It was a message that hardly needed to be spelled out to Barkshire, Jenkins and the rest of the new market's leadership. But, as Melamed rightly implied, the big question was whether LIFFE's *membership* would persevere – especially if the investing institutions, potentially so important as end-users, continued to decline to come off the fence. The *FT* on the Friday morning featured some discouraging assessments. David Wildsmith, managing pensions for British Airways, observed that trustees, often with a non-financial background, could hardly be expected to understand this complex new market. Another, unnamed pension fund manager blamed LIFFE for having failed to clarify the tax position of the institutions if they used the market. David Malcolm of Royal Insurance said that he was looking at LIFFE 'with a degree of caution'. And Mick Newmarch of the Prudential said that he would be taking 'a regular rain check' and that 'if the market becomes liquid

Opposite: The *Standard* billboard, 30 September 1982.

we might take part'. Granted that the founders had conceived LIFFE as an essentially *institutional* market, these and other similar evaluations meant there was little chance of euphoria lingering beyond opening day.

The year that followed was neither boom nor bust. The exchange traded a total of 86,033 contracts in its first four weeks of operation, and by 1 December trading was taking place in all seven contracts. After a downturn in volume in December, it took 67 working days to reach the first quarter million contracts (on 5 January 1983); 56 to reach the second; 50 the third; and at 11.01 am on Friday, 5 August 1983, after a further 42 working days, the one million target was hit. The board's expectation at the outset was that this was likely to take a full year, so the pleasure was undisguised. Naturally, daily trading volumes also increased, eventually running at almost 7,000 by the end of the first year.

Yet for all this overall growth, with the value of seats holding up fairly well, and the fact that the market opened every day that it was supposed to and functioned efficiently, there were some bad moments. This was especially the case in spring 1983, at about the six-month stage, after a period in which average daily volume had been making painfully slow progress: 4,177 lots (the alternative term to 'contracts' as a unit of measurement) in January, 4,566 in February, and 4,207 in March. Firstly the merchant banks Morgan Grenfell and Charterhouse Japhet, hitherto supportive, left the trading floor; and then on 9 April the *Economist* declared without equivocation that LIFFE 'has been a flop' and 'is doing little more business now than when it opened its doors'. It blamed the uncertain tax situation rather than the exchange itself, but the accompanying photograph of the trading floor was captioned 'the funny-jacket brigade'. Barkshire's short, effective reply denied that volume was static and emphasised 'the steady growth of open interest', in other words the number of contracts held over from one trading day to the next. Rightly identified by Barkshire as 'the best measure of the genuine commercial business that is being transacted', open interest had shown continuous growth every month, from 3,100 contracts at the end of October to 12,000 by the time of writing.

Confidence, however, was undoubtedly at a lowish ebb – and average daily volume in April was only 4,554 lots – at which point Margaret Thatcher did her bit on 10 May by announcing a general election for 9 June. 'The election has proved a timely bonus for LIFFE,' remarked Alex Murray in a *Sunday Telegraph* piece ('City banks on a Tory triumph') eleven days before polling day: 'As the "long gilt" contract offers the only real opportunity both to buy and sell the gilt market forward, the demand for it has been soaring.' Average daily volume for May was a much healthier 5,495 lots, and on 9 June itself, as

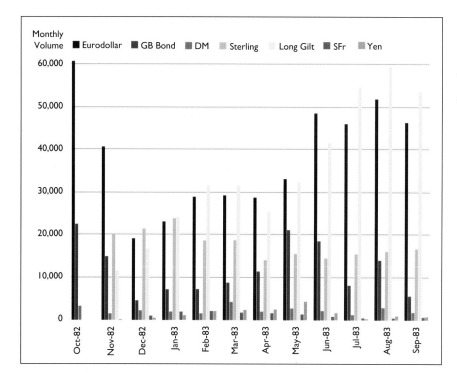

Monthly Volume ■ Eurodollar ■ GB Bond ■ DM ▨ Sterling ▨ Long Gilt ■ SFr ▨ Yen

The first year's growth at LIFFE.

Thatcher duly triumphed, a record number of transactions took place, with 7,952 contracts traded.

Throughout the first year Jenkins in particular kept a watchful eye on the membership, but altogether there was only a handful of significant defections. 'Chicago mob pulls out of LIFFE' was the headline in the *Investors Chronicle* after GNP Commodities decided to withdraw due to 'highly competitive commissions' and 'insufficient volume'. Business for non-members did gradually increase – by the end of the year over 40% on the gilts contract and some 20% on the Eurodollar and short sterling contracts – but most business remained member-driven. A worrying proportion of the membership stayed almost entirely passive. An internal survey in March 1983 ascertained that about 50% of the volume was attributable to twenty members, 75% to forty members, and 90% to sixty members. However, by August the number of active members had doubled to roughly 120.

Who were the market leaders? *Futures World*, after the first month's trading, reckoned that Salomons, CSFB and Citifutures (a subsidiary of Citicorp) were 'the names most frequently heard' in Eurodollars, though with Goldman Sachs, Conti, Cargill and Smith Brothers also recording a high turnover; while once trading began in gilts on 18 November, Wedd Durlacher and Akroyd & Smithers naturally emerged as the two leading players, seeing off Smiths but to the jobbers' annoyance having to contend against a strong challenge from Salomons. The March 1983

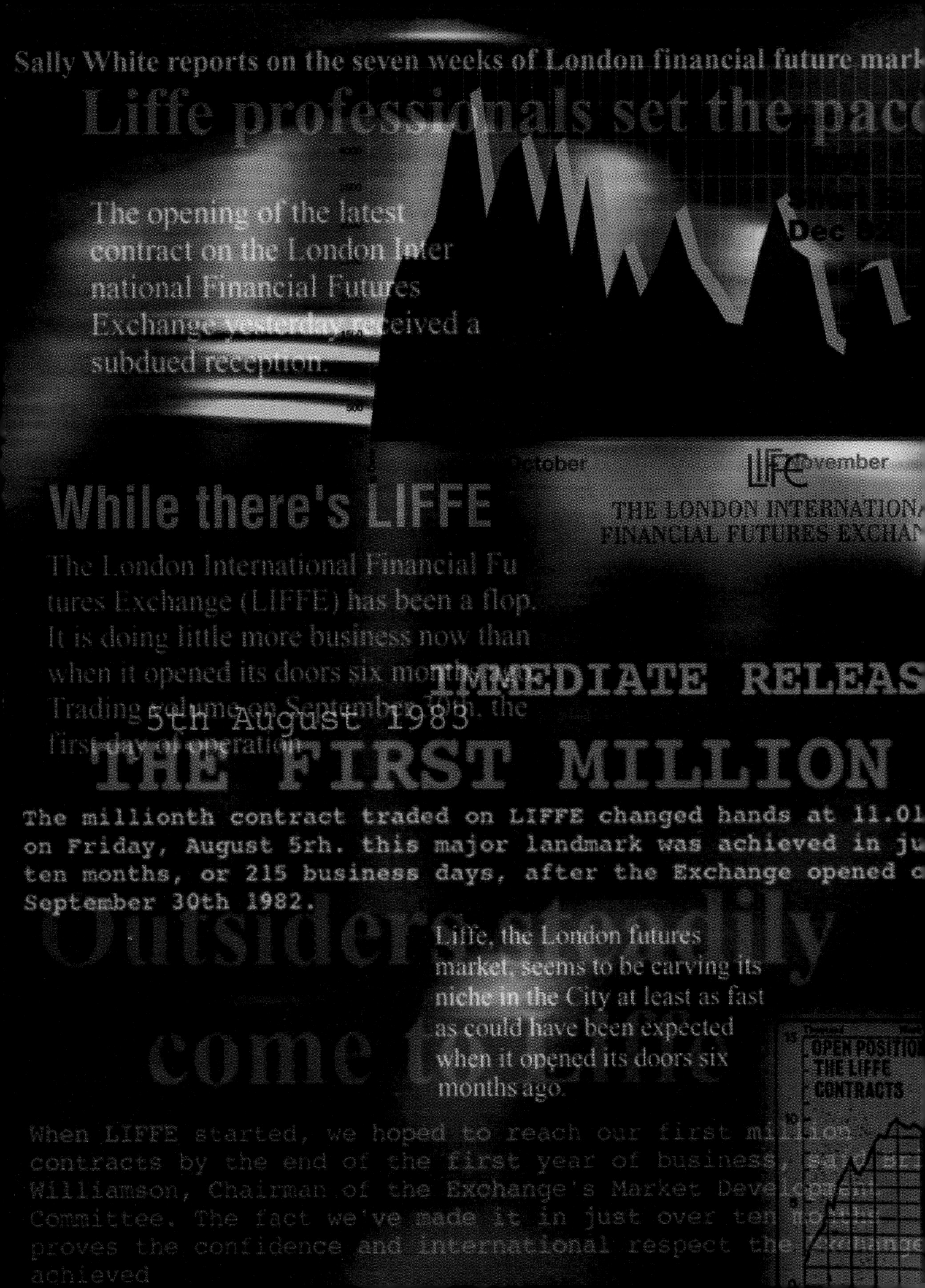

Sally White reports on the seven weeks of London financial future mark

Liffe professionals set the pac

The opening of the latest contract on the London International Financial Futures Exchange yesterday received a subdued reception.

Dec 8

October

november

THE LONDON INTERNATIONAL
FINANCIAL FUTURES EXCHAN

While there's LIFFE

The London International Financial Futures Exchange (LIFFE) has been a flop. It is doing little more business now than when it opened its doors six months ago. Trading volume on September 30th, the first day of operation

IMMEDIATE RELEAS

5th August 1983

THE FIRST MILLION

The millionth contract traded on LIFFE changed hands at 11.01 on Friday, August 5rh. this major landmark was achieved in ju ten months, or 215 business days, after the Exchange opened o September 30th 1982.

Outsiders steadily

come to Liffe

Liffe, the London futures market, seems to be carving its niche in the City at least as fast as could have been expected when it opened its doors six months ago.

OPEN POSITION
THE LIFFE
CONTRACTS

When LIFFE started, we hoped to reach our first million contracts by the end of the first year of business, said B Williamson, Chairman of the Exchange's Market Development Committee. The fact we've made it in just over ten months proves the confidence and international respect the Exchange achieved survey, conducted for the purpose of reviewing booth allocations, listed those members who in the early part of the year had traded regularly and whose transactions amounted to at least 2% of the total volume of contracts traded in a specific pit. The list of 44 names makes, from a latter-day perspective, interesting reading:

Allied Irish Investment Bank Ltd
Alan James Dickinson
Alpine Intercurrency Services Ltd
Australia and New Zealand Banking
  Group Limited
Akroyd & Smithers (Futures) Ltd
Bache Guinness Mahon Futures Ltd
E. Bailey Commodities Ltd
Barclays Futures Ltd
Butler Harlow (Financial Futures) Ltd
Boustead Commodities Ltd
Cater Allen Futures Ltd
Anthony Paul Caton
Central Trustee Savings Bank Ltd
ContiCommodity Services Ltd
Citifutures Ltd
COMFIN (Commodity & Finance)
  Company Ltd
Continental Illinois National Bank &
  Trust Company of Chicago
Cargill Investor Services Ltd
Commarco Ltd
Drexel Burnham Lambert Ltd
Charles Fulton Futures Ltd
GNI Ltd
Grindlays Futures Ltd

Hambros Bank Ltd
J. Aron & Company (UK) Ltd
Johnson Matthey Bankers Ltd
J.H. Rayner (Mincing Lane) Ltd
London Commodity Futures Ltd
Marshall, French & Lucas Ltd
Marshall, Rouse, Woodstock Ltd
Midland Bank Plc
National Westminster Financial
  Futures Ltd
Nordic Bank Ltd
Phillips & Drew Futures Ltd
Pacol Ltd
REFCO International Futures
  (London) Ltd
Rudolf Wolff Financial Services Ltd
Singer & Friedlander Ltd
Salomon Brothers International
Smith Brothers (Financial Futures) Ltd
Trade Development Bank
Tullett & Riley (Futures) Company
  Ltd
The Union Discount Company of
  London Plc
Wedd Durlacher Mordaunt Futures
  Ltd

Opposite: The ups and downs of the first year.

There were some conspicuous omissions, including all the Japanese members following a negative directive from the financial authorities in Tokyo. Moreover, quite a number of those on the list were struggling to make a profit, let alone decent money. Mike Stiller, floor manager for Tulletts, would subsequently recall the 'big pain barrier' that most broking companies were having to go through at this time and indeed for some years to come; Nigel Ackerman (working for E. Bailey) returned to commodity trading after about six months, feeling that he was not missing a lot; Clara Furse, on the financial futures desk at Phillips & Drew, would remember one early day when she carried out a 70-lot order for one client in gilts and as a result 'was an absolute star'; and even the chairman's outfit, Marshall Rouse Woodstock, had to go through some painful rationalisation, finding like other money brokers that banks ceased to be clients when they had their own presence on the floor.

Overall, in terms of commitment to the market matched by resources, it was thank goodness for the American banks. This was symbolised by the election to LIFFE's board in March 1983 of Charles McVeigh of Salomons, huge supporters of the Eurodollar futures contract in particular. Soon afterwards B A Futures, the futures arm of Bank of America, doubled its seats to four; Paul O'Hanlon of Citifutures told *Futures World* in July that his business on LIFFE 'could double' in the next 18–24 months; and later that month Steve Balsamo, manager of the Continental Illinois futures division, insisted to *International Banker* that 'LIFFE is a liquid enough exchange for people to use' and that 'I still think there's a chance the Eurodollar volume will double by the end of the year'. Unlike the British banks, ambivalent at best as to whether they wanted the currency contracts in particular to succeed, there were no or few mixed feelings – and, one should add, this attitude of the American banks wonderfully vindicated the internationalist assumptions on which the market had been created.

Futures trading was the very opposite of an impersonal business, and the success or failure of members owed much to the quality of the traders they employed. John Hutchinson and Alan Clayton, for example, were a formidable pair of born traders who contributed largely to the edge that Wedds soon came to enjoy in gilts; Roger Simmons was a big, aggressive trader for Bank of America; while Colin Alexander, an able spread trader from the commodity markets, handled gilts business for Salomons to great effect. Two other outstanding early traders, who would become permanent features of the market, were Russell Geary and John Jones. Many of these traders – such as Marc Bailey, working at first for E. F. Hutton but soon moving to GNI – came to find the floor a passion, in which they could play out to the full skills and instincts otherwise only latent, and this particularly applied to the small, slowly growing corps of locals. By late summer 1983, in a survey of its floor traders, the exchange had identified 20 individual locals (trading entirely on their own account) and another 20 corporate locals (involved in a profit-sharing arrangement with a sponsoring clearing member). Salomons was again important, with Ted Ersser on behalf of it pushing a lot of business the way of locals, knowing he would get the keenest execution. In general, these locals fed on market movements, making decisions in the trading pit for their own account as opposed to solely following back office or customer instructions; and the exchange reckoned that by this time these locals accounted for as much as 45% of turnover, of which a third was contributed by individual locals.

Most locals, then as later, were young, physically active, mentally tough, forthright and extremely confident of their own abilities. All these attributes applied, *par excellence*, to Alan Dickinson, one of the two individuals in the 2%+ list of March 1983 and reputedly the first trader on LIFFE to become a millionaire. His background was commodity trading, and two months earlier, still in his twenties, he had (he would relate to the *Wall Street Journal* in October 1985) 'put down his family savings of £15,000 and borrowed an additional £30,000 to buy a seat'. With business initially fairly sparse, he would not have survived without backing from Salomons, who got him to do business for them, but in due course Dickinson emerged as one of LIFFE's emblematic figures. 'I'm a very reactionary trader, a gut sort of trader,' he told an interviewer in 1988. He usually closed out his positions at the end of each day: 'I have enough worry during the day; I don't particularly want to take it home as well.' And he had learned by then rarely to run a position into a government announcement: 'I see no point in working day after day

Alan Dickinson.

– scalping the market, jobbing it, trading it – and then going in and rolling some dice over a figure that could cost you two or three weeks' hard work… The main thing to do is not lose all your ammo in one go.' Or as the market saying went – provenance unknown – about the abiding danger of gradually amassing profits but then losing them all in one disastrous trading session: 'Feed like a pigeon and shit like an elephant.'

Inevitably there were tensions within this new trading community. Initially at least, the attitude of many of the salaried traders towards the locals was that they were at best a regrettable necessity, at worst merely regrettable. Almost certainly this was far less because they were seen as an unhealthily speculative influence, much more because of jealousy, the unpalatable idea that someone had the freedom not to work for an organisation and the potential to make a lot of money. Nor – though depending much on personal background – did there tend to be an instinctive affinity between traders working for banks and traders working for commodity firms. The former were inclined to assume a superior financial knowledge and perhaps social status, the latter a superior grasp of how to operate in an open outcry market. Some of the financial elements of the City, John Bradney of Boustead Commodities had mused publicly in July 1982 about the market that was taking shape, 'are even learning that commodity brokers don't actually carry knives in their socks', but mutual suspicions did not die overnight. Also suspicious, to the eyes of some, was the relationship that the Stock Exchange jobbers (especially Wedds) enjoyed *vis-à-vis* the cash market. The essence of the complaint, which tended to come with an American accent, was that they had much better and certainly more immediate price information on the cash gilts market, which they were then able to use to their advantage in the futures market. 'Sour grapes on the LIFFE' ran a *Daily Telegraph* story on this theme as early as December 1982, and the rumblings continued to persist.

Even so, notwithstanding these various grievances, there was a very real camaraderie that built up on the trading floor during these pioneer times. No doubt this was largely attributable to the simple fact that this was a new market in a new trading environment, in which everyone was having to learn new things, but arguably there were two other significant elements involved. One seems to have been the feeling, on the part of some traders anyway, that they were semi-discards, put on the LIFFE floor by firms who did not much believe in the future prospects of this new market and were therefore assigning to it their less highly valued traders – an enforced gathering, as it were, at the last-chance saloon. The other element was a sense of being *contra mundum*, or at least *contra* the Stock Exchange and other conservative parts of the City. 'The ongoing pyjama party' was the bankers' nickname, while 'two ice-lollies' was a favoured ironic cry that greeted traders in their coloured jackets as they stepped outside the Royal Exchange; 'the ice-cream man' and 'the store clerk' were others. They might not have admitted it, and of course one can only surmise, but the probability is that during LIFFE's early years many Stock Exchange members wanted it to fail. That, anyway, was how it seemed to traders in the stripling market.

Ken Heymer as floor manager had the unenviable task of maintaining discipline on the floor, and with the exchange less than a month old issued a circular to members warning 'that all forms of personal gaming are prohibited within the Trading Floor Area'. That and a host of other behavioural offences were liable to lead to punishment, and in the course of the first year one of the corporate locals employed by Smiths was fined £50 for using 'foul and abusive language in a malicious manner' while trading in the long gilt pit. More seriously, Heymer and Jenkins were concerned about trading standards generally. Jenkins in December 1982 asked one of his staff, Sandra Steele, to report on trading in the gilts contract, and she found that when price movements were volatile (moving 10, 15 or even 20 points from one bid/offer to the next) 'inexperienced traders enter the pit and accept a price, without waiting to establish whether or not the price they heard called was actually at market or whether it was a "rogue" price'. The following month, on 11 January, the long contract became the first major contract to experience (because of excessive volatility) a full limit move during trading hours, and Heymer reported afterwards that 'an apparent lack of traders' knowledge in how the limit procedure works may have led to an artificial support of the market between 10.45 and 11.25', in that 'there appeared to be signs of traders buying in at the limit price purely to keep the contract open'.

By spring 1983 a new approach to trading standards had been adopted, involving more detailed training, more stringent exams, and generally greater surveillance of those learning on the job how to trade. There was also set up a trading standards panel, non-disciplinary but intended (as Jenkins explained in September 1983 to the chairman of Grieveson Futures) 'to draw the attention of individual traders to situations where an apparent lack of awareness of trading procedures or practice may be undermining standards in the pit'. The occasion for his letter was an incident the previous month when, on entering the long gilt pit, the Grievesons' trader, 'without questioning where the market was, heard an offer at 102.06 made by another member of your dealing staff and proceeded to book the offer when the market was clearly offered at 102.05'. 'It is hoped that a discussion of shortcomings at Panel meetings is constructive and its over-riding aim is educational,' Jenkins added, though the question of trading standards would remain at the best of times a difficult and somewhat nebulous one. Some help, however, did come in due course from the floor committee, whose chairman by 1984, Chris Henry, was a responsible, constructive influence.

Katie Blount.

The new community was not only on the trading floor, though that inevitably was the focus of most attention. There were also characters off the floor. 'John the Apostle' was a big, swarthy, bearded maintenance technician who had once had a part in Zeffirelli's *Jesus of Nazareth*. 'Bucket John' was an old Irish labourer on the Royal Exchange site who had stayed on as a general factotum, his habit being to collect cups in a bucket, not on a tray. And, at the other end of the social scale, there were the charming, well-bred young girls – sometimes known as 'the daughters of the discount market' – who comprised a not insignificant proportion of the staff. One, a graduate of Mrs Thomsett's Secretarial College in Oxford, was Katie Blount, responsible for compiling the daily summary of market fluctuations. 'The best thing about LIFFE from my point of view,' she told *Harper's and Queen* in May 1983, 'is it gives you slightly more opportunity and the bosses are incredibly easy to work for. It's not purely secretarial work. *They do their own photocopying!*' Nothing, however, epitomised the new community more than the Greenhouse, a tiny champagne bar just by the traders' entrance. Also selling smoked salmon sandwiches and quails eggs, it was until LIFFE's opening the almost exclusive preserve of Stock Exchange members. That now changed, as the proprietor Miles Maskell found he had a goldmine literally on his doorstep. More hard drinking was done by the traders at the Cock and Woolpack in Finch Lane, but it was the Greenhouse that had a symbolic quality.

LIFFE was poised to become a social phenomenon. When in early 1983, for Channel Four, Gerald Priestland gave a series of television essays on practical ethics, pictures of the Tory Party Conference provided the visual backdrop for politics, and Blackpool for sex, while LIFFE performed the task for business. At about the same time, on 27 February, the *Mail on Sunday*'s colour supplement ran a feature called 'Philip's golden future'. The introductory blurb set the tone: 'The City has produced a new breed of broker. He swaps millions at the flick of an eye in the rainbow-hued Financial Futures Exchange. He's young and brash and sometimes without an O-level to his name. Mike Durham meets one...' The broker in question was Philip Hyde – 24 years old, born in Stepney but living at Rainham in Essex, no qualifications to his name, now trading for Akroyds. He was 'young, aggressive, extremely energetic', as well as 'sharp-witted, slim and athletic, a casual dresser who looks like an off-duty footballer'. He claimed not to have read a book in his life and his self-professed motto was 'make it and spend it', often at La Valbonne or Stringfellows. Expecting shortly to be earning £35,000 a year, he preferred not to take the long view: 'When I've had enough of financial futures, I'll look around for something else. I see LIFFE as a ladder; you keep on climbing and when the time's right, you jump. There's always another pot of gold, another rainbow.' Yet, as the *Barking and Dagenham Post* noted a few days later in its version of the story, 'despite the huge salary and City night life there is nothing Philip enjoys more than a good knees up with his family and friends'.

Hyde and all the other traders were open for inspection from the visitors' gallery, and not surprisingly many came to stand and stare, and were usually fascinated, during the first year. Among them was Alan Brien, researching an article on the changing City for *Punch*. 'There are,' he wrote in September 1983, 'four raised rings, known as "the pits", resembling smallish garden ponds, and the brightly-clad boys and girls seem to have a marvellous time acting out the drama of their exchanges.' He noticed that chewing gum was not forbidden, unlike in the Metal Exchange, and that 'there was a certain amount of rather school-yard prankishness, digs in the ribs, mild cat-calls, a pellet of paper or two thrown in good-humour, and roars of encouragement and congratulation when a particularly smart job was executed'. Presumably Brien did not know it, but a century earlier he would have written much the same about the prevailing atmosphere on the hectic, boisterous, febrile, rumour-ridden floor of the Stock Exchange, if he had been allowed in to see it. It was a historical continuity that, it is tempting to argue, both markets should have appreciated more than they did. There was, however, at least one crucial difference. Unlike the old Stock Exchange in its prime, where the concept of a woman on the trading floor was unthinkable, LIFFE by September 1983 had in various capacities around 150

Philip's golden future

The City has produced a new breed of broker. He swaps millions
at the flick of an eye in the rainbow-hued Financial Futures
Exchange. He's young and brash and sometimes
without an O-level to his name. Mike Durham meets one

*The calm
and storm
of futures
trading*

THE LONDON INTERNATIONAL FINANCIAL FUTURES EXCHANGE

A t 24, Philip Hyde is some- | money in a short time. But he will be
thing in the City. Some- | likely to stand the pace for more

Mail on Sunday,
27 February 1983.

women on its floor, though outnumbered 4-to-1 by the men. And as Neeta
Brambhatt, dealing on the floor for Citifutures, told that month's *Cosmopolitan*,
to succeed as a female trader 'you've got to be shrewd, forceful, precise – and
above all daring'.

On 17 January 1983, three and a half months after opening, the Bank of England's
financial statistics division summarised progress to date: 'The market's volume has
not so far grown as fast as optimistic proponents forecast at the outset; turnover
on all contracts together falls short of that normally seen in Chicago for the frozen
concentrated orange juice contract. The London currency contracts in particular
attract very little business…'

The four currency contracts had indeed been a huge disappointment, at least
for anyone who had imagined they might flourish. In January itself, they managed
a volume of only 12,269 between them, of which over half the trades were on the
sterling contract. By contrast, the other three contracts achieved a volume over
the month of 71,262 lots, with little to choose between them, though as the year
progressed both the gilt and Eurodollar contracts pulled away from the short
sterling contract. Yet for all contracts, whether relatively successful or distinctly

unsuccessful, the crucial question was how to achieve – or begin to achieve – the virtuous circle of low costs, good liquidity and high turnover. With virtually all brokers losing money in the market (and the money brokers Exco publicly revealing in April that they were doing so), it was a matter of considerable urgency, though few imagined there were either easy or quick solutions.

Transaction costs were an especially critical area, granted that five of the contracts were almost interchangeable with the CME's, and there took place endless discussions between LIFFE and ICCH. As early as January 1983 both parties agreed to substantial cuts in charges in order to reduce the cost of a round trip in currencies (in other words, the total transaction in and out of the market) from 70p to 10p. Three months later, after much hard bargaining, a compromise was reached over a larger package: on the one hand, ICCH would start paying interest on initial margin deposits left with it by LIFFE members, and this would apply to all contracts; on the other hand, ICCH would increase its registration fee on interest rate contracts from 25p to 35p, in order to compensate it for having to pay interest on margin. The level of margin itself, however, remained a contentious question, as Webster of the Bank reported to Dawkins on 12 April following a conversation with de Guingand. Jenkins, he had been told, 'sees the retention of heavier-than-necessary margins as an inhibition to expansion of trading'; and as a result 'ICCH noses are clearly out of joint', for 'in their view level of margin is their concern not LIFFE's, for the simple reason that it is ICCH who have the neck on the block'. Not long afterwards, not only did initial margins come down (e.g. from $2,000 to $1,000 for the Eurodollar Contract), but ICCH agreed in principle to accept collateral other than cash to be put up for trading, though to the disappointment of some members gilt-edged stock was not deemed acceptable.

Jenkins himself remained frustrated by the relationship and seems to have felt that a huge opportunity was being missed. Paying a visit to the Bank on 22 August, his thoughts were paraphrased by Dawkins:

> LIFFE's principal source of income, apart from subscriptions, is the 20p it receives for each round turn, except on currency contracts, for which it gets nothing. Recent studies have shown that this will not be sufficient for LIFFE's longer-term needs. Experience elsewhere suggests that the really profitable functions are the services provided by clearing houses. LIFFE, of course, has a contract with ICCH, which still has four years to run. ICCH operates a labour intensive system using obsolete technology. It needs substantial expenditure (£2m?) to bring it up to date. Internationally ICCH is seen as fat and slow.

A day or two later, annotating the Dawkins memo, the Bank's B. J. Presland was sceptical: 'I confess to having thought that LIFFE, more than ICCH, was looking increasingly "fat"... I also suggest that LIFFE's view of the ICCH's technology is unrealistic. LIFFE have concentrated on individual computer systems for each task, whereas ICCH's has to be fully-integrated.'

A particular vexation for Jenkins and the board was that ICCH's costs were shrouded in mystery, in that it refused to charge LIFFE direct for clearing services on the grounds that to do so would constrain independence and hence its profitability, as McGaw made clear to Jenkins on the 25th. Five days later Jenkins wrote a particularly frank memorandum. Against the background of the exchange's increasingly strained finances, liable to limit the development of the market, he argued that the present split of clearing fees for a full-price round trip (ICCH taking 70p to LIFFE's 20p) was 'inequitable' and ignored three cardinal facts:

a) *LIFFE, in running the matching system, makes a substantial contribution to clearing not offered by other exchanges.*

b) *The split allows ICCH to make a profit when LIFFE is suffering a substantial loss.*

c) *Although the major investments in the market (e.g. marketing and promotion, new technology, new contracts, lobbying for tax law changes etc.) are made by LIFFE, the bulk of the return on that investment goes to ICCH.*

Jenkins also itemised what he saw as ICCH's four fundamental failings that explained why it had hitherto failed to benefit fully from economies of scale in its clearing operations, let alone pass any substantial benefits on to LIFFE. In addition to the point he had already made to Dawkins about its backward, labour-intensive clearing system, he claimed that the calibre of some of its technical staff was 'mediocre'; that its present shareholders, having paid too much, were 'looking for a return of around £10 million per annum'; and that 'ICCH has commitments to other markets that appear to be a lot less demanding than LIFFE'. Taking comfort from the thought not only that LIFFE by contrast had shown itself 'very flexible in how it tackles new problems', but also that it was in 'a reasonably strong bargaining position' in that 'ICCH wants LIFFE more than LIFFE needs ICCH', Jenkins therefore concluded:

LIFFE should press for

a) *A different relationship than ICCH has with other exchanges. LIFFE should be the sole interface with members on fees.*

b) *A higher share of clearing fees starting in 1983/84.*

c) *A joint approach to a complete re-design of administrative system. This would mean starting with a clean sheet of paper.*

In fact there were some capable people at the clearing house, which throughout these years had to balance preserving its financial integrity (including in relation to the independent guarantee, for which there was no specific charge) with endeavouring to help the market; but it took the organisation as a whole a long time to appreciate that LIFFE would have to be treated as a separate animal.

The pursuit of liquidity inevitably demanded a close statistical examination of the use of existing contracts, how that use might be extended, and what new contracts might profitably be introduced. For all its marketing efforts, however, the exchange for its first nine months had no research staff; and when at that point Kim Albright arrived, at first on a consultancy basis, to look after business development, she found no computer available for research analysis.

A prime focus of concern was still, as it had been from the start, the moribund currency contracts, in relation to which three important initiatives were taken or discussed in the first year in addition to the reduction in the cost of trading in February. Firstly, even before that reduction, there was on the sterling currency contract a cut in the 'tick size' (the minimum price movement) from 5 to 1 basis points, bringing the value down to $2.50 as against $12.50 for the other currency contracts. This change (implemented in January 1983) was intended to encourage a tighter spread in line with the cash market and was a victory for the view that LIFFE's currency contracts should essentially be a wholesale market, dominated by banks and institutions, as opposed to a semi-retail market in which the leading players would be smaller banks and commercial/industrial organisations. The second initiative, also favoured by those who wanted to go down the wholesale route, made less progress. 'There is an urgent need to increase the size of the Currency contract amounts from £25,000 (or currency equivalent) to £250,000,' Rodney Bass of the Midland Bank's group treasury wrote to Burton on 22 October 1982. 'At present, the futures market cannot possibly compete with the Foreign Exchange market and I believe that contract design has been influenced too much by the Chicago market. Indeed, it is perhaps surprising that the Sterling Currency contract has traded to the extent that it has. The deutschmark is a complete waste of time.' LIFFE stayed its hand, but Bass and others continued to argue over the next year that there was no alternative to 'jumbo' contracts if the currency contracts were to attract professional business. The third initiative concerned the possible introduction for the currency contracts of what was termed an ex-pit transaction facility [EPT]. These transactions might take place at any time and, Foyle proposed in April 1983, would be permissible 'provided that there is a simultaneous corresponding (i.e. opposite) cash transaction between the two parties to the EPT'. He noted that the IMM had an equivalent facility and argued

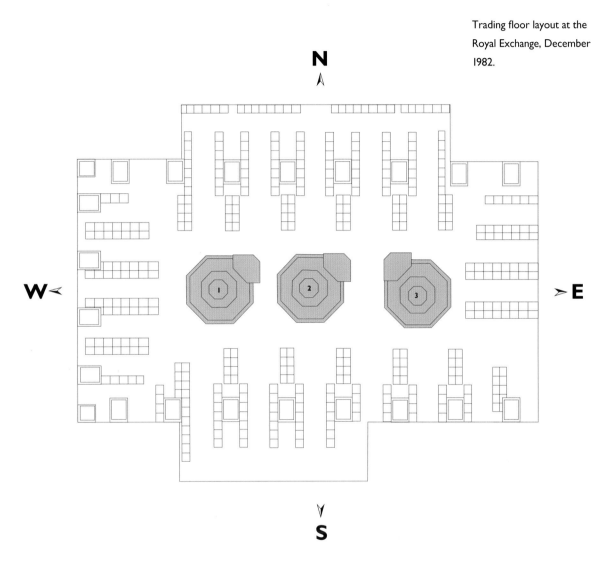

Trading floor layout at the Royal Exchange, December 1982.

KEY

1 Long Gilt

2 Eurodollar/Short Sterling

3 Currencies – Yen, British Sterling, Deutschmark, Swiss Franc.

387 Booths

that an EPT facility in London 'would offer valuable additional flexibility to those LIFFE members who are making a market in the currency contracts but who are not major participants in the cash and forward markets', making it much easier to avoid or control overnight exposures or overnight open positions. By July the facility was scheduled for implementation in the autumn. At the start of September, however, it emerged that the Bank of England 'did not appear to be enthusiastic' about the EPT facility and that 'their researches had indicated that it was not widely used'. For the moment the proposal went on hold; and the view of the market development committee of 28 September was that 'although it may become necessary to terminate the currency contracts, now would not be the appropriate time'.

The Eurodollar contract, in complete contrast to the currency contracts, was initially the star turn. In October 1982 it achieved a volume for the month of 61,035 lots, as against 42,042 for the Eurodollar contract that the IMM had launched the previous December. However, the gap narrowed sharply in November: 40,921 on LIFFE, 39,244 on the IMM. And very soon, the assumption that London would dominate in Eurodollar futures because historically it was the home of the cash market was shattered. However paltry in Chicago terms, it was the IMM contract that now moved decisively ahead: 40,012 lots in December to LIFFE's 19,178; and over the following nine months, though LIFFE's volume steadily grew, it was never more than 39% of total IMM/LIFFE monthly volume in the contract. Why did this reversal – permanent as it happened – take place? It may simply have been because of what the financial futures industry would come to know as the 'first mover advantage', by which once an exchange has succeeded in establishing a contract and securing liquidity in that contract, it is extremely difficult for any competitor exchange to take that liquidity away from them. Against that, it would seem that LIFFE did briefly have a window of opportunity in its early months or perhaps only weeks – an opportunity it squandered.

If that indeed was the case, perhaps the crucial factor was the absence of locals in anything like adequate numbers to give the new contract a speculative fizz; although Barkshire himself has argued that the reason the big London Eurodollar users failed to get involved in the futures contract was precisely because the London cash market was so good and there was thus less need for a futures market, rather as with the London forward market and the currency contracts. Yet liquidity was surely the crux, and arguably in this contract it never left Chicago. 'Our business in the U.S. is increasing because of LIFFE,' John Harangody, head of Drexel Burnham Lambert's London futures operation, told the *Wall Street Journal* in early February 1983, explaining that London customers were willing to carry positions into the close because they knew they could lay them off in Chicago. To which Sandor, also now at Drexels, added: 'LIFFE has done a very big education job. They've alerted a lot more people to the futures market. That's brought more people into using the American contract. They're attracted to the Chicago exchange because of the liquidity.' If that analysis was correct, as it may well have been, it hardly made comforting reading for those responsible for spending LIFFE's education budget, as the IMM's Eurodollar volume in January–July 1983 soared to a total of 437,000 lots, compared with 124,000 in the same, pre-LIFFE period in 1982.

But in any case, what is clear is that LIFFE was running second to the IMM in the Eurodollar contract *before* the IMM's parent, the CME, reached an agreement, announced in July 1983, with financial leaders in Singapore that it would back the establishment of a financial futures market there, ahead of a projected one in Hong Kong, in return for a mutual offset arrangement by which a deal done in one market could be reversed out by a deal in the other – and long before that pioneering link took effect the following year. Yet just conceivably, London might have clambered back if the Merc had not forged the link with SIMEX, as Singapore's exchange would soon be known as. That at least is the view of Melamed, recalling the circumstances of early 1983:

For Far Eastern participants, we were not equals. The London time zone allowed LIFFE to open each day during the tail end of the Asian business hours, while in Chicago we were still sleeping. That made LIFFE very attractive to Asian bankers and other futures market participants. For the moment, the LIFFE advantage wasn't critical since the IMM's Eurodollar contract was so much more liquid. Traders tend only to use markets that are liquid. But the handwriting was on the wall. With every passing month, I could see the open interest in Eurodollars at LIFFE inching its way up toward the IMM's. Since from the outset I was certain that Eurodollars represented perhaps the most important futures contract of all time, LIFFE's time zone advantage made me very concerned.

The result was full speed ahead on the Singapore connection, a link probably envisaged originally in May 1982, several months before LIFFE began. One can only guess whether or not the link was crucial in determining that the long-term future of the Eurodollar contract lay in Chicago not London. In terms of open interest, LIFFE was indeed creeping up in its first years: from 10% of the total IMM/LIFFE open interest in the contract at the end of October 1982, to 13% at the end of January 1983, to 15% at the end of March 1983, to 18% at the end of May 1983. Yet can one really assume that, all other things being equal, that would *inevitably* have led, at some future point, to London winning the battle? At the least it is a large assumption to make.

There was, from LIFFE's point of view, an immediate, intriguing coda to the link. Within days of its formal announcement the Merc was letting it be known that it had already begun preparations for a similar arrangement with LIFFE. 'The world is shrinking and becoming one vast marketplace,' stated Melamed, 'and no market operates in a vacuum today'. He seems to have been envisaging a move towards 24-hour global trading – but very much on his own terms. 'IMM has indicated that it will be unwilling to enter links with LIFFE if we establish links with Hong Kong, CBOT etc.,' the development planning group was told on 29 July. 'The Chairman reported that he would be in Chicago next week and would visit both the IMM and CBOT to discuss possible areas for co-operation. The meeting's initial view was that the best approach, if sustainable, would be to establish links with various Exchanges in respect of particular contracts.' Soon afterwards, in Chicago, Barkshire told the local columnist Jerome Idaszak ('Along La Salle St.') that though the increasing internationalisation of financial futures was 'the way the world will go' and that 'there will be more international links between exchanges', LIFFE itself was having 'no official talks with anybody' and needed '12 months with its nose focused on London', though of course 'one is always talking to others'. At the next board meeting, on 15 August, 'it was concluded that it would not be satisfactory to enter discussions with the Chicago Mercantile Exchange on an exclusive basis which would prevent the exchange from holding discussions with other exchanges'. Soon afterwards it emerged that the Bank of England would want to be involved in any 'substantive discussions' about links with another exchange.

Thirteen years later, in his memoirs, Melamed would claim that prior to LIFFE's opening he and Barkshire had 'envisioned an eventual link-up between the IMM and LIFFE' and that 'our imagined grand design was that, ultimately, our two exchanges could dominate the world's financial futures business', with each dominant in its own time zone. In fact, LIFFE in summer 1982 had insisted that it wanted to get its own market up and running before discussing any formal co-operation; while it is impossible to be sure how committed Barkshire was to this grand design, though the Englishman was as convinced as the American of the general proposition that the way ahead for financial futures lay in globalisation. In any case, by summer 1983 the infant but growing London exchange was determined not to be swallowed up by either of the Chicago behemoths, which assuredly it would have been had it accepted the IMM's demand for an exclusive agreement. Back in February, in the *FT*, John Edwards had put his finger on the crucial point. Noting that in relation to LIFFE 'a somewhat patronising view is taken in Chicago', he had gone on: 'U.S. exchanges are very conscious of the need to expand internationally, as well as domestically... They see LIFFE as a good medium for introducing and encouraging potential users in the European time zone who will then be tempted into the "big league" in Chicago.'.It was not, from the vantage point of the Royal Exchange's mezzanine floor, an enticing prospect.

Irrespective of possible links, there was never any question that the initial portfolio of contracts – the moderately magnificent seven – would not be given a full twelve months in which to prove themselves. There was also from the outset an acceptance that almost certainly at least some would fail – just as had been the case on the Chicago exchanges. Indeed, from almost the day the exchange opened active consideration was being given to additional contracts. In June 1983, as almost her first act after coming on board, Albright outlined various pros and cons about broadening LIFFE's product range. Apart from its intrinsic interest, her paper serves as a reminder that the whole business of identifying contract opportunities and then drawing up specifications in order to implement them was and is an art as well as a science, an exercise involving instinctive as well as rational faculties:

	Pro	*Con*
NEW CONTRACTS IN GENERAL	• *We want to have the latest & most appealing contracts for our market*	• *Overwhelming member view is to get liquidity in existing contracts first*
	• *Might need to pre-empt another market*	• *Longer lead times to get results than changing an existing contract*
OPTIONS CONTRACTS	• *Highly successful in U.S.*	• *Are we exclusively a futures exchange?*
	• *Many users prefer them to futures as they are much simpler*	• *Education problem with members and users*
		• *Regulatory/tax problems?*
EUROBOND FUTURES	• *Strong commercial interest as hedgers*	• *Technical problems of delivery, supply which bonds etc.*
	• *Commercials may also be speculators*	• *Hedging can be done with cash U.S. Governments or CBOT Note futures*
	• *Cash market growing substantially*	• *No competitive threat*

EUROBOND FUTURES (contd.)	• *Bring new players to market (Eurobond dealers)*	• *Too narrow appeal*
SHORT GILT FUTURES	• *New users to market (banks and discount houses who trade only shorts)*	• *Dilute liquidity in long gilt*
	• *Spreadable vs long gilt*	• *No competitive threat*
	• *No contract design or education problems (basically it's just like the long gilt)*	
	• *Speculative trading in cash market focuses on shorts*	
FT INDEX FUTURES	• *Wildly successful in U.S.*	• *Gaming Act risk*
	• *Bull market in shares*	• *Will FT agree?*
	• *Bring in new users, both commercial & retail, hedge & spec.*	
	• *Easy to understand*	
	• *Must pre-empt Stock Exchange*	

There were other possibilities that Albright weighed up – gold futures, FT Index options, gilt options, FX options – but for a combination of reasons they were less plausible candidates. As yet, contracts based on Japanese or Continental European financial instruments were not even conceived of as possibilities. At this stage the assumption of Barkshire and the rest of the board firmly remained that the core of LIFFE's business would be in domestic products, plus Eurodollars/Eurobonds as, as it were, honorary Brits. Barkshire would later blame himself for not identifying the potential *international* products quickly enough, but he was in good company.

Designing a new contract was an immensely complicated, often frustrating process, as the Eurobond saga amply showed. When thinking began in 1982 about a long-term dollar-denominated future, the obvious move was to introduce a

London version of the CBOT's extraordinarily successful Treasury Bond contract. However, it was soon felt that futures trading in London in the bonds of a foreign government would present major difficulties, and instead thoughts turned to a contract based on the highly familiar Eurobond market – a London-based market with an average daily turnover approaching $1 billion yet lacking appropriate hedging instruments, especially for underwriters. A Eurobond sub-committee, chaired by Roy Evans of Merrill Lynch, began meeting in October, and Robert Miller made the first stab at a possible design for the contract. A key problem was quickly identified as the shortage of suitable deliverable stocks, the heterogeneity of Eurobonds being such that the quality of some bonds put forward at delivery was liable to be totally unacceptable to the buyer. Following constructive advice from Hambros, the sub-committee decided in January 1983 that the contract would be based on a 'basket' of high-rated bonds and that 'at delivery the seller must offer a "deliverable" bond from the "basket"', at which point 'the buyer has the option to take delivery of that bond or take a cash market settlement', the hope being that 'this buyers' cash option would solve the problem of the heterogeneity of the bond market'. Devising the value of the cash market settlement would be no straightforward matter ('some complications in this are not necessarily a bad feature provided it is not beyond a reasonable level,' Foyle wrote optimistically to Evans in February), but progress was being made.

The spring was occupied by not only statistical research into the price behaviour of the Eurobond market but also the canvassing of market opinion. This was somewhat disheartening, especially when Barkshire on 5 May received important advice from Ronald Pearrow of Salomons. On the basis of 'five years direct experience of all sides of the financial futures market', he argued strongly against introducing a Eurobond contract at this time:

> Different types of futures users enter the market at different times. This pattern of entry into the market is very consistent and indicates the groups that are likely to be the immediate users of a new futures exchange. The first group to enter the market is always the speculators, both institutional and individual. At the institutional level, the speculators are usually found in the dealing room. They trade currency, deposits, gold and anything else that is likely to allow them to make a trading profit which means that trading financial futures is a small step. Virtually all of the futures business in Europe is speculative in nature even if it is by banks. The relative success of the Gilt contract is due entirely to the presence of institutional speculators…
>
> The point of this explanation is that introducing contracts with hedgers in mind is not the way to create a viable contract. Hedgers come into a contract after the speculators have made it popular and enough time has passed to legitimise the market. In order to have a reasonable chance of success, any new contract introduced should be targeted directly at the speculators.

If you accept my analysis of the market, the criterion for any new contract is straightforward. The primary considerations for speculators are liquidity and movement. They want enough liquidity to make getting into and out of positions easy and enough price movement to make the game worthwhile. Based upon these two considerations, a Treasury Bond Contract like the one traded on the Chicago Board of Trade is much more likely to generate the necessary trading volume than a Eurobond Contract.

The long term Treasury Bond Contract is the most liquid futures contract in the world. It draws speculators like a magnet. Most futures salesmen in Europe do more business in Treasury Bond Futures Contracts than any other contract. There is a substantial volume of business into Chicago from Europe every day. Tapping and enlarging the flow of business that already exists in the Treasury Bond Contract is easier than creating a new flow of business in another contract...

In short, though hedging by end-users was the market's ultimate economic purpose, there had to be a liquid market in the first place for those hedgers to use.

By July if not earlier, the Eurobond sub-committee had been renamed the Eurobond/T-Bond sub-committee, with James Wilmot-Smith of Salomons as its new chairman. The general expectation, however, was that a Eurobond contract would be introduced by the end of the year, and the Eurobond market itself began to show signs of impatience. 'Eurobonds need LIFFE, does LIFFE want Eurobonds?' asked *Futures World* in early August, arguing that 'given the clear economic need for an effective way of hedging Eurobond positions on the futures market, LIFFE will be missing out on a chance to increase turnover substantially, if the challenge of designing a workable contract is not met soon'. The sub-committee completed a third draft specification in September, but there remained the fundamental problem of the limited number of Eurobonds suitable for inclusion in the contract basket. 'It may indeed be possible to design a Eurobond contract,' a progress report concluded, 'but the contract will undoubtedly be complex in its working and thus likely to have appeal to a limited group of users, namely the inner sanctum of professional Eurobond dealers. It is unlikely that with the limited supply of tradable stock open interest will be substantial...'

The same report noted that the sub-committee was becoming increasingly favourable towards the possibilities of a T-bond contract ('although perhaps a collective sigh of relief from studying the complexities of the Eurobond contract!'), and reiterating some of Pearrow's bull points observed that 'it is now common practice for Eurobond dealing houses to express their view of dollar interest rates by buying or selling US Treasuries'. Significantly, the attitude of the CBOT itself seemed benign. Initially somewhat concerned at the possibility of competition from London diluting the market, it was reported by the *Investors Chronicle* in late September as feeling that 'with growing interest among European investors and traders the effect would be to increase trading hours rather than reduce trading volumes in Chicago'. It was not yet an either/or situation between a Eurobond and a T-bond contract, but the latter was perhaps just starting to become the favourite.

The other new product in the pipeline involved less agonizing but was both complicated and contentious. Trading in stock index futures had begun in February 1982 on the Kansas City Board of Trade, followed soon afterwards by the CME and the New York Futures Exchange. The CME's Standard & Poors 500 stock index contract was soon dominant, attracting considerable business once the great bull market of 1982 got underway in mid-August, with over 36,000 contracts being traded one day in late October. The following May, in *Futures World*, Nic Stuchfield of Wedd Durlacher argued strongly that the time had come to introduce a UK equity index future, not least because it 'would hasten the acceptance of the hedging (and trading) techniques on which the success of *all* LIFFE's contracts so crucially depends'. Stuchfield did not doubt the potential demand: not only would a stock index future offer a cheaper mechanism than dealing in unit trusts, but 'holders of large broadly-based portfolios anticipating a decline in the market will be able to hedge more cost-effectively than by divesting and will still be able to maintain their desired balance between various components into the bargain'. Not long afterwards, with Wigglesworth to the fore as chairman of the Contracts Committee, the board decided to explore the possibilities; and Jenkins was able to report on 15 July that Dawkins saw LIFFE (as opposed to the Stock Exchange) as 'the logical market for such a product because of its method of trading and the arrangements it had for margining etc.', apparently confirming *en passant* 'that the Bank was not in favour of London markets offering directly competitive products...not so much because it was against competition but it wished to avoid unseemly squabbling'.

Later that month an equity contract working party under the chairmanship of Bob Openshaw of Wood Mackenzie (the biggest equity brokers) met for the first time. One of its members was Peter Jones, a partner of Wigglesworth's at Greenwells and a fellow of the Institute of Actuaries. On 8 August he submitted an important paper on the choice of index:

All other things being equal, we should opt for the FT-Actuaries All-Share Index. It is clearly the 'correct' portfolio hedge. But it is less well known than the FT 30 and liquidity is an essential ingredient of a successful contract. It seems relevant that the Chicago markets have opted for the Standard & Poors 500 and not the Dow Jones Index. (They are broadly comparable respectively to the FTA All Share and the FT 30). Chicago is also going to trade a future on a new 100 stock index, specially created by Standard & Poors; I take it to be significant that the number of securities is as high as 100 – making it virtually certain that the contract cannot be manipulated by activities in the cash market.

The question remained, however, whether it would be realistically possible to convert into real time the 747 share prices of the much larger index, intrinsically preferable to the unweighted, geometric Thirty-Share Index; and an enormous amount of work still needed to be done on that and other problems – much of which work would be done, as with the design of the other early contracts, not by LIFFE staff but by 'outsiders' like Jones who wanted the new market to succeed.

Of course, Jones and other members of the working party belonged to member-firms and were thus only quasi-outsiders. So, to try to gauge the attitude of real outsiders, *Money Management* in October 1982 put to 72 financial specialists – mainly investment managers, life assurance managers and financial advisers – the proposition 'that LIFFE is just a casino and will not make a real contribution to London's role as the centre of the financial world'. Fourteen agreed (two of them 'strongly') and another 14 were don't knows, but the other 44 disagreed (10 of them 'strongly'). But for all the relative lack of outright hostility – and for all LIFFE's increasingly systematic attempt to educate end-users, especially once it realised that members themselves could not be relied upon to undertake the task – there persisted a critical lack of external awareness, knowledge and confidence. 'The problem with London is that many of LIFFE's potential customers are undereducated at the moment,' James Adams of GNP justly remarked in March 1983 when his broking firm quit the trading floor. The corporate treasurers of large, often industrial companies continued on the whole to watch and wait, not surprisingly finding it an uphill task (even if they attempted it) to persuade their boards that using LIFFE was not a matter of taking on new financial risk, but about the *management* of risk through dealing with speculators and thus shedding risk to them. Buying and selling foreign exchange forward was one thing, being done through a company's bank and involving tangible dollars or whatever, but buying and selling interest rates was quite another matter. 'In their shoes I suspect I might have reacted in the same way to a totally new, as yet untried concept in London,' would be Barkshire's not unsympathetic retrospective assessment. 'A dollar that you're going to need in six months' time, you can almost talk to it and dust it and see it and take it off the shelf, and know it's there. It's money that's going to be there. An interest rate isn't money.'

There were other institutional thorns in LIFFE's side. Building societies, under existing legislation, were not empowered to use the contracts they might have wished to use (such as the long gilt and short sterling), while there was no tax-free exemption for the pension funds. By early May the government expressed willingness to move in that latter area, but within days the general election intervened and any possible legislation was deferred until the following spring. 'We

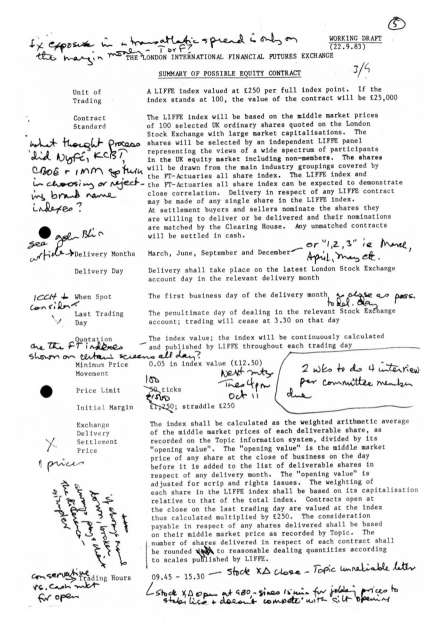

Getting the detail right:
early work on the FTSE
futures contract,
22 September 1983.

are rather disappointed,' Jenkins admitted, but at least the principle had been conceded – and importantly so, with its implicit acceptance that undertaking hedging operations on LIFFE was a genuine 'investment' activity. The suspicion remains, however, that these and other tax and legislative uncertainties offered convenient camouflage for end-users reluctant to enter the new market in any meaningful way. A conference on financial futures on the eve of the first anniversary featured some well-publicised and distinctly damaging remarks by

R.C. Wheway, deputy chief general manager of the Halifax Building Society. Describing himself as 'only a potential user, and very much as a sceptic at that', he stressed that he thought 'most other building societies feel the same as we do' and that in his opinion 'an investment in a LIFFE contract by a building society would be illegal and immoral'. Trading (or speculating) in the new market was obviously out of the question, nor did Wheway see any need for hedging in it, arguing that although building societies borrowed short and lent long there was no mismatch because they also borrowed at variable rates of interest and lent at variable rates. While as for the future: 'I think that building societies will break out and may well surprise their competitors over the next few years, but I think that they will do this independently of LIFFE and I should be surprised to see us using LIFFE contracts in conjunction with our mainstream activities.' To which one might add that fixed-rate mortgages were still unavailable in the early 1980s, and building societies failed to appreciate until later the potential facility that LIFFE gave them.

Potential end-users could also argue, with some plausibility, that the regulatory framework remained inadequate. In June 1982 the Bank of England had requested the six main futures exchanges – the Grain and Feed Trade Association, the International Petroleum Exchange, the London Commodity Exchange, the London Gold Futures Market, LIFFE, and the London Metal Exchange – to establish, as soon as practicable, a client compensation fund and codes of practice covering relations between member-brokers and clients. This would provide an appropriate basis for not only LIFFE to be recognised as an association of dealers under the Prevention of Fraud (Investments) Act 1958, so that LIFFE's members could do business on the long gilt contract, but also for an exemption from the Banking Act for the members of all the futures markets, in order to resolve doubts as to whether collecting margins in cash constituted deposit-taking under the Act. In response to the Bank's suggestion, a committee, the Joint Exchanges Committee [JEC], was set up under the chairmanship of the LCE's David Harcourt. LIFFE (in the person of Foyle) was represented, and by spring 1983 the JEC had proposed the formation of a Futures Brokers' Association [FBA] and a range of measures to protect private investors. LIFFE in turn called for comments from its own members. It was a process whose urgency was hastened by the failure on 8 June of one of those members, the commodity brokers Commarco, largely as a result of disastrous speculations (in aluminium futures and in the foreign exchange interbank market, not on LIFFE itself). Even so, it was quite a messy failure; and LIFFE was perhaps fortunate that at the time the *FT* – then the only paper that covered its affairs on a regular basis – was in the middle of a protracted strike.

The banks, predictably, were less than enthusiastic in their responses to LIFFE, especially about funding a compensation scheme that would protect the clients of the less reputable commodity firms, of which there were quite a few. 'An FBA without the banks, and many other large commodity brokers who do not handle *private* clients, might appear to be a "poor man's club",' wrote Foyle, attempting to hold the line, to Rodney Bass of the Midland in early August. 'Better, perhaps, if all market members join up and thereby publicly give support and subscribe to the codes of conduct. Fees and levies will need to reflect the nature of each member's involvement.' LIFFE in general was not unduly wedded to the JEC/FBA route – for example, Jenkins told Dawkins in July that the exchange planned anyway to have a system for segregating client accounts ready for implementation by 1 April 1984 – but it seems to have been keen to stay in the City mainstream, at a time when, with the Gower Report on Investor Protection due to be published shortly, some fundamental, possibly pre-emptive decisions were being taken. In late July or early August, Sir Basil Engholm of Comfin put down on paper some thoughts, duly forwarded by Whiting to Foyle, that give a clear sense of the Square Mile deciding how best to play its hand in the context of an emerging, potentially uncomfortable dispensation:

The unfortunate happenings at Lloyd's, and on the Stock Exchange, in recent years have inevitably made the City markets vulnerable to criticism, of which there has been a good deal from many quarters, including moderate ones. Only in the last few days Mr Roy Hattersley [shadow chancellor] has added his voice to those of the critics, and said that self-regulation is inadequate, and that City dealers should be licensed. The tide is running against the continuing freedom of the City institutions to regulate themselves. I am sure, therefore, that it is right for the Exchanges to come forward voluntarily with proposals for self-regulation which may, in the longer term, provide a safeguard against more drastic ideas. And the time seems to me propitious, with a government sympathetic to the concept of self-discipline, and a report by Gower coming out in favour of self-regulation within a framework of statutory Governmental supervision...

The first anniversary of LIFFE provoked a flurry of assessments, few broadly out of line with Michael Blanden's opinion in the *Investors Chronicle* that 'the exchange has established its credentials as a serious market with considerable potential, and with a reasonable if not yet sufficient level of turnover it has laid a strong basis on which to build'. Williamson, talking to *Euromoney*, stressed the American contribution: 'It's difficult to imagine how different LIFFE might be if Salomon Brothers hadn't committed itself so much at the beginning'. Melamed in the same magazine said 'I believe it will make it. I just don't want anyone to get cold feet. It's already a small miracle...'; but according to Kidder Peabody's Joe Speiler, liquidity on LIFFE was still very thin – 'Sometimes you sell ten lousy contracts to four different people. It's crazy.' – and the only answer was more

THATCHER CALM AMID CITY NERVES

Sterling touches record low point

By *JAMES WIGHTMAN Political Correspondent*

THE Prime Minister yesterday gave the Commons a calculated demonstration of calm in face of another bout of nervousness in the City and Westminster about sterling. oil prices and the timing of the General Election.

REAC
OFFE
MOSC

By RICHARI
in Wash

PRESIDENT
his State
address to th
night said he
for a positive
relations wit
Soviet leaders
But he linked
a tough warnin
Union that it m
deeds as well
commitment to
rights of sovere
"Responsible
the world com
threaten, or inva
bours, and they
allies from
said'in a

LIFFE hits the front page; *Daily Telegraph*, 6 January 1983.

locals. *Futures World* marked the occasion by a questionnaire to members. How did they assess the performance of LIFFE so far? Very good: 9. Good: 72. Fair: 28. Poor: 2. Did they think existing contract designs were adequate? Yes: 39. Fair: 5. No: 30. How might they be improved? Increase forex size: 27. Which new contracts would they like to see in the next twelve months? Eurobonds: 45. Stock index: 44. Short gilt: 41. Jumbo forex: 25. T-bonds: 7.

All these things mattered greatly to market participants, but something else was afoot by the autumn of 1983. July had seen the Parkinson-Goodison agreement, to dismantle the Stock Exchange as generations had known it and pointing the way directly ahead to the 'Big Bang' of October 1986. That was the future – a future that to some significant degree already existed on LIFFE, with its open, widely based membership, dual capacity and absence of fixed minimum commissions. Indeed, there was already anecdotal evidence that a substantial chunk of the short-term speculative trading in gilts on the Stock Exchange had moved across to LIFFE. 'There are even reports,' Hamish McRae and Peter Rodgers wrote in the *Guardian* on 5 August, 'of brokers giving virtually commission-free trading on LIFFE as a hidden discount to customers on the Stock Exchange.' In short, the City was changing in fundamental ways, and LIFFE's emergence was part of that change.

Yet in most eyes LIFFE was still a small fish that might or might not turn into a bigger fish. 'THE EXCHANGE REACHED ITS MILLIONTH CONTRACT TARGET TWO MONTHS EARLY,' Williamson telexed an Australian well-wisher in October, 'BUT FORTUNATELY HAS NOT BEEN SO SUCCESSFUL AS TO CAUSE ENVY AND RESENTMENT IN THE CITY.' It was, to change the metaphor, a good position to be in: unfancied, and coming up on the outside.

Chapter Four

In the Money

OVER THE NEXT four years – October 1983 to September 1987 – the baby grew up. The pattern was one of steady, occasionally spectacular, growth. Having taken 215 business days to reach the first million contracts on 5 August 1983, the two millionth contract was recorded 151 business days later, on 9 March 1984. Four months later, on 10 July, a new daily record of 20,876 contracts was set. Average daily volume during 1984 ran at 10,220, almost double the 1983 average of 5,400. Progress continued in 1985: on 30 October a new daily high (34,590 contracts) and a daily average of just under 14,000. Then, in early 1986, came a further lift-off, with the daily volume twice over 39,000 in the first half of January; over the next few months further daily records continued to be set (including 48,113 on 13 May); and the 1986 total volume of 6.95m contracts represented a 96% increase over 1985. The pace was kept up in 1987 – in March over a million contracts traded, and on 14 April the magic six figures hit for the first time in a day – and by the time of the fifth anniversary daily average volume was running at 51,978 contracts, more than double that in the same period the previous year. Undeniably a propitious background existed for this second phase of LIFFE's history. These were the years in which the world's financial boundaries conclusively dissolved, in which national governments began to quail before what Denis Healey called in June 1985 'an atomic cloud' of footloose and speculative capital flows, and in which attempts by finance ministers to stabilise exchange rates frequently left interest rates to take the strain of market volatility. Nevertheless, not only was there nothing pre-ordained about LIFFE's success in these years – there were serious problems *en route* and no shortage of disappointments – but that success itself needs to be seen in a salutary global context. By May 1984 the exchange's share of world financial futures trading was 2.5%, and soon afterwards Jenkins made it an objective that a figure of between 10% and 15% should be reached by the end of 1987. By the fifth anniversary, with only three months to go, at best the lower target was going to be hit. LIFFE was doing well, in other words, but perhaps not *quite* as well as it might have hoped.

On 13th January, 1984

LIFFE

exceeded 10,000 contracts

BA Futures

Citifutures Limited

GNI Limited

Phillips & Drew Futures Ltd

Salomon Brothers International

Wedd Durlacher Mordaunt Futures Ltd

Clearing members of the London International Financial Futures
Exchange are pleased to be associated with this new record.

Advertisement in *Financial Times*, 16 January 1984.

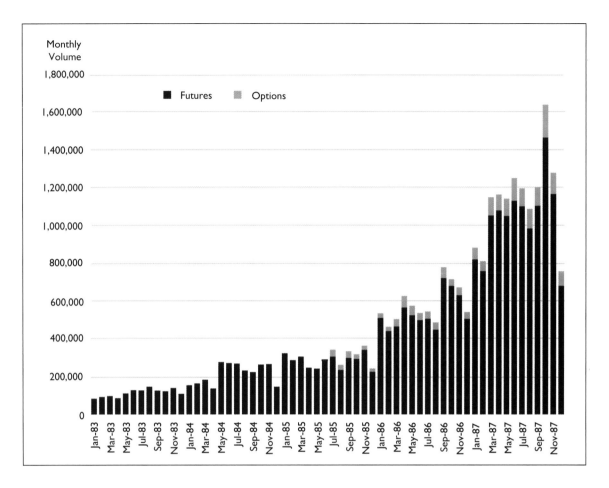

Monthly Volume

■ Futures   ▨ Options

John Barkshire continued as chairman until March 1985, when he stood down and was succeeded by Brian Williamson. The new chairman's background was the discount market; he knew almost everyone who mattered in the City, and with an engaging, somewhat quixotic manner he had a gift for public relations which he exploited relentlessly in the cause of the exchange. He also had a good brain – sometimes, in the best City tradition, disguising the fact – and sensibly appreciated that the quasi-autocratic approach of his predecessor was no longer possible as the institution grew. As for his board, there had already been significant changes since the first anniversary. Jenkins after the 1983 elections had expressed his unhappiness about the absence of actual traders, an unhappiness shared on the floor, but in March 1984 Chris Henry, Phil Barnett and John Chitty – all active traders – were elected, with the board itself expanding from 13 to 19 members. This expansion also allowed for more practitioners generally, including at this time Nick Durlacher of Wedd Durlacher and Tony La Roche of Cater Allen. A year later the board acquired its first female face, in the person of Rosalyn Wilton of Drexel Burnham Lambert, following a suggestion from Jenkins that she stand.

The growth of LIFFE business, 1983–87.

On the executive side there were several key recruitments during these years: Roger Barton and Peter Mather were brought in on a permanent basis on the technology and clearing development side, where they supported Gerry Rodgers and Neil Blurton on the operational side generally; Nick Carew Hunt and Phil Bruce became important figures in product development; and Mary Lou Carrington, a London-based American, came from the First National Bank of Chicago as marketing director, in effect succeeding Bernard Reed. LIFFE from 1986 also had a personnel manager, in the person of Helen Jenkins. A particular source of satisfaction to Michael Jenkins was a Bank of England survey in 1987 of members' views, which found that 'the day-to-day administration of the Exchange was thought to be excellent' and commended 'the interchange of ideas and general communications between LIFFE and its members'. A predominantly youthful team was responsible for a decidedly youthful market, and the prevailing ethos discouraged undue solemnity almost as much off as on the floor. 'Trivial Pursuits game in boardroom at 5.45 against Coward Chance,' noted the internal diary on 5 February 1985. 'Spectators unwelcome.' And two days later: 'Librarian's cat, Walid Jumblatt, is one year old.'

Brian Williamson.

The value of a seat on LIFFE rose rapidly. In January 1985 it was still as low as £35,000, but a year later two seats were sold at £70,000 each. By August 1986 the going rate was £100,000, in June 1987 a seat was sold for £165,000, and by the fifth anniversary (following an upsurge of Japanese interest) seats were changing hands for around £250,000. The process of amalgamation generated by 'Big Bang' meant that the total membership declined somewhat – by May 1987 down to 189 members and 13 associate members – but this mattered relatively little. The creation of Kleinwort Grieveson Futures, for example, did not lead to an overall reduction of floor presence. Indeed, far from suffering from economies of scale, LIFFE benefited *inter alia* from 'Big Bang' in that practically all significant components of the restructuring were now represented.

Within the membership there were some discernible shifts in the balance of power – perhaps most notably away from the commodity firms, which by spring

1987 had zero representation on LIFFE's board. Indeed, in his 5th anniversary overview for the *FT* later that year, Alexander Nicoll baldly stated that 'the financial houses' had 'essentially taken over the futures business from commodities traders'. British clearing banks were becoming more active – as, by about 1984, profits became squeezed, capital ratios deteriorated, and there was a move to off-balance-sheet financing that benefitted derivatives as opposed to the cash market – but according to *Futures and Options World* in December 1986 it was the investment houses and broking firms that still held a tight grip over the market. Right up to 1987 it remained very difficult to make a purely broking profit: in February that year the Bank of England's survey of 18 firms, representing a cross-section of LIFFE's membership, found that commissions were extremely competitive, that according to one estimate only 25% of London financial futures broking business was profitable, and that 'casualties were predicted if commission rates did not recover'. It was an old tune, and would not go away, for in the event LIFFE would *always* be over-broked, to the considerable competitive advantage of the market as a whole. Moreover, as life in the cash market changed fundamentally in 1986, with the end of minimum commission, such a regime came to be seen as the norm rather than the exception: no longer was there that painful discrepancy between, say, a £300 commission on a 100 lots of gilts and the £1,500 commission on an equivalent cash order. Not surprisingly, this changed broker attitudes in the City as a whole, in terms of the respective merits of the cash and futures markets.

Above: Roger Barton.
Below: Peter Mather.

None of this was a revelation to the Americans, already well versed in ratio problems and deregulated commissions, and as a national group they remained almost certainly the most powerful players in the market. J. Aron, Bache Commodities, B A Futures, Bankers Trust, Chase Manhattan Futures Corp, Citifutures, Dean Witter Reynolds, Donaldson Lufkin & Jenrette, Drexel Burnham Lambert, Heinold Commodities, E.F. Hutton, Kidder Peabody, Merrill Lynch, Morgan Futures, Paine Webber Mitchell Hutchins, Phillip Brothers, Refco, Salomon Brothers, Shearson Lehman American Express, Trade Development Bank – this January 1985 *Futures World* list of principal US futures brokers in London was a useful pointer to the top twenty. And, of course, the American impact affected all aspects of the City in the mid-1980s. As Neville Wood, a partner of Messels which was in the process of being acquired by Shearson Lehman, wryly put it in 1985, 'I have to get in at 8.00 am now – before the Americans arrived the working day started at 9.15. I arrive before the tea-lady now.'

Locals remained, for some time anyway, relatively unimportant in the official scheme of things. Jenkins had traditionally been a supporter, but as late as January 1987 he told the *Banker* that inadequately capitalised locals were a burden to the market if they traded just 'ones and twos', adding that 'we introduced the local concept to the London market, we would like more of them, but the main pillars of our market are the institutions'. Soon afterwards the Bank of England's survey indicated that most member firms 'believed that there should be fewer locals', on the grounds partly that 'there was not the right capitalist atmosphere in the UK to support large numbers of active locals' and partly that 'some of the existing ones were not useful'. It was also 'stressed that it was essential for LIFFE and General Clearing Members to keep a close control over locals at all times'. The question of control was one that Williamson implicitly touched on in June, addressing the American industry's lobby organisation, the Futures Industry Association. 'I happen to think that Europe has the advantage of not having to satisfy a pit population,' he observed, almost certainly an allusion to the way in which much of the effective power at the CBOT rested in the hands of its myriad locals, often making it very difficult to plan and implement long-term policy.

Nevertheless, LIFFE in the mid-1980s did to a modest but significant degree encourage the growth of locals. In July 1983 a paper by Albright had shown that, under the existing cost structure, a local had to be 'right' (i.e. buy the market when it ticked up, or sell it when it ticked down) 82% of the time in the long gilt contract in order to break even and 130% of the time (clearly an impossibility) in the short sterling contract; whereas under the Chicago cost structure the percentages would have been a more encouraging 61% and 77% respectively. Accordingly, in February 1984, specifically following the CBOT's example, the exchange introduced zero charges for personal locals on scratch trades completed within a day, in other words those round trips in which both transactions were made at the same price; though the ICCH was unwilling to make such a concession and charged 15p per round trip per lot on scratch trades. The facility undoubtedly helped – by January 1987 there were some 65 genuine locals on LIFFE contributing around 16% of pit volume – but the local revolution was far from complete.

For the press, of course, the locals were a source of much interest. In October 1985 the *Investors Chronicle* interviewed Adrian Bone, who had started his own company a year earlier: 'I took the view, why should I be paid a salary when I can earn commission and have the freedom of being my own boss? The job after all is no different whether I work for de Zoetes or myself.' He had leased a seat, established that he had a minimum net worth of £25,000 ('and that is not borrowed money!'), and by now reckoned that he did about '75 per cent jobbing and 25 per cent broking', the latter, being a local, only for members of the exchange. 'Do you scalp as a rule or take positions?' he was asked. 'I take positions. I don't like scalping – where you just make one tick. I frequently take positions home overnight. I'm one of the few who do. And it's easier – overnight the market generally moves up or down, no messing around – while it fluctuates continually during the day.' *Euromoney* in April 1986, as part of its supplement on LIFFE, focused on various locals, including Nigel Ackerman, who nine months previously had returned from the commodity markets – 'I like to spend my time in markets

Above: Nick Carew Hunt.

Below: Mary Lou Carrington.

that are active and volatile... I decided there were more opportunities for me here.' Having originally leased a seat, he had now borrowed the money to buy one, arguing that the macro-economic outlook for Britain and America was so uncertain that there would continue to be sustained activity in financial futures.

Soon afterwards *Intermarket* featured three 'American Pit Bulls in London', namely Mark Stanton, Tony LaPorta and Tom Theys, survivors from the original ten or so American traders and by this stage of the game all operating as locals. 'The tough part about what we do is the discipline involved in cutting your losses,' Stanton told his interviewer. 'You've got to do it no matter how much it hurts. You can't let your ego get in the way... I try to play within myself, to be satisfied, not to get greedy.' The American trio had all been with Smith Brothers when the exchange began, while Guy Whittle had also worked for jobbers, in his case Akroyd & Smithers, before going it alone in September 1983. 'It was taking quite a risk,' he recalled to the *FT* in March 1987. 'LIFFE had only been open for a year and volumes were very low.' Concentrating on gilt futures he aimed to turn over between 30 and 200 contracts a day, he reckoned to be on the floor more or less all day (9 to 4.15 in the gilt market), would never think of taking more than half an hour off for lunch, and calculated that ten years was the upper limit on a local's trading life.

Arguably though, there were four peculiarly emblematic figures among the LIFFE locals of the mid-1980s. One was Alan Dickinson, jobbing the markets and filling the orders in an aggressive, manifestly successful way that others were keen to emulate. Another, who had been in the market from the first day and represented a rather different strain, was David Morgan. He was already in his mid-forties and had had a variegated business past, selling an export-import business and a restaurant in order to finance himself on LIFFE when it opened. Invariably dressed in a suit, and seeing himself as something of a father figure to fellow-traders, he was soon deeply committed to his new way of life and in September 1986 spoke at length to Izabel Grindal of *Futures and Options World*:

Above: Nigel Ackerman.
Below: Mark Stanton.

> *I was attracted by the possibilities of not needing a huge staff, stocks and assets. You are relying purely on yourself and your own value judgements as to whether you produce any profits... It is the independence of being able to walk into the market with a few ideas and a blank piece of paper, and just start trading... It has to be a full-time commitment if you are going to be successful. You have to assimilate different views, take your position and hold on to it even when the market is going against you, confidence is vital... I have had two dreadful days in four years but my losses have never been greater than £10,000. I found it difficult early on but as the markets have developed so has my ability to trade profitably and I have been able to increase my commitment to the market... There is enough liquidity in the market for locals to operate as long as*

they don't feel intimidated by a 'fat landlord syndrome'. There isn't a Them and Us attitude at LIFFE, it is an extremely homogeneous market, particularly considering how far more 'institutional' London is than elsewhere... There are dull periods and you have to get through them but generally speaking I enjoy coming into the market. You meet a hell of a lot of nice people, more than I ever thought would exist in a competitive market.

Typically, it was Morgan (along with Simon Raybould of NatWest) who in the mid-1980s organised the annual LIFFE Traders' Dinner, with The Brewery in Chiswell Street as its regular venue.

The third emblematic figure was Phil Barnett, by 1984 not only trading entirely on his own account but the first local on the board. 'You can be concerned about a situation but you mustn't let it interfere with your trading,' he told *Futures and Options World* in October 1987. 'A lot of people come to grief because they lack the strength of character to react sensibly, contain themselves and get back up after a knock. Survival depends on staying on an even keel, keeping a clear, level head and continuing to trade in a logical manner.' Asked which animal best described a local, he chose as his reply the elephant for its strength, wisdom and knowledge, the cheetah for its speed, the mongoose for its ability to make a quick kill, and the hyena because it lives off the pickings.

Above: Tom Theys.
Below: David Morgan.

Finally, there was David Kyte, who became a local because, he claimed, 'I didn't want to have to laugh at other people's jokes'. A North Londoner born in 1960, he traded first for Comfin and then Tulletts before starting as a sole trader in January 1985. 'I trade anything that moves' was his philosophy, he informed *Euromoney* the following year. In 1987 he talked to the *Sunday Times Magazine*. 'If I lose £10,000 now, there's plenty more where that came from,' he was quoted as saying. 'If I make £10,000 it's not going to make such a great advance on my equity. I don't think of it as money any more. It's just points. If I'm up it gives me more to play with, that's it.' The apparent brashness belied an essential seriousness, and like Dickinson, Morgan and Barnett, he did not intend to be an ephemeral presence in the market.

On the floor itself there was plenty of fun still to be had – imaginary games of snooker around the octagonal-shaped pits, arm-wrestling matches between the English and Americans, and pantomimes organised by David Morgan, with Ted Ersser's booth decorated like a bamboo hut. 'As the festive season approaches,' a notice to floor members from Ken Heymer, floor operations manager, rather wearily reiterated on 10 December 1985, 'we would again request the co-operation of Members in keeping celebrations, on and around the Trading Floor, within acceptable limits.' After warning that 'damage to computer terminals and booth equipment can very easily arise as a result of the discharge of foam and streamer aerosols,' he especially asked traders to look after their price reporting board: 'It may not always be right up to date, but it is the only one we have, and the repair or replacement costs, I do promise, will be just a little bit higher than any fine imposed so far.'

More importantly, the question of trading standards was an increasing concern as the exchange's volume grew so markedly. The introduction of fines (up to £100) from July 1984 for members failing to comply with the routine mismatch procedures led to some temporary improvement, but in January 1986 Rodgers was compelled to tell the board 'that the high volumes of recent days had confirmed the need for a reassessment of the standards of discipline and conduct on the floor'. Noting that the saturation of the LIFFE and ICCH systems on the busy days had resulted in considerable delays in the matching and clearing of trades, he stated that 'these problems had been caused mainly by some members failing to submit clearing slips on a timely basis, including some who had delayed doing so until after the close of trading'. He was supported by Barnett, who argued that 'the problem lay as much with traders as with the system' and that 'the level of fines and the degree of discipline imposed was not sufficient and bore little relation to the advantages which might be gained by ignoring the rules'.

Later that month Rodgers and Heymer produced a lengthy 'Review of Systems, Facilities, Disciplines & Standards at the Royal Exchange'. The general thrust of their review was that all four areas needed substantial upgrading. There was a particularly key (if rather convoluted) passage:

Above: Phil Barnett.
Below: David Kyte.

LIFFE's public image and identity in terms of regulation and credibility has consistently been high, with few if any controversial issues. The performance of LIFFE's operational systems and management to date has been above average to high. Disputes and resultant arbitrations have as a result been significantly low. The three basic levels of operational dictate have all been of an acceptable to high standard, i.e. Trading Rules, Trading Procedures, Trading Etiquette.

The existence of the above physical conditions has given rise to an evolutionary process in which the major resourcing effort has consistently been directed into non-operational areas. The supervisory level therefore that might reasonably be expected has been below average to low, with a very heavy dependency upon exchange officials alone to take the initiative and exercise control.

This situation coupled with the inescapable fact that the financial futures and options industry in the UK is now experiencing growth in excess of the availability and quality of suitable personnel gives us a position in which:

'Senior traders' attract premium reward packages against which there are little if any incentives to participate in a formal exchange disciplinary or supervisory capacity.

Pit Committee strength and effectiveness is low.

Floor Committee strength and effectiveness is less than acceptable.

Exchange staff to at least middle management level are constantly vulnerable to a head-hunt.

Consistency, continuity and development of exchange staff is less than effective and against present employment/recruitment criteria is difficult to achieve.

The Rodgers/Heymer argument was in effect twofold, if only implied rather than fully fleshed out: firstly, that an ideal open outcry floor should be populated by *knowledgeable*, technologically supported traders, as opposed to those just filling orders, and that as far as possible back office functions should be moved off the floor; secondly, to achieve this, the exchange would have to aim consciously at *balanced* growth, in which the training of people and the development of technology were as important as the volume of contracts. In practice, however, volumes – and liquidity – remained everything in a globally competitive industry; and people and technology had to adapt or be adapted as best they could.

A competitive trading cost structure was crucial to that pursuit of liquidity, and LIFFE's management spent a significant part of the mid-1980s engaged in what was not far short of guerilla warfare with ICCH. In August 1984, after a joint clearing study undertaken by the two organisations had failed to produce any tangible results, and with ICCH sticking to its position that a reduction in fees (bringing down its clearing fee from 70p per round trip to 50p) was contingent on an extension of its contract with LIFFE, the board agreed that Barkshire should go direct to the Bank of England and ICCH's shareholders. Jenkins drafted a paper ('LIFFE's Clearing Arrangements') that would be his ammunition. It argued that LIFFE was facing 'sharply increased competition' from other financial futures exchanges; that on the basis of the present share of income received from clearing, the exchange would become insolvent during 1985; that neither subscription rates and other charges to members could be significantly raised nor costs significantly reduced; and that, in the context of intense pressure on the profitability of members of international exchanges, 'the costs of using LIFFE must be competitive with other international exchanges in order for LIFFE merely to maintain its existing market share'. The paper then turned to the deficiencies of ICCH itself:

By any standards, the charges for ICCH services covering clearing and performance guarantee are very high. Its current charge for clearing – 70p for a round trip – is ten times that of the most expensive US exchange. In defence of its present charge it has been claimed that the ICCH service is more comprehensive, eliminating additional work in members' offices. This claim has not been substantiated, is disputed by many clearing members, and is certainly not required by all members. This increases the charges to all for the possible benefit of a few...

Banks and other financial institutions which predominate on LIFFE as members and clients, particularly resent their high margin costs. European banks in particular do not understand why they should place deposits with a clearing house owned by UK banks, who thereby make 1½% on their funds…

ICCH has stated that the cost of providing a clearing service to LIFFE in 1983 was £1.47m. Apart from the questionable validity of the method of arriving at this figure (one-third of ICCH expenditure reflecting LIFFE's one-third contribution to volume), it is unbelievably high. A comparable figure for NYFE is £600,000, which includes data processing, reconciliation, margins and fund management, and financial surveillance. LIFFE has no reason to doubt that it could operate its own clearing system at a similar cost and has received a quotation to do so from a US clearing house [Options Clearing Corp]…

On 1 October, in a second-anniversary piece in the *Daily Telegraph* called 'LIFFE Needs Rich Uncles', Christopher Fildes called on Stuart Graham, chairman of ICCH, to be uncle-in-chief and cut charges.

Possibly after some persuasion from the Bank, and faced by the apparent threat of LIFFE going elsewhere, ICCH and its shareholders agreed to major concessions, as Jenkins informed members on 22 November. Henceforth, for each lot up to a monthly average of 15,000 lots per day, the 90p transaction fee per round turn for all contracts except currencies would be split 64p to LIFFE and 26p to ICCH; and once the average rose above 15,000 lots, then 70p would go to LIFFE. At the very least LIFFE's financial survival was assured, with break-even likely to be achieved at average daily volumes of around 12,000 lots. Furthermore, members would benefit directly from three other changes, to come into effect from the start of December: the first tranche of initial margin (in cash, up to £50,000) would attract no interest; bank guarantees and UK Treasury bills could still be used to cover initial margins in excess of the first tranche, even though the existing

Daily Telegraph,
1 October 1984.

LOMBARD STREET   By Christopher Fildes

LIFFE NEEDS RICH UNCLES

TWO CANDLES on the cake at the Royal Exchange today, the usual deafening turmoil on the nursery floor and, among the grown-ups, an anxious search through the parcels to see whether the rich uncles have weighed in. Anything from Stuart? Anything from Nigel?

This is the birthday of the London International Financial Futures Exchange, L I F F E is the biggest gamble on a brand institutions — are still dabbling their toes in the water. We would like, says a treasurer, to be sure, first that we know what we are doing in L I F F E and secondly that if we used it to our full potential it would be big enough for what we need.

But the real push will be for the international business written into L I F F E's full name but not, as yet, so legible in its books, and going after the business will be Stuart Graham, who used to run the Midland Bank and is now chairman of the International Commodities Clearing House. Payments on L I F F E are cleared through I C C H, which acts for the major commodity markets and, belonging to the Big Four banks, is strong enough to underwrite any market's credit.

But its services are not cheap, Chicago futures markets charge less than L I F F E for a trans-syndicates who lease a seat on the Exchange, take a view, lease another, perhaps buy one . . . This business is growing.

It would grow faster if an accident of tax law did not treat profits from futures trading as though they were income. You pay at the top marginal rate and capital losses, other than from futures trading, cannot be offset against your liability. Traded options on the Stock Exchange, by contrast,

1½% accommodation charge on non-cash margin was to be abolished; and cash-covered initial margins in excess of the first tranche would attract interest at a competitive rate set daily so as to appeal to clearing members as an alternative to using bank guarantees. It was a crucial battle that Jenkins and his board had fought.

Henceforth the focus would be less on ICCH choking the young market in a financial sense, much more on the even more invidious question of whether it was up to the job of satisfying that market's increasingly voracious functional needs. A letter in March 1986 from Williamson to David Walker of the Bank of England forcefully outlined the new agenda, if arguably exaggerating ICCH's failings:

> LIFFE needs to make a radical change in its clearing arrangements. The existing system does not meet requirements, is unreliable under pressure, has insufficient capacity and cannot be changed easily. In considering how LIFFE will proceed we are influenced by our perception of ICCH as a clearing organisation. Except on one or two occasions it has been unresponsive to meeting LIFFE's requirements. We have never had confidence in ICCH's technical capability, in their systems and programming and we are not convinced that they carry out their basic monitoring role competently. Sadly, we feel they have fundamentally weak management. In the past year these traits have become more pronounced.
>
> In summary, while we are very happy with the guarantee function provided by shareholders, we have very little confidence in what goes on in Crutched Friars. We are not alone in this perception, it is shared by The Stock Exchange and a number of members of the London Commodity Exchange...

Williamson added that LIFFE would shortly inform ICCH of its intention to give notice to terminate the existing clearing agreement and that later in the year it would invite two or more organisations to tender for its clearing business. 'We conclude at the moment that unless there is a very radical change in the management of ICCH, we cannot envisage ICCH being successful in getting LIFFE's business.'

Undoubtedly, perceived operational constraints, affecting LIFFE's further growth, now featured heavily in the exchange's thinking. 'The volume highlighted the technical shortcomings of the ICCH clearing system,' Jenkins noted in May about the peak trading periods already experienced that year. But in the event, like competitors in a three-legged race, the odd couple stayed together. Barkshire – interested, typically, in how a reorganisation of ICCH's international as well as domestic business could benefit London's overall competitive position – became chairman of ICCH in September. It was an appointment blessed (possibly initiated) by the Bank, willing to see what this creative man could do. Over the winter of 1986/7 it became apparent that though Barkshire believed in principle that new owners were required, there was no unanimity over the question of ownership on the part of either the banks or the exchanges, the latter desiring neither to take on the ownership function themselves nor see it passed to ICCH's clearing members. The result, accordingly, was impasse.

In the course of the spring, the exchanges successfully asked the Bank of England to persuade the shareholders to retain ownership for the next 18 months or so while plans could be laid for what Jenkins called 'an orderly transfer to new clearing arrangements for London'. And in August 1987, following considerable constructive input from LIFFE, especially in the person of Barton, those new arrangements were publicly unveiled by ICCH: the raising of the clearing guarantee from £15m to £100m (as a result of which, declared *International Financing Review*, 'the London capital market perceives that the British clearing banks have a moral investment in ICCH') and a reorganisation into a number of separate operating subsidiaries, one of which would provide services to the London markets. It was also agreed that ICCH would enter into a joint venture with LIFFE to design a new system to meet LIFFE's clearing needs – jointly funded, but with LIFFE to have the controlling interest. All problems would not suddenly vanish. Nevertheless, the very worst of the LIFFE/ICCH relationship was over, partly thanks to the efforts of David Hardy, brought in by Barkshire soon afterwards to be managing director of the London clearing division.

The protracted imbroglio over the clearing house, allied to a natural tendency to glamorise personalities, contracts and atmosphere, helped to mask the fact that the exchange could not have grown as it did without a remarkable level of technological responsiveness and improvisation. 'Though we have only been open two years,' Rodgers told the *Sunday Times* in October 1984, 'we are having constantly to innovate. You cannot afford to stand still.' And he looked ahead to the introduction in the short to medium term of microcomputers being installed in the booths, extending the range and mix of real-time data, market calculations and communications available; to the reduction of paperwork through further automation; to the introduction of multi-channel radio in order to eliminate physical contact between dealer and messenger; and to computerised voice recognition techniques. The 1980s was the decade when technology came to the City in a big way, and addressing an *FT* conference in April 1986 on 'Technology and the Securities Markets' Jenkins was characteristically pragmatic. Arguing that by starting late LIFFE had gained advantages, including reliability and systems that were highly adaptable, he went on: 'When we ran into capacity problems with our matching system recently, we were able to double capacity in a couple of weeks. Do not pioneer. Use proven hardware and software wherever possible and keep a finger on the needs of the market.'

Such were the dictates of the market that it soon became clear that, despite all the various upgradings, the first-generation systems needed replacing. The upshot was the Trade Registration System [TRS], an under-appreciated cornerstone of LIFFE's history and a tremendous achievement by Peter Mather in particular. Originally introduced in September 1987 for options only, it would be implemented for all contracts by the end of 1988. Essentially designed to facilitate the time-consuming, relatively unautomated task of trade processing, the new system combined the functions of LIFFE's floor-based trade matching system and those of ICCH's back office-based matching and confirmation system, Intercom. The way that TRS worked was through details of each trade being input either by exchange staff on the floor via clearing slips or by members themselves using input terminals while matching was performed automatically, with mismatched trades being displayed on-line for resolution by members. Back-office automation offered three major advantages: one, obviously, was savings for members in terms of costs and time, with all trades able to be matched and confirmed within an hour of execution; the second was that TRS provided a real-time feed of trades to any client accounting system that wished to participate in the market, thereby allowing members to make an objective choice about which accounting system suited them best; and the third was that, through TRS terminals in back-offices interacting with the central system, it enabled members to view their own trades, allocate trades, claim allocation give-ups, and assign trades to client, house and local accounts. TRS involved an investment of some £1.5m (ICCH declined to commit itself to a joint venture), and – far ahead of the competition – it was one of those rare cases of every penny well spent, for all the paucity of headlines it attracted.

Of the original septet of contracts, the four currency futures remained largely in the shadows, sometimes all but forgotten, with the partial exception of the British pound. By July 1984 it had achieved a total cumulative volume of 245,383 lots, compared with 51,707 for the deutschmark, 26,659 for the yen and 22,922 for the Swiss franc. By then it was clear that the Bank of England was unwilling to allow the exchange to introduce an EPT [ex-pit transactions] facility for the currency contracts and that it preferred all transactions to continue to take place in the pit on the exchange floor. Meanwhile, the notion of introducing jumbo-sized currency futures seems to have been quietly forgotten. Talking to *Euromoney* in early 1986, Williamson remained publicly defiant – 'Every journalist I see asks me why we don't get rid of our currency futures contracts... We accept that they're the least successful, but they're much more successful than is generally thought, because they make a valuable contribution to the breadth of products available on the floor.' – but the members themselves continued to grumble. 'Most, including one of the biggest players in the currency contracts at present, said they would not regret the loss of the contracts altogether,' the Bank of England's February 1987 survey reported. In July that year the four contracts managed between them only a pathetic 1,412 lots, and it was becoming a question of how long the sentimental attachment would persist.

Such was not the case with the short sterling interest rate contract, which after a somewhat disappointing start rarely failed to pay its way. By autumn 1983 the possibility was being actively canvassed – by Albright in particular – of doubling its size to £½m, in order to give it a tick size that made it attractive to locals. This was opposed by Burton, on the grounds that low activity was the result of the control over sterling rates exercised by the Bank of England, and by Foyle arguing that the crux was lack of price volatility and that there were better ways of cutting dealing costs, but the change was implemented in January 1984. Progress after this change was solid rather than remarkable, but in January 1986 the contract received a major fillip when the British government intervened heavily in the currency markets, through massaging interest rates, in order to prop up the pound in the face of falling crude-oil prices. 'The short sterling contract has come into its own for the first time,' noted 'Lex' on the 11th, 'trading on average around 6,000 contracts daily for a nominal turnover of about £6bn a day' – a nominal turnover in the contract higher than in sterling bills and certificates of deposit. 'On that sort of volume, the futures market is more liquid than the cash market, and while it may not yet be large enough for banks like NatWest or Barclays to hedge their whole books, there is quite enough liquidity for most of the other money market operators.'

Thereafter the short sterling contract settled down as one of the exchange's linch-pins. In June 1987 it was the third most popular contract, in July the second (142,925 lots). Over the years its longevity would give it one of the market's most diverse as well as established user bases. It became invaluable for London-based treasury operations with sterling exposure, for example, and eventually it provided the means whereby banks and building societies offered fixed-rate mortgages – a key instance of the effect LIFFE had on the financial services market right through to the retail sector. It also served as a punting tool, often being the first contract to show sentiment and its enhanced size not proving too big for locals. The flagship domestic money market product, it would tend to be unfairly overlooked during the whirlwind internationalisation of the late 1980s and early 1990s.

In the Eurodollar contract, LIFFE had fallen behind the IMM in December 1982 and, in the event, never recovered its all-too-brief ascendency. Volumes themselves were by no means unsatisfactory: in 1984, for example, 54,491 in January, 84,718 in March, 134,173 in May; yet in that latter month the IMM's volume was a staggering 568,862, over four times the London total. In September 1984 the mutual offset system started operating between the CME and the Singapore International Monetary Exchange [SIMEX]. And not long afterwards, there was another significant development when the CME further extended its trading hours, starting to open ten minutes earlier at 1.20 London time – strategically important because this was ten minutes before the American economic figures came out, hitherto the regular high point in LIFFE's Eurodollar trading. In May 1986 *Futures and Options World* surveyed the state of competition: 'The Merc has all the advantages of volume and liquidity to keep it in premier position. London, by contrast, has a time zone advantage in that much Eurodollar cash market trading is done in the City's morning, and therefore corresponding hedging or trading is carried out on LIFFE until Chicago opens.' These were valid words perhaps, but the disparity in volume was now huge: 2,341,471 on the CME for the first three months of 1986, compared to 260,601 on LIFFE. The SIMEX volume for the same period, incidentally, was 79,892, hardly suggestive that the forging of the mutual offset link was *the* turning point. There was still plenty of London business to be done in Eurodollar futures (192,775 contracts in April 1987, for example), but in global terms the horse had bolted.

The long gilt contract, early front-runner in LIFFE's history, was by 1985 lagging well behind the Eurodollar. That autumn, however, 'Big Bang' hove rapidly into sight, as the Bank of England named the 29 primary dealers in gilts who would be permitted to trade on the Stock Exchange from 27 October 1986 – the end of the cosy jobbing duopoly enjoyed by Wedds and Akroyds. 'It's no coincidence that all of these prospective dealers are members of LIFFE, although a third have been excluded from the Stock Exchange,' commented Jenkins. The confident expectation was that the revamping of the cash market would bring considerable new hedging activity to the futures market, and soon afterwards LIFFE surveyed its members about the desirability of bringing forward the opening time of the long gilt contract, which currently began trading at 9.30 (an hour and a quarter after some of the trading began elsewhere on the floor) in deference to that being the Stock Exchange's opening time.

Only a handful – including Wedds and Akroyds – disagreed with the proposal that gilt trading should start earlier, and the report noted 'a degree of resentment that the present late opening of the cash and futures markets is primarily to the benefit of the dominant jobbing firms'. Almost all of the 29 nominated primary dealers were firmly in favour of an earlier start, as some of their responses eloquently showed:

Would like to see 8.45 opening at latest. 5 cash market players known to be quoting firm prices to Far East then... In office from 8.00 and there is No Reason for them not to be open longer... Would be absolutely delighted if they were opened at 8.30 with the rest of the market. Come in at 8.00, make decision what to do, want to trade at 8.30, can't till 9.30 by which time good overnight position, more often than not, has gone against them... Do believe that prices are being made from 8.45 and business coming in from Far East. 'Waiting until 9.30 helps no man!'... Suits me! 9.00 would be great. Shouldn't be tied by Stock Exchange – it has been proved that good volume is done after the jobbers pack up at 3.30... No objections to it but there will be opposition to it from the cash market... Very, very good idea! anything to take power away from jobbers!

Despite a certain temptation to the contrary, LIFFE held back from a unilateral move, and following some high-level dialogue both it and the Stock Exchange moved to a 9 o'clock start for trading in gilts, beginning on 28 April 1986. LIFFE's 'forbearance' had, Eddie George wrote appreciatively to Williamson that day, 'been well rewarded by the fact that the time change has come about without great grumbling and hostility from elsewhere in the City'; though informally, George let it be known that if LIFFE came back and pushed for a further 30 minutes, it would not be appreciated.

Meanwhile, in terms of the larger picture, it was not just a case of a tedious countdown to the fabled 27 October 1986. 'It's been frustrating to hang around waiting for Big Bang,' Williamson told Fildes in July, but already in the first half of 1986 the long gilt's 958,866 contracts represented a 178.2% increase over the first half of 1985. Over the next two months new single-day records for the contract were set, partly attributable to the primary dealers (now reduced to a slightly more circumspect 27) gaining experience in gilt futures ahead of the restructuring of the cash market. On the day itself there were as many as 40 to 50 people, including on the research side, concentrated on the gilt-edged table at Kleinworts, and that was not untypical. The revolution did not disappoint: amidst much hedging of positions, there ensued in November a series of record days in long gilt futures, culminating on the 20th when a total of 31,480 lots were traded, worth £1.57bn, representing a 20% rise over the previous record set the day before. The mood music also helped, with (the *FT* reported) 'concern over a further decline in the value of sterling and the growing prospect of higher interest rates' as well as 'continued election fever and an opinion poll which showed that the Labour Party had moved back ahead of the Conservative Party'.

The long gilt had now become easily the exchange's dominant contract, and it remained so through the winter of 1986/7, on the back of the cash market nearly trebling in turnover since deregulation. In March 1987 the contract traded a daily average of 31,660 lots (compared to 8,555 a year earlier). 'The advantage we have in London is that the majority of risk is in the long end,' Mark Eynon (of Warburg Securities) commented, 'rather than in medium or short term, and we have a long-term gilt futures contract that is almost a perfect match to the cash gilt. It is a perfect vehicle for hedging and trading.' By this time the capacity of the long gilt pit had been increased by some 30%, and over the summer the good times continued to roll. A new daily record was set on 23 June (57,876 lots), and for

Today's Big Bang changes the London securities market irrevocably. The prize within the City's grasp is the leading position in the European time zone in a seamless market extending around the wor

Monday October 27 1986

THE CITY REVOLUTION

the first nine months of 1987 volume was some 225% up on the corresponding period in 1986. In September alone long gilts accounted for 1,197,565 contracts, an average daily volume of more than 54,500. The much-touted bloodbath in the cash market had failed to materialise; and with profits there distressingly meagre compared to the fat old days, all seemed set fair in long gilt futures, barring an outbreak of virtue on the part of the British government.

In summer 1984 the exchange launched its first two wholly new contracts since the opening flurry. The first was the FTSE 100 futures. The equity index working party, in tandem with LIFFE staff, had continued its labours the previous autumn, including taking the market pulse and discovering that a real time index transmitted directly to all interested parties – the only way in which the pit trading community as a whole would have access to the same information at the same time as Stock Exchange members – debarred the FT-Actuaries All-Share Index because of price collection impracticalities. The FT 30, although the best-known index, had already been ruled out by the investment institutions, strongly of the opinion that it was not a serious measure of portfolio performance. Accordingly, it was decided that an index formed of the shares of the 100 companies with the largest capitalisation would best serve the purpose of the proposed new contract. The problems of price collection and real time calculation were tackled through establishing a joint working party with the Stock Exchange, interested for its own purposes in developing a new, real time index. Meanwhile much time was spent worrying about the possibility that Gaming Act implications might preclude cash-only settlement for the contract, and accordingly a delivery option was devised in which buyers and sellers wishing to go into delivery would nominate shares they might wish to receive or deliver.

Jenkins in early February weighed up to the board some of the pros and cons of launching this new contract:

There is a strong feeling among members that it is essential for the exchange to introduce a new contract in the first half of 1984. This will keep momentum going... The vast majority of the turnover in U.K. equities takes place in London. Furthermore, there is strong competition for the management of funds with increasing publicity being given to the performance of individual funds and fund management groups. This is particularly true in the pension funds field. A financial product that can assist in the management of risk and in increasing return on investment is unlikely to be ignored... Potentially there is a very wide range of users for this contract. This is also evident by the enthusiasm of some LIFFE members for the exchange to introduce the contract. However, it is a radically new

Opposite: Big Bang.

financial product that is bound to be greeted by significant professional scepticism. Many pension funds, unit trusts, etc, may have to change their trust deeds before they can participate and there will be uncertainties in the treatment...

Overall, however, Jenkins recommended a buy, and after a revised, more positive, legal opinion had been obtained the board decided on 17 February to press ahead, on the basis of cash settlement only. Three days later it was announced that trading in the new contract – to be called the FTSE 100 – would start on 3 May.

Behind those apparently innocuous four letters there lay quite a story. In essence the Stock Exchange tried to squeeze the *FT* out of the frame – as it was perfectly entitled to attempt – and might well have succeeded but for LIFFE's resistance. An internal note by Jenkins in November 1983 reflected what was at stake:

From a LIFFE viewpoint, there are a number of arguments in favour of the proposed index having an FT prefix.

i) there is a close association between the FT and Stock Exchange indices. It will be easier to market an index which retains that association. Put in another way it may be difficult to explain convincingly why the Stock Exchange has not followed precedent and involved the FT. Since the FT is likely to be hostile to a Stock Exchange 100 index, it may not be above impugning lack of objectivity to the new index.

ii) the FT will be very upset if they are not involved. I do not believe that it is in the Stock Exchange's interests or in LIFFE's to fall out with the FT. They have been particularly supportive of LIFFE and we need that support to continue.

iii) the FT have an attractive offer from a Chicago exchange (I believe it to be the CME but it may be the CBOT) to trade the FT-30. This is certainly not in LIFFE's interest and not in the City's either. A much more sensible arrangement would be for the FT to be involved with the new contract and for that to be used by both LIFFE and the CME if necessary.

There do not appear to be any strong arguments for excluding the FT:

i) the FT have accepted that it will be essential for the Stock Exchange to collect prices and to calculate the index in real time. In their mind there is no question of this being done by their existing price collectors.

ii) the FT would clearly want to be on the Steering Committee and have a say in the constituents and the maintenance of the index. I cannot see any objections to this.

iii) it has been mentioned that having an index with FT in the title restricts its acceptance by other newspapers. I think this argument would be difficult to sustain. All papers quote the FT index and it is synonymous in the public's mind with Stock Exchange indices.

'I only hope the *FT* and the Stock Exchange will reach an accommodation,' Jenkins wrote to Wigglesworth on 7 December, reiterating his view that 'LIFFE's overriding concern is to avoid any deterioration in relations between the Stock Exchange and LIFFE on the one side and the *FT* on the other', adding that it was 'not impossible' that the *FT* 'might promote their own index in association with Reuters or some other information carrier'.

For the first few weeks of the new year the Stock Exchange continued to refer stubbornly to the new index as the 'SE 100'; but on 10 February, three days before it was publicly unveiled, an accommodation was reached. 'We are expecting that the index will be called the FTSE index,' the Stock Exchange's chief executive, Jeffrey Knight, duly explained at the launch. 'We have been talking to the *FT* for some time. We recognise the value of having the *FT* associated with the new index.' The *FT*'s stubbornness, allied to LIFFE's own needs, had enabled the paper to cling on by the skin of its teeth – vitally, as it turned out, for the new index rapidly became the dominant measure of market sentiment and indeed a household name. The acronym 'Footsie' played its part in that acceptance. The first sighting seems to have been on 14 February, when 'Lex' (probably Martin Taylor) declared that 'the new FTSE Index – "footsy" to its friends – answers an obvious need for a market measurement which is both comprehensive and up-to-the-minute.' By the end of the week the spelling had changed, with the *Investors Chronicle* referring on the 17th to how 'the index, not yet christened officially, is expected to be called the FTSE 100, but the market has taken the hint from this mouthful of initials and has named it "Footsie"'. Unlike LIFFE the pronunciation was not in doubt, and a new benchmark was born.

> The new FTSE Index — "footsy" to its friends — answers an obvious need for a market measurement which is both comprehensive and up-to-the-minute. The impetus for
>
> *Financial Times,* 14 February 1984.

Even before the traders woke up on the first Thursday in May, Christopher Morgan had been hard at work publicising the launch of the new contract. In the small hours of the night he oversaw five teams putting down pink footprints leading from the City's five main stations to the Royal Exchange; he then rang up the *Today* radio programme; and shortly before the market was due to open, he managed to fob off an understandably irate representative from the City Corporation. The Stock Exchange's chairman, Sir Nicholas Goodison, was also busy that morning. First, in his own patch, he opened London's first stock index options, before hurrying across the road to open LIFFE's new futures contract. The *FT*'s reporter allowed himself a bit of fun:

Sir Nicholas's role in opening both markets meant that LIFFE had to postpone the debut of its contract until 9.45 am.

Right on cue, Sir Nicholas raced on to the LIFFE floor. Meanwhile, traders *from the gilt pit flooded the FTSE, or "Footsie", one and turned it into a seething mass of brightly coloured blazers.*

Sir Nicholas picked up the megaphone. Time for a few words? Not a bit of it. The traders did not even allow him to give them the off. At 9.45 precisely, the yelling started and it was not until 9.45.03 that Sir Nicholas managed to ring the starting bell. By that time, even if the megaphone had been nearer to his lips, he would not have been heard over the din.

Seventy-five people crammed into a space the size of a large paddling pool and within seven minutes, 200 contracts had changed hands…

Pink feet in the City.

'Sir Nick legs it to play footsie' was the *Standard*'s memorable headline, but more serious press comment was divided about merits and prospects. 'Imitating the fecund inventiveness of the American commodity markets does not necessarily serve the needs of London nationally or internationally,' thundered *The Times* on the 3rd itself, arguing that LIFFE had only invented this latest product because it 'seemed to be losing momentum'. 'Lex' was kinder the morning after the launch, contending that though 'institutional investors may take some convincing before they make heavy use of the FTSE contract' – unsurprisingly, granted that 'both pension fund managers and insurance men take about as long to change course as a super-tanker' – nevertheless the new contract had 'the advantage over the ill-starred currency contracts, since there is no ready made liquid market corresponding to the inter-bank forward currency market, where the action has remained'.

In the event it proved a desperately slow burner, even after (following research partly funded by LIFFE) E. Dimson and P.R. Marsh of the London Business School published a paper in the *Journal of the Institute of Actuaries* in September demonstrating that the minute-by-minute calculation of the FTSE 100 could be used to read off the value of the All Share index with virtually 100 per cent certainty – in other words, that the new contract could be used as a highly efficient hedge of the wider cash market. In the first eight months of 1985 total volume was only 56,187, and a variety of explanations began to be put forward, both privately and publicly. They included the high cost of arbitrage with the underlying market; the lack of incentive for stockbrokers, with minimum commission still obtaining in the cash market, to use it; the slowness of fund managers to adopt hedging strategies; the continuing tax uncertainties; and the quality of the index itself, by now being criticised by some as a flawed investment tool on account of its missing small company component, its lack of a dividend yield calculation (important for institutional investors), and the fact that it was based on mid-prices, not traded prices. This failure was all the more galling in the context not only of Chicago's phenomenal volume with stock index contracts (some 15 million S&P lots in 1985), but also the strong bull market in London equities.

Would 'Big Bang' do the trick? The sharp reduction in stockbrokers' commissions would obviously be a help, while there were confident expectations of greater price volatility in both markets and thus enhanced need for hedging. However, October 1986 proved a false dawn, especially as the Inland Revenue still could not get its head around the notion that a pension fund using a FTSE 100 future for hedging purposes was engaged in investment, not trading. Even so, there was *some* improvement, and by spring 1987 monthly volume was up to some 25,000 lots, appreciably better than the 10,000 or so monthly lots of a year earlier. It was satisfactory up to a point, in other words, but those pink footprints had been expected to lead to something more exciting.

Sir Nicholas Goodison launches the FTSE Index futures contract, 3 May 1984.

The other new contract introduced in 1984 was US T-bond futures. By the previous October the board had decided that a Eurobond contract was no longer – temporarily at least – a runner: 'The relatively small number of bonds available to be included as deliverable continues to give cause for concern that the contract price may be susceptible to being unduly easily influenced through transactions in the cash market.' Therefore, 'the work on a possible US Treasury Bond contract is now being pursued as a matter of urgency'. Soon afterwards the views of some of London's primary dealers in US government securities were sought, and there was unanimity that the contract should be modelled as closely as possible on the immensely successful CBOT 30-year contract – liquid, volatile and well understood. The ultimate goal, it was generally agreed by the dealers, should be fungibility (i.e. interchangeability) with the Chicago contract, on the grounds that the convenience and simplicity of knowing they were trading the same instrument outweighed any possible volume that might be generated through arbitrage if the contracts were fundamentally different, for example in terms of delivery months or price factors.

Further encouragement continued to come from the CBOT itself, and though by February there was some concern on the board that there might be relatively little price volatility during morning trading prior to the opening of American markets, McVeigh of Salomons 'expressed the view that the secondary trading desks are likely to use the contract, even though the primary trading desks and syndicate underwriters might not do so, and that this should ensure an adequate market'. Soon afterwards 21 June was set as the date; and the press release explained that a futures contract in London covering long US interest rates would 'allow the ever-increasing number of holders of U.S. Government securities outside the U.S. to hedge their portfolios prior to the opening of the U.S. markets each day'.

'The Yanks Are Coming' was the headline to a Fildes piece on 18 June, and three days later, at a sprightly 8.15 am, the CBOT's chairman, Tom Cunningham, rang the bell to open trading in the contract. 'You do not see a successful London market as taking business away from Chicago?' he was asked later in the day by the BBC's Vincent Duggleby. 'No, I see it actually as enhancing the business in

Chicago. There will be an overlap here of one hour where the chaps in London will be able to trade with the people in Chicago and there will be, we presume, a great deal of arbitrage business between the two exchanges.' Business in the first fortnight ran at a mildly encouraging 1,100 contracts a day, and against expectations it was not concentrated in the one-hour window of arbitrage opportunity (2–3 pm) when both LIFFE and the CBOT were open. By the autumn, volume was running at around 2,000 lots a day, and Albright told the brainstorming session that though LIFFE would never rival the CBOT's daily 100–200,000 contracts, the exchange had 'carved out a niche with very little cash market to build on' and offered 'a needed service' to the European time zone.

Thanks for the T-Bond: Tom Cunningham (centre) receives a present from LIFFE following the launch, 21 June 1984.

In fact, the latter part of 1985 provided a sudden, unexpected take-off, against the backdrop of prevailing uncertainty about American interest rates and an ever-climbing US debt mountain. By December it was doing almost 10,000 contracts a day and becoming, Carew Hunt told *Intermarket*, 'close to our number one contract', jostling for poll position with Eurodollars and long gilts. During much of 1986 it continued as LIFFE's fastest-growing contract, forging ahead of Eurodollars but not quite matching the long gilt's trading. Total volume in the first eight months was a very healthy 1.13 million contracts. However, there was soon a downturn, and volume of 660,089 in the first half of 1987 represented a fall of nearly a quarter on the same period the previous year. The contract's moment in the sun had almost passed.

'How do you decide what products to bring in?' *Euromoney* asked Williamson in April 1986:

There's a constant clamour, among our members, for new contracts [Williamson replied] and in deciding which to introduce, we have three criteria. First, there has to be a commercial demand for the product and we need to be able to design a contract that will effectively meet that demand. The second is to rely heavily on our membership surveys, which give us a very accurate view of the potential use of a contract because our members themselves are the major potential users. Whereas some other exchanges might say, 'our clients would like this,' we have our members saying, 'we would like this.' Thirdly, we require commitment from a nucleus of floor members that they will support the contract in its early days.

Williamson perhaps exaggerated the 'constant clamour', for less than a year later the Bank of England's survey of members' views noted that 'there was an overwhelming call for quality of contracts, defined in terms of volumes and liquidity, not continuous development of multifarious new ones', and that 'the feelings on the subject were very strong and almost totally against any larger number of contracts than at present'. Either way – and almost certainly there were sharp collective mood swings on the subject – the whole area of developing and establishing an appropriate range of contracts was a vexed and permanently knotty one. Kim Albright was wont to quote from Darwin's *The Origin of Species*: 'Owing to this struggle for life, *variations*, if they be in any degree profitable to the species, will tend to the preservation of the species... The more diversified the species becomes, the better will be its chance of success in the battle for life.' Or in other words, as she put it to a brainstorming session in late 1984, 'We must constantly diversify our product base to compete with formidable competitors in a fast-changing environment.'

That diversification continued on 27 June 1985, with the launch of two options contracts. Back in April 1978 the Stock Exchange had made a somewhat ineffectual response to Amsterdam's just-opened European Options Exchange [EOE] by starting its own traded options market, introducing call options on ten leading equities. For several years trading was thin, and the general perception was that the Stock Exchange Council was failing to get behind the market and give it adequate resources. Daily volume pottered along at a few thousand contracts, at best; and David Steen, the market's spearhead for the first eight years, found it a depressingly uphill task to convince his fellow-members that traded options were not merely a potential playground for speculators. Yet it was precisely these undesirables who were needed to complement the very gradually growing institutional use of the market for hedging purposes, in particular for the protection of portfolios. 'The number of speculators required to balance the market is still woefully inadequate,' noted 'Lex' in June 1982. 'The mismatch between hedgers and speculators had led to low premiums, reducing the attractions of writing options for institutions.' General election uncertainty the following May led to a daily record of 9,727 contracts, and the same sharp-tongued columnist declared that 'if the Stock Exchange were to devote half as much energy to traded options as it has to the USM, the market might really take off'.

LIFFE's interest in traded options began in November 1982, when Robert Miller was asked to write a paper on the possibilities. His tone was optimistic

('Currency option contracts would offer a wholly new service to a highly sophisticated foreign exchange market.'), but as the exchange bedded down over the next year and a half, all went quiet on the options front. Then in May 1984 the board decided that the development of an options product should be given a high priority, with bank members in particular pushing hard for the introduction of a currency option. There ensued a more systematic survey of members' views as to which options contract or contracts to introduce first, with the report in the autumn noting that the opportunity for LIFFE to be an innovator in this field had gone: 'By the end of 1984 it is probable that a range of currency options will be trading on the CME, the EOE, the PHLX [Philadelphia Stock Exchange] and possibly the CBOE [Chicago Board Options Exchange]. Eurodollar options will be trading on the CME and the PHLX.' The survey found that 'the options products of greatest interest to members at present are currencies and Eurodollars'; while in terms of which currency product to develop it concluded that 'an option on LIFFE's £/$ futures contract stands a reasonable chance of success as this is by far our strongest currencies futures contract, showing nearly respectable volumes from a small but committed group of members, including several banks'.

Press reports, meanwhile, indicated that the traded options market was also thinking along the same lines, wishing to introduce currency options, and Jenkins told the board in November that he had spoken to David Steen 'to advise him that LIFFE was developing currency options products and held the view that it was more appropriate that such contracts are traded on LIFFE'. This warning was politely ignored, and in the event the Stock Exchange introduced currency options in May 1985, several weeks ahead of LIFFE. 'We are now an exchange going out there to grab business on a world scale instead of being a market with walls around it,' asserted Steen shortly before this gratifying achievement.

From LIFFE's point of view there were many complications involved in launching options – including, partly for tax reasons, creating a subsidiary company, LIFFE Options plc, with members being invited to apply for 'B' shares at £7,500 each – but none proved insuperable. In the pre-opening publicity much stress was laid on the margining system that had been developed, 'probably the most advanced in the world' and 'the first system of its kind that can margin options on the same principles as futures'. Specifically, and applying to long as well as short option positions, it would 'enable buyers of options not only to enter into positions by placing a deposit margin rather than paying the full option premium on purchase, but also to receive any accruing gains on a daily basis rather than having to exercise or sell the option to access the profit'.

There was not universal enthusiasm for this innovative, risk-sensitive, cost-efficient system of delta margining, as it was called. 'It is a very complicated system for the trader on the floor,' John Mullett of Messels told *International Financing Review* in April. 'Not everyone has a computer behind his back. You want the

Norman Tebbit launches options on LIFFE, 27 June 1985 (Sterling-Dollar and Eurodollar).

punter, the speculator, to play the game and make it a success.' It was a perceptive criticism, and came only a few months after Albright in January 1985 had privately speculated as to 'What LIFFE might look like by mid 1986'. Part of her vision was 'fewer seat-of-the-pants traders' and 'more mathematically proficient traders (due to the nature of options and the interrelationship of options and futures)'. In that sense, the introduction of options was about the creation of a more sophisticated trading community.

Norman Tebbit, Secretary of State for Trade and Industry, rang the bell on 27 June to start trading in the options contracts on the sterling-dollar exchange rate and Eurodollar futures. Neither the bell nor his words could be heard, as trading went on regardless in other pits; reputedly he remarked about the din: 'This is worse than the House of Commons – which I suppose means that noise can conceal order as well as disorder.' At the press conference he praised LIFFE as 'a success story for Britain, with its remarkable continuing rate of growth', its monthly turnover by now running at £170 billion. By this time 175 'B' shares in the options market had been sold, including some to non-futures members. Who would win the City's options war? The general opinion was that, despite the Stock Exchange's emphasis on fungible contracts with the Philadelphia Stock Exchange (the leading currency option market), the superior fire-power lay in the Royal Exchange, not least because of the heavy investment made in LIFFE's success by the banks, the major players in the world options markets.

Over the next few weeks the Eurodollar option (which of course the Stock Exchange did not trade in) got off to a poor start, partly reflecting quietness in the Eurodollar futures contract, but the sterling option quickly built up liquidity, attracting quite a stable pit population. In the five weeks to the end of July, LIFFE's average daily volume was 1,502, compared with the Stock Exchange's 641 in its rival sterling option product – a particularly commanding lead granted that the LIFFE contract was worth £25,000, twice that of the Stock Exchange. 'We will be the major options exchange outside America,' Williamson predicted to the press. 'I think that Philadelphia now has a serious competitor on its hands.' Nor was the chairman content with getting optimistic forecasts inserted into the newspapers. 'It seems incomprehensible to me that whilst all editions of the *Wall Street Journal* publish LIFFE Option statistics, Britain's premier financial newspaper does not,' he admonished the *FT*'s chief executive, Frank Barlow, on 2 August, and corrective action was soon taken.

1985 also saw a new futures contract launched. It had long been intended that LIFFE should have a sterling-denominated interest rate contract in the medium maturity range of the yield curve, in order to fill the gap between the short sterling (three months) and long gilt (twenty years) contracts. In 1983 John Lewis chaired a working party, which developed a contract specification for a short gilt future but concluded in September that year that it should wait until the long gilt futures market had matured further. Soon afterwards members in the gilt market complained that not enough priority was being given to the development of the short gilt contract, but Jenkins insisted that it would be a mistake to introduce it before the building societies (the largest holders of gilts in the cash market) were able to use LIFFE contracts. In spring of 1985, even though futures still did not count as authorised investments for building societies, work began again under Wigglesworth's direction, with substantial input from James Capel and Greenwells on the research side. A survey of potential users indicated considerable enthusiasm:

Stockbrokers/Jobbers   *ASAP please. It would add net liquidity, should be £100,000 and 1/64. Must get it going in time to get option on it before 'Big Bang'. Would welcome it as a way of attracting Building Societies; sooner rather than later.*

Insurance Brokers   *Would be able to use a short future, cannot use present long.*

Clearing Banks   *Would use it extensively and not only for trading as is the case with the long. Customers want it quickly.*

Building Societies   *Hope to use it.*

Discount Houses   *All favour introduction in May.*

US Banks   *Will use it to hedge cash books.*

A May 1985 start was originally planned for the short gilt contract; but this was postponed to 10 September as a result of uncertainties about how it would be handled within the Bank of England's proposed market-maker risk measurement system. The size of the contract (based on a 10% British government bond with a maturity of 3 to 4½ years) was indeed set at £100,000, twice that of the long gilt contract, reflecting the less volatile underlying cash market in short-term gilts; but with the 'tick', or minimum price movement, being set at one sixty-fourth of a percentage point, compared with one thirty-second for the long gilt, this meant that the minimum price movement on both contracts would be £15.625.

On 10 September it was Sir Peter Middleton, permanent secretary to the Treasury, who did the honours. Initial signs were good, and Jenkins looked for a daily volume of 2,500 contracts, but during the first eight months of 1986 – just as the *long* gilt contract took off – total volume was a depressing 49,919. That autumn the deregulation of the cash market failed to make a significant difference; legal authorisation for the building societies continued to be delayed; and by summer 1987 trading in the short gilt effectively ceased. The contract had proved superfluous to requirements, attributable partly to the abundant liquidity in the cash market for short gilts, but perhaps also to an undue emphasis in the contract design to the hedging use of the contract.

Win some lose some, and when Middleton rang the bell in September 1985 it was the exchange's twelfth contract to be launched. Few believed at this point that the mix was quite right, and there began to be felt a serious worry that LIFFE was in danger of becoming a dollar-dominated exchange (Eurodollars and T-bonds) – a worry replaced about a year later by the equally strong anxiety over the undue concentration of business on long gilt futures. 'With the large growth in the volume of the long gilt contract we are in danger of becoming a single-product exchange,' Jenkins would warn the board in February 1987. By late 1985 at the latest, there was much talk of the need to diversify, and no one pressed the theme more strongly than Albright. Members were subjected that autumn to an exhaustive product and development survey, and a product plan was prepared. Some fundamental discussion ensued at the board meeting on 11 December:

The Chief Executive noted that the product plan had been developed after seeking the views of members. Members had supported the introduction of a range of new products but had also indicated their concern that certain existing products are obviously not successful at present and that to introduce new products which will require support may result in the exchange having a number of less than successful products. In regard to existing products, the firm intention is to strengthen the performance of weak products by increasing the available resources for marketing these products.

Ms Albright noted that the introduction of new products had been important to the exchange's development. To be successful in the future the exchange should have as an objective the provision of a full and comprehensive range of products to enable members to take advantage of the European Time Zone and to provide a 'one stop' full service exchange. New products should be regarded as the generator of future increases in volume and the costs incurred in developing and launching them as an essential part of widening the appeal of LIFFE to potential users.

Mr Edwards [John Edwards of Citifutures] noted that Ms Albright's paper did not propose an active review of existing products – whilst considering the introduction of new products. There is a danger that the exchange would suffer from a wide range of less than successful products unless it gave some consideration to delisting failures. 1986 is likely to be sufficiently demanding in time and resources as members develop their plans for 1986 and the 'Big Bang'. It may be wiser to allow members to develop these plans without requiring them to support and invest in new products which will require further investment and education.

Mr Wigglesworth noted that it would be expedient to have new contracts available prior to the 'Big Bang' in order that in the new competitive environment the exchange could offer from the start a comprehensive and full range of products and be in a position to benefit from the changes in the environment.

Whereupon Williamson in the chair proposed that the product plan, envisaging the fairly rapid development of a broad range of new contracts, should be adopted; and by eight votes to three it was.

No plan ever quite works as expected. One of its main elements was the Eurobond contract, plans for which had been abandoned in 1983. 'Contract design had developed substantially in the interim,' Albright assured the board, 'and design would therefore be easier than previously,' adding that 'a Eurobond contract would bring substantial volumes to LIFFE from the European market and would be an innovative contract for LIFFE'. By improvements in contract design she was almost certainly referring to the CBOT's recent successful introduction of a futures contract based on an index of municipal bonds, a plausible model for creating a Eurobond index. Soon afterwards LIFFE and the CBOT began to work together closely on the problem, aiming to launch a contract that would trade interchangeably on both exchanges; and in September 1986 the board received an optimistic report from Phil Bruce, who anticipated the introduction of a Eurobond index futures contract the following spring. But the appalling heterogeneity of the Eurobond market remained a Becher's Brook, and in early 1987 Bruce conceded to *Intermarket* that 'we are at a fairly early stage in trying to devise an index contract that will be commercially useful'. By July, however, the Association of

International Bond Dealers [AIBD] had agreed to co-operate with LIFFE and the CBOT, and this made it at least theoretically possible to establish the index upon a reliable price reporting system. On the fifth anniversary the confident expectation was that a Eurobond futures contract was – at last – just around the corner.

There were no such problems about introducing three new option contracts early in 1986, each as a direct result of the December 1985 decision to expand significantly the exchange's portfolio of products. The introduction on 30 January of a dollar-mark option contract (accompanied by a parallel dollar-mark futures contract) was followed on 13 March by the simultaneous launch of option contracts on US T-bond futures and long gilt futures. The latter options represented a fairly obvious development, given the current success of the T-bond and long gilt futures. 'We look for bond options to trade more at first,' anticipated Richard Morrish of Kleinwort Grieveson Futures, 'as UK institutions need to be educated in the use of options.'

However, it was not only the institutions that found puts and calls conceptually challenging, as a memo by Albright in April 1986 made clear:

It appears that we have 15–20 market makers [MMs] in options at present, including both corporate and personal locals. This is a reasonable start, but is not enough to support 5 contracts, especially since the more successful contracts tend to draw MMs away from the weaker products.

Further, professionalism and even attendance by our MMs varies greatly from day to day; certain option contracts sometimes do not have prices for up to 1½ hours after their official opening time; some MMs do their pricing matrices the night before and are unable to price any options the next morning because the underlying has moved significantly; bid/offer spreads can be very wide; hours can pass without an update of options screens. LIFFE's competitors' (i.e. Philadelphia, CME) prices update on an almost minute by minute basis.

It is widely recognised that there is a lack of practical options trading expertise among traders on the floor including among futures brokers and traders who are unfamiliar with options but often need or want to know more… Another constraint on potential users of options is the inability of some back office staff to cope with the LIFFE options and futures margining system.

It was a frustrating situation. Back in November 1984, outlining LIFFE's options strategy, Albright had argued that the exchange 'must look outside its present membership to augment the number of active options traders' and that 'new members should be actively recruited from existing options markets around the world'; but for a variety of reasons, this had not happened as much as might have been hoped. While in terms of actual market makers in options, LIFFE – still operating under significant financial constraints – had failed in these early stages

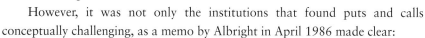

to provide sufficient incentives to encourage them, in effect suppressing its misgivings and hoping that it could get away with trading options in the same way as it traded futures, even though they were very different products.

Nevertheless, LIFFE launched a sixth option contract on 30 September 1986, namely on the FTSE 100 futures. Like most of its fellow-options, the new contract failed to achieve an early lift-off. 'With the exception of the Long Gilt,' Jenkins noted gloomily in October, 'LIFFE options are ailing through lack of liquidity. Not surprisingly, LIFFE's small full time band of market makers tend to concentrate on our one successful product.' They did indeed, and for 1986 as a whole the long gilt contract accounted for more than 57% of options volume – a volume that itself represented less than 7% of the exchange's total volume. 'We are having difficulty educating the basic floor population as to the intricacies and the attractions of options,' Phil Barnett conceded to *Futures* in January 1987. Soon afterwards scratch trading facilities were introduced on options, and gradually the picture did become less bleak. In July 1987, for example, total option trading was 95,404 lots (compared with 36,585 lots the previous July), but it was hardly healthy that 85,584 of those lots were in the long gilt option. Options, in short, remained *terra incognita* for many inside as well as outside the market.

Another part of LIFFE's diversification was Japan, supported rather than initiated by the November 1985 product plan. Japan in the mid-1980s was perceived as the world's slowly awakening financial giant, and Williamson in particular very much wanted LIFFE to be part of the action, which in turn would send a clear signal to the American financial futures industry that the London exchange was by now a major player on the international stage. In his early interviews on becoming chairman he pointed out that there were more Japanese banks in London than in New York and that LIFFE had 'a lot to gain through cooperation with the Japanese'. In September 1985 he hosted a delegation from the Tokyo Stock Exchange [TSE], looking for practical guidance shortly before the opening of its futures market in domestic government bonds; and the following month, in Tokyo for that opening, he announced that LIFFE and the CBOT had signed an agreement to develop a Japanese government bond contract that could be traded on both exchanges. To an extent the agreement was born out of mutual frustration, the two exchanges having found it hard to make headway with the Japanese financial authorities. But there was also, as Michael Prest noted in *The Times*, a straightforward economic motivation: 'The Japanese government is accumulating a vast pile of debt, growing at the staggering rate of $100 billion annually. It is attractive, therefore, that some way be found of helping holders or traders in that debt to lay off their risks.' An active and growing London cash market in Japanese government bonds, together with Japanese officials apparently becoming less outrightly hostile to an overseas yen bond contract – it all seemed very attractive, provided such a contract could come to fruition.

A session that Jenkins had in Tokyo in April 1986, at the Ministry of Finance [MOF], indicated some of the problems:

MNHJ commented that so far as the rationale for JGBs [Japanese Government Bonds] on LIFFE is concerned, the analogy is of the introduction of T Bond, growth of primary dealers in cash and futures markets in Europe. Informatory meetings with Fed and U.S. Treasury were held prior to introduction.

Mr Nishikata understands but JGB primary market is Tokyo, and MOF have to carefully consider implications and impact of LIFFE/CBOT action to introduce JGB futures...

MNHJ commented that it is the market participants who want the contract. We certainly intend to continue technical research, and have no firm timetable for introduction yet.

Mr Nishikata acknowledged all.

MNHJ then asked when there may be relaxation of rules prohibiting Japanese access to overseas futures markets. Any chance of changes in rules in the near future. Mr Nishikata says trend is favourable. International Securities Bureau looking at it on behalf of the hedging opportunities, but not speculation! The review proceeds.

MNHJ understood but commented on the difficulty of defining 'hedging'!

Mr Nishikata said that with only 6 months JGB futures, experience is low in Japan. He appreciates the help LIFFE has given to the learning process of Jap. Sec. Houses. Must support a healthy development of the market.

Later that month LIFFE gave a dinner at The Savoy to its Japanese members, memorable for a celebrated exchange as Wigglesworth swapped cards with one of the guests, Hiroshi Nakajima of the Bank of Japan. 'What does "Wiggle" stand for, Mr Wigglesworth?' he was asked. 'I'll tell you if you tell me what "Naka" stands for in Nakajima,' came the reply. The dinner also enabled Williamson to outline the exchange's plan to introduce a yen bond contract, and he received assurances of support. Such an attitude on the part of the Japanese securities houses in London was very welcome, but as Jenkins pointed out a few weeks later to the board, 'the Tokyo Stock Exchange is likely to look upon the contract, and the likely competition it represented, with less favour'.

Meanwhile, serious work began on the extremely taxing contract design, more of it done in London than in Chicago, with the CBOT indicating that it would be happy to see the JGB contract 'bed in' on LIFFE before trading the contract itself. The target launch date was November 1986, and Williamson

The London International Financial Futures Exchange
Table Plan for Dinner in the Beaufort Room, The Savoy Hotel, London, WC2
Monday 21st April 1986

| Kim Albright
Development
Director
LIFFE | Mr N Fukuda
General Manager
Sumitomo Trust
& Banking | Mr M Ishikawa
Financial Minister
Embassy of Japan | Brian Williamson
Chairman
LIFFE | Mr H Nakajima
Deputy Chief
Representative
Bank of Japan | Mr F Ishii
Associate
Managing Director
Nomura International | Nick Carew Hunt
Contracts
Development
Manager
LIFFE |

Mr S Hotta Associate Director Yamaichi International (Europe) Ltd	Mr H Kase Deputy General Manager The Mitsubishi Bank	Mr K Masuda Assistant General Manager The Mitsui Bank	Mr F Fujimoto Senior Dealer Mitsubishi Trust & Banking Corporation
Mr T Tsuchiya Assistant General Manager The Sanwa Bank	Mr T Mitsuhashi European Editor Nihon Keizai Shimbun (Japan Economic Journal)	Mr Y Rai Executive Director Daiwa Europe Ltd	Mr T Matsutani Joint General Manager The Fuji Bank
Ron Porter Director LIFFE	Mary Lou Carrington Marketing Director LIFFE	Mr S Shinjo Assistant General Manager The Bank of Yokohama	Charles McVeigh III Director LIFFE
Mr Y Nishikawa Deputy General Manager Daiwa Bank	Mr K Seiki General Manager The Industrial Bank of Japan	Patricia Duncan Executive Assistant LIFFE	Mr H Moriyama General Manager & Director The Long Term Credit Bank of Japan Ltd
Mr S Matsumoto Chief Dealer The Taiyo Kobe Bank	Mr Y Yoshida Manager Nippon Credit Bank	Mr T Asai Deputy Managing Director New Japan Securities Europe Ltd	Mr T Komizo Assistant General Manager The Toyo Trust & Banking
Mr K Oyama Managing Director New Japan Securities Europe Ltd	Mr K Yoshida Executive Director Nikko Securities Company (Europe) Ltd	Mr Y Tsutsumi General Manager The Mitsui Trust & Banking Company	Mr Y Yamagata Manager Treasury Department The Tokai Bank Ltd
John Edwards Director LIFFE		Mr I Arihara Senior Manager & Chief Dealer The Dai-Ichi Kangyo Bank	Jack Wigglesworth Director LIFFE
Mr H Kitagawa General Manager The Saitama Bank			Mr K Okawa Senior Deputy General Manager The Kyowa Bank Ltd
Mr Y Edahiro Manager of Money Markets The Bank of Tokyo			Mr R Nakatani Joint General Manager The Sumitomo Bank Ltd

| Michael Jenkins
Chief Executive
LIFFE | David Burton
Deputy Chairman
LIFFE |

The seating plan of the Savoy Hotel dinner for Japanese members.

telexed in July to the British Embassy in Tokyo that 'so far no objection has been placed in our way by the Ministry of Finance, and whilst we are very nervous we have no reason to believe that they will prevent us from going ahead at the last moment'. He added that, with a rumour in the air that Japanese residents were soon to be allowed to trade on foreign exchanges, 'I would be very grateful to know if you get any gossip on whether MOF is likely to make such an announcement'. By September the launch date had been put back to 1987: not only, Carew Hunt reported to the board, had certain technical problems emerged relating to the procedures for delivery, but a host of other complications had arisen, reflecting the fact that 'the interactions necessary to develop a suitable and potentially successful product involve LIFFE, CBOT, ICCH, The Board of Trade Clearing Corporation [BOTCC], Japanese entities (Bank of Japan, TSE and *indirectly* the Ministry of Finance), esoteric Japanese cash market practices, Japanese securities houses etc, LIFFE and CBOT members etc'.

Gradually the pieces fell into place. In December 1986 the MOF gave its permission (important, even if not strictly needed) to the trading on LIFFE of Japanese government bond futures; from May 1987 it allowed domestic financial institutions to deal in foreign financial futures and options markets; and that same month Jenkins told the board that 'there has been a clear change of attitude in Tokyo' and that 'both the TSE and MOF are now keen to see LIFFE introduce the contract and this appears to be a consequence of pressure from within the Japanese financial community rather than external pressure'. Moreover, some significant technical wrinkles had been ironed out: Japan's anachronistic retention of withholding tax meant that the contract had to be designed for cash settlement, despite some misgivings in the market, while the TSE's reluctance to supply LIFFE with closing futures prices on the last trading day for an expiring maturity changed following some MOF pressure. In late May the launch date of the JGB futures contract was publicly set for 13 July 1987. 'We've got to be more than just an east end of the American markets,' an excited Williamson told Fildes. 'It puts us at the crossroads.' And: 'We'll be the first futures market in the world with contracts on three major bond markets. We already have systems to settle in many currencies so another one is easy. The three most liquid bond markets in the world, all being traded in one place... I think it will change people's perceptions of London. There's now a decisive reason for using London.'

Japanese ladies, who by mistake had been asked to dress in what were pyjamas rather than kimonos, handed out badges to passers-by; Shiro Uramatsu (executive vice-president of the Tokyo Stock Exchange) did not take offence at this embarrassing error of etiquette and rang the bell; and during the first half hour the Japanese institutions, especially Nomura, piled in. A remarkable 36,065 JGB contracts – many of them 'congratulatory' – were traded during the first day, easily a record for a new contract. Quickly, however, trading volume fell back to around

4,000 contracts a day, and it was widely felt that London's Japanese houses – for so long dormant members of the exchange – did not yet have the staff and systems in place for large-scale futures dealing in London. Moreover, as *FOW* noted in August, locals were conspicuous by their absence from the JGB pit: 'Only two to date are thought to have braved the £41 tick size to trade the contract for their

own account. Compared with tick sizes of £15 for long gilts and £19 in bonds, £41 for every price movement is a large trading risk to take especially in a contract which has shown some erratic price movement and is backed by a cash market not yet fully understood outside Japan.'

By early September barely 500 contracts were changing hands each day, and the *Economist* ran a negative piece with the dramatically gloomy headline 'Death at LIFFE'. Recalling the same magazine's notorious 'LIFFE has been a flop' article of

The launch of the Japanese Government Bond futures contract, 13 July 1987.

four and a half years earlier, Williamson wrote to the editor that 'contracts do sometimes take time to catch on, but not so slowly as your correspondents'. Nevertheless, the exchange was palpably disappointed, and soon afterwards *IFR* put forward the explanation that the big Japanese houses had been 'more active within the Tokyo time-frame' and were 'disinclined to deprive the Tokyo Stock Exchange of business although dealing costs on LIFFE are considerably lower'. Back in July, on the eve of launch, the *FT* had reckoned that if any new futures contract had 'the ingredients of a sure-fire success' it was the JGB contract, but so far it had generated prestige rather than business.

One financial system was arguably an even more somnolent giant than Japan's. In the mid-1980s the common perception in London – and a view shared by Barkshire and Williamson – was that the German financial system was fundamentally arthritic. Even such unexceptionable financial instruments as zero-coupon bonds and floating-rate notes in deutschmarks were, in 1985, still forbidden. There was no financial futures market, nor a realistic prospect of one in the near future. When Sara Scott of Bank of America Futures toured Luxembourg in autumn 1984 to develop business from German banks, based there because of its looser regulatory and tax regime, she found (as Albright noted in December) that though there was 'quite a lot of interest' in the idea of LIFFE developing a DM deposit futures contract, these bankers felt the German authorities might well oppose such a contract's development: 'The Bundesbank does not welcome futures, and the Bundesaufsichtsamt [für das Kreditwesen] (which regulates banks directly) is even more negative, referring to "those nasty speculative instruments – futures, options and FRAs"'. As for the possibility of a futures contract on German government bonds – attractive, because 'as a long term instrument they should be more volatile than deposits' – the hard fact was that 'the long end is even more closely controlled by the German authorities'. Albright, who since the summer had been getting interested in the idea of a German initiative, then added her own thoughts: 'Despite the lack of official enthusiasm, I think we ought to pursue the possibility of DM contracts seriously but quietly. They could expand our range beyond domestic products and products which compete head-on with Chicago.' The date was 13 December 1984, an epochal moment – though no one knew it – in LIFFE's history.

'Quietly' was the word, however, and the historical trail then runs dry until 21 August 1985, when a delegation of German bankers visited the exchange. Two months later, on 28 October, fortified by some informal encouragement (including from Richard Bown, treasury manager of Schroders) over the notion of futures products in London, Albright and Carew Hunt paid an exploratory visit to the Bundesbank in Frankfurt:

We talked [Albright reported] about possible new products which LIFFE might introduce. In summary, a deutschmark deposit contract at the moment would not be looked on very favourably by the German authorities. The confusion over how to regulate financial futures trading at present does not make them favourably disposed towards any additional instruments which the German banks might want to try. Mr Kurt Seifarth said that the German authorities would very much like LIFFE to ask themselves and the Ministry of Finance first before considering the launch of deutschmark futures... He further added that if there were to be such contracts in deutschmark instruments, he felt that the Germans might prefer to start such a market of their own. However it's hard to see this occurring under the present regulatory regime.

We will have to proceed very carefully with the German authorities. Logically, it is difficult to see how the Bundesbank or the Bundesaufsichtsamt could ultimately oppose a LIFFE Euro deutschmark contract... However, the easiest route to get German bank participation on LIFFE under the present regulatory structure would be to offer a $/DM option for which there are no present restrictions for German banks.

By the time she wrote this the membership survey had indicated substantial support for a dollar/mark option contract, and the ensuing product plan pushed it hard, arguing that it should be quoted in European terms – i.e. deutschmarks to the dollar – in order to attract continental users. The board agreed with all this at its pivotal meeting in December (though Barnett thought that European-style quotation 'represented an additional unnecessary complication for traders'), and the launch of the dollar/mark option, along with a parallel futures contract, was fixed for 30 January 1986. The contracts were very much tailored to the needs of German banks, and such was the abiding financial conservatism there that neither really took off in the course of 1986.

'In the things we're good at,' Williamson remarked to Fildes that July about the fact that less than half of LIFFE's European business came from the European Community, 'travel, insurance, financial services, we don't get any reciprocity. It's a fact of life.' The conventional wisdom in the exchange remained, in other words, that it was necessary to look further afield. It was a conventional wisdom – an instinctive assumption – born largely out of history: Britain's in general and the City's in particular. Albright, as an American, did not share it, especially in the light of her recent involvement in the major fact-finding and marketing effort on the Continent that had preceded and accompanied the launch of the dollar/mark option. She had been struck by the fact that although there was no shortage there of dealing rooms full of traders, LIFFE had practically no products to offer them. Most of the dollar trading in the European time zone was done from London, and virtually no one on the Continent traded sterling instruments. However, the northern countries all had deutschmark books, usually at the short end, but often also at the long end – in other words, in German government bonds (Bunds) and their relations; while in the southern countries, the ECU was becoming a sort of shadow second currency. The other obvious fact was that Germany was the largest economy in western Europe, and yet there were no deutschmark derivative products. Soon afterwards, in April 1986, she produced a matrix showing the continuing enormous gaps in the exchange's existing international product range; and the following month she read an article in the *Sunday Times* by Robert Heller. Called 'Why Can't We Think Big?', and castigating British management for its lack of ambition, it made a huge impression on Albright, seemingly crystallising her frustrations at LIFFE's apparent reluctance to grasp the Continental nettle. From about this time, 'Europe' became a very personal mission on her part.

Again, however, there was a pause in the story, broken by Dresdner Bank announcing early in 1987 that it was buying a seat on LIFFE, only the third German bank to do so and the first to establish a floor operation. Indeed, Dresdner's Rolf Willi had already given the exchange much help and encouragement, even opening the dollar/mark option the previous year. One of the other two German banks that were members was Deutsche Bank. Its managing director, Barthold von Ribbentrop, told *Euromoney* in July 1987 that if the German financial authorities did not move quicker to establish a futures contract in German government bonds, then the government would find it increasingly difficult to obtain attractive rates in the cash market for their bonds. He spoke

Kim Albright.

against a background of two recent issues having flopped, and the same article quoted Miles Slater, president of Salomons in London: 'For all the world benchmark government markets, you need to have liquid futures and options. You can't do without them. This becomes particularly apparent when things get difficult.' Significantly, von Ribbentrop added that a futures contract in German government bonds 'would be helpful wherever it is traded' – seven words that Albright underlined in her copy, as she did his thoughts about the cash market: 'As an internationally operating bank, we can't concern ourselves only with the problems of Frankfurt. We will trade wherever it is most efficient. If the threat is really there, you will see us trading government bonds in London.'

Deutsche Bank itself now played a key role. Very soon afterwards, on 21 July 1987, Jenkins, Albright and Carew Hunt were visited by a Deutsche trio (Hung Tran, based in New York and head of Deutsche's bond research department, Jurgen Dietze and Nigel Pearson). They had somehow heard of a report on deutschmark derivative possibilities that Albright had commissioned the previous summer from a German student, Andreas Moellendorf; and they made it clear that if LIFFE was going to develop a new German product it had to be a government bond contract.

On 9 September a LIFFE trio (Albright, Carew Hunt and Sandra Steele) went to 150 Leadenhall Street to pick the brains of Larry Anderson, economist of Deutsche Bank Capital Markets. They learned much, Albright memoed, about the cash market in German government bonds and the possibilities for a futures contract:

> *German traders are unable to go short, except by trading* outside *Germany through Euroclear. For this and other reasons, there is a better market in London than in Germany, and about 70% of German Government Bonds are traded in London. While changes are expected in Germany within the next two years, there is no certainty of this.*
>
> *Dr Breuer [of Deutsche] has contacted the Bundesbank. He has told them that he sees no disadvantage to having a contract traded in London, as this would not preclude trading in Frankfurt when the law is changed. At the Bundesbank Herr Köhler, who is responsible for overseeing capital markets, is favourable. However, he needs to persuade his colleague, the Chief Economist, Herr Schlesinger. The chances of a positive reaction are judged to be better than 50/50. A decision is expected within the next few months, and certainly before the end of this year.*
>
> *The attitude of the other German banks is positive. They would ideally like the contract traded in Frankfurt, but recognise that this might not be until the 1990s. They would therefore like to see the contract traded as soon as possible on LIFFE, as this is within the European time zone.*

Put another way, a major battle was taking place within the German financial system, and LIFFE was the potential beneficiary.

Gradually in the course of the 1980s most of the various taxation and legal problems attached to the use of financial futures and options were resolved, but it was a fairly slow and tedious process. From 1984 pension funds were given exemption from income tax on financial futures, but the *FT*'s Clive Wolman was fiercely critical in May of the Inland Revenue's failure to clarify the tax treatment of the newly launched FTSE 100 contract. His piece was called 'More speculators needed', and he argued that this negative approach (in marked contrast to the tax privileges for Lloyd's underwriters) reinforced 'the conservatism of UK financial institutions and their unwillingness to understand the operation of futures markets'; and that consequently there was not enough hedging capacity (i.e. through the offloading of risks on to speculators) in the financial system to allow institutions like building societies and pension fund managers to pass on the risks they invariably faced. By 1986, however, this and various other taxation obstacles had been removed, and the focus turned to internal restrictions hampering certain organisations.

In particular there was the vexing matter of the building societies, still precluded by the Registrar of Friendly Societies from using the LIFFE market. 'We have exhausted our reserves of tact and expertise (such as they are) in trying to persuade the Registry to give us a fair hearing on the subject,' Williamson wrote to Middleton at the Treasury in September 1986, five years after the first meeting between LIFFE and the Building Societies Association. Several of the societies themselves were becoming, by this time, almost as exasperated – 'We share your annoyance and dismay,' Michael Tuke of the Woolwich wrote to Williamson – and it was another two years before building societies were allowed (though still on a restricted basis) to use LIFFE in order to hedge risk and thus be on anything like an equal footing with other financial institutions.

Education and marketing remained a vital area – the impact not always easy to gauge, the effort sometimes undervalued. There was a ceaseless programme of self-financing seminars, conferences and courses; LIFFE executives had a full diary of speaking engagements as well as contributing frequently to the specialist press; and the gallery overlooking the trading floor served a useful function, with visitors in spring 1985 for example including Prince Hiro of Japan as well as a 25-strong party from Pinner Townswomen's Guild. The institutional rather than individual user was kept firmly in view, and guidance was made as practical as possible. Often it was a case of building bridges, perhaps especially in relation to the FTSE 100 contract, with the exchange working on performance measurement and portfolio valuation on behalf of the institutions. In other words, it was a case less of LIFFE directly selling its product, rather of offering a problem-solving partnership in order to overcome obstacles to the institutional use of a product.

Was enough being done? In the course of 1985 there took place what Williamson that autumn called 'a switch from education to marketing', there being 'enough educated people now who need to be persuaded'. The marketing budget was significantly upgraded, and Carrington was appointed as marketing director in November. She saw her task, she told *FOW* in March 1986, as twofold: on the one hand 'to familiarise the targeted audience with the services and products we have to offer', on the other 'to differentiate our exchange from others'. The early weeks of the year had already seen an ambitious European road show to publicise the dollar/mark contracts; and undoubtedly the marketing tempo now increased, with financial institutions still firmly the target, not the retail market, in continuing deliberate contrast to the Chicago model.

LIFFE in its early years was often criticised as being little more than a glorified system of members taking in each other's washing, so wherever possible publicity was given to the growth in open positions held by non-members of the exchange.

At the start of 1984 these comprised some 27% of all open positions, but by the end of the year were up to some 40%; and at the close of business on 28 April 1986 open interest was 100,102 contracts, the first time the number of unliquidated contracts had broken the six-figure barrier and prompting Williamson to claim that 'over £20 billion's worth of business is being hedged by commercial and financial institutions through LIFFE's contracts'.

Arguably two outside figures were particularly influential in the gradually increasing institutional use of the market. One was George Dennis, who ran the Post Office's gigantic pension fund and also helped to lead the campaign for tax exemption. 'Our argument to Revenue focused on two main points,' he told *Pensions* in April 1984. 'If London is to remain a financial centre, it must develop sophisticated markets, so the first argument is a macro-economic one. The other is we feel the financial futures market is a market which pension funds could enter for legitimate investment reasons.' The second helpful person was Colin Stiasny of the Prudential, which by autumn 1985 had committed itself publicly to an increasing use of stock-index futures, particularly on LIFFE. It was a significant commitment on the Pru's part, for at about the same time one London broker told the *Investors Chronicle* that the reception so far for stock indices in Britain had been 'absolutely amazing in terms of apathy' and that 'fund managers' attitudes are prehistoric'. LIFFE was doing its best to penetrate the consciousness of the UK fund management community. A cocktail party it gave a year or two later at the NAPF [National Association of Pension Funds] Investment Conference in Eastbourne was notable for the presence of a six-foot inflatable LIFFE trader. The following morning it had gone, last seen deflating and making rapid progress across the Channel.

Financial conservatism, unlike inflatable traders, did not dissolve overnight. 'Some fund managers,' Jenkins tactfully put it to *Pensions* in March 1987, 'just don't want to hedge. They are using their judgement on stock selection and don't want to lose out on any potential profit.' As for corporate treasurers and finance directors, on the whole instinctively more open-minded about financial futures, John Parry argued in *Corporate Money*, on the occasion of LIFFE's fifth anniversary, that 'despite serious efforts by LIFFE staff and exchange brokers to encourage corporate treasurers to use futures for hedging, they have not generally picked up the offers'. Instead, faced by exposure dates requiring precise hedging, they had tended to use the rapidly growing Over-the-Counter [OTC] market in risk management, with its tailor-made hedges (often created by non-clearing banks like Hambros) that did not expose clients to daily variation margin payments nor require expensive staff and systems. Parry failed to point out that many of the banks offering these tailor-made hedges were managing the risks thus created for themselves by carrying out their own direct hedging on LIFFE. He did not deny LIFFE's overall importance in the business of managing corporate treasury risk –

above all 'its role as a safety valve to relieve pressure build-ups in the cash market' – but it was clear that here, as in other institutional areas, the landscape was permanently shifting and LIFFE needed to be on the *qui vive*.

It was an undeniable plus for professional end-users that LIFFE, for all its speculative image in the eyes of the wider public, managed to stay remarkably scandal-free. The major exception was a tax scam that resulted in August 1987, following an eight-month investigation, in five member firms being fined and nine traders suspended. The scam involved a number of different schemes designed to move trading profits offshore through pre-arranged trades executed outside the pits, and the heaviest penalty (a one-year suspension) was imposed on Keith Catchpole, former LIFFE floor manager of Cargill Investor Services, the British broking subsidiary of the American giant Cargill. There was criticism in the market that the disciplinary action had been inadequate, but Jenkins contended that 'it must be considered on the scale of things the traders could have done' and that 'in this case the pre-arranged trades did not deny any business to the pit or affect any customers'.

Certainly it was small beer compared with some of the more notorious City scandals of the mid-1980s, their frequency hastening the evolution of a new regulatory environment. In January 1984 the Gower Report put flesh on his earlier discussion document, with its suggested establishment of a series of 'self-regulatory associations'. That October the Association of Futures Brokers and Dealers [AFBD] was incorporated, as one of the handful of recognised self-regulatory organisations [SROs], while it was announced that the Securities and Investments Board [SIB] would be established in advance of legislation in order to oversee the SROs. In January 1985 the government published a White Paper on investor protection, and in December 1985 the Financial Services Bill started out on its long passage to becoming law as the Financial Services Act. LIFFE, as both a new institution and a hybrid, tended to play a cautious hand through all this, simultaneously seeking to reconcile conflicting interests within the futures industry; to maintain its traditionally good relationships with the Bank of England and the DTI (the latter ensuring that the Act resolved any remaining legal worries about the impact of the Gaming Act on the validity of LIFFE contracts); and to minimise any possible interference with its own control over its own market.

In November 1983 LIFFE agreed, unlike the London Metal Exchange [LME], to participate in the formation of the AFBD (that body succeeding the putative Futures Brokers Association), even though Barkshire told Dawkins that, as he informed the board, 'it had been LIFFE's original preference to devise its own scheme for segregation and compensation and that this approach might produce a better scheme for LIFFE, more quickly and at lower cost, than the joint approach'. The three other founder members of the AFBD were the London Commodity Exchange, the London Gold Futures Market and the Grain and Feed

Trade Association, with Alistair Annand, former managing director of the Manbré and Garton sugar company, becoming chief executive. 'Now we are persuaded by the Bank of England and Professor Gower that we should have more regulations on the private client side,' commented David Harcourt, chairman of the LCE. '"Caveat emptor" is not considered to be adequate these days.' Soon afterwards the actual Gower Report noted that some 50 commodity firms were currently under official investigations of one kind or another, and he quoted the Old Bailey judge who had recently described the world of commodity dealing as 'a jungle suitable for hunting for large and experienced animals but one in which the small animal is at very serious risk', so it was a timely conversion. In the course of 1984 the LME came on board, and in November *The Times* praised the AFBD's formal incorporation as marking the first time that 'all of London's main commodity exchanges will treat their private clients in the same way'. Annand himself stated that 'our policies will be geared to the greatest possible flexibility in adapting to changing market conditions and situations, whilst encouraging members' responsibility for their own behaviour and integrity' – a clear nod to his main constituency's strong, abiding attachment to the most local form of self-regulation.

The Joint Exchanges Committee remained in being, with Foyle as its secretary, and Williamson and Jenkins were LIFFE's representatives in April 1985 when it met Sir Kenneth Berrill, chairman-designate of SIB. Peering into the new, post-Gower world, he reassured the JEC that 'the government wishes the system to be based on practitioner involvement and not a civil-servant based system such as that in the USA and in Japan'; while Jenkins 'commented that the AFBD's primary role was that of investor protection' and that 'for it to be responsible for the running of the Exchanges would be a major distraction from this task'. Inevitably the question of which LIFFE members qualified for membership of the AFBD, as opposed to an alternative SRO, proved both difficult and contentious; but a compromise was adopted, by which membership of the AFBD on a provisional basis would be provided to all existing members until legislation was passed some time in 1986/7, though the exchange itself had not yet aired the question of AFBD membership generally with its bank members.

A board meeting in September discussed the continuing state of play:

The Chief Executive pointed out that there remained a considerable absence of information regarding the contents of the Act. However until details became clear LIFFE should support the AFBD in the knowledge that LIFFE may in the future decide to follow a different course in the interests of its members.

The Chairman noted that after its efforts to contribute to the formation of the AFBD LIFFE could be seen to be far ahead of the other London exchanges. The SIB in its assessment of the impact of the regulatory system had not discounted totally the possibility that LIFFE would apply for authorization as an SRO. LIFFE would have the opportunity to contribute to the shape that the AFBD will take and to enjoy political credibility from participation in the enhancement of the regulatory environment.

Accordingly, though against some opposition from bank members (reluctant to participate in compensation arrangements potentially involving commodity brokers), the exchange insisted that all those eligible had to apply to join the AFBD, albeit on a temporary basis.

There was a fundamental problem involved, however, and in December 1986 LIFFE reacted angrily on being informed by SIB that its members could *not* choose between the AFBD and The Securities Association [TSA], the latter being the SRO born out of the recent merger between the Stock Exchange and the London-based international stock and bond dealers. The exchange's view was that at the very least a choice should be given, granted the intimate connection between financial futures and the underlying cash market; but Berrill defended his AFBD-compulsory policy by claiming that 'a future is a future is a future'. LIFFE won the day, with Williamson informing the board in January 1987 that SIB 'had agreed that The Securities Association should have their scope extended to regulate financial futures and options', and that accordingly members could choose which SRO they wished to join. 'What is likely to happen,' Jenkins explained to the press soon afterwards, 'is that some of our members will have to be authorised by The Securities Association and some by the Association of Futures Brokers and Dealers... The logical thing is that whoever regulates the cash market ought to also regulate the associated futures.' While as for those involved in *both* commodities and securities, he simply said that 'nothing goes into neat little boxes' and they would have to make a choice. There, for the moment, the matter rested, pending parliamentary endorsement of the SROs as a whole.

One revealing as well as important episode showed the extent to which LIFFE's spiritual centre of gravity by now resided almost as much to the west of Leadenhall Street as its physical home indubitably did. LHW Futures Ltd, incorporated in 1981, was the creation of Colonel John Lockwood, John Hughes and Jeremy Walsh (Lockwood's stepson). The Oxford-educated Hughes, who had learned about futures broking while working for S & W Berisford as a coffee trader, was managing director and probably the driving force. LHW quickly established itself as the first City firm to make a systematic attempt to market commodity futures to private investors, and in 1982–3 it achieved pre-tax profits of £1.2 million. Already a member of several London commodity markets, LHW sought in 1983 to acquire a seat on LIFFE. The exchange conducted a detailed investigation, and in October the board granted admission to membership, conditional on LHW agreeing 'to cease its current practice of making unsolicited telephone calls to potential non-professional clients ("cold calling")' and to supervise its junior account executives more closely. LHW objected to both conditions, and the application was refused.

The business itself continued to prosper, notwithstanding unfavourable talk of LHW's high-pressure selling techniques and exceptionally high commissions, and in June 1985 it was a mark of incipient respectability when Hughes was recruited to one of the LCE's committees. 'The reason is that this company has done more than any other to bring more private investor business to the markets,' an LCE source told *FOW*. A new application to join LIFFE was already on the table, and the board discussed it on 15 July:

Mr Porter [Ron Porter of the National Westminster] pointed out that he had been informed that frequent queries regarding this company from National Westminster Bank customers had been received and that many of these gave cause for concern about the applicant's style of operation...

The Chairman [Williamson] stated that the acceptability of private client business should not be considered to be in question. Such business should be accepted and encouraged, although the function of the market primarily benefited professional users.

Mr Wigglesworth pointed out that traditionally the Stock Exchange members viewed institutional investors and private clients as totally different types of client. Accepting a private client's account laid obligations upon the Broker to be aware of the total circumstances surrounding the client and to offer advice based on a prudent and responsible assessment of the client's exposure to risk...

Mr Eynon pointed out that the Membership and Rules Committee had found no evidence that the applicant failed to comply with the criteria for membership stated in the Rules.

Mr Whiting recorded his support for the application as a referee for the company and suggested that admission of the applicant would bring significant benefits to the exchange...

Mr Barkshire stated that he opposed the election to membership of the applicant. All business on the exchange should be encouraged, whether institutional or private. However, to admit the applicant would be likely to result in damage to the reputation of the exchange. The style and conduct of its business and the manner in which clients were induced to invest in high risk contracts by newspaper advertisements should not be considered good practice. The reputation of the company itself was, in his view, unsatisfactory for a member of the Exchange.

The discussion concluded with Williamson stating that LHW should be told that 'it was likely in the future that the board would consider with favour any further application from LHW when the reputation of the company was more acceptable'.

LHW was not prepared to wait and formally appealed against the decision, thereby invoking the procedure in LIFFE's rules by which the governor of the Bank of England appointed a commissioner to adjudicate on the case. This was Sir Anthony Rawlinson, a former permanent secretary at the DTI, and LIFFE made its formal submission to him on 18 December, laying heavy emphasis on the frequency and seriousness of the complaints made by LHW's clients, several of those complaints recently aired on the BBC Radio 'Checkpoint' programme. A ferocious article by Andrew Alexander in the *Daily Mail* on 7 January strengthened the exchange's case. 'The time has come to put a clothes peg over my nose,' he began his piece, 'get out a barge pole and spray the surrounding columns with disinfectant. For I am going to write about LHW.' He then described the company's methods and cited some real-life stories, which were given chapter and verse the following day in a selection of readers' letters ('LHW: What the victims tell us'). The picture that emerged was one of skilful and very persistent telephone selling and of unusually high commissions whose only justification was a guaranteed 'stop-loss' system, whereby the client's position was closed without further loss if prices moved rapidly against him – a system that, according to the letters, seemed to work in theory rather than practice.

LHW made its own submission to Rawlinson soon afterwards. This defended in some detail the company's procedures for client protection, countered the

Daily Mail, 7 January 1986.

Daily Mail, Tuesday, January 7, 1986

Beware the LHW smooth approach

By ANDREW ALEXANDER

THE TIME has come to put a clothes peg over my nose, get out a barge pole and spray the surrounding columns with disinfectant. For I am going to write about LHW.

In case you have not heard of LHW or have had no dealings with them — and count yourself lucky in the latter case — I should explain that the firm carries out commodity trading, concentrating particularly on private clients. And while the firm's methods are wholly legal, they are in other senses a disgrace to the City.

LHW has an ingenious way of parting investors from their money. Picture the scene :

You receive a leaflet, perhaps through the post, about LHW or read about them in an advertisement (not in the Daily Mail since we, unlike most of the Press, will not carry their advertising).

You read what sounds like sage advice, fatherly

losing more than your initial stake and that the investment can be exciting and profitable.

Impressed by the cautious preamble, you perhaps contact LHW. Then the telephone salesmen really go to work and, frankly, you should run for your life.

The voluminous lists of complaints from our readers should warn you. First, the salesmen are suave and polished — 'upper crust' as one reader put it—skilful and extraordinarily persistent.

They are not so strong on expertise. Reader after reader reports being put into losses.

Nor does the responsible approach implied by the initial LHW literature last for long. One reader proposed to invest £5,000 (having been urged in by an acquaintance who later lost £30,000).

But a 'senior account executive' quickly urged him to . . . put all his

figure in many cases) that it can operate the guaranteed 'stop-loss' system, whereby the clients' position is closed without further loss if prices move rapidly against him.

True. But the crucial converse is that when so much goes in commission, it only needs a more modest loss before the clients' position has to be closed out and his money is gone. LHW's commission was described by one commodity dealer yesterday as outrageous.

Tactics like these employed against the financially sophisticated amount to a joke in bad taste. But deployed against some of the readers who write to us—simple folk disposing of modest savings—they are utterly contemptible.

I know that City Editors are supposed to be a hard-bitten lot, but I must honestly tell you that some readers relate experiences which would move you to tears. There was the cripple who invested some of his compensation with LHW, the salesmen who lost all his savings and finally his job and his wife, the bus driver who lost all his money put aside for his daughter's wedding—and so on.

But, oh, it's all so profitable. It is not just the smart young salesmen of LHW (one of whom admitted to us he knew little about commodities) with various media criticisms, and observed that 'LIFFE is not a club where applications for membership may be rejected out of hand and for no good reason'. Rawlinson also received a letter from the LCE's chairman, Saxon Tate, who pointed out that LHW had been 'outstandingly successful in introducing retail customers to London's Futures Exchanges', and he argued that though the company had made mistakes it was now 'making a very determined effort to run its business ethically and properly in a sector which, by its very nature, generates complaints'. Indeed, 'I believe that the company will be able to satisfy you that the level of complaints justified and unjustified is lower than that which would be expected by similar firms operating in the United States.'

Rawlinson issued his judgement on 4 February 1986. He rejected LHW's appeal, essentially on the grounds that, fairly or unfairly, its reputation was such that LIFFE was justified in denying it membership. 'Some of the comment may be tendentious or unfair or inadequately based in fact; but it is in itself a fact that LHW have attracted significant adverse public comment. Reputations often outlast, at least for a while, the factors which generate them.' LIFFE emerged from the episode without an unwanted member, but not unscathed. Michael Prest argued in *The Times* that it had perpetrated 'a good, old-fashioned blackball' – reflecting the fact that 'despite its newness, LIFFE was founded by the elements of the City Establishment' – and that LHW's thriving business, with a gross commission income in 1985 of over £30 million from some 6,500 clients, 'cannot withstand adverse publicity and rejection by the City for ever'; while according to *FOW*, LIFFE was being foolish in continuing to turn its back on private clients, as well as now needing to take note of Rawlinson's criticism that it should have framed a code of conduct against which LHW or any other applicant for membership could have been measured, instead of waiting for the AFBD to devise such a code. Over the next three years, amidst continuing unfavourable publicity, LHW (renamed Burgon Hall in 1988) tried and failed to acquire AFBD membership. And though Hughes had remarked defiantly after Rawlinson's judgement that 'the LIFFE rejection does not stop us making money', in the end it proved the turning-point in this flawed enterprise's history.

LIFFE's relations with other parts of the City also came under scrutiny because of the mildly absurd options situation. 'The exchanges are making it not just harder for each other, but also for themselves,' observed 'Lex' in April 1985 about the preparations of LIFFE and the Stock Exchange for rival options products. There was an obvious case for some rationalisation, but over the next fifteen months little if any progress was made. 'There is no indication as yet that The Stock Exchange Council has any serious interest in reaching an agreement with LIFFE on a division of the options playing field,' concluded Jenkins in July 1986 in the context of formally proposing the introduction of the FTSE option contract. 'LIFFE has always been the one to take the initiative and whilst we have received acquiescent noises, no action has resulted.' And he added that 'even if agreement was reached with the Stock Exchange on which market particular types of options should be traded, it is unlikely that LIFFE would give up trading options on its own futures contracts'. Options on the FTSE index were already traded on the Stock Exchange, which issued a somewhat frosty press release following the announcement of LIFFE's new contract. 'What price a unified London Options Exchange?' asked Kenneth Fleet in *The Times* soon after the contract's launch, speculating that 'any pressure for a joint options market is likely to come initially from the Stock Exchange where there are no sacred cows left'. In fact, fitful talks took place during the second half of 1986 at both chairman and chief executive level, to discuss areas of mutual co-operation such as regulation and clearing, and Bernard Reed (by now options manager of the Stock Exchange) told *The Times* in early December that 'there is no longer any argument about a merger, only when and how'. The Stock Exchange's traded options market had just traded its ten millionth contract, following a sharp upturn of business in equity options since the British Telecom privatisation in late 1984, and it probably saw itself as the natural senior partner in any such merger.

Jenkins reported progress to the board in January 1987:

He had agreed with the Chief Executive of the Stock Exchange the outline of a paper for the two Chairmen. It is their view that whilst the two exchanges existed essentially in competition there would be little scope to co-operate in the immediate future. The Chief Executive said a long term approach would require that a single financial futures and options market be established in the UK. He said that two particular problems which would require examination existed, the question of how such an exchange would be regulated and the structural problems which would arise from the two existing differing memberships.

The Chairman pointed out that the Bank of England would probably support LIFFE if a difference of view with the Stock Exchange occurred.

By March the two chief executives had prepared their paper. One section (drafted at the insistence of the Stock Exchange) referred to the creation of 'a separate autonomous market like other parts of the Stock Exchange'. The clear implication of this, Jenkins told the board, was that 'any combination of the LIFFE and SE options markets would be likely to come under the jurisdiction of the Stock Exchange – a suggestion that is clearly unacceptable to LIFFE'. To which Williamson suggested that the Stock Exchange, with 'its sizeable overheads', had an economic motive: 'If a unified LIFFE/traded options market was absorbed into the Stock Exchange it is likely that the increase in overall Stock Exchange costs would be significantly less than the additional revenue which they would derive from the LIFFE activity.' And he added that 'if a unified market was independent of the Stock Exchange, the Stock Exchange might need to find a way of reducing its overheads and this might prove very difficult for them to achieve'.

Following several months of drift, matters at last started to come to a head in early July, when LIFFE received a fairly detailed proposal from the Stock Exchange about the creation of LFOM, the London Futures and Options Market. Providing dealing facilities for all the instruments currently traded on LIFFE and the Stock Exchange's traded options market (which was starting by this time to be called the London Traded Options Market, or LTOM for short), it would operate 'with a very high degree of autonomy' within the structure of the Stock Exchange, an autonomy to be 'ensured by drawing up very broad Rules and financial policies within which it would develop its own detailed procedures, operating practices and budgets'. Goodison, in his accompanying letter to Williamson, emphasised that 'it is better for our two markets to develop products and systems together, and to fight the world competition together, than to be distracted by local competition between us', and that 'it would be good news for London generally if we can succeed in developing a strong unified world market in London in derivative products'. As for the possible fears on the part of some LIFFE members about being brought under the aegis of the Stock Exchange, he expressed confidence 'that any fears can be allayed during discussions about the details after the decision is taken in principle to work towards an integrated futures and options market'.

Pending LIFFE's response, the press began to run with the story. 'Why LIFFE should want to marry into the Stock Exchange baffles the imagination,' commented the *Daily Telegraph* on 14 July. 'To merge the two would create the City's equivalent of Asda-MFI – a growth business matched to one that is looking flat-packed, if not Completely Knocked Down.' When the board met six days later there was unanimous agreement over the unsuitability of the Stock Exchange's existing proposals, especially in relation to the loss of autonomy that would be involved. Significantly, it emerged in the course of discussion that whereas the Bank of England until recently had been leaning towards the idea of a merged market under the umbrella of the Stock Exchange, it was now 'more open-minded as to the most appropriate solution', a shift partly prompted by the recent JGB launch, which it was felt might not have been possible under Stock Exchange auspices. The major contribution came from Barkshire:

It would be in London's interest that LIFFE and the traded options market should get together in order to concentrate efforts and resources in respect of product development, trading floor facilities, clearing, back office procedures and systems generally. However, this would not necessarily be best achieved by arrangements under the umbrella of the Stock Exchange. Indeed this could be the worst solution and might stifle the development of the markets. He would therefore be concerned if the solution involved operating under Stock Exchange auspices. Mr Barkshire added that it was important that LIFFE should not now be seen as being unresponsive and that we should not concentrate upon criticising, or proposing changes to, the Stock Exchange paper. We should instead start with a clean sheet of paper and recapture the high ground by developing and putting forward a new proposal.

Over the next fortnight LIFFE expressed to the Stock Exchange its clear preference for the creation of a unified and independent market, but was unable to persuade the Stock Exchange that this was the way ahead. Instead, the two exchanges agreed to commit themselves publicly to a programme of joint development and co-operation, which might or might not result in an eventual union. Separate, poorly co-ordinated press conferences were held on 6 August. 'The situation is somewhat embarrassing,' conceded Goodison. 'We have agreed to disagree on the fundamentals.' While Williamson commented about his failure to convince the Stock Exchange of the value of an independent derivatives market: 'It is obvious they are in the midst of a major reorganisation, and they aren't willing to give up any of their critical mass.'

The outside world was fairly unimpressed. 'Carry on up the City' was a headline in the *Independent*, critical of 'a quarrel which should never have broken out and shames all involved'. But at the same time the paper found an explanation for the disunity in 'the fundamental institutional difference' between the Stock Exchange and LIFFE. The Stock Exchange 'is a self-consciously important public institution which has undergone traumatic and largely involuntary changes', whereas LIFFE 'is run comparatively on a shoestring, believes its decision to be independent has been crucial to its success, and sees contracts derived from cash, bond and money markets as requiring different management from equity-based markets'. This analysis, emphasising the cultural as well as functional differences between the two exchanges, was surely correct. Looked at from LIFFE's side, the young meritocratic upstart inevitably regarded the Stock Exchange, for all the rapid process of change that had recently been forced on it, as still run by the old guard and still unnecessarily bureaucratic. Nor, as it happened, was the personal chemistry between the two chairmen particularly good. 'We did not wish to become part of the Stock Exchange,' Williamson explained a few weeks later to

Carry on up the City

The Stock Exchange and the London International Financial Futures Exchange yesterday launched a co-operation programme amid scenes of rampant disunity. At separate press confer-

Independent, 7 August 1987.

the *Sunday Telegraph*. 'We need to be independent in order to survive and the future of LIFFE entirely depends on many underlying markets.' Granted LIFFE's history – a young market that had prospered precisely through avoiding, somewhat fortuitously, the clutches of the Stock Exchange at an early stage – there could plausibly have been no other response to the prospect of becoming what Prest in the *Independent* aptly called 'a semi-autonomous province within the Stock Exchange empire'. 'Can Toffs and Oiks really mix?' *FOW* had asked in its August issue – and as yet, the toffs were not willing to admit to the disturbing possibility that the future might lie with the oiks.

A similar wish to retain freedom of action also governed LIFFE's often rather tortuous relations with the two giant Chicago exchanges. The outstanding issue by 1984 was whether LIFFE would get involved as a possible third leg in the CME-SIMEX mutual offset agreement. The Merc continued to insist on a measure of exclusivity, in other words that LIFFE should not establish another link with a rival American exchange. Discussion of any LIFFE link with the CME was terminated in April, when the Merc decided that until its link with SIMEX had been operating for a year, no other links would be explored. That September the CME/SIMEX mutual offset system at last began operating.

Fourteen months later, on a visit to London in November 1985, Melamed and his colleagues got the ball rolling again, but Albright's account of the discussions indicated that there was no great meeting of minds:

> *The CME's bargaining position was to concentrate on the prospects for fungibility between new and future contracts on our two exchanges… We said our principal interest was fungibility in the Eurodollar future; this was what members and end users want… 'Their' Eurodollar is clearly the jewel in the crown at the CME. They believe that they have much more to lose than we do in making a fungible arrangement on this contract, and are very reluctant to do so. We made clear that we would really only be interested in a deal which includes a Eurodollar future, possibly in a package with other contracts.*

The Merc had softened its line over exclusivity, but over the next two months the question of the Eurodollar contract proved the sticking point. Visiting Chicago in January 1986, Jenkins and Albright found that the only possible basis for fungibility would be if LIFFE stopped trading the contract prior to the Merc opening, i.e. at 1.20 London time – a singularly unpalatable prospect from LIFFE's point of view. 'Although LIFFE's Eurodollar volume still makes it our strongest contract,' noted Jenkins on his return, 'its market share has steadily declined. At its current level of around 12%, any sharp change in its perceived liquidity could damage its volume irretrievably.' Accordingly, discussions ceased for the time being – Jenkins's opinion being that the Merc had declined to put the Eurodollar on the table in any meaningful way not only because of the sensitivities of the Chicago traders, but also because it 'had concluded that LIFFE was fairly desperate for a link and that they did not consider it necessary to offer any concessions'.

One link that did actually happen came directly out of the failure of these talks. In September 1985 the Sydney Futures Exchange [SFE] had broached the idea of trading LIFFE's Eurodollar futures contract on a fungible basis, as part of its plan to maximise the advantage of being two hours ahead of Singapore and thereby attract business from US houses in Japan. In particular it would allow Sydney to exploit the fact that it was the first market to open each Friday after US money supply figures came out, a key source of SIMEX volume. The SFE, Jenkins observed to the board in December, was 'intrinsically less attractive' as an alternative to the CME, but it would 'require comparatively little executive time' to develop a link with it, a distinct advantage. There followed the failure of the CME talks, and in May 1986 the board formally decided to adopt that alternative strategy, especially in the light of Sydney's willingness to provide the bulk of resources to implement a link. 'LIFFE's planned Australian link brings 24-hour trading closer' was the *FT*'s headline, and Williamson was in Sydney in October to inaugurate the proceedings, managing in his enthusiasm to pull the handle off a brass bell in the trading pit. 'Since positions opened on one exchange may be closed on either, trading in the two different time zones will now become as cheap as trading on LIFFE,' he told a press conference. 'This cost efficiency, coupled with the immense flexibility of the 17-hour trading day, will bring considerable gains all round.'

Early reaction came from the *West Australian*, a Perth daily. Its headline was 'London link a fizzer – SFE dealers', which sounded good but in fact was vernacular for a flop. By January 1987 the average daily volume had fallen to 20 Eurodollars and 30 T-bonds. It was all too clear that the lack of a domestic US T-bond cash market was a vital defect in terms of fungible T-bonds, while in relation to the Eurodollar battle with SIMEX the solid volume that had already been attained in Singapore gave it a decisive edge in that time zone. The Sydney traders, in short, found it easier and more profitable to stick to Australian contracts. 'I can go some way to explaining the failure of the [English] cricket and rugby teams,' Williamson at the end of his chairmanship in 1988 would write to Leslie Hosking of the SFE, 'but find it more difficult to spot the real reason why our joint venture didn't take off. I really thought that would be a winner partly because it seemed to make sense but also because I felt we had a good understanding between us in spite of being 12,000 miles away.' In April 1989, with volumes nugatory, the SFE formally suspended trading in its two contracts linked to LIFFE.

It was Chicago that really mattered, and over the years LIFFE looked mainly to the Board of Trade, a relationship cemented in the mid-1980s by joint work over the yen bond and Eurobond contracts. But in the same way that the Eurodollar contract was the indispensable component of any meaningful link between LIFFE and the CME, so it was the T-bond contract that would make or break a possible LIFFE/CBOT link. The Tokyo agreement of October 1985 referred to the development by the two exchanges of 'mutually beneficial trading opportunities', but from the first there was a question mark as to whether the CBOT would be able to secure member support for fungibility of the T-bond. Moreover, there was also the whole larger question – equally applicable in relation to either Chicago exchange – of whether LIFFE wanted to develop internationally in partnership or to go it alone. Albright distilled her thoughts in a December 1985 memo to Jenkins:

> A partnership could be extremely powerful, since it would combine our very complementary strengths (they have locals, we have the cash market; they have money, we have the strong membership; they're in the U.S., we're in Europe). Our chances of achieving a dominant international position in derivative products seem small without such a partnership. However, it is questionable whether a partnership in international development is achievable, or if achieved, is workable. Reaching agreement on practical issues on a continuing basis could be very difficult; we could see their views as parochial, they would see ours as institutionally dominated. To some extent, there is an inherent appeal in being able to chart our own course, unfettered by the need for consensus with a very different market, even if that means our destination isn't Utopia...

It was a fundamental dilemma, and one that LIFFE, for all its instinctive leaning towards independence, found it difficult to resolve conclusively.

Certainly there was no wish to abandon the possibility of links with Chicago. In January 1986, at the same time as the CME talks ran out of steam, LIFFE decided to press ahead with active co-operation with the CBOT on the Eurobond front in particular, in the hope that if a workable fungible contract in that was up and running, then the CBOT's floor members might abandon their opposition to a fungible T-bond. Joint work on both the Eurobond and yen bond contracts continued through 1986, and by October that year the CBOT had a major proposal to make to LIFFE. Having concluded that it would be impractical to envisage 24-hour trading on its Chicago floor, but still wishing to trade there derivative products representing the major capital markets of the world, it intended to develop its links with overseas exchanges and wanted LIFFE to be its partner in the European time zone. In theory it might have chosen the Paris financial futures market – Marché à Terme Instruments Financières (MATIF) – which had opened in February and was doing quite well, though mainly in domestic government bonds. The CBOT's proposal encompassed fungibility in a broad range of contracts, including T-bond futures.

Albright in her briefing memorandum to the board recommended acceptance – the advantages including 'a strong partner, an opportunity to divide up the clock and avoid a trading hours war, a very strong combination to face the Japanese as their influence in financial markets expands radically, and an opportunity to solidify a niche in international products in the European time zone' – and Williamson scribbled 'delighted but suspicious' on his copy. Some tough negotiations ensued, before on 9 February 1987 the two exchanges signed a memorandum of understanding to develop a wide-ranging linkage agreement. Interchangeable contracts to be traded, once a mutual offset system had been developed, would include the T-bond. Williamson stressed to the press that LIFFE's independence would not be compromised, while the *Wall Street Journal* quoted Thomas Baldwin, one of the most active professional traders in the Board of Trade's bond futures pit: 'What do we need London for? I don't see how it can benefit Chicago at all.'

The hope was that the linkage would be in place by early 1988, but in July 1987 Jenkins felt compelled to complain to the CBOT's chairman, 'Cash' Mahlmann, about the way in which LIFFE's prospective partner seemed to be dragging its feet. Mahlmann denied that the CBOT was having second thoughts about the link, and at the next board meeting Jenkins sought to allay anxieties:

Wall Street Journal,
10 February 1987.

THE WALL STREET JOURNAL, TUESDAY, FEBRUARY 10, 1987

Chicago Mart And Liffe Agree To Linkup Pact

Exchanges Plan to Develop Interchangeable Contracts For Trading of Futures

By MATTHEW WINKLER
Staff Reporter of THE WALL STREET JOURNAL
LONDON – Seeking to boost their transatlantic business, the London International Financial Futures Exchange and the Chicago Board of Trade agreed to develop interchangeable contracts.

The accord represents one of the broadest lin... ...chan...

Negotiations that led to the linkage agreement began several years ago, according to Liffe officials. "Although we may be on different sides of the Atlantic, we share about 30 major clearing firms as members of both exchanges," said Michael Jenkins, Liffe's president. "Many of our members have urged this idea of compatible futures contracts on us for some time."

However, international linkages between U.S. and overseas futures exchanges have yet to draw much interest from traders and speculators. A recent accord between Liffe and the Sydney Futures Exchange to trade an interchangeable U.S. Treasury bond contract has proven a big disappointment so far.

Since its Oct. 23 launch, average daily volume has plummeted to about 50 contracts from an initial daily volume of 2,100 contracts.

Lack of Liquidity

The ... ...t stem...

The position was unclear. CBOT members had approved the linkage concept in principle late in 1986 although it remained to be seen whether they would approve the detailed proposals… The successful introduction [on the CBOT] of evening trading sessions and the continuing dull performance of LIFFE's T-Bond contract may have affected opinions at the CBOT. However, the CBOT had taken the initiative in proposing the link and their fundamental problem of having, in the financial area, a single dominant product, still remained. LIFFE's position has, if anything, probably strengthened.

Ms Albright added that the growth in long gilt volumes and the successful start made by the JGB contract reinforced that view.

Several thorny issues still needed to be resolved in relation to trading practices and clearing arrangements, but progress was made over the next two months, and by late September the two exchanges were publicly committed to unveiling by the end of the year their detailed plans, including to their respective memberships. The dream of multi-contract fungibility – enabling a position to be opened and closed on separate exchanges but necessitating only one set of transaction and margin costs – was still alive.

The Merc did not watch all this passively. In October 1986, in the context of the CBOT's attractive proposal, Albright predicted that 'it is probable that once they realise the door was closed on co-operation with LIFFE, all-out war would be waged'. In fact, LIFFE over the next few months kept a back-door open, insisting that the Eurodollar contract be kept at arm's length from the linkage agreement. On 6 February 1987, practically on the eve of the LIFFE/CBOT announcement, Melamed rang Jenkins to say that, after all, there *was* a possibility of having a fungible Eurodollar, in other words involving an overlap in trading hours, previously always resisted by the CME:

He said [Jenkins noted] that the CME had commissioned a study to quantify the effects of having a mutual offset arrangement with London. The professor who undertook the study apparently concluded that whilst it might initially have a negative impact on volume, there would ultimately be a larger pie. Leo thought this would be good ammunition to persuade floor members to look favourably on a fungible link.

I said that the conclusion of the study did not surprise me; we had long held that view. I said that we remained interested in a fungible Eurodollar but that our main priority at the moment was engineering a link with the CBOT. We had limited resources and could not move on too many fronts at the same time.

Leo said that CME views on a link with LIFFE were bound to be influenced by any arrangement LIFFE might announce with the Board of Trade. I said that LIFFE had always been consistent in eschewing exclusive arrangements with any one exchange…

The announcement was duly made on Monday the 9th, and two days later Melamed wrote to Williamson:

As you no doubt heard from Michael Jenkins, it had been our intention to begin a committee review process toward the possibility of an eventual Eurodollar mutual offset link with LIFFE… Unfortunately, your recent CBOT/LIFFE announcement puts a very definite crimp in our plans. The announcement included markets that had been CME territory since the advent of financial futures. Thus, some of our members will no doubt view certain aspects of your announcement as a competitive move. Accordingly, the present environment would make any proposal for a connection on Eurodollars politically quite difficult. I'm sure you understand these realities.

It was not long before Melamed had his own announcement to make, a genuine bombshell. On 2 September 1987 the CME and Reuters announced 'a long-range agreement in principle to create a global electronic automated transaction system for the trading of futures and futures-options before and after regular U.S. business trading hours'. Melamed called the agreement 'the ultimate and logical response to the demands posed by technology and the globalization of trading' and stated that its implementation, when combined with the Merc's regular trading hours, 'could result in a literal 24-hour transaction system'. He added that 'we will make every attempt to develop the concept on an international basis and invite every financial center to join these efforts toward a unified global trading system'. This was the system that the world would soon know as GLOBEX, short for Global Exchange; and to Melamed's intense relief – knowing the instinctive antagonism that open outcry traders felt towards the 'black box' – the Merc's members endorsed the concept at a special meeting a few weeks later. The price of their endorsement, however, was that the CME (locked in a constant competitive struggle with the CBOT) would retain control over GLOBEX's structure and restrict any advantage to the benefit of its own members.

The announcement was a particular shock for Williamson, who during the summer had believed that he was on track to do something similar with Reuters (i.e. after-hours screen trading) specifically in relation to the Eurodollar contract. That initiative was now dead, but together with Melamed's apparent coup it showed that automation – as opposed to conventional, SIMEX-style linkages – *might* represent the way ahead in terms of capturing global market share. 'We took another look at trading links and concluded that they are stop-gap measures that don't fully address international trading,' the Merc's president, Bill Brodsky, told the *Wall Street Journal*, arguing that the main problem with most links was that they married strong and weak markets, with the smaller of the two exchanges having little chance of building sufficient liquidity to attract many of the bigger exchange's customers. By contrast, he argued, the just announced after-hours electronic trading system, scheduled to start in early 1989, represented a more comprehensive response to traders' needs.

Which way would the future point? No one really knew, but a passage from Melamed's memoirs gives a sense of the potential high importance of the moment:

Just as I had done in 1972 when I entered the murky waters of currency trading with the IMM, I was now asking the futures industry to follow me on yet another odyssey, over oceans, across continents, and through the channels of high technology. I had learned long ago that if my goals weren't big, then neither was my vision. After all, what is vision other than imagination extended to a future. Take the science fiction novel I wrote, The Tenth Planet, *in which the central character is Putral, an all-powerful computer that runs five planets in its galactic world. I began writing the novel in 1983 and finished it in 1986, just at the time I fostered the concept of GLOBEX, a kind of Putral of the futures world as I had envisioned it...*

'Top salaries in the City fair make one gasp, they are so large,' Margaret Thatcher told *Newsnight* in summer 1985, as the City geared up for Big Bang. It was becoming the time of the 'marzipan set' (high-fliers below the icing but above the cake), of the 'golden hellos' (six-figure signing-on fees), and of the 'BOBO' (Burnt Out But Opulent). There is no reliable guide to what LIFFE traders earned in the mid-1980s – not least because basic salaries often bore little relationship to total earnings – but without doubt the exchange and its inhabitants now became (in middle-class eyes anyway) an unmistakable symbol of changes taking place not only in the City but also in society at large. In March 1986 Michael Cockerell reported for BBC 1's *This Week Next Week* on City big earners, making much of how LIFFE's dealers enjoyed showing off their new-found wealth by marching into Green's Champagne Bar with a wad of notes and ordering 'two bottles of your best shampoo, please'. These dealers, according to Cockerell, were almost all 'young men in their twenties and early thirties' who came 'from working-class homes in the East End or the suburbs of London' and, working on commission or incentive payments, 'earn from £15,000 up to £200,000 a year for a handful of the very top traders'.

Soon afterwards a *First Tuesday* programme for Yorkshire Television went into production, going behind 'the sedate columns of London's Royal Exchange', as *TV Times* put it, and enabling the viewer to 'follow Mick, Bob and Nigel as they hurl themselves into a billion-pound maelstrom', in which 'frenzied atmosphere they are all too aware of their own futures and that they are working on borrowed time'. LIFFE managed to exercise some editorial control – though Ackerman's reference to the prevalence of market rumours 'like Ronnie Reagan has had a heart attack when they mean Lonnie Donegan' stayed – before the programme was shown on 3 June. To the *Sunday Mirror* 'it looked and sounded like a prep school bun-fight in Petticoat Lane', while for Nancy Banks-Smith in the *Guardian* 'it was like being a dog biscuit in Battersea':

The din was indescribable, the screen full of faces and fists. Everyone was yelling and, as no voice could be heard above the hubbub, signalling with their fingers. Splayed fingers covered the camera, stabbing fingers, clenched fists, open mouths. All young, male and barking.

The odd thing is that I have no idea what they trade in nor, stranger still, has a trader. What is a financial future? Silence like a poultice came to heal the blows of sound. Mick, the first barking face we saw and a nice young dog off-duty, thought about it for some time. He read the ceiling. He gave up. 'You'll have to cut this. There's a good answer but I don't know it.'

The whole exercise did not impress Heymer, who before the programme went out predicted 'a hard core negative response to the film from members, particularly floor traders who, not for the first time, would ask: "Why did the exchange let this happen?"'.

Access policy subsequently tightened up, but media interest did not abate. The *FT* noted in March 1987 how LIFFE's locals were finding it increasingly 'tiresome lately being interviewed by journalists for "East End boy makes millions"-type stories', while *FOW* commented soon afterwards that 'facing a potential TV audience of millions to brag about salary, Porsche and docklands flat is nothing compared to the experience of facing the inevitable barrage of jokes and derogatory comments from the LIFFE pits following the broadcast'. But some traders were willing to brazen out the jeers, and that autumn there appeared the spread on 'A Man of the Futures' in the *Sunday Times Magazine*: 'David Kyte is new-breed City. Classic product of the Big Bang. For the past year he's been cleaning up on the financial futures market. But he's already 27... how much longer can he go on?'

Going beyond ephemeral journalism, there were two major representations in these years of futures trading. One was largely sympathetic, the other somewhat less so. *Trading Places* was a huge commercial success in the States in summer 1983, and that December the film was released in Britain. It had a pleasing plot – white Philadelphia executive Louis Winthorpe III (Dan Akroyd), working for two millionaire uncles, both brokers, 'trades places' with black, off-the-street Billy Ray Valentine (Eddie Murphy) – and Nigel Andrews in the *FT* called it 'the best Christmas-timed comedy America has produced in recent years'.

Portraying the world of futures trading as a thoroughly positive and democratic experience, John Landis's film gave the whole industry a huge if immeasurable shot in the arm; and Jenkins in an article on marketing in 1985 noted approvingly how its theme was 'the ascendence of the young dynamic approach over that of the establishment'.

Two years later, in March 1987, Caryl Churchill talked to the *London Daily News* about her new play, shortly to open at the Royal Court: 'We wanted to show the energy, skill and wit of this world. I think we were all surprised by how attractive the City is. I deliberately wanted to make all the characters as bad as each other. They are villains, but they're likeable villains…' The play was *Serious Money*, and quite a lot of the action took place on the floor of LIFFE, which she and the actors had visited for research purposes. Written in verse, with no shortage of what Michael Billington in the *Guardian* called 'satirical exuberance and ensemble attack', it had a complex plot, one of whose strands featured a LIFFE dealer Scilla Todd, daughter of a wealthy, conventional stockbroker. 'It's a cross between roulette and space invaders,' she explains to her father, who is appalled by the barrow-boy company his daughter is now keeping. Frances Cairncross in the *TLS* praised Churchill for having not only 'deftly caught the feel of the trading floor at LIFFE' and its language, 'a mixture of obscenity and gambling', but also managing (near the end of act one) to explain 'accurately and in verse, the workings of futures markets in general and of financial futures markets in particular'. Cairncross also noted that 'everyone in the play is driven by greed, or fear, or both'; and indeed, the moral force of Churchill's anti-City critique was undisguised. Nevertheless, the City in general, and LIFFE in particular, loved it. 'Tickets are the hottest property in the market,' Fildes noted at the start of June. 'LIFFE's member firms have taken to block-booking the theatre, and take their brightly jacketed dealers along on works outings.' Soon afterwards, as the unlikely theatrical hit of the year, the play transferred to Wyndham's Theatre in the West End. Whatever the validity of its perspective, *Serious Money* had captured a defining moment in the City's history, a moment in which LIFFE was literally centre stage.

'Five more glorious years,' the chorus called for at the end of the play, and on 11 June 1987, less than three months after it had opened, the electorate obliged. That day many of LIFFE's traders sported stickers proclaiming 'We all say YES to Maggie', and Bruce Clark of Reuters listened to some of Thatcher's children:

Opposite: Five years old.

Serious Money poster, 1987.

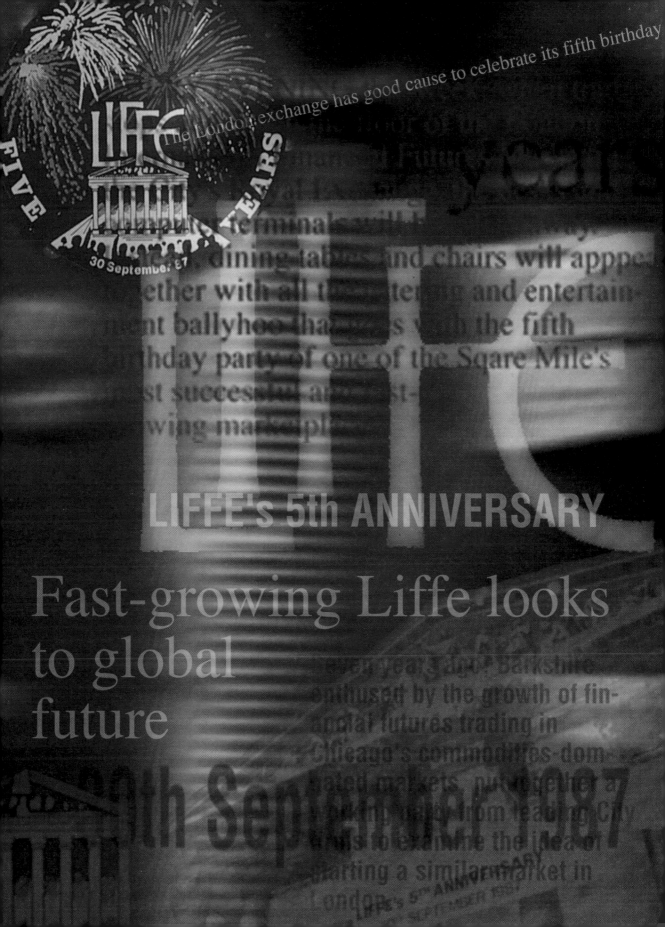

'It's so capitalist down here, you can't get away from it,' said 19-year-old trader Nick Prentice. Like many of his colleagues, he is fearful of Labour's taxation plans eating away at the salary he hopes to be earning in a few years time. 'If the Conservatives don't win, you won't see half the people down here,' said a 23-year-old English trader with an American bank. 'Why should people risk 100 per cent of their money and then pay most of their gains in tax?' 'LIFFE definitely typifies Thatcherism,' said 26-year-old Martin Frewer, one of the few traders to have been educated at one of Britain's elite private schools. 'In a good way, of course', he hastens to add...

The summer of 1987 was in retrospect the high tide of Thatcherism, and the exchange's fifth anniversary celebrations in the last week of September reflected the exuberant mood. They were Williamson's brainchild, abetted by Christopher Morgan, and implemented with his usual combination of panache and attention to detail by Gerry Rodgers. The cost of the celebrations was equal to one day's revenue for the exchange, and *FOW* described them:

Every afternoon, once trading ended, carpenters built a raised floor over the pits, curtains were hung, flowers arranged and lights were dimmed to create what looked like the City's first nightclub. Cocktails and dinner were followed by a Cecil B. DeMille style history of the Royal Exchange, beamed in glorious technicolour onto all the prices screens. After a quick brandy guests were dispatched with a LIFFE trading button firmly pinned to their chests to wait for the tenth birthday celebration...

From Monday to Thursday members supplied most of the guests, but Friday night was traders' night. 'Staff at the Royal Exchange knew only too well,' *FOW* commented, 'that it would take at least a weekend to clear up after that event.' They were right. Rik Mayall (star of television's *The Young Ones*) was given a rough ride when he came on to perform; John Wells (doing his Denis Thatcher impersonation) just about survived; and at the end of a tumultuous evening, Williamson and Rodgers were relieved men that Tite's masterpiece was still standing.

Chapter Five

Storm, Crash and Bund

THURSDAY, 15 OCTOBER 1987 was a record day on LIFFE – a volume of 114,031 lots, easily beating the 14 April record of 101,510. The immediate cause was disappointing US trade figures, allied to a general sense that ambitious talk of currency co-operation between finance ministers was failing to mask the increasing lack of interest rate co-operation.

The following morning the south-east of England woke up to a scene of devastation. Telephone lines were down, trees lay across roads, trains were not running. By 8 o'clock the only senior person who had made it in to the exchange was Gerry Rodgers, by now deputy chief executive, who had already been there for two or three hours. He knew that LIFFE, being in the business of risk management, could not afford not to be open, and he had managed to summon enough technicians. Now, following a fairly fruitless visit across the road to the Bank of England, where he found that practically the only person inside was a functionary in a pink uniform, he pressed ahead. The first member of the board to arrive was Williamson, who on the basis that the computer and clearing systems were working normally endorsed Rodgers' decision, telling Reuters that 'we see no reason to close'. With barely a handful of traders present at the outset, and not very many more later straggling in, volume was extremely thin, with activity at a virtual standstill by mid-morning, though in the end some 10,000 lots were done. Nevertheless, crucially helped by ICCH being open, it was a far more impressive

Financial Times,
20 October 1987.

performance than almost anywhere else in the City: the London clearing system was suspended, halting all payments between Britain's banks; trading on the Stock Exchange barely functioned, with hardly anyone present to man the screens in the dealing rooms; and the London Metal Exchange, the International Petroleum Exchange, and most of the London Futures and Options Exchange (the former LCE) all failed to open. The contrast proved excellent publicity, with *The Times* referring to LIFFE as 'irrepressible', the *Sunday Telegraph* to it as 'triumphant'. It also, on the Friday itself, encouraged people with an exposure in the cash market to hedge their positions in the futures market – thereby saving a few fortunes, as it turned out.

The Crash of '87 – the most sensational event in the world's financial markets for over half a century – took place on the Monday and Tuesday of the following week. Trading on the LIFFE floor was hectic on the 19th (especially in the afternoon, as the CBOT went 'limit down' and business poured into the LIFFE T-bond), but unbelievable on the 20th, as 180,212 contracts changed hands. Heymer reassured the press that trading had been 'quite orderly considering the very rapid fluctuations in supply and demand', but no trader who was on the floor that day was likely to forget the experience. 'You could smell the fear in people,' Marc Bailey would recall. 'There are some who're well down,' an anonymous trader told the *Evening Standard* at the time. 'I know one who's £130,000 adrift.' Yet whatever the individual dramas, it was quite quickly clear that overall the crash was an enormously beneficial development for LIFFE. Of critical importance had been the decision two years previously to abolish price limits (brought into operation on some nine occasions since 1982), on the grounds that they had been 'felt to be a hindrance rather than of assistance in a volatile market'. This meant that – as long as the systems and clearing mechanism continued to function effectively, which for the most part they did – LIFFE was able to offer a continuous market, unlike the Chicago exchanges or in effect the Stock Exchange, albeit a continuous market with wide spreads trading at one stage at an enormous discount to underlying value, as the FTSE 100 future went for a time into free fall. This was potentially very embarrassing, but amidst the wider drama being played out received relatively little publicity. The *Evening Standard* published on the 27th a characteristic letter from David Morgan:

Is it not time to realise the difference between the Stock Exchange and the Financial Futures Market? LIFFE has weathered the weather and cashed in on the crash by being open throughout, quoting tight prices and breaking both records in volume and open interest this past week.

Please note we don't hide behind unanswered telephone calls. Open outcry in the pits ensures a true and fair market with anyone able to hedge their equities or government bonds in the Footsie, or gilt pit. Stop knocking the City.

Underneath the rhetoric these were, from LIFFE's point of view, fair claims; but inevitably, the inquests on how the markets had conducted themselves during the crash were only just beginning.

Anxious that derivatives might be made a scapegoat for the stock market crash, as seemed likely to happen in the States, the Options and Futures Society held a seminar as early as 18 November at which a succession of speakers denied that the equity market had fallen more than it would have done without futures and options. Desmond Fitzgerald spoke for the meeting as a whole when he asserted that 'there was a speculative bubble in the cash market, now corrected, but I do not accept that futures and options trading had much to do with it'. Jenkins agreed, noting that the bull market in bonds had been a major contributor to LIFFE's record volume, as brokers switched out of equities and into bonds; while as for the FTSE 100 futures contract, he argued that, accounting as it did for a relatively small proportion of LIFFE's volume, it had probably not been a significant factor in the cash market's misfortunes. Nevertheless, it was obviously a key relationship, especially to the investing institutions, and Quintin Price, head of options research at James Capel & Co, some months later put it under the microscope in a thoughtful piece for the *Local Government Chronicle*:

The FTSE 100 future traded the record 9,111 contracts on 19 October and a further 9,251 contracts the following day. Volume in the week directly preceding the crash averaged 2,400 contracts per day. The higher volume of those two days was not enough to save the futures contract from reaching a near 400 point discount, equivalent to about 20% of the day's opening value, to the cash market on Tuesday morning (a result of pressure of the 'sell at open' orders that many brokers were obliged to execute on behalf of clients). However, this situation was momentary and although the future continued to trade at a discount to the cash market, the differential in percentage terms was less than a number of equity related futures contracts traded in the USA and elsewhere. When the future dropped below 1500 (FTSE equivalent) the institutions began to question the logic of the size of the discount and when it fell below 1400 the buyers came in...

At about the same time, early in 1988, LIFFE made substantial contributions both to the Stock Exchange's report on the crash and to a confidential report that the DTI prepared for ministers. Index arbitrage was a particularly hot potato, and in both reports LIFFE was able to establish convincingly that in the distinctive UK context this arbitrage was to be encouraged, not only as the basis for connecting the cash and derivative markets but also as a means of providing a liquid market for hedging. In addition, there was also no support for the fashionable nostrum of circuit breaking, seen as contrary to the fundamental principle that markets whose underlying rationale was the trading of risk needed most to be open when risk was at its highest. 'LIFFE is a crisis exchange,' Williamson told a Cambridge University magazine in February, 'which works well precisely because we have capitalised, well-audited members. They provide the liquidity, unlike in Chicago, where the local traders do this. LIFFE can thus take greater strains.' LIFFE was also at last able – in the new, risk-averse environment – to get across its wider message, that the underlying purpose of the market was for hedging, far more effectively than at any time since opening. Coming so soon after all the *Serious Money* publicity, when 'speculation' seemed the only word on everyone's lips, this was a timely antidote in every sense.

One by-product of the crash was that the CBOT put on ice its proposed link with LIFFE. It was a situation that the London exchange was willing to tolerate, aware of the intense regulatory pressures now on the Chicago exchanges, until it emerged early in 1988 that the CBOT was thinking of introducing early morning T-bond trading (conceivably at 8 am London time). Such trading, Williamson wrote to Mahlmann in February, 'would make unnecessary and indeed counterproductive a link with LIFFE'. Soon afterwards Williamson and Jenkins were in Chicago, where to their surprise they found that the CBOT was still hoping that LIFFE would continue to support the link even if the Board of Trade did bring in early morning trading. In May the CBOT decided to defer the introduction of an early morning session – almost certainly reflecting continuing internal uncertainty as to whether its approach to international trading should be to run a continuous market in Chicago or to forge links with exchanges in different time zones – and LIFFE remained mildly hopeful about the link, still seeing it as the most likely way of expanding the total market for its products.

Williamson, writing to Mahlmann in June, sought to clarify LIFFE's position:

Of course, you are absolutely right that the Memorandum of Understanding did not contain any restriction on trading hours. We both thought that some overlap was acceptable and even desirable and were not particularly bothered whether it was one or two hours. However, the possibility of the CBOT opening for an early morning session was never mooted and it never entered our heads that you envisaged doing this. Such a move would certainly reduce the attractions of a linkage for LIFFE.

An effective linkage agreement between two or, as we hope, three [i.e. including the Tokyo Stock Exchange presumably] parties around the World presupposes that none of those exchanges is open for more than its own trading day (however liberally that may be interpreted). It is not clear from statements coming out of the Board of Trade that this is accepted...

Two days later, at a board meeting, there took place 'a broad discussion, the consensus of which brought into question the whole viability of the link, which appeared to some members to be very much on CBOT's terms, and queried the benefit which would accrue to LIFFE'. Following the next board meeting, on 11 July, the firm decision was taken that Williamson's successor, David Burton, should inform Mahlmann that there was no longer a common basis for implementing a linkage agreement. 'The LIFFE Board,' he accordingly wrote, 'find it difficult to interpret the CBOT intention to extend its trading hours other than as a move that would frustrate the operation of a linkage, and would hurt LIFFE's T-Bond business'.

By the end of August no reply had been received, yet soon afterwards, at the industry's annual get-together at Bürgenstock, Jenkins's discussions with CBOT people suggested that, in the Chicago mind at least, the link was still alive:

> They argued that the CBOT had no current plans to open before 7.20 a.m., that there were logistic problems that they were not sure they could overcome if they were to open earlier and with the number of traders likely to come in, liquidity would be limited, probably less than on LIFFE. Nevertheless, the CBOT felt it could not agree to any restriction that might limit its freedom of manoeuvre on the T-Bond.
>
> Tom Donovan conceded that the CBOT would probably be willing to agree to restricting hours in respect of LIFFE products. The quid pro quo would be that LIFFE would not put these products on a screen for out-of-hours trading. They also conceded that it was unlikely that they would list such products unless there was fungibility with LIFFE.
>
> It is never easy to fathom CBOT motives or to know how much reliance to place on them, but it is clear that their primary objective is to prevent LIFFE trading T-Bonds out of hours on a screen-based system such as GLOBEX.

There, for the moment, the on-off saga rested.

Jenkins' mention of GLOBEX reflected how, in the year following Melamed's dramatic announcement, it had come to dominate much of the industry's agenda. Back in October 1987, LIFFE's board considered a strategy review that had been commissioned from Kep Simpson, former managing director of P A (the management consultants) and introduced by Rodgers. This looked ahead to the world as it might be five years hence:

> The world's largest private telecommunications carrier (Reuters), in conjunction with CME, has now completed three years operations of its global electronic trading network. Announced in September 1987, the development of this system has followed the pattern originally envisaged:-

March 1989   –   Start up operations
September 1989   –   Fully operational system
July 1991   –   System made available to all exchanges
for products not competing with CME.

The exclusive agreement between Reuters and CME relating to the latter's products still has 7½ years to run until it expires in A.D.2000.

In a pre-emptive move, CME launched sterling-denominated products in 1990 designed to attract liquidity from LIFFE. It achieved considerable success in diverting institutional business originating from members' dealing rooms. It also ensured that LIFFE could not use the Reuters network for its major products for the rest of this decade.

By now, the Reuters/CME network has successfully demonstrated the following:

- *its effectiveness not only as a complement to, but as a substitute for an open outcry market*
- *the dramatic cost reductions achievable by members through staff economies, as well as lower exchange tariffs*
- *the appeal to regulators, users and exchange management of its automatic audit and supervisory features*
- *the power and utility of a system which enables simultaneous dealer room transactions in both underlying and derivative markets*
- *the system's ease of extension to new products, and especially to new centrally-cleared services related to Forward FX, Interest Rate SWAPS, etc., which used to be called 'Off Exchange'.*

Scary stuff, and the board, suitably softened up, decided there was no alternative but to comply with the review team's recommendation that the exchange develop a system of Automated Pit Trading [APT] in parallel with increasing the capacity and quality of the open outcry market. A few weeks later Roger Barton was authorised to develop a working model of the APT system for demonstration purposes.

Sounding out opinion in December, Bruce Clark of Reuters found sharp divisions about the future of open outcry trading. 'Being pro-screen trading and working at LIFFE is like a pacifist being Secretary-General of Nato,' was the uncompromising view of David Morgan, supported by another local, Trevor Clein, who asserted that 'open outcry has a proven history of being far more efficient than any other system'. Many members made much of how LIFFE's floor had functioned during the recent crash, in contrast to Stock Exchange market-makers refusing to answer the telephone. At the other end of the spectrum was Nick

Durlacher of BZW: 'I wouldn't say the days of the pit trader are numbered, but I would say the years of the pit trader are numbered. I'm not prejudiced against open outcry, but in the end it will give way.' And when it was put to him that open outcry had unique features, he replied crisply, 'so did the dinosaur'. Durlacher was backed by another board member, Phillips & Drew's Rupert Lowe, who argued that 'automated trading will come because of the reduced cost per trade'. It was the start of a debate that would run and run – a debate in which full rein was given to deeply entrenched instincts and assumptions.

By March 1988 the APT model was completed, having been developed entirely in-house and using advanced technology to simulate the main principles of open outcry with a screen-based system. 'To the best of our knowledge it is unique,' Barton informed the board. 'No other exchange or systems organisation has to date developed an automated facility which emulates open outcry in this way.' Later that month the board discussed the long-term aim of APT, in the course of which Barkshire commented that 'while it could not be predicted with any certainty what would happen in the long term concerning automated trading, it was important that the Exchange be fully prepared for such developments by putting in place an automated trading capability'. The board agreed to this flexible approach – essentially a defensive response to the CME/Reuters initiative – and Barton was authorised to implement a pilot operation of APT. Details of the system remained secret, but Williamson informed the press that 'we are convinced we are a long way ahead of everyone else'.

Over the next six months and beyond, LIFFE adopted an essentially five-pronged approach: trying to establish whether the CME and Reuters were serious about their new-found wish to open up GLOBEX to other exchanges, and on what terms; assessing whether GLOBEX would actually work and what it could do; developing APT itself as rapidly as possible; reassuring traders, especially locals, that APT represented no immediate threat to open outcry and was indeed based on the principles of open outcry; and fifthly, seeing whether other exchanges (in particular MATIF) might be willing to develop jointly an out-of-hours trading facility, in effect as a rival to GLOBEX. At Bürgenstock in September, Jenkins talked with MATIF's chairman, Gérard Pfauwadel, who not only confirmed his exchange's keenness to use APT but also agreed to liaise on a negotiating stance with the CME. 'The view of MATIF is similar to our own,' noted Jenkins, namely 'scepticism that restriction on freedom of manoeuvre will be outweighed by the advantages.'

International relationships may have been getting increasingly problematic, but at least there was now a quiet period vis-à-vis both ICCH and the Stock Exchange. LIFFE had been largely responsible for the restructuring of ICCH in August 1987 – splitting it into six smaller units, in order to achieve greater transparency – and in April 1988 the board agreed to commit itself to a new two-year agreement with the clearing house. As for the Stock Exchange, and in particular its traded options market, the name of the game was co-operation in specific areas, though LIFFE for its part still sought a merger with LTOM in order to create a new, independent exchange – possibly but not necessarily on the floor of the Stock Exchange, where the traded options dealers were becoming used to a state of splendid isolation. Discussion documents proliferated during the winter of 1987/8, but no great progress was made.

This lack of momentum is partly explained by the fall-out from the October crash, which may have been beneficial to financial futures in terms of their use as a risk management tool, but was appreciably less so in terms of options. This particularly applied to LTOM, where there had been some spectacular cases of investors, having adopted apparently low-risk option positions in order to squeeze a little extra income out of equity portfolios, suddenly incurring huge losses. However, in October 1988 LIFFE and LTOM at last published a new set of joint initiatives, of which the most important was the proposed common use of the Trade Registration System [TRS], which had been developed by LIFFE and was in its final stages of implementation there. Moreover, LIFFE agreed to withdraw its option on the FTSE 100 future, in return for LTOM withdrawing two gilt option contracts. There was also talk of rationalisation in the area of currency options, hitherto disappointing products on both exchanges. 'Physical collaboration is vital,' insisted LTOM's chairman, Geoffrey Chamberlain; but at the same time his colleague Tony de Guingand (now director of traded options at LTOM) remarked, 'I think the merger question has been shelved.' From LTOM's perspective, that would remain the case pending a recognition on the part of the market's masters that the post-colonial age had dawned.

Undeniably dawning was a new era in City regulation, amidst some very mixed feelings. 'City policeman under fire' was the *FT*'s headline on 5 January 1988, reporting on a campaign to oust Sir Kenneth Berrill as chairman of SIB. It was a campaign based on a widely held belief in the City that Berrill was seeking to impose an unworkably complex and unacceptably intrusive regulatory system. There is no evidence that LIFFE was involved. By the end of February it had been announced that Berrill's tenure would not be renewed, just as the deadline was approaching for would-be members to make their applications to the SROs. LIFFE members divided, as predicted, between The Securities Association and the Association of Futures Brokers and Dealers. As for LIFFE itself, there was never any serious doubt that SIB would recognise it as an investment exchange, but perhaps somewhat more uncertain was whether the Office of Fair Trading would give LIFFE's rule-book a clean bill of health. Sir Gordon Borrie's standards were famously exacting, but on 13 April he informed Lord Young, Secretary of State for Trade and Industry, that he had 'found nothing in the rules that can be said at this stage significantly to restrict, distort or prevent competition or to be likely or intended to do so'. In particular, although 'the restrictions on membership of LIFFE in principle operate as a barrier to entry I note that there is a market in such seats which provides a mechanism for prospective new applicants to gain entry to LIFFE while taking account of the need to safeguard the original investment by members in setting up the exchange'.

Just over a fortnight later, on 29 April 1988, there took place the long-awaited, much-delayed A-Day, the implementation day for the 1986 Financial Services Act. 'The level of investor protection in the UK will improve significantly from today,' the *FT* predicted, trusting that Berrill's successor, David Walker from the Bank of England, would not permit 'the pendulum to swing back too far towards cosy City self-regulation'. LIFFE, it is fair to say, was not wildly enthusiastic about the new set-up as a whole. 'We remain concerned that whilst wholesale markets continue to be regulated by the Bank of England their associated exchange-traded derivatives come under the supervision of the Securities and Investment Board,' stated the 1987 Annual Report, published soon afterwards; and it added that as between TSA and the AFBD, with many LIFFE members having to be members of both, 'there is a need for a further rationalisation amongst these two self-regulatory organisations'.

In the immediate future however, while the new system bedded down, there remained plenty of scope for day-to-day self-regulation. In August the board approved new rules concerning cross trades, as well as giving the go-ahead for the introduction of a ground-breaking system of video logging of pit trading activity and the audio logging of all telephone lines into the trading floor. The proposed introduction of video logging was a dramatic step. However, the floor committee was persuaded by Foyle – correctly, as it turned out – that in addition to improving the audit trail it would greatly assist in the resolution of trading disputes. With the support of its chairman, Chris Henry, the floor committee unanimously

Financial Times,
29 April 1988.

Clive Wolman introduces the City's new legal structure

recommended to the board the introduction of video logging of all trading pits. Video and audio logging were bold moves to strengthen the audit trail, but in the new post-FSA environment LIFFE had both to prove itself and to be sufficiently ahead of the game to enable it to help the regulators understand what was, after all, one of the City's more challenging markets.

Borrie might not have been so sanguine about LIFFE's membership arrangements if it had not been for the exchange's impending expansion of trading rights. Jenkins and Foyle had outlined their thinking to the board in June 1987:

Without a significant expansion of the trading population the exchange will find it difficult to meet increasing demand for its successful products and also expand the size of other contracts. This is particularly relevant as far as attracting new locals is concerned but it also applies in the case of corporate members.

On the other hand it is desirable that the new issue should not cause any significant decline in the value of seats. A strong seat price is a major psychological benefit to the market. We need to strike the right balance between expanding the trading population, reducing the cost of entry to new products, and protecting the seat price.

The need to expand trading rights was urgent. Foyle proposed a repeat of the technique to circumnavigate the tax problem that had been developed earlier, when LIFFE Options plc had been created and 'B' shares had been issued to members. Accordingly, on 6 July 1988, LIFFE issued a prospectus inviting its members to apply for 'C' shares in a new subsidiary company, LIFFE Futures plc. A total of 373 'C' shares were offered – i.e. one for each seat on the exchange – with each costing £10,000 (roughly one-eleventh of what a full seat now cost). Members would be able to apply for one share for each seat held; and each share would entitle the holder to apply for a restricted futures trading permit, giving him the right to have one trader on the floor to trade all new futures contracts and all of the existing futures contracts, *except* for the four major ones, that is the long gilt, T-bond, three-month sterling and Eurodollar contracts. A significant incentive was that from September 1990 holders of 'C' shares would have the option, on a four-to-one basis, of converting into 'A' shares. The issue was oversubscribed by 32%, prompting Burton to comment:

I am delighted that the Rights issue has been so well received. The main aim is to improve liquidity by creating additional trading capacity. This should particularly help the existing less successful contracts and new contracts... Our second aim is to reduce the cost of entry to the market in order to attract new traders to the floor. This should be evident after 1st September when the shares will become transferrable and the trading permits will be able to be leased out...

David Burton, still with Warburgs, had become LIFFE's chairman in late May 1988. His background was more meritocratic than either of his predecessors, and in several key ways he had a clear sense of where he wanted the exchange to go. One of those ways was giving a greater weighting to the locals, and even though the expansion of trading rights had been planned before he became chairman he much encouraged this significant deviation from the traditional conventional wisdom that LIFFE should be an almost entirely institutional market. Obviously he was not alone in his thinking, but equally obviously the rapid rise of the local – arguably *the* LIFFE phenomenon of the late 1980s – was materially helped by having a sympathetic figure at the helm.

Volume continued to grow inexorably in LIFFE's sixth year. October 1987 was the busiest month the exchange had yet experienced, November 1987 the second busiest; and in the first seven months of 1988 over 8.8 million contracts were traded, compared with 7.6 million in the corresponding period in 1987. Back in early 1987 the Bank of England's survey of members' opinions had reflected the inevitable accompaniment of this growth:

LIFFE's premises were generally thought to be a problem for the future. Facilities such as trading booths were cramped. The layout of the pits was not ideal. The floor was cramped. This last detail was good for the open outcry system, but could not cope with any further trading developments. The general feeling was that the Royal Exchange was aesthetically distinguished, provisionally satisfactory but unduly restricted for the future. LIFFE would have to move in the next few years.

The space problem was equally acute for the staff. Although offices had been acquired at 28–29 Threadneedle Street, which helped, when Ian Nash arrived in December 1987 to be Foyle's assistant he found that there was no desk that he could call his own. In general, it was significant that when Jenkins was outlining for the board in April 1988 the main issues involved in the expansion of trading rights, he was insistent on the need 'to avoid an immediate and dramatic increase in the number of traders which might impose intolerable strain on the available capacity of the exchange's facilities'. As Burton soon afterwards put it to the *Sunday Times*, 'sometimes it's like the rush hour on Waterloo Station on the trading floor'.

In terms of that floor, and the fundamental constraints on space imposed by the site, what was to be done? Williamson in August 1987 played down to *The Times* rumours of a move to new, larger premises: 'The danger of getting off a bar stool and getting into an armchair is that you might go to sleep.' Serious thinking, however, was under way by early 1988, though clouded by two major uncertainties: the question of how a possible merger with LTOM related to the obvious possibility of occupying the Stock Exchange's floor; and over and beyond that, the larger question of whether the possibly imminent advent of global screen trading might render the very concept of a trading floor redundant.

If the Stock Exchange was the obvious option – all that empty floor space barely 100 yards away – it was not an option that Jenkins for one relished. Referring to the Stock Exchange's 'bureaucracy' in a memo in early March, he noted that 'it wants to provide a furnished apartment whereas we want an empty floor with vacant possession'. Soon afterwards Rodgers reported to the board that three possibilities for a long-term home for LIFFE were being evaluated: the Royal Exchange itself; the Stock Exchange; and the new Cannon Street development, on top of the station. He added that 'because of substantial operating cost', and because the Stock Exchange 'was expected to redevelop the floor in 3–4 years', the Stock Exchange 'could not be viewed as a long-term home for LIFFE'. At about this time, moreover, it emerged that the Stock Exchange was proposing an initial charge of £10 million to cover the cost of modernisation and refurbishment, a proposal that went down poorly. Granted that the Cannon Street development, even if suitable, would not be available until 1990 at the earliest, the board decided in May that there was no alternative but to stay put for the time being. 'The Board has approved a series of steps to increase the capacity of the floor and to improve its flexibility,' noted Jenkins, and later in 1988 a lease was taken out on the offices in Finch Lane that had once housed Greenwells. It was, in other words, a case of make do and mend.

David Burton.

That September the exchange's premises manager, Edward Hillyard, explained 'The Facts of LIFFE' to *Premises Management*:

As a result of continuous growth, our premises team are engaged in a constant cycle of improving accommodation and building new quarters into every available corner. This means staff have to work every evening and weekend to avoid interrupting trading... A constant problem in the Royal Exchange is that we haven't got the space to provide more offices and support systems. We are having to compact as much as we can into every conceivable space in the best possible way. I would say that we have now reached saturation point... We have our own computer and electrical engineering workshop to carry out essential repairs to the network of 235 monitors in the trading areas and back-offices, and there is a permanent 10-strong team of Telecom engineers to keep 3,000 voice and data lines and 294 dealer boards in working order. Underfloor cabling has mushroomed, and now is well in excess of 100 miles. With the introduction of more and more technology, we expect that the original 100 per cent of spare cabling capacity will be filled within the next 18 months... We are looking for very flexible people to work in a very flexible environment. LIFFE requires a lot of commitment from its people. We never know what is around the corner. There is always a big element of the unknown, and that carries on right down to the premises function...

One near certainty, though, was that trading activity would generate ever-more bags of paper rubbish – 150 bags every day as Hillyard spoke, disposed of in three daily collections.

Not enough of that wastepaper related to JGBs. 'The contract has not set the world on fire,' Carew Hunt conceded to *FOW* in December 1987, while Nicholas Baker of Daiwa observed that local Japanese institutions were still relatively unsophisticated in their use of financial futures: 'These institutions are going through the same learning process that the Europeans went through three or four years ago. They need to become more accountable and there is a move now for them to move off balance sheet.' By March 1988 turnover in Japanese government bond futures was still no greater than about $\frac{1}{15}$ th of the Tokyo Stock Exchange's bond futures market, when (according to *IFR*) it was 'generally believed' that the listing of JGBs on LIFFE 'cannot be termed a success unless trading volume reaches about one-tenth that of the TSE's contract'. Among several reasons being given for this low turnover – about 450 lots a day – the most popular was the contract's lack of deliverability, being cash-settled only, as a result of Tokyo's procedures and tax laws. This meant that it could not be offset against Tokyo's contract, a serious defect. There was also a continuing view that the size of the contract was too big – 'with such a large tick size, it can be very expensive for locals if the market goes against them,' argued Clara Furse to *FOW*. But whatever the causes, its failure by this time was a serious disappointment.

1988 was also the year when not only did volume on the Eurodollar contract on SIMEX surpass the volume of LIFFE's Eurodollar contract, thanks to Singapore's fungibility with the CME, but also when, quite suddenly, the long gilt future lost its commanding ascendency. Alexander Nicoll, in the *FT* on 10 March, called it 'the backbone of the exchange', but that month saw a significant decline in volume, and by September it was no longer top dog. Conditions in the course of the year became increasingly grim in the underlying cash market, as new government issues virtually dried up because of the low PSBR, which indeed for a time even went into surplus, the government becoming a net buyer of gilts; and in the early autumn, Bob Tomkins of Tullett & Tokyo explained to *FOW* the market's expectation that the long gilt would soon 'cease to be the most significant contract because there is going to be no deliverable stock out there in the big volume long gilts this time next year'. Instead, the new pace-setter was that old faithful, the short sterling future, prospering generally and in September trading a record 436,430 lots, an increase of 276% on September 1987. The prime cause of the contract's return to prominence was a renewed bout of British interest rate volatility, with uncertainty compounded by the prolonged fall-out from the celebrated Thatcher/Lawson row in March 1988 over the Chancellor's policy of shadowing the deutschmark, a row that led directly to the uncapping of the pound.

LIFFE had therefore chosen a propitious moment when on 5 November 1987 it listed an option on the short sterling future, the exchange's seventh option contract. Members had been pressing for it for some time, and the expectation was that it would provide UK corporates and banks with an attractive instrument to hedge their sterling interest rate risk. It quickly settled down as the second most popular option, though way behind the long gilt option, and from January to September 1988 achieved a reasonable volume of 274,057 lots. The other new contract introduced in the winter of 1987/8 was the medium gilt future on 7 January, aiming to fill the yield curve gap between short sterling and long gilt. 'The medium dated sector of the cash market,' Carew Hunt informed the board shortly before, 'has become of increasing significance with greater participation by overseas investors (10 years is regarded as a *long* bond maturity in many overseas euro-markets), and the maturity structure of outstanding gilt stocks has become increasingly biassed towards medium-dated stocks.' The contract was based on £50,000 nominal value of gilts, with a 9% coupon and delivery of any gilt with seven to ten years until maturity.

Initial volume was encouraging ('It's like any new contract down here,' a local told *IFR*, 'traders get in the pit to get on the cameras.'), but the contract was soon in trouble. Accordingly, Wigglesworth sounded out some of the top long gilt players who in December had committed themselves to medium gilts (all being then in favour except Phillips & Drew), and reported to the board in March:

A number of people expressed disappointment at the low volume, lack of liquidity and wide spread or touch compared with earlier hopes. One was highly critical that other big names had not been showing 2-way prices as he had. Some pointed to a lack of retail interest and one, who said he had known it would not work, to the dearth of natural long position holders. A small number described how difficult it had been to close client positions. One summed it up as proving that people want liquidity more than they want a hedge.

Despite the above comments a majority expressed hope that it will work, that the reasons it was introduced remain valid, that it is a sound contract and that Building Societies will use it [i.e. once they were permitted, later in the year, to do so].

In the short term we can do little to help in terms of radical measures. The suggestion of a fee waiver is not likely to motivate locals because they would most probably regard the saving of 90 pence fee as insignificant when compared with the chance of making even a one tick turn, worth £15.625, in the liquid long gilt pit where they can expect to deal on a close spread at all times.

It is vital in the short term that perhaps board members pledge their teams to do everything that is commercially possible to ensure reasonable volume.

Soon afterwards the board agreed that there was nothing specific that could be done; and though there were hopes that the issuing of 'C' shares would help in due course to attract locals to the contract, the stark facts were that in June only 2,096 lots were traded and in July a pitiful 84. Still, at least there was a contract in existence, unlike the fairly wretched saga of the Eurobond contract. The October 1987 crash severely affected the London cash market, making it so illiquid as to distort prices and jeopardise any index, and the following May the project was effectively shelved, or put on the 'back burner' as Jenkins told *Euromoney*.

None of this, however, had anything to do with the strategic plot unfolding in year six – the pivotal year, as it turned out, of LIFFE's history. In October 1987 the strategy review argued with the utmost emphasis that over the next few years LIFFE needed to establish itself beyond question as the dominant financial futures exchange in the European time zone. 'Throughout Europe,' it asserted, LIFFE needed to 'develop local membership and products, and market international products, so as to anticipate the formation of potentially competitive exchanges', of which 'the obvious immediate example is in Germany'. The message sank home, for at the board meeting (with Burton in the chair in Williamson's absence) to discuss the strategy review, when 'it was questioned whether LIFFE should take a more global approach rather than concentrating on European markets', it was 'generally agreed that London ought to establish itself as the dominant European Futures exchange and that this in itself would represent a major challenge'. Burton succeeded Williamson as chairman the following spring, and almost certainly he was appreciably keener than his predecessor to focus LIFFE's efforts on the competitive European goal rather than trying to construct ambitious alliances dependent on a seamless world of 24-hour trading. Of course it was only a difference of emphasis, but it was an important difference.

Undeniably the overall mood in summer 1988, his first few months as chairman, was somewhat edgy. MATIF was doing sufficiently well in French government bonds for Goodison to claim in late May that Paris had overtaken London in financial futures, with a daily volume of 65,000 contracts as compared with LIFFE's 55,000; over the next few weeks there were some well-publicised defections (including Exco) amongst the membership; GLOBEX continued to pose

an imponderable, rather ominous threat; no one now imagined that the glory days
would return for LIFFE's dollar-denominated products; and quite suddenly the
long gilt future was no longer the surefire winner that it had recently been. Put
another way, if the European strategy was really to work, what was now needed
was a new, knock-out product – a product that would be LIFFE's own, as opposed
to a scrap from someone else's table, and have a wide European appeal. Happily,
through a mixture of planning, determination and luck, that very product was
being designed. It was of course the German government bond future.

How the Bund contract came to be traded on LIFFE is one of the more fascinating
episodes in contemporary international financial history. In October 1987, three
months after the Deutsche Bank initiative that unofficially but decisively reopened
possibilities, it was still very much Albright's baby. On the 14th she talked on the
telephone to Mario Francescotti, head trader for Bunds (i.e. German government
bonds [GGBs]) at Morgan Stanley in London and, according to Albright's report,
not only 'arguably the biggest trader of cash Bunds in or outside of Germany' but
also 'very keen on a Bund futures contract'. His briefing on the politics of the
situation could hardly have been more helpful:

- *The Bundesbank sees its role as promoting non-inflationary economic
  growth in Germany. It does not believe it exists to protect the German
  banking system from change or competition.*

- *So the Bundesbank may think a LIFFE GGB future is okay. The MOF
  [Ministry of Finance] in Bonn may object, however.*

- *Mario feels that a deliverable contract might encourage the development
  of a repo market in Bunds, which the Bundesbank opposes as they fear
  this would cause further increases in the money supply.*

- *The Bundesbank's main concerns are its ability to control the money
  supply, the German money markets and the exchange rate. LIFFE's plans
  for a GGB must address these areas of concern.*

- *A cash settled contract would mean that no large capital flows would
  result from delivery. Also the Bundesbank would be able to intervene at
  the FSE [Frankfurt Stock Exchange] fixing and thus feel in control of
  contract pricing. Cash settlement would also be a convenient way around
  the difficult German legal environment.*

- *The views of the German banks may not be that decisive in stopping LIFFE. The banking lobby is weakening in Germany – public perception is that banks are fat cats deserving no special favour.*

- *Morgan Stanley cannot openly support LIFFE however. They will not do anything to upset either the Bundesbank or the big German banks. They need the latter to off-load large client positions.*

In short, the project was politically possible, but would need considerable acumen if it was to be steered through.

On 22 October – the Thursday after the crash – Albright and Mary Lou Carrington were in Frankfurt for three important meetings. At the Deutsche Bank they were unable to see von Ribbentrop 'due to the state of the market', but Hung Tran was available, and Carrington recorded his thoughts:

The official view on a LIFFE GGB is that we should pursue it ourselves. Although they gave us the idea four [in fact three] months ago, they are strong backers of a local exchange [plans for the German Options and Financial Futures Exchange (GOFFEX) had been announced in August] and don't want to send mixed signals to the Bundesbank. This does not mean that they wouldn't use the contract on LIFFE.

Advice on approaching the Bundesbank – Be open about our plans citing the strong interest expressed by all the German banks. Have prepared case studies on how trading problems from the past week could have been alleviated by using futures and options.

They would support LIFFE doing courses in Frankfurt and would send their traders.

Albright reported on the other two meetings. At Salomons the managing director of the bank's Frankfurt operation, Peter Coym, was wonderfully unequivocal:

Do it – everyone wants a GGB contract.

Bundesbank strategy. Go in at highest possible level – Pöhl (or failing that, Köhler) – with LIFFE Chairman.

Pay no attention to underlings saying no.

Don't let anyone else speak on your behalf. Go in yourselves.

Coym would be very surprised if Köhler or Pöhl said no.

Might not be a bad idea to give them some idea of our thinking in advance, i.e. the alternative contract design structures. Keep the pressure on and the momentum up. If we can do a contract in 3 months, this is a tactical advantage. The closer our timing becomes to GOFFEX's, the less likely we'd get a 'yes'.

Tell everyone you're going to do this, and put the pressure on. This is an unusual business opportunity for LIFFE but must be pursued NOW.

When LIFFE Chairman visits Frankfurt, he should see the capital markets board members *for each of the largest banks.*

Nor did Heinz-Jurgen Rentsch, a vice president of Bank of America, hold back:

Go for it! We must have GGB futures ASAP. If not Frankfurt – go ahead in London. You've already got infrastructure, experience, reputation.

He prefers cash settlement based on FSE fixings – deliverable contract could have more legal problems.

Why ask the FSE about using their prices? Everyone else uses them, i.e. all retail business in GGBs is done at FSE fixing prices. If we ask, that gives FSE the possibility of saying no. Also, FSE has many committees, therefore much delay. Factions – big banks vs. stockbrokers vs. regional banks. They won't agree easily even among themselves.

He bets a bottle of good German wine that Bundesbank will say no – after a lot of polite discussion, exchange of information and time, because they fear loss of control to overseas forces. But TRY. As a last resort, send the Bundesbank a letter with a concrete, thoroughly researched proposal. They HATE letters because then they have to say in writing why they don't like the futures proposal, and they would be very reluctant to do that as they'd look retrogressive.

Altogether it was a thoroughly encouraging trio of responses. The following day, however, the two American women pitched up at the gloomy and forbidding surroundings of Wilhelm-Epstein-Strasse 14, home of the Bundesbank. There they were seen by a director, Kurt Seifarth, who had been fairly discouraging two years earlier and was much more so now:

Bundesbank's official position is that futures and options are O.K.; if the banks want Bundesanleihen [i.e. German government bond] futures they should have them: Bundesbank is working with the Federation of German Stock Exchanges and the big banks on GOFFEX. When GOFFEX is ready, the world will have a GGB future. Until then, Bundesbank does not want anyone else to start one.

It was a brief report (by Albright) on a brief meeting, a *mauvais quart d'heure* that ended on a chilly, ultra-formal note. Carrington's reaction on leaving the building was to forget the whole thing, but her companion was adamant that they should persist.

Albright now concentrated on writing a lengthy paper about the proposed contract, sent to Jenkins on 3 November and in turn passed on to the board. She gave details of how the cash market in German government bonds was 'one of the largest and most international in the world', with turnover greater in London than in Germany. 'The stable political climate and strength of the deutschmark have made GGBs very attractive to foreign investors in recent years,' she explained, and accordingly 'the price moves in the market originate from foreign buying and selling, not from the domestic investors.' It was also, she claimed, a 'quite volatile' market, 'showing approximately a 6 point trading range in the first 9 months of 1987 and an 8 point range in the abnormal conditions of October 1987'; yet 'there are few hedging mechanisms for Bunds, all of them inadequate', which explained why all the major traders of Bunds, in both London and Frankfurt, whom she had met 'strongly feel they need a futures contract in Bunds at the earliest possible date'. Albright then outlined the somewhat confused regulatory and political climate in Germany for futures and options, discussed alternative design structures for a GGB futures contract, and asked for support in trying to launch the contract as quickly as possible. 'We know that MATIF, the CBOT and even Luxembourg are also eager to trade a GGB future,' she noted, 'so we need to pursue the opportunity expeditiously'. She concluded by recommending that the Bank of England be kept in the picture and that a meeting be arranged with the Bundesbank at 'the highest possible level'.

Williamson always relished acting at the highest level, and he now picked up the challenge. In mid-November he set up a meeting on 14 December with Professor Claus Köhler at the Bundesbank (Pöhl being unavailable); and he wrote to David Walker expressing 'concern' that 'the Bundesbank may approach the Bank of England as a result of LIFFE's overtures to them for "permission" to trade a German Government Bond on LIFFE', or put more bluntly that one central bank might nobble another.

Soon afterwards, on the 23rd, Phil Bruce and his colleague Laurie McGilvary spent a busy day in Frankfurt sounding out three more banks. Roland Hemmerich, head of bonds at Commerzbank, saw GOFFEX 'as a long way off', claimed that 'the financial community in Germany will definitely use a GGB contract', and expressed 'intense enthusiasm' for LIFFE going ahead but 'would not openly support such a move at this stage'. Josef Wertschulte, head of institutional investment at BHF Bank, who 'was very well prepared for our visit and had done his homework', thought that a GGB contract traded on LIFFE 'would be met with overwhelming success but the Deutsche Bank would not approve', and claimed that he himself had 'no problem with coming out of the closet' in terms of openly supporting the contract. Finally, Klaus-Dieter Rohricht, in charge of bonds at Dresdner Bank, said that although the Bundesbank 'views futures and options and also LIFFE as a bit on the shady side', and Dresdner itself 'could not openly support a LIFFE GGB venture', nevertheless 'they would completely support and trade the contract in London' and he was 'confident of such a contract's success'.

The board met the following day. Albright's paper was 'noted', Williamson said that he would be telling Köhler of LIFFE's wish to proceed 'in conjunction with the German banks', and 'it was felt that it could take between 18 months and 3 years to complete the appropriate legislation before GOFFEX would be in a position to commence trading'. It would seem that the board was willing to back Albright's project, but without any great enthusiasm.

On 14 December, before going to the Bundesbank at 2 o'clock, Williamson, Jenkins and Albright spent some time with their overt and covert allies in Frankfurt. Hemmerich at Commerzbank and Wertschulte at BHF both advised on tactics ('Be prepared to reassure Köhler on reputation of exchange/independent guarantee,' Williamson scribbled in biro on a piece of graph paper), and Coym met them for an early lunch at the Frankfurter Hof, where no notes were made. Then came the big one. Köhler, an influential member of the Bundesbank board and responsible for capital markets, was flanked by two officials, one of them Seifarth. Albright described this memorable encounter:

We explained our development as a market for financial institutions to hedge a wide variety of cash market financial risk in internationally traded instruments. Given this focus, various members (including Deutsche Bank but also several non-German banks) had suggested we provide a GGB futures contract. After 32 meetings with German and foreign banks both inside Germany and in London, we had found very broad and very enthusiastic support for a GGB future on LIFFE, and it was our intention to respond to this market need by providing such a contract.

Professor Köhler explained that the Bundesbank's concern re deutschmark securities focuses on the 'issuing' market. For example, the Bundesbank does not want to see the equivalent of a yankee or bulldog bond market arise for DM bonds. However, the 'trading' (i.e. secondary) market was free to develop as it wished, and LIFFE's proposal fell in the latter category.

Professor Köhler asked if we know about GOFFEX, and RBW said yes, and that we were quite happy to help them in any way we can. Further, that we have no intention to trade options on German equities.

Reinhard asked if we'd seen MOF in Bonn and RBW said we wanted to see the Bundesbank first.

Seifarth asked if we did not encounter opposition to our plans in some departments of German banks even if others indicated support. KA responded that in the bond trading areas of the banks we visited we had found universal support, in small as well as large German banks.

Note to the GGB file
From: Kim Albright
Meeting: 14 December 1987 at Deutsche Bundesbank, Frankfurt

Bundesbank: Professor Claus

Professor Koehler explained that the Bundesbank's concern re DM securities focuses on the "issuing" market. For example, the Bundesbank does not want to the equivalent of a yankee or bulldog bond market use for DM bonds. However, the "trading" (i.e. secondary) market was free to develop as it wished, LIFFE's proposal fell in the latter category.

1. We explained our development as a market for financial institutions to hedge a wide variety of cash market financial risk in internationally traded instruments. this focus, various members (including Deutsche Bank but also several non-German banks) had suggested we provide a GGB futures contract.

2. etings with German and foreign banks both Germany and in London, we had found very broad enthusiastic support for a GGB future on and it was our intention to respond to this market need by providing such a contract.

3. Professor Koehler explained that the Bundesbank's concern re DM securities focuses on the "issuing" market. For example, the Bundesbank does not want to the equivalent of a yankee or bulldog bond market for DM bonds. However, the "trading" (i.e. secondary) market was free to develop as it wished, and LIFFE's proposal fell in the latter category.

Professor Koehler asked if we know about Goffex, and RBW said yes, and that we were quite happy to help them in any way we can. Further, that we have no intention to trade options on German equities.

Reinhardt asked if we'd seen MOF in Bonn and RBW replied we wanted to see the Bundesbank first.

6. Seifarth asked if we did not encounter opposition to our plans in some departments of German banks even if others indicated support. KA responded that in the bond trading areas of the banks we visited we had found universal support, in small as well as large German banks.

NAME OF FIRM: BUNDESBANK
PERSON SEEN: Kurt Seifarth
TITLE: Bundesbankdirektor

Bundesbank's official position is that futures and options are O.K.; if the banks want Bundesanleihen futures they should have them; Bundesbank is working with the Federation of German Stock Exchanges and the big banks on Goffex. When Goffex is ready, the world will have a GGB future. Until then, Bundesbank does not want anyone else to start one.

7. Koehler said that though his colleagues (indicating Reinhardt and Seifarth) did not agree with him, "I really believe we cannot say "no" to you." He added elt the Bund cash market needed a futures act and should have had one two years ago. He at he would have preferred that the German ad organised such a market expeditiously, but repeated that he couldn't say no, and that "it's up you" to decide what to do.

MARKETING REPORT
Salomon Brothers A.G.
PERSON SEEN: Peter Coym

o it - everyone wants a GGB contract.

undesbank strategy
o in at highest possible level - Poehl (or failing that,
with LIFFE Chairman.

ay no attention to undetlings saying no.

on't let anyone else speak on your behalf. Go in yourselves.

oym would be very surprised if Koehler or Poehl said no.
hone Poehl's office to set up meeting and ask for his advice re
ho would be best for our Chairman to see (and ask them to get
ack to us).

ight not be a bad idea to give them some idea of our thinking in
dvance, i.e. the alternative contract design structures. Keep
he pressure or and the momentum up. If we can do a contract in 3
onths, this is a tactical advantage. The closer our timing
ecomes to Goffex's, the less likely we'd get a "yes".

ell everyone you're going to do this, and put the p
his is an unusual business opportunity for LIFFE bu
ursued NOW.

8. Reinhardt wanted LIFFE to discuss the contract detai with the Bundesbank before finalising proposals. Koehler said that Reinhardt would be the man to liai with on this.

9. Regarding Bonn, Koehler said we need not wait until all contract details were finalised to see them. He "I think you have done your research and you are rea to Koehler."

10. We agreed we would go to Bonn to tell MOF of our pla and to review our detailed proposals with Mr. Reinha when they are ready.

BANK OF ENGLAND
LONDON EC2R 8AH
E.A.J. GEORGE
EXECUTIVE DIRECTOR

Very many thanks for your letter of 15 December reporting or positive outcome of your meeting with Professor Koehler at t Bundesbank. This seems extremely satisfactory from every of view, and I wish you every success.

REPORT PREPARED BY: Kim Albright

ith good wishes for Christmas and the New Year.

Handwritten notes:
NOTH HOLD TAX ? JAN89
M.O.F. Wingham
ONLY BONDS.
HOW CAN BUNDESBANK MANIPULATE?
FIXING v B.H.F.
COMPONENT

Köhler said that though his colleagues (indicating Reinhard and Seifarth) did not agree with him, 'I really believe we cannot say "no" to you'. He added that he felt the Bund cash market needed a futures contract and should have had one two years ago. He said that he would have preferred that the German banks had organised such a market expeditiously, but repeated that he couldn't say no, and that 'it's up to you' to decide what to do.

We agreed we would go to Bonn to tell MOF of our plans and to review our detailed proposals with Mr Reinhard when they are ready.

'You see I've gone too far for my officials,' Williamson would recall Köhler as saying, and the London trio left the meeting in the warm knowledge that they had not been refused. Köhler was on the side of shaking up the German financial system, and almost certainly he viewed LIFFE's proposal as a useful weapon.

Once home, Williamson thanked Köhler for his 'frankness' and filled in Walker and Eddie George at the Bank of England. Köhler, he reported, 'accepted the realities and said that provided we had involved the German banks (which we have) he "would not wish to say no"'. George's reply was warm – 'This seems extremely satisfactory from every point of view, and I wish you every success.' – and Köhler himself informed Williamson on the 30th that he had spoken to the Ministry of Finance about LIFFE's plans, adding that 'I consider the co-operation you are envisaging with the originators of GOFFEX and your close relationship with the German banks to be very useful'.

But if the politics so far were going surprisingly well, the worry remained that the contract might be launched in a fanfare of publicity and apparent goodwill, and then flop embarrassingly, just like the recent JGB experience. Albright addressed these concerns in a progress report on 6 January 1988:

A contract could be ready for launch in the Spring, but whether it will be possible to do this successfully depends to a significant extent on whether LIFFE will have adequate trading capacity to provide support for this product. There appears to be significant demand for the product and no competition from either the cash markets or other exchanges. However, if we can design a first-rate contract and effectively market it, our efforts will still be wasted if there are not enough floor traders to execute the trades. We can anticipate both the demand for seats from German banks who aren't already members and also a need for seats by existing members who will have to buy or lease another seat to trade a GGB. In my view, we cannot rely on present traders who are already dedicated to a pit (e.g. long gilt, Eurodollar) coming into the GGB pit on an occasional basis to support the GGB.

Opposite: Exploring prospects for the Bund.

The expansion of trading rights was of course in the offing, but at this stage no one knew exactly when it would happen or how effective the creation of 'C' shares would be in ensuring that new contracts were given a fair wind on the floor.

Jenkins and Albright met Waldemar Mueller-Enders of the Ministry of Finance in Bonn on 14 January. It proved neither comforting nor utterly disastrous:

MOF wants the contract to start in Frankfurt first. Then, after seeing how it works, they might consider allowing such a thing elsewhere. In that light, we (LIFFE and MOF) should have our discussion.

MJ said we are in a position to start in three, four or six months. Our discussions with many German and foreign banks have shown that there is a need now for such a contract. We have the infrastructure in place already, including clearing. We understand the desire to have a futures contract begin first in Frankfurt and Frankfurt is the logical place ultimately. As an exchange, however, we are the servants of our members and are obliged to introduce the products they require.

Mueller-Enders then asked a series of questions – on the riskiness of margin trading, on Big Bang, on whether futures increased cash volatility, on whether the cash market would move to London if futures were there, on tax problems for people using futures, on the events of October, and whether there was enough volatility in Bunds to make a futures contract successful – which Jenkins and Albright answered as best they could, as well as explaining (with the MOF apparently not wholly in the picture) that the Bundesbank had said that the cash market needed a futures contract, that it would prefer to see the contract in Germany first but that could be some time away, and that LIFFE should keep it informed of any plans. Whereupon:

After further discussion, Mueller-Enders said we had changed some of their thinking and he would report the content of our meeting to Mr Tietmeyer, his boss. He said he was sorry Mr Tietmeyer had been unable to see us this time. He said we couldn't have expected to get a 'green light' from them on the first visit.

Mr Mueller-Enders tried to leave the impression that we needed to come back to Bonn and that they would decide when that would be. He thanked us for answering all their questions. MJ said we would be happy to come back and see them again.

Albright was fairly downcast, but four days later she received some invaluable advice from Coym of Salomons. It was, as paraphrased by her: 'Write a letter to Tietmeyer, explain what we're going to do, advantages for health of Bund mkt. To avoid confusion, could they confirm no objection to LIFFE's plans… MOF may not answer the letter, but they would be v. reluctant to say no in black & white.' Williamson accordingly wrote to Tietmeyer on the 20th. He formally outlined the proposal to introduce the contract, emphasised that LIFFE had no wish to 'pre-empt' a financial futures market developing in Frankfurt, and referred to 'the detailed co-operation we have had from the major German banks'. Coym's prediction proved quite correct. There was no reply – and therefore no veto.

So far none of this had got into the press, but that was about to change. 'LIFFE eyes D-Mark business' was the *FT*'s headline on 18 February, with Haig Simonian breaking the story about LIFFE's intentions and noting that so far the signals from Germany's leading banks had been somewhat 'confusing'. One figure whom he identified as now definitely antagonistic was Rolf Breuer, not only a board member of Deutsche Bank but also one of the driving forces behind the development of GOFFEX. 'If LIFFE were to go ahead,' Simonian reported, 'Deutsche Bank would not trade its futures contract.' The following day (with Bruce at a technical meeting at the Bundesbank to go through the contract's draft specifications) the German press published an interview with Breuer in which he stated that he and his fellow-bankers were convinced that GOFFEX was on course for opening by the end of 1989, that 'we don't need a deutschmark contract before that at LIFFE', and that 'I can't imagine that a London contract without participation of the leading German institutions is going to work'.

The atmosphere was accordingly rather sticky when, in Frankfurt on the 22nd, Williamson, Jenkins and Albright had a meeting with Dietrich-Kurt Frowein, a member of the Commerzbank board of managing directors and on the GOFFEX steering committee, and two of his colleagues:

> Frowein said everyone agrees a Bund future is needed 'so let's come to the point'. We said we were well aware of GOFFEX plans and would like to co-operate with GOFFEX, perhaps in providing compatible systems, procedures, etc. for a common contract.
>
> They asked if we'd seen the Bundesbank and we told them about our meeting with Professor Köhler. They seemed not to want to believe that we'd been told by the Bundesbank some weeks ago that they 'would not stand in our way'.

Financial Times, 18 February 1988.

They also asked what our timing was (we said mid-year). Frowein confirmed GOFFEX start in late 1989 with futures added after that.

Frowein said it was impossible for GOFFEX to talk to anyone else right now. He said they are in the process of finalising their agreement with SOFFEX [the Swiss Options and Financial Futures Exchange due to open in Zurich] and this takes precedence over all else. We tried again to put the case for co-operation with LIFFE. Eventually Frowein said he would mention this to Dr. Breuer.

Frowein said 'we don't want to be unfriendly', but that LIFFE's activities and plans had come at a very unfortunate and difficult time given their own plans.

GOFFEX was in the process of being renamed Deutsche Terminbörse [DTB], with most of what was a considerable capital investment coming from the main German banks. 'On the one hand, solidarity with DTB is expected of us,' a senior German banker, asking not to be named, told the *Wall Street Journal* in an article published on the 25th. 'On the other, we say, "if there's an instrument already available, why shouldn't we use it?"' And the same article, to LIFFE's considerable pleasure, quoted Köhler: 'We would have been very pleased, of course, if this had been a German exchange, but as it turns out, the project is from London and we shan't say no.'

Albright noted in her progress report on 8 March that it was 'important to defuse the political aspect of LIFFE's plans so that the German banks are able to view our efforts as being complementary to their Bund trading activities'; but her main emphasis was now more functional, being the need over the next few weeks to 'speak to GGB traders and LIFFE brokers to review the contract design alternatives with them, seek a consensus on contract design, and enlist their specific "Day 1" support for the contract'. There ensued a period of considerable doubt and even soul-searching as to whether the contract should be a cash-settled index (as per the original design) or a deliverable contract. The protracted inquiry and debate delayed the launch by some three months, but it was crucial to get this right. The main pressure for a deliverable contract came from American firms (including Louis Dreyfus, Goldman Sachs and Merrill Lynch), arguing that people knew how to trade cash-and-carry, in the fashion of T-bonds, and that this was crucial for the contract's liquidity. The technical problem with delivery was that most German bonds were poorly or tardily delivered; but help came from J.P. Morgan in Frankfurt, where Nick Pugh (head of non-government dollar bond trading) said that it would act as delivery agent there, an offer which made it much easier for Bruce to transform the Bund future into a deliverable contract.

At no point does the board seem to have made a formal, final decision on whether or not to launch the contract, but on 27 April it received threefold reassurance from Albright: seven member firms had already agreed to become designated brokers (i.e. members prepared to commit a full-time broker to the

Bund pit for a minimum of three months); it was looking as if it would be possible to design a deliverable contract; and Deutsche Bank, she explained in response to a specific query, 'were on record as saying that they would not boycott LIFFE's contract'. Almost certainly an undertow of scepticism lingered, with doubts being expressed privately if not on the record about the plausibility of traders thronging around a Bund pit. While from the trading community itself, 'Why should we do anything to help the Germans?' was reputedly the response of one prominent local.

The contract was publicly announced on 7 June, to be launched on 29 September, as usual with new contracts a Thursday. Details of the designated brokers scheme were also published, with 16 members (none of them German) making a firm commitment by the end of June. The scheme was a direct result of what had happened after the misleadingly euphoric JGB launch, but Leslie Sutphen of Pru Bache complained to *FOW* that it was an unhealthy precedent, in that a broker might be committed to a contract but still not wish to commit one person to the pit at all times. Soon afterwards, on 11 July, Jenkins told the board that at his recent meeting in Paris it had been 'apparent that MATIF had been hoping to introduce a GGB contract but had been pre-empted by LIFFE'. With the Banque de France, concerned about Franco-German relations, having blocked that possibility, this was an obvious source of satisfaction; but the crucial question remained the attitude of the German banks once the contract actually started trading. Simonian in the *FT* on the 13th referred to a 'ban' on the part of Deutsche and other banks sponsoring the DTB, but was careful to put that emotive three-letter word in inverted commas, pointing out that how easy the boycott would be to maintain 'remains to be seen', given this long-awaited chance to hedge exposures in German government securities. A fortnight later the *International Herald Tribune* quoted a seemingly relaxed Breuer: 'We're not worried about London competition this fall. They first have to show what they can do.'

The weeks leading up to 29 September featured an intensive round of courses and briefings in Germany and elsewhere in Europe on the new contract, with a key role being played by the recently recruited Ralf Herklotz, a German who, as a graduate of the leading management school INSEAD, spoke fluent French. Most of the presentations were oversubscribed, especially in Frankfurt, and at Carrington's insistence each started with a German lawyer stressing the legality of the new contract, in other words in terms of institutions trading derivatives. Altogether it was a massive operation, with many ramifications. There were, for example, no technical words in German for certain English expressions relevant to the nascent futures industry in Germany, so these had to be specially invented. Well over a thousand traders and back office people had to be educated – mainly in Germany, but also in London – and Price Waterhouse helped in Germany by setting out accounting principles and tax procedures, without which it would have been difficult for futures trading there to have gone ahead.

Norman Lamont (second
from left) launches the Bund
futures contract,
29 September 1988.

On 19 September an internal circular at LIFFE announced a fee holiday for
the Bund contract, and in the last few days before the launch there was
considerable press attention, including much speculation about the likely
behaviour of the German banks. Ulrich von Schilling of Bailey Shatkin was quoted
as saying that all the German banks were willing to use the contract, whatever the
party line. 'They are not being very public about it, but I think there will be German
trading come Thursday,' agreed Linda Glover of Midland Montagu Futures. 'It's
not a market they can ignore.' While according to an unnamed German banker:
'It's so easy to do it without being seen. You just give a call to another broker and
have it done on your behalf.' The official attitude of the German banks was strictly
non-committal, but there were probably few observers who would have disagreed
with the maxim that was now quoted, from an unnamed vice-president of an
American bank in Frankfurt, that 'profits speak louder than pride'.

A burst of noise greeted Norman Lamont, Financial Secretary to the Treasury,
as he rang the bell at 8.10 am to signal the start of trading. 'It sounds more like a
revolution than an extension of capitalism,' he remarked afterwards. 2,939 lots
were traded in the first hour and a half, and total volume for the first day was a
perfectly respectable 9,097. LIFFE on the eve of its sixth anniversary had become
the first financial futures exchange in the world to have bond contracts in the four
most actively traded currencies, at last giving full validity to its claim to be a
genuinely international exchange. It was also LIFFE's first non-UK European
contract, and both Lamont and Burton talked of it as a significant step by the City
of London in preparation for the single European market of 1992. But would it
succeed? Alan Dickinson, with his trader's instinct, had his doubts, and he was
not on his own. Even in a market devoted to guessing the future, few saw history
in the making.

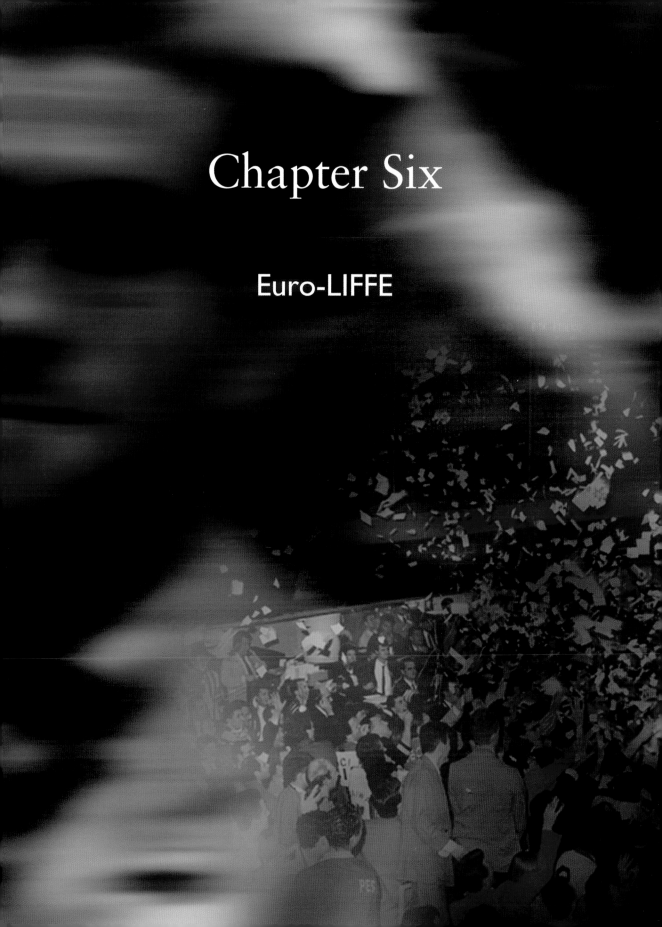

Chapter Six

Euro-LIFFE

THE CITY OF London was a nervous place in the late 1980s and early 1990s, adjusting to painful realities that the reckless expansion and structural transformation of the mid-1980s had largely concealed. 'Will the City ever recover?' asked *Institutional Investor* in November 1989, looking back on twelve months of redundancies, readjustments and much reduced profits. 'Big Bang bred overambition that not even the crash fully cured – until now,' ran the blurb below. 'Chastened and suffering, the City has lately spawned a survivor culture…' And the story quoted Duncan Duckett, chairman of Marshall & Co: 'Imagine London like a village. It had a fish-and-chip shop and a couple of corner cafés. Then suddenly in come French restaurants, McDonalds, pasta joints and sushi bars. Hell, people can only eat three meals a day.'

But apart from the domestic digestive problem, there was also the international aspect. The larger purpose of Big Bang, after all, had been to bolster London's position as an international financial centre. Had it done the trick? 'Reports of London's relative decline as a financial centre are premature,' argued 'Lex' in October 1989, on the event's third anniversary, but LIFFE's board was not so sure when it discussed the City's prospects the following June:

In the short term the outlook appeared to be favourable for the City. Deregulation will benefit London as markets are opened up. The use of English as the prime international language, and the available investment expertise, will continue to ensure that benefits accrue to the City. However, in the longer term the outlook was difficult to predict. There was concern that the role of sterling may diminish; the advantages of the City may be eroded by the introduction of new technology; the City's ability to innovate to meet changes in market conditions was not guaranteed, nor was it possible to predict the level of government support in the future.

By 1991, with '1992' and the single market sneaking up fast, and also the possibility of a single currency in the more distant offing, the press was awash with articles gauging London's chances of fending off the competition from other European financial centres, above all Frankfurt and Paris. Sir Martin Jacomb, writing as chairman of BZW in the *Independent* in April, caught what was becoming the prevailing tone among the City's more thoughtful practitioners:

Today it is no longer obvious that London will be the only place for international business. With instant communications and no exchange or capital controls, such business can be done anywhere. We need to work to keep it here.

Merely proclaiming that London is the only financial centre of Europe does little more than excite the competition. It does not create much incremental business, but brings home to the governments of France and Germany, and indeed of Spain, Italy and the Netherlands, how important invisible earnings are – and naturally they want to avoid losing domestic business to London.

Five years later it would be pretty clear that the battle had been won; but in the early 1990s there was no such sense of certainty.

LIFFE, bucking the City gloom, was already playing a significant part in that battle. In the first half of 1989 no less than four months produced a record monthly volume (including 2.41m contracts in June); on 16 October, amidst falls in world equity markets, a new daily record of 382,209 lots was established, comprehensively demolishing the record set a few weeks earlier of 200,446 lots; and the total 1989 volume, some 24m contracts, represented an increase of 53% over 1988. Growth only slightly abated during 1990 – volume up by 44%, with over 34m contracts traded – and more records continued to be set in 1991, including in February a volume of 3.7m lots that easily beat the August 1990

The growth of LIFFE business, 1987–91.

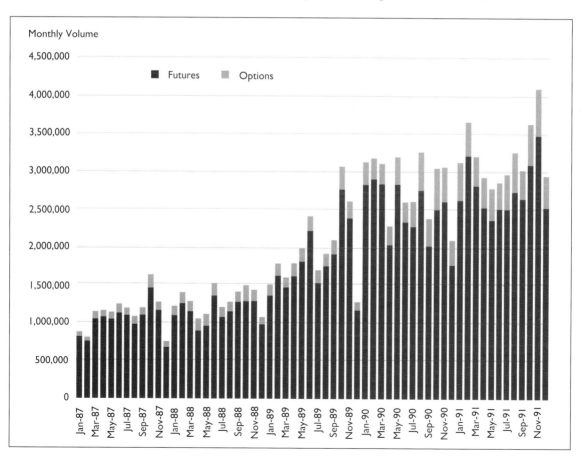

record of 3.3m. Volume for the first half of the year was 18.6m contracts, a 6% increase on the same period in 1990; and for 1991 as a whole, the turnover of nearly 38.6m contracts was a 12.9% increase on the 1990 level. It was LIFFE's ninth successive record year, a remarkable achievement, and for the second year running it was named as *International Financing Review*'s International Exchange of the Year.

Nevertheless, the sobering fact remained that, amidst the rapid and far-flung proliferation of financial futures exchanges, LIFFE by autumn 1991 enjoyed a share of the global market that was only some 7.8% – compared to London's roughly 20% of the insurance market and cross-border banking market, 30% of the foreign exchange market, 50% of the shipping freight market, and at least 70% of the international equity market. The American exchanges may have been starting to worry that their traditional ascendency was beginning to be eroded by the upstart European exchanges, but in 1991 their share of the world derivatives market was still almost two-thirds, compared to Europe's one-fifth. The European competition was increasingly what mattered to LIFFE, but in global terms it was a struggle between minnows.

There were some memorable days and weeks during this period, when agitated traders dealing in high volume responded to major, uncertainty-inducing events in the world at large. In Britain there were the death-throes of the Thatcher government, marked by Lawson's resignation, Thatcher's reluctant entry into the ERM, and her fall a few weeks later; in Europe, there was the even more seismic fall of Communism, the reunification of Germany, and the dramatic coup against Gorbachev; and in the Middle East there was Saddam's invasion of Kuwait and the ensuing Gulf War. 'The world has a great deal of problems,' remarked Melamed in early 1991, adding that 'futures are in the forefront to protect against upheaval'. And upheaval, like fate in *Gentlemen Prefer Blondes*, kept on happening.

A more or less final set of obstacles was removed during these years. Already in July 1988 the Inland Revenue had published a Statement of Practice that had sought to clarify – especially for portfolio managers – the tax treatment of futures and options; while from 1 October that year, building societies were at last allowed, subject to the approval of the Building Societies Commission, to use the short sterling and gilt futures and options contracts as part of their treasury risk management. 1989 saw the dismantling of particular regulatory restrictions preventing the offer and sale of LIFFE's products in the US. Then in 1990 a protracted campaign (that had culminated in October 1989 in a submission to Nigel Lawson just before he resigned as Chancellor) at last bore fruit, when that year's Finance Act enabled UK pension funds and authorised unit trusts to use futures and options without fear of uncertainty as to the taxation consequences.

Did end-user attitudes decisively change along with these enhanced opportunities? 'No place to hide' was the title of a July 1990 piece in *FOW* by Neil Wilson, who argued that there were 'already signs that the Brave New World may not come quite so fast or the change be quite so profound as the more optimistic pundits suggest', having found that the traditional caution of UK fund managers was changing only very slowly. He quoted Roger Marshall of the National Association of Pension Funds: 'There will probably be a lengthy learning process.' Nevertheless, over the next year or so there was a perceptible change. Early in 1991 a survey by KPMG Management Consulting of the leading pension funds found that nine out of the UK's ten top pension funds used futures and options in their funds, with seven out of ten saying that they were likely to increase their use over the coming twelve months. 'It's just possible UK pension fund managers are getting the hang of derivatives,' wrote Wilson in *FOW* soon afterwards; while according to Tracy Corrigan in the *FT* in November 1991, UK fund managers were finally 'waking up to the applications of derivatives, particularly in areas such as individual stock selection or asset allocation'. She quoted the investment director of British Rail's pension fund: 'We certainly don't have a knee-jerk reaction against derivative products. We have a stipulation that derivatives should be used for investment purposes.'

In practice, the touchstone of institutional attitudes remained their willingness or otherwise to use the FTSE 100 future. Addressing a no-doubt sceptical NAPF audience in 1990, Andrew Threadgold of PosTel Investment Management explained its merits:

Index futures provide a convenient mechanism to obtaining cheaply and quickly economic exposure to a market. Typically, the aim is to buy the futures contract when it is at a discount to fair value and roll in to the underlying stock when the futures are at a premium... We learned one or two useful things during the October 1987 crash. We were long of index futures and were reluctant to sell them when they were at a truly substantial discount to the cash market. We now know that the futures were giving a truer picture of the cash market than the cash market itself... Increasingly we see the equity futures market reacting before the spot market to changes in market sentiment. When there is divergence between the two, we tend to believe the futures price.

Very gradually the message was getting home. It was still a highly professional market – 'the day when the average punter bets on the FTSE future rather than Desert Orchid is still a distant prospect,' noted 'Lex' in January 1991 – but turnover on the contract in 1990 was 40% up on the previous year. Daily volume was still only some 6,000 lots, but at least the trend was in the right direction, and it continued into 1991. As for outside use of the product range as a whole, traditionally measured by open interest, at the end of February 1991 it stood at 763,942 contracts, a 33% increase over end-February 1990.

Of course, potentially overshadowing all these moderately encouraging signs, there was the larger question of whether, as some claimed, LIFFE and its fellow exchanges were threatened by the growth of over-the-counter [OTC] deals in derivative products. Both then and later, as far as one can tell, LIFFE's attitude seems to have been broadly relaxed. In June 1990 the board anticipated that, as far as derivatives as a whole were concerned, 'capital adequacy rules would give some bias towards exchange-traded products compared with OTC products' and that 'there would be closer integration with OTC markets'. The following spring Burton publicly dissociated himself from the CME/CBOT view that OTC derivatives should be more strictly regulated in order to curtail their spread: 'It is rubbish to say that the OTC market is taking away volume from the exchanges.' According to Desmond Fitzgerald, by now head of arbitrage at Mitsubishi Finance in London and also talking to *IFR*, it was a case of *vive la différence*: 'My view is to let the OTC continue to develop tailor-made contracts while the exchanges should stick with the simple products... Pit traders are extremely simple souls. If they don't understand the contract, they won't trade it.' Put more kindly, whereas exchanges offer standardisation of contracts and liquidity – what has been called a 'centralised bucket' – OTC is a credit-risk market with few participants, mainly well-capitalised banks; and, as Burton implied, OTC business often leads to hedging on the exchanges, whether on money market contracts or on options. In other words, broadly speaking (with the possible exception of private client business), they have played a complementary role.

The intensity of regulation was of course a key difference, and LIFFE like the rest of the City more or less got used to living with the consequences of the Financial Services Act. Relations with SIB seem to have been good, especially following its push for simplification; while as for the AFBD it was generally accepted that in late 1988, under the chairmanship of Christopher Sharples, it made a manful attempt to weed out the applications of the commodity cowboys, most of them operating a retail, LHW-style business. Nevertheless, even though the securities houses had naturally gravitated to TSA, it was still felt that the AFBD was unduly weighted towards the commodity interest; and following keenly contested council elections in October 1989, Burton told the board that the results had been 'particularly disappointing as far as the candidates identified mainly/wholly with financial futures and options business were concerned'. Accordingly, LIFFE was not opposed to the plan to merge the AFBD with TSA, a plan publicly mooted in June 1990, voted for in November, and implemented in April 1991, creating the Securities and Futures Authority [SFA]. 'It is expected', noted that year's *British Derivatives Markets Handbook*, 'that this will produce more effective and coherent regulation at lower cost for participants in the securities and derivatives markets'. It was a merger that could not have happened without an efficient, well-orchestrated campaign on the part of both the original SROs: many of the stockbroker members of TSA did not want to have anything to do with futures, feeling particularly threatened by financial futures; while the commodity firms who belonged to the AFBD tended to see stockbrokers as condescending and liable to exercise undue clout in a merged body. In the end, though, over 90% of both sides did vote in favour of merger.

LIFFE itself continued to remain enviably scandal-free – in contrast to not only the Chicago exchanges, subject of a lengthy FBI investigation into allegations of widespread corruption and racketeering in the futures pits, but also the London Futures and Options Exchange [London FOX, the former LCE], where in October 1991 it was found that there had been artificial inflating of volume in the exchange's recently launched property contracts. Market surveillance remained a high priority. By early 1989 the new video logging system was working well, while by late 1991 the capacity existed to record simultaneously up to 1,440 channels of telephone conversation between dealers on the trading floor and clients telephoning through instructions.

There remained, though, a question mark over dual capacity trading, i.e. allowing brokers and traders to conduct business on behalf of their own as well as their customers' accounts. An internal survey in May/June 1990 asked whether members would support the introduction of a single capacity requirement, and it found that 'views were divided, with those in favour of moving to single capacity slightly in the majority'. A year later, in the light of the FBI inquiry in Chicago, a working party was set up to re-examine the question, and *IFR* found that LIFFE's brokers and traders remained 'divided on the issue, with some arguing that it adds liquidity and volatility to the market, while others say it merely invites price manipulation'. Nick Buckmaster, senior manager at Daiwa Europe, was insistent that London was not Chicago: 'In Chicago order fillers are about 90% to 95% independent, whereas on LIFFE most brokers retain their own order fillers. So far there has been no problem with dual trading on LIFFE.' Many believed that the introduction of single capacity trading would lead to a reduction in the number of locals, on the grounds that jobbing provided much less security than broking, and that therefore, in the words of one trader, 'liquidity will be reduced because it won't have the local going in and tightening up the market'. The case to the contrary was put by Tony La Roche of Cater Allen: 'I think single capacity trading is quite a good idea. It will remove any doubt that traders are jobbing customers' accounts and making ticks for themselves.' It was a debate that had plenty of mileage left in it.

The rapid rise of the local – usually providing a broking service as well as jobbing for himself (not often herself) – was well under way by spring 1989. By then there were over 100 independent floor traders, and the annual board elections produced what one member described as 'a decisive vote for the floor population', with a greater emphasis on trader representation than had been the case before. The reasons for this surge of locals were probably threefold. Firstly, the new availability of trading permits through the buying or leasing of a 'C' share had unblocked the logjam of access to the market as well as decisively lowering the cost of entry. Secondly, the right product was at hand: 'The Bund is a fantastic contract and you can trade it for nothing,' one new local, Mike Carrington, told Reuters in March. And thirdly, the chilly City climate, with recent major job losses at Exco, Morgan Grenfell and Security Pacific Hoare Govett, meant that many salaried employees on the floor were tempted to set up on their own before the axe fell; there was also a pool of traders recently made redundant who had sufficient financial muscle to enter the market on an independent basis, especially as the cost of leasing a full seat was now only about £10,000 a year, following the steady decline in seat prices from the high point of 1987. A fourth consideration may also have influenced some of LIFFE's dealers into going local, David Morgan telling Reuters that 'the threat of the electronic age has jolted them into thinking that perhaps there's not that long to go, if they want to make serious money'. The rise of the local was a trend that the board now wholeheartedly welcomed – a trend much encouraged by Juliette Proudlove in her role overseeing membership – and Jenkins reported in April 1989 that a review was currently being conducted to examine ways by which the number of own account traders could be further increased.

In terms of broking as such, it was an easier market in the late 1980s in which to make money than it had been in LIFFE's first five or so years, but that halcyon interlude seems to have ended by 1991. 'The London Futures Market – over-broked?' asked *IFR* in February, detailing how increasingly cut-throat competition had led to dwindling broker commissions, with the commission fee for one contract, including clearing and floor broking, down from about £7.50 per round trip at the start of the new decade to as low now as £5–6.50, depending on the client. 'The error risk of trading such contracts is enormous,' remarked one trader with a UK house. 'If there is one out trade, it can wipe out three or four months commission.' Alex Cooper of Crédit Lyonnais Rouse said: 'I think the market is suffering from a surfeit of brokers, though there is always room for well-qualified brokers.' As usual, an imminent shake-out was predicted – and as usual, it largely failed to materialise, presumably because the financial futures industry as a whole was still on such a steep growth curve that it seemed foolhardy to abandon it.

LIFFE itself underwent a fundamental corporate reconstruction in July 1989. The existing company, The London International Financial Futures Exchange Limited, a company limited by guarantee of £10 per member, continued to run the market. A new holding company, LIFFE (Holdings) plc, was put in place.

Members exchanged their original seats for 'A' shares of £20,000 each in LIFFE (Holdings) plc, their 'B' shares in LIFFE Options plc for 'B' shares of £5,000 each, and their 'C' shares in LIFFE Futures plc for 'C' shares of £5,000 each in the new holding company. The voting rights were all in proportion to the nominal values of the new shares. It had become apparent that the original corporate structure had serious disadvantages – including VAT on the issue of seats and on transfers, CGT on the net proceeds of seat issues, and the problem of entering any major property commitment or raising finance for the future through a company limited by guarantee. The reconstruction meant that a company limited by guarantee was replaced by a company with a substantial share capital and that the VAT and CGT burdens were removed. Essentially the reconstruction was about tax, but it did not attract any tax liability for members or the exchange and was not a matter of controversy. It was a sensible solution, masterminded by Foyle, and subsequently the company operating the market was renamed LIFFE Administration and Management.

GLOBEX loomed large in these years, even though it progressively showed every sign of turning into a huge white elephant. Towards the end of 1988, Jenkins reported to the board not only on the CME's latest terms, but also a field trip to New York that Albright, Barton and Mather had undertaken to evaluate the system itself that Reuters was developing:

It was clear that the GLOBEX system was not a substitute for APT; it is a relatively slow-speed order-matching system based on Reuters' dealing system for foreign exchange and US Treasury Bonds. Mr Melamed had explained [on a recent visit to London] that CME membership had insisted that its Board had a majority control over GLOBEX. He recognised that this would give problems to other participating exchanges, which they were trying to tackle...

Early in 1989 the board reached a 'consensus' against participating in GLOBEX 'unless the current terms could be substantially improved', with board members expressing 'particular concern about the loss of independence and the restrictions likely to be imposed on product development'; soon afterwards MATIF made it clear that it was intending to join GLOBEX rather than accepting LIFFE's offer of having APT on licence; and at the next board meeting, on 13 February, the decision was taken that, while options should remain open in terms of an arrangement with one or other of the Chicago exchanges, the important thing was to maintain freedom of action and to press on with APT.

The CBOT itself was now pursuing the development of automated trading (having to eat many of its 1987 words in the process), but following rival presentations by it and the CME at the FIA's Boca Raton meeting in Florida in early March, the LIFFE view was that, if there was to be an involvement with either system, then GLOBEX had the edge over the CBOT's Aurora system. For a time it looked as if negotiations with the Merc were getting somewhere – over trading hours, products to be put or not put on GLOBEX, and a start date of September 1990 – but the basic, unpalatable fact remained that as a sub-licensee LIFFE would not be a party to the CME/Reuters agreement, whose terms could therefore be changed without reference to LIFFE, and furthermore not only would limitations be imposed on the expansion of LIFFE's membership but also the GLOBEX board, on which the CME would have a controlling interest, would be responsible for setting all GLOBEX fees, admitting new exchanges and approving all system changes. There was also the question of whether APT was viewed by the Merc as compatible, even if used only in London, with plugging some of LIFFE's products into GLOBEX. Almost certainly it was, from the Merc's standpoint, incompatible. In May the negotiations were broken off, apparently by the CME but not to LIFFE's sorrow.

Despite the formidable CME propaganda machine, and in particular Melamed's persuasive salesmanship, LIFFE's was a negotiating position based on technological strength as well as native obstinacy. 'After watching a demonstration of APT,' wrote Prest in the *Independent* on 2 May, 'one has the suspicion that GLOBEX is out of date before it has started.' And he explained that whereas GLOBEX 'essentially matches orders, removing much of the flexibility of pits', APT's 'prime virtue is that it tries to emulate the rules and practice of pit trading on the screen', above all the open outcry principle that bids and offers should be executed 'while the breath is warm'. LIFFE and the CME now pursued their separate approaches, though soon afterwards there was some ill feeling caused when the London exchange unsuccessfully attempted, on anti-competitive grounds, to persuade the DTI to refuse recognition of the CME as an overseas investment exchange and thereby being allowed to install GLOBEX terminals in London.

On 2 October the board formally decided to launch APT on 30 November 1989, having been told that 42 members had ordered 50 terminals, that the simulated trading sessions had shown that APT did indeed provide a realistic trading environment, and that a number of 'vendors, including Reuters, had promised to report APT price information'. A week later members were invited to the Savoy, where they were given a demonstration of APT in action. The emphasis of the presentation was on reassurance, showing how use of the 'mouse' on a colour graphics screen would enable extremely high-speed, absolutely fair trading, both short-term arbitrage, day trading and scalping and long-term position building and liquidating. It was also of course emphasised that APT had been implemented in order to supplement – not replace – open outcry trading.

From all points of view that was a thoroughly well-advised emphasis, for barely a week after the Savoy presentation there was the astonishing day, on 16 October, when LIFFE's volume hit 382,209 lots, nearly double the previous daily record. 'Fucking automate that if you can,' one exhausted local challenged Barton at the end of the day, and for all the crudity he had a point. APT itself went live smoothly enough on 30 November, with an evening trading session (4.30–6.00) in the Euromark futures contract (introduced earlier in the year). It was a system that, under Mather's impressive direction, had been built on a shoestring, costing only £1.6m; and from the start it worked very well, the envy of many other futures exchanges. 'LIFFE is very proud of this achievement,' announced Burton on the first day, and it was right to be.

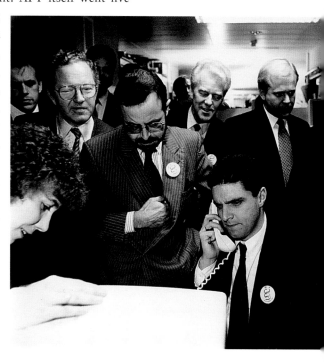

APT's launch day, 30 November 1989. Clockwise from left: Vana Leonard, Ian Nash, Jack Wigglesworth, John Foyle, David Burton, Ian Bush, Mark Williams.

Yet in a sense APT would become over the years rather like the front room in a northern working-class home, much admired, much dusted, but rarely used. Or put another way, the board loved it, the traders ignored it. Certainly every effort was made in APT's first twelve months or so to allay traders' sensitivities. In particular, a process of wide consultation with traders preceded not only the gradual phasing in of the range of contracts on to APT (including trading the Bund electronically prior to the DTB doing so in Frankfurt), but also the much trickier matter of deciding whether to operate APT during floor trading hours for the less popular contracts. On this latter issue, the board agreed in February 1990, 'there would not be a referendum amongst members' but 'members would be fully consulted on their views before any such decision was considered'. The inevitable survey followed, with 119 members responding, and there was overwhelming opposition to the T-bond, Eurodollar and FTSE contracts being moved on to APT for daytime trading, but general acceptance that the JGB could benefit from such a move. This indeed happened from April 1991, by when APT was executing an average of some 5,400 contracts a day – not exactly negligible, but only a small part of LIFFE's overall volume. Still, on occasion it could really come into its own, most notably for the first time on Friday, 5 October 1990, when just two minutes before floor trading was due to end the Treasury made its surprise announcement that sterling would enter the ERM. 'It took everybody by surprise,' a trader from Midland Montagu told *IFR*. 'By the time everybody had time to read the announcement, it was almost too late to do anything.' About quarter of an hour later APT began, traders were ready, and volume soared (especially in short sterling futures), with the system registering 31,659 lots. It was an episode that amply justified the existence of APT, quite apart from the general boost to LIFFE's credibility that the system gave.

Credibility was a commodity increasingly denied to GLOBEX, as delay followed upon delay in its implementation. Indeed, the joke in the Chicago pits was that when people asked when GLOBEX would start up, the answer was

APT Terminal 'going live'.

always 'May – or may not'. Melamed did his best to take the high ground. 'The delay in launching GLOBEX is of little consequence if one considers that it will change the way business is done for ever,' he told a Swiss conference in September 1990 – but it was becoming an awkward hand to play. By this time the CBOT had joined forces with the CME and Reuters to develop an electronic trading system, and with MATIF also involved it was inevitably a somewhat cumbersome coalition with which to do business. LIFFE during 1990 continued to weigh up the options, instinctively disliking the global carve-up of financial futures products that GLOBEX was essentially about, but still uncertain whether it would benefit LIFFE to be in that cartel or out of it. A significant element of the membership (and not just the Americans) still saw it as the way of the future, and the LIFFE executive, for all the underlying scepticism, felt the continuing need to keep checking it out.

Early in 1991 Burton was in Chicago, where (he told the board) 'he had a number of positive meetings particularly regarding GLOBEX' and 'had expressed the hope that the CME would re-open negotiation with LIFFE on this issue, although it was recognised that exclusivity would continue to be a potential problem'. In March, at Boca Raton, he and Jenkins had the first formal session with the CME and CBOT on GLOBEX. 'The meeting had been friendly,' Burton told the board, 'but the two exchanges were seeking exclusive rights on all contracts (other than energy), including those awaiting formal approval'; and 'in general the terms appeared to be less attractive than in 1989'. Realistically, there was probably now no chance of a deal – even if the terms were right – until GLOBEX went live and proved itself. In early November the two Chicago exchanges held a news conference in London, announcing that the system would go on trial in January 1992 at 250 key stations, with a projected launch in the summer. Melamed put most of the blame for the delays on Reuters, but insisted that 'they're spending a lot of money, and they want to finish this thing'. For LIFFE the problem remained one of exclusivity, as Burton told the *FT* at the same time. Specifically, LIFFE would not be allowed to trade on GLOBEX those products already listed by the CME or the CBOT unless it already had over half the global volume in that particular product; and furthermore, even in such a product (such as the Bund future) LIFFE would not be able to trade it on GLOBEX during regular Chicago trading hours. Even so, he did not rule out the possibility of an agreement, remarking somewhat ambiguously that 'we have to do what is in our members' best interests'.

Inevitably, the introduction of APT and the ongoing GLOBEX saga overshadowed the considerable amount of technical progress that – day-in, day-out – met the challenge of rising volume and increased the efficiency of the market as a whole. December 1988 saw the full implementation of the crucial Trade Registration System [TRS], enabling the rapid matching, allocation and confirmation of trades, continuously throughout the day, as well as providing an on-line method of monitoring the status of all trades. TRS was, the exchange claimed, 'one of the first successful implementations of high volume transaction processing systems based on relational database technology'. By autumn 1989 there were over 250 TRS terminals installed, with the system allowing 200,000 lots to be matched within one and a half hours of the closing bell. Moreover, building on TRS, LIFFE now developed in 1989 the Clearing Processing System [CPS], further extending the post-trade support available to members. CPS's facilities included real-time position keeping (including delivery and exercise instructions), margin calculations, and end-of-day processing of deliveries, exercises and settlements. As for the trading process itself, this hectic period of technological activity (1988–90) also saw the implementation of not only the new Futures Reporting System [FRS], speeding up the capture, display and dissemination of prices, but a new order-routing system ('LIFFElink'), enabling client and member orders worldwide to be routed automatically to TRS terminals on the floor or to members' offices. Altogether this package of facilities, including APT, added up to a fully-integrated support and trading system, known by the generic term 'LIFFEforce'.

A little later, coming onstream in spring 1991, there was the introduction of SPAN. It was the acronym for the 'Standard Portfolio Analysis of Risk', had originally been developed by the CME, and now replaced the delta-based margining system that had been used for options since 1985. Appreciative of the portfolio approach inherent in SPAN, LIFFE and LCH took up the Merc's margining system; and Barton assured the readers of *Risk* that, through its more accurate reflection of risk, it gave 'better cover for your bucks'. He did not need to add that the Merc had developed SPAN after the October 1987 crash, when those holding futures and options portfolios which were broadly market neutral were forced to liquidate positions as a result of traditional margining systems and the extent to which cash was locked up in premium value. It is worth noting that even with SPAN, the US exchanges have not overcome the latter problem through the futures-style margining of options that LIFFE had adopted in 1985.

The clearing house did not involve itself in the development of the CPS, and Jenkins spoke to the board in January 1989 about 'the disappointing relationship between ICCH and the exchange'. The problem was once again financial as well as technological, and a new study was initiated into the cost of LIFFE undertaking its own clearing. A few months later the London Clearing House (as the London markets part of the ICCH operation was now called) was asked to provide a breakdown, and Jenkins informed the board in June that LCH's analysis had shown 'that the revenue it receives from LIFFE business greatly exceeds the cost of providing clearing services'. Accordingly, he recommended that LCH receive a fixed annual fee for providing clearing services to the exchange. This more favourable approach was implemented, and in June 1991 (a year after the end of Barkshire's fairly low-key chairmanship of ICCH) the clearing house was, once again, restructured. ICCH ceased to exist; a new holding company had two wholly owned subsidiaries, one of them The London Clearing House Ltd; LCH's financial backing was increased from £150m to £200m; each of LCH's markets was to be treated internally as a separate profit centre, and each would have its own management committee, consisting of exchange representatives, LCH officials and clearing members. The primary impetus for these management committees, Jenkins told *FOW*, came from LIFFE, adding that he wanted 'to ensure that there is a partnership between LCH and the exchange over the efficient operation of post-trade services'.

Yet despite all this, the old dream did not die. When, two months later, Jenkins informed the board that he had been asked to join the board of LCH, and argued that this would be advantageous in giving LIFFE 'a greater say in the policy of LCH and greater control over the costs of clearing', Durlacher 'noted that a continuing debate was whether the exchange should conduct its own clearing services'. Jenkins in the event did join the board of LCH, but the debate would continue intermittently as long as the somewhat unsatisfactory situation obtained in which the clearing banks were reluctant owners of the clearing house – a state of affairs given an added lease of life by the way in which, by the early 1990s, back-office risk became a major policy issue in the world's financial markets and among central bankers. LIFFE's executive knew that it was not a responsibility to assume lightly.

All the contracts had been subject to periodic review and technical amendments in order to reflect users' requirements and changes in cash market characteristics. However, in some cases underlying demand withered. The exchange's first contract to be delisted was the option on the FTSE 100 future, on 22 March 1989, and it was followed in 1990 by the suspension of nine other contracts: the original four currency contracts; the two currency options; the dollar/mark future; and, a source of considerable disappointment to those who had held out high hopes, the short gilt and medium gilt futures. These delistings were a recognition of market realities, not a reflection of any diminution of LIFFE's aim to provide as broad as possible a range of financial futures and options products. Indeed, in June 1990 the board explicitly committed itself to seeking to 'strengthen the standing of LIFFE as a one-stop exchange, thereby pre-empting other markets trading LIFFE's core products, protecting LIFFE's deutschmark product base, improving liquidity in the exchange's US dollar and Japanese yen products, and encouraging greater participation by members' overseas offices'.

In practice, improving liquidity in the JGB future was no easy matter; but eventually in April 1991, following lengthy discussions with the Tokyo Stock Exchange, a new JGB futures contract was launched that was not only more closely linked to the TSE's parent contract, but in London would be traded solely on APT. The LIFFE contract was revolutionary in that, although not fungible, it provided scope for directly linked activity on LIFFE and TSE by expiring overnight at the Tokyo opening price; this one-day lifespan led to it being called the 'mayfly' contract.

Financial Times, 3 April 1991.

The old contract having latterly often failed to trade even 200 contracts a day, the new one fared appreciably better though not sensationally so, managing almost 10,000 lots in its first month. As the contract settled down, the improvement would be sufficient to justify the bold APT-only decision, taken largely in deference to the wishes of LIFFE's Japanese members, more used to screen-based trading and in some cases not wishing the greater expense of mounting a floor operation. 'It was recognised that listing the JGB on APT all day would be setting a precedent,' the board hardly needed to be told in July 1990; but the recent membership survey had indicated acquiescence on the part of the membership as a whole.

There were no magic solutions to dwindling liquidity in the US dollar products. The Eurodollar future peaked in 1989, with just over two million lots that year, and in 1990 managed only 1.24 million, compared with SIMEX's 3.46 million and the Merc's 34.69 million. The downward trend continued in 1991 (994,000 lots), and a working party was set up to try to reverse it. The T-bond was likewise dogged by market indifference: from November 1988 the CBOT opened its T-bond trading at 7.20 local time, a cruel blow to the London market;

384,641 lots in the first four months of 1989 was well down on the 613,062 in the same period in 1988, and *IFR* referred to it in August as by now a 'normally lame duck contract'; while by 1991 the total volume for the year was barely 463,000 lots.

It was a less bleak picture in LIFFE's 'core products', in effect the short sterling and long gilt futures. Short sterling had some amazing days between 1988 and 1990, against the background of deep schisms within the British government and in particular the formation of monetary policy. A landmark was 25 May 1989: 77,734 short sterling futures changed hands – at the time the most contracts ever traded in one LIFFE pit on one day – as base rates rose one point to 14 per cent to support a tumbling pound. Even in 1991 (after Thatcher's fall) it managed an extremely healthy volume for the year of 8,064,000 lots, barely 3% down on 1990. The long gilt continued to have a more chequered time, but it was a help when from December 1989 the specification was changed, so that instead of being deliverable against a basket of stock with maturities of 15 to 25 years, the contract was delivered against issues with specific maturity dates – a change made in response to the shortage that brokers had been experiencing of deliverable stock against the contract. Over the next two years, as the cash market somewhat revived, annual volume ran at some 5.7 million lots: it was still an important contract, in third place in the exchange's pecking order, but no longer the phenomenon that it had been at the time of Big Bang.

None of this was of negligible importance, but what really mattered in these years was Europe, as there took place a keen, occasionally ferocious three-cornered tussle between London, Paris and Frankfurt, with the Swiss exchange (SOFFEX) as a bit player. The bottom line was that LIFFE was determined throughout to safeguard its position as Europe's leading financial futures and options exchange, an objective that was to be attained, the board agreed in June 1990, 'by either co-operation or competition'. In practice, it was usually by competition.

Very quickly after its launch on 29 September 1988, the Bund future became the contract which LIFFE was prepared to fight tooth and nail to defend. An impressive 107,643 contracts were traded in October 1988, on the back of bid-offer spreads being kept to within two pfennigs, making it at once the exchange's fifth largest contract (overtaking the Eurodollar); and over the next few months it averaged more than 5,000 lots a day. Arbitrage trading was the main reason for this initial sizeable turnover, *IFR* argued in January 1989, pointing to 'the relative cheapness of the Bund future relative to the French 10-year government bond future traded on MATIF'. The contract had 'exceeded all our expectations,' Bruce informed Reuters at the same time, noting that the small tick size of 25 marks was attractive to locals as it meant that they could limit their price risk. The German banks, as on launch day, used the contract – probably providing about a sixth of the volume, according to an informal LIFFE survey – but in a low-profile way, almost all their orders being filled quietly through brokers. 'They go to extraordinary lengths to cover their tracks,' one observer told the *FT*, declining to be more specific.

January 1989 itself was the month of real lift-off – 196,166 contracts, compared to 83,195 in December – as the Bund moved into third position, its progress much helped by the Bundesbank's considerate hike in the discount rate. February saw a further dramatic leap – to 300,409 contracts – with at one point the March Bund future almost reaching the stage where the cost of carry was such that pure arbitrage was possible between the cash and the futures. On 8 March 29,869 contracts changed hands, a new record for the Bund, as the Bundesbank set a fixed-rate securities repurchase agreement tender below the 6 per cent Lombard rate, and the *FT* noted that, amidst a wave of profit-taking on European bond markets, 'a changing relationship between cash and futures prices meant that traders were unwinding arbitrage positions, selling futures and buying cash'. Volume for March as a whole nudged up to 312,171 (ahead of the long gilt and now only behind the short sterling), and on 13 April turnover in Bunds hit a new daily peak at 34,673 contracts, on news that Bonn was reconsidering the 10 per cent withholding tax that had recently been imposed on German financial instruments. By this time it had become increasingly clear that the Bund had arrived in the nick of time. 'We must innovate,' Jenkins had told reporters earlier in the month. 'We practically have no domestic bond market anymore.' And on the 20th, as a natural development, LIFFE launched an option contract on the Bund future.

This was all very satisfactory, giving LIFFE an invaluable lead while the DTB in Frankfurt had not yet opened, but the more immediate problem was MATIF in Paris, which in 1988 reportedly traded 16.3 million contracts against LIFFE's 15.6 million, in turn meaning that MATIF was growing at nearly double the rate of LIFFE's 20% annually. Soon afterwards, on 20 January 1989, MATIF rejected LIFFE's proposal of co-operation – the licensing of APT, mutual product access, and joint development of new products – and told Albright, in justifying the intention to join GLOBEX, that (as Albright reported to the board) 'they viewed London as a competitor and therefore considered that they must face the future alone'.

It was probably very soon after MATIF's courteous declaration of war that LIFFE heard that the Paris exchange was planning a three-month deutschmark contract; and this led to a rival contract being designed very quickly by Carew Hunt and Bruce, in the first instance on the back of a cigarette packet at Balls Brothers wine bar in Threadneedle Street. On 14 February it was announced that LIFFE would be launching on 20 April, along with the Bund option, a three-month Euromark interest rate future, thereby complementing the 10-year Bund future at the short end of the yield curve.

It was a decision taken with some reluctance: the board would have preferred, despite the success of the Bund future, to have delayed the launch of two more European products so soon after that one; the systems people already had enough on their plate; and there was not universal enthusiasm for another huge round of European roadshows. Again, it was Albright, with 'Europe' on her brain, who gave the crucial push. She saw the immediate situation as being intensely competitive; while having discovered (from Richard Bown of Schroders) as long ago as 1983 that the short DM market was bigger than the short sterling market, she believed that introducing a three-month future would not only consolidate LIFFE's hold on the infant Bund future, but extend the range of LIFFE's German products and bring in a whole host of new continental cash market traders, from the short end of the banks' trading operations. In addition, a Bund option would finally get the Dutch option traders to London – vainly hoped for since 1985 – and perhaps also some French options traders. Partly for tactical reasons, she now played the GLOBEX card as hard as possible – arguing that an aggressive European strategy would enable LIFFE to negotiate with GLOBEX on LIFFE's terms – and almost certainly this was an important factor in the board giving its consent.

The proposed launch date had its problems, it being belatedly realised that it was the centenary of Hitler's birth, but objections were overruled. Two important developments occurred before the launch: one was that Dresdner Bank agreed to be among the 16 designated brokers, though emphasising that it would not cease to be involved in the as yet unlaunched DTB; and MATIF found itself unable to begin floor trading of its almost identical contract until 9 May, though it said it would introduce the contract on an unofficial over-the-counter basis on 19 April. 'Inevitably the French banks will trade on their home exchange,' predicted Jenkins, 'but I believe that most of the other players will come to London.'

The 20th itself went well – an entirely unexpected rate rise in Germany about an hour before closing taking first-day volume on the Euromark up to 11,944 – but Katharine Campbell in the next day's *FT* stressed the seriousness of the continental competition. MATIF had aggressive traders, supportive banks that had rapidly assembled sophisticated trading operations, a liberal supply of government bonds to trade, and a government that saw the exchange as an important plank in its project to establish Paris as the leading European financial centre; she even quoted one London fund manager, according to whom 'you still tend to get better fills on MATIF, as people will often step away in active markets on LIFFE'. While as for Frankfurt, although 'a bearish and difficult trading environment, together

Financial Times,
21 April 1989.

Liffe and the Matif bare their knuckles
Katharine Campbell on the mounting futures rivalry between London and Paris

with the sudden realisation of the enormous investment in training required to bring the German financial community up to date in derivatives, has brought considerable new business to LIFFE this year, and pushed up the attendance of LIFFE Euromark promotional [and educational] seminars in Germany' – given in German – the fact remained that the German banks were making a huge commitment of capital to their own exchange; and, in terms of deutschmark products, it represented 'a considerable threat to LIFFE in the long term'.

During the rest of 1989 the Bund option performed respectably – by the autumn reaching monthly volumes of almost 90,000 – while the Bund future continued to show its paces, notching up 5.33 million contracts for the year as a whole, second only to the short sterling future. The closing months of the year saw the rapid, unexpected crumbling of the Iron Curtain, the end of the Berlin Wall, and a mood of huge, often irrational fluctuations in sentiment about German economic prospects. It was becoming a particularly good time to have a strong market in deutschmark products, and the Euromark contract accordingly benefitted, though never looking like attaining the same sort of volumes as the Bund future. LIFFE tried all sorts of incentive schemes (including weekly champagne prizes) to get locals to move from the thriving Bund pit to the less liquid Euromark pit, but met with only mixed results. Even so, the Euromark contract had the edge on MATIF's competitor, in September for example being ahead by 132,812 lots to 84,808, as well as attracting some 83% of the open interest between the two exchanges. It was an important edge, for that same month MATIF overall traded 2.16 million lots (of which well over half were 10-year government bond futures), just pipping LIFFE's 2.12 million lots. Of that volume on LIFFE, around 35% was contributed by the Bund future and option and the Euromark future, so there was no mistaking the revolution in the exchange's product character that the launch of the Bund future a year earlier had signalled.

Another dimension was given that autumn to the larger European battle when LIFFE introduced on 26 October 1989 an ECU three-month interest rate contract. It was a contract with quite a history. Back in June 1985, following rapid recent growth in the amount of ECUs [European Currency Units] in issue, LIFFE had publicly committed itself to introducing an ECU futures contract. This seems to have been partly because the Bank of England had expressed its concern that competition from the US might result in an ECU contract being traded first outside its prime areas of interest; and at the board discussion 'it was pointed out that the ECU existed as a politically inspired currency with no real institutional interest'. Later that year the product plan downgraded ECU products to the second tier of priority, on the grounds that 'in the absence of competitive pressures' there were more important products to be developing. 'We tend to base new products on the size of the underlying cash market, and we feel that it isn't large enough yet,' Carew Hunt told *Intermarket* soon afterwards, though conceding that with the CME now

trading an ECU future it was 'surprising that we haven't committed to an ECU product'. In July 1986 a survey of both the membership and the London cash market found little demand or support for an ECU derivative product on LIFFE, and the board in September somewhat reluctantly concurred, Burton pointing out that 'if LIFFE did not introduce an ECU based product, it is likely that another European Exchange would seize the initiative'.

A pause ensued until January 1988, when Albright pushed hard for a three-month ECU future. She pointed out to the board that there were by now 13 ECU clearing banks and that the ECU was 'virtually a second currency in Italy', and argued that an ECU product would not only 'give LIFFE something to sell in France, Belgium and Italy', but also, 'coupled with a German government bond, it would put us in a very strong position to be *the* international market serving this time zone'. The matter was put on hold, but that summer the discussions that took place on European monetary co-operation, together with the British government's announcement that it would issue ECU-denominated short-term Treasury bills, gave renewed impetus to the possibility of an ECU contract. MATIF by now was also thinking ECU, and at Bürgenstock in September the two exchanges agreed (noted Jenkins) 'that there would be advantages in jointly listing an ECU'. That, however, was before the competitive dispensation took effect, and in April 1989 each exchange announced its intention to launch an independent ECU contract before the end of the year. 'If London wants to do an interest rate ECU we will do one as well,' MATIF's managing director, Gilbert Durieux, told *FOW* soon afterwards.

Behind LIFFE's ECU announcement there existed a more or less veiled agenda, and again it belonged to Albright. Determined to push ahead as far and fast as possible on all feasible European fronts, she had her eyes firmly set on Italy as well as Germany by early 1989. She saw Italy as a country ripe for the taking: the third biggest economy in western Europe (possibly tied with Britain), huge cash markets, stupefyingly large cash bond market and PSBR (more outstanding government debt than anywhere in the world except America and Japan) – but no derivatives. Yet while exchange controls remained in force, and only a tiny proportion of its government bonds were held by international investors, Italy was not a place that the City of London took a serious interest in. With no realistic prospect of Italian products until these conditions altered, Albright instead wanted to prepare the ground for such products. In practice, this meant getting the Italians used to the idea of interest rate futures, making contacts with Italian banks in both Italy and London, and persuading them not only to start trading futures but to think about devising a sensible regulatory system. For all of which purposes, the ECU future was the only product almost at hand, notwithstanding its weak cash market (though less so in Italy than elsewhere) and relatively limited appeal. Its collective mind concentrated by the fear that MATIF would launch an ECU product first, and at the same time encouraged by the Bank of England's positive support for an ECU future, the board was willing to give the green light; but to Albright, it was the Italian dimension that was crucial.

LIFFE went firm on 11 September, announcing the launch date, and according to the *Independent* 'you could virtually hear the gnashing of teeth in Paris'. Three banks had agreed to act as designated market makers. Two were Belgian (Banque Belge and Kredietbank), reflecting the relative enthusiasm there for the ECU; and the third was Italian, namely the Istituto Bancario San Paolo di Torino [San Paolo Bank], whose London manager, Mario Cotto, was especially helpful in terms of the contract's ulterior purpose. These three recruits were important in terms not only of the board's acceptance of the contract, but also LIFFE's European membership base, hitherto expanding with painful slowness. Later in September, MATIF announced that it would soon be launching a futures contract based on France's ECU-denominated long-term Treasury bonds, but said that the precise date would depend on when the French Treasury held its next auction of the bonds. *IFR* at the end of the week quoted Thierry Coussieu of the Banque Nationale de Paris [BNP], who taking the broad view commented that 'London has scored one mark, but what really matters is the further expansion of the ECU'. LIFFE itself was careful not to talk up prospects excessively, but did undertake another vigorous, multi-lingual European roadshow. A crucial figure here was Paolo Cuniberti, hired from a Milanese business school, and in all sorts of ways LIFFE was shedding its final inhibitions about foreigners and foreign languages.

In the event, after Eddie George had rung the bell on 26 October 1989, 2,030 contracts were traded on the first day, and over the next few weeks daily volume settled down at about 500 lots. During the next year or so it became clear that, in strictly commercial terms, the contract was unlikely in the near future to become an outstanding success; and thereafter it became the accepted version of events that LIFFE had launched it only because of pressure from the Bank of England. No doubt there was an element of truth in that, but two qualifying points should be made: firstly, that LIFFE before taking its firm decision carried out a survey of 66 banks in 8 European countries and found 60% support for the contract; and secondly, it was a strategic as well as commercial product, in the sense not just of Italy, not just of the existing European battle as a whole, but also with the prospect of monetary union in mind, in other words a sensible way of hedging bets just in case the ECU became *the* European currency. Moreover, LIFFE had launched its ECU product ahead of MATIF, which by the end of 1989 still had not moved. 'We see MATIF mainly as a French exchange listing French products, traded in the main by French members, and used in the main by French clients,' was how Burton drove home the point to Reuters in December, adding that by contrast 'LIFFE is a well-spread exchange, listing a range of international products.' Nevertheless, the uncomfortable fact was that LIFFE in 1989 traded

The launch of the Three Month ECU futures contract, 26 October 1989. From left: Eddie George, David Burton, Dominique Rambure.

23.86 million contracts, rather less than MATIF's 25.65 million. There was, moreover, a further cloud on the European horizon: the much-delayed, but now imminent start-up of the DTB.

It began on 26 January 1990, for software reasons trading equity options only to start with, thereby giving LIFFE a further, priceless breathing space to continue building up the already impressive liquidity of its deutschmark products, above all the Bund future. An electronic exchange based on Switzerland's SOFFEX – 'a Swiss clock clad in German armour plate,' someone remarked – the DTB got off to a good start, no doubt encouraged by LIFFE sending it a framed antique print of Frankfurt to mark the occasion. A few weeks later, on 1 March, LIFFE initiated an option contract on the Euromark future; but it was the Bund future that celebrated the start of a new decade by soaring into the stratosphere in the course of 1990. Against a rapidly evolving political and economic background – the sudden move towards German reunification (monetary first, then political), rising interest rates, increasing German government debt – the contract flourished even more than before. Over one five-day period it was trading in a range of 200 ticks a day – 'It was quite a slaughterhouse,' Herklotz would recall. The atmosphere in the extremely crowded pit was feverish. 'There had been rumours that the Bundesbank had requested LIFFE to suspend dealings in the Bund contract and even that Bundesbank officials had entered the LIFFE pit to "calm things down"', Jenkins told the board on 12 February. And he added: 'He had spoken to Professor Köhler at the Bundesbank to ensure that they were aware of the rumours. Professor Köhler had been aware of the rumours which he dismissed as ludicrous.' Still, the rumours were not altogether surprising, granted that (as the *Economist* observed in April) 'since the opening last November of the Berlin Wall, it is the government *bund* futures contract, busily traded on LIFFE, that has been the financial barometer of the political drive towards German unity.'

By May it was averaging almost 40,000 contracts daily, and in late July (soon after currency union) the DTB announced that it was having to postpone the launch of its Bund future, which had been set for 10 September. Nevertheless, there was no complacency, and by this time a 'Defend the Bund' project was well under way. An important aspect was trading hours, especially once it became clear that the DTB intended to trade in Bund futures from 7 am London time. The views of members had already been sounded out, in anticipation of the DTB's move, and the overwhelming majority were willing to shift to an earlier opening time in order to match Frankfurt. 'The Board appreciates that opening the market at 7 am will pose considerable difficulties and inconvenience to members' staff,' a circular to members conceded in September, in anticipation of starting 65 minutes earlier once the DTB contract finally came on stream. 'Just about everyone affected is mega-upset,' one trader at a major German bank in London told *IFR*. 'People are feeling fairly used and abused right now. LIFFE is putting the squeeze on what little social life we have left outside of the office.'

But if the main battle with DTB was still to be fought, using alarm clocks as well as pits and screens, an important one with MATIF was over. 'We have lost the battle for the Euro-DM,' admitted Pfauwadel in June 1990. 'When we launched the contract [i.e. the future], our share was 50%. Now we have 10% of the market.' In fact, the disparity for June as a whole was even greater than that – 14,112 contracts on the MATIF floor, compared with LIFFE's total of 224,401 lots. It was a more even contest in the option, prompting *IFR* to remark that 'this may prove the claim that the French have a better understanding of the maths of options than the British'. However, that was probably thin comfort, with LIFFE also now starting to show ahead in terms of overall volume, by 21% in the first eight months of the year. Few imagined that MATIF's belated ECU future, a contract on ECU-denominated long-term French government bonds to be launched on 18 October, would make a decisive difference, with the ECU itself obstinately failing to develop into a widely used commercial currency.

In October 1990, however, the main focus was on Frankfurt. 'We would not be so foolish to make more than a 150 million deutschmark investment if we were not ready to continue until we have a success,' *Securities Week* was informed in early October by an official with Commerzbank, one of the five major stakeholders in DTB. And he asked rhetorically: 'In what other country are the bonds of that country traded in another country? It is absurd.' By the end of the month a firm date of 23 November had been set for the DTB to start trading Bund futures, and

IFR reported that 'among German dealers and analysts, the feeling is that the DTB contract will eventually become more actively traded than its counterpart in London'. Or in the words of a London trader with an American investment house: 'I think the German banks will do everything to force their guys to use the contract, whether they like it or not. They have invested a lot of time and money into this contract.' On 6 November, at a board meeting, Burton called on as many members of the board as possible to make the ultimate sacrifice and be present on the floor on the 23rd for the first day of 7.00 am opening. The DTB's chairman, Rolf Breuer, meanwhile put his trust in technology. 'We have greater transparency here,' he told a news conference. 'We are a computerised bourse. LIFFE is only now developing into a computerised exchange.' To which Jenkins almost immediately countered: 'We think open outcry will work better than a screen in periods of intensive trading. With a computer system it takes a long time to key in bids and offers.'

On the first day the DTB traded just over 4,000 contracts in the Bund, compared with nearly 25,000 on LIFFE, and it was soon apparent that much would turn on whether the top German banks, who were estimated by this time to do about 30% of LIFFE's business in the contract, would really put all their backing behind the DTB even if liquidity continued to stay in London. In mid-December – with the DTB's average daily Bund volume running at only 2,500 contracts, less than a tenth of LIFFE's – the Deutsche Bank acted, explicitly reversing its earlier decision to trade where the market was most liquid and stating that it planned to 'give preference' to the DTB. 'But,' noted Katharine Campbell in Frankfurt, 'most traders are reluctant to bow to "political" pressure, preferring to deal where they can make money, namely in the more liquid market.' There was no doubt where that liquidity was, with LIFFE for 1990 as a whole trading 9.58 million Bund futures – and becoming in the process the exchange's top contract, over a million ahead of short sterling, though in global terms only the world's 15th most traded futures contract, with that league table headed by the CBOT's T-bond future (75.49 million contracts).

The pattern of LIFFE's dominance in the Bund contract remained fairly constant in early 1991, and at the start of March the exchange took pity on its traders by agreeing to open the Bund half an hour later, enquiries having revealed that there had been little activity in the first half-hour of trading each day. At about the same time, nine German banks adopted what one banker described as a 'gentlemen's agreement' to make a market in Frankfurt's faltering Bund future, in an attempt to narrow the spread between bid and offer prices, hitherto far wider than in London. The agreement made an impact, with March volume for the DTB Bund up to 113,873 contracts, almost double the January total, while LIFFE's Bund futures business, which had been seven figures in February, slipped in March to 908,556 lots. The differential, however, remained huge; and Barton told the board on 2 April that 'the gentlemen's agreement had been less effective last week', while

Opposite: The Battle for the Bund.

Liffe vs DTB: will it go to penalties?

In the second of a two-part feature on European markets, FOW takes a look at recent developments at LIFFE, and produces the annual directory of LIFFE's members. With the coming of futures trading to the DTB, Liffe's open outcry system will also be facing direct competition on the Bund contract from the new electronic exchange in Germany. In light of the likely sharper competition in the European future especially between Liffe and

A TIMELY REMINDER

From November 27, you can trade LIFFE Bund futures and options from 7 a.m.* (London time) Set your alarm clocks accordingly.

In Bund Futures Contract Battle, Screaming Trounces the Machines

COMPUTER SCREENS may be the wave of the future, as many specialists claim.

But waving is trouncing the electronic sound of a battle between London and Frankfurt to trade the popular german government bond, or Bund, future

Frankfurt fights to regain bunds

Marc Bailey 'noted that one bank which had been doing 40% of the volume had now withdrawn from a gentlemen's agreement'. Nevertheless, it was still early days. 'Its international rivals at heart believe that the DTB will be made to work,' Campbell wrote in the *FT* in March, adding that the German banks 'may not have been using the Bund on LIFFE as actively as was thought' and were now 'only just gearing up to derivatives'. The jury, moreover, was still out over the respective trading systems, though she did quote one Frankfurt trader who criticised the DTB's software as *too* sophisticated: 'It's like Tolkien – fascinating, but do you need it?'

The battle for the Bund was intensely preoccupying, but there were significant developments elsewhere on the European front in the winter of 1990/1. In October the board considered a product strategy paper by Victoria Ward (the new director of product development), who argued that if LIFFE wished to retain its position as the leading European derivatives exchange it needed to launch a new wave of international products. These should be mainly interest rate in nature, including three-month Euroswiss and Eurolira contracts, but she also advocated an ECU bond contract and a European stock index. During the discussion, reservations were expressed about the Euroswiss and Eurolira contracts, on the grounds that 'they would only have a limited amount of activity'; but at the same time, 'recognising that these contracts would be introduced and traded on some European exchanges over the next two to three years emphasised the need for the exchange to be both innovative and entrepreneurial'. Accordingly, the consensus was to push ahead as much as possible with these new products, 'to be supported by liquidity-providing schemes'.

Two months later, shortly after SOFFEX had said that it would start trading a Swiss franc short-term interest rate contract from 22 March 1991, LIFFE jumped in and announced that it would be trading an almost identical contract from 7 February. The immediate impetus was a visit that, following SOFFEX's announcement, Burton had received from representatives of the leading Swiss banks in Switzerland. They had told him categorically that LIFFE should be the exchange to list this contract, and that even if LIFFE listed after SOFFEX it would still quickly win the battle. Two of the Swiss banks – Swiss Bank Corporation [SBC] and Union Bank of Switzerland [UBS] – agreed to act as market makers; and Steve Sparke of SBC told *FOW* that 'the demand for a futures contract lies here', pointing to not only Swiss interest rate volatility, but also how 'the Swiss franc is one of the most traded currencies outside the ECU market and there's a big Euroswiss franc deposit market in the UK'. On the day itself, John Redwood, Minister for Corporate Affairs, rang the bell ('This is another good choice. I want to see London flourish as one of the big three world markets in financial services. Derivatives are crucial to that success in the 1990s...'), and in the early weeks the contract averaged just over 2,000 lots a day, slightly higher than expectations.

The winter's more important launch, though, was the 6 March 1991 start of the ECU Bond future, over four months after the MATIF and trading in the immediate slipstream of a 2.5 billion ECU bond issue by the British government. Back in October the board had noted that it was now the Bank of England's 'intention that London should be the centre of the ECU bond market in the future', and soon afterwards John Major as Chancellor had confirmed that the UK was planning its first issue of ECU bonds. 'MATIF ECU starts well, but LIFFE lurks' was one October 1990 headline; 'LIFFE gives the French a fright over ECU trade' was another; 'MATIF stakes its claim on the ECU' was a third. LIFFE formally made its intentions clear in November. The *Wall Street Journal* quoted Bob Tyley, bond market analyst at Paribas Markets in London: 'The ECU has become the currency of Europe. There's no way both the exchanges aren't going to go after that market.' National pride was at stake, and few quarrelled with the view of Bruce at LIFFE that 'there may not be room for two contracts'. The stakes were higher for MATIF, not only because of its narrower product range but also in the light of the 1990 overall volume figures, showing LIFFE at some 34 million and MATIF at 28.6 million. By February the general expectation was that, with the MATIF contract managing only some 3,000 lots daily, LIFFE would sweep the board, especially with its contract's greater choice of deliverable bonds.

'LIFFE marches into ECU battle,' was the *Evening Standard*'s headline on launch day – Francis Maude, Financial Secretary to the Treasury, getting the early call – and Tracy Corrigan wrote in the *FT* that it 'may not enjoy heavy volume immediately, but there are hopes that it will in time become the most actively traded futures contract in Europe'. If there were indeed such hopes, they could hardly have been more mistaken. Average daily volume settled by mid-April at some 300 lots – compared to MATIF's 2,350 lots – and Nick Buckmaster of Daiwa Europe Futures remarked acidly to the press that 'if LIFFE did not put the ECU in a broom cupboard and perhaps moved it next to the Bund it could generate more interest'. Over the coming months the MATIF contract, though it never really took off, continued to fare much better than LIFFE's, and after a revamping of the contract had made little difference it was reluctantly accepted that this was a battle lost – arguably because it was the French Treasury that had the greater political will-power.

By contrast, LIFFE's pre-emptive strike against SOFFEX proved a success, with volume on its Euroswiss franc future running by the end of 1991 at some three to four times that of Zurich's similar contract. There was no joy, however, for the only contract that LIFFE launched between May and August 1991, in the always tricky field of stock indices. This was the FTSE Eurotrack 100 Index futures contract, which started trading on 26 June, an irritating twenty days after SOFFEX and the Amsterdam-based European Options Exchange had both launched option contracts on a rival stock index, EuroTop 100. The contract itself was a joint

Francis Maude rings the bell for the ECU Bond futures contract, 6 March 1991.

venture with LTOM, and the Eurotrack index had been launched in October 1990, being denominated in deutschmarks and mainly comprising German, French, Dutch, Swiss and Italian stocks that were quoted on the Stock Exchange in London as well as in domestic markets. 'Dealers and investors will be unfamiliar with the technical complexities of the new contract and the present softness of European stock markets is likely to discourage futures trading,' commented the *FT*, though adding that 'dealers are optimistic about the medium to long-term growth of the Eurotrack contract'. In fact the contract started inauspiciously – only 500 lots in the first three days – and got worse. By the end of 1991, SOFFEX had posted 23,956 EuroTop options, the EOE 9,632, and LIFFE only 2,721 lots in its Eurotrack future. LTOM had launched its own option in October, but had managed only 1,467. The general view on LIFFE was that it was a contract ahead of its time, certainly ahead of most fund managers, and hard on the heels of the ECU Bond flop, it was another blow for the notion of a pan-European product.

Far more was at stake with LIFFE's next product initiative, arguably second in importance only to the Bund launch of 1988. This, of course, was the Italian job, less than two years after the ECU futures dummy run. Foreign exchange controls were at last abolished there in 1990, and without a pool of captive savings to rely on the Italian Treasury began to look abroad. Its first step to attract foreign investors came in February 1991, when the government issued Italy's first ten-year fixed-rate domestic bond, whereas previously four years had been the longest fixed-rate bond. This, the *Economist* noted in May, not only made it 'easier for foreigners to assess the relative value of the Italian market', but 'in time could provide the basis of a futures contract'. Italy itself had no financial futures market – which naturally further whetted the appetite of Paris as well as London.

During the spring and early summer there was much talking to leading players in the cash market and general sounding out of opinion. This process included an interview with Lamberto Dini, deputy governor of the Bank of Italy. LIFFE at this stage was thinking in terms of a three-month interest rate contract as the first Italian step, and Dini in effect said that he was happy for it to go ahead if the exchange was sure it would be a success, but that he did not want this initial contract to be a flop. This had the effect of making LIFFE think again, and the weight of opinion shifted towards the long-term bond instead. In early June the board discussed the feasibility of introducing an Italian government bond contract. Jenkins explained that there was now 'a political dimension' involved, in that whereas 'discussions had previously been held regarding the assistance LIFFE could offer the Italian authorities in setting up a futures exchange', this was 'before the potential competition had arisen from MATIF', inevitably making the situation much more urgent from LIFFE's point of view. 'The Italian authorities,' Jenkins added, 'were keen to have their own futures market to trade government bonds in Italy, and were reluctant to see this market move "offshore".' However, 'it was considered that there would be little the Italian authorities could do if LIFFE were to introduce such a contract, other than discourage its use by Italian Institutions (although this was thought to be unlikely)'. Moreover, though the trading floor on the Royal Exchange was by now becoming almost intolerably crowded, 'it was not considered commercially or politically possible to wait until the floor was relocated [at the end of the year] before the exchange launched such a contract', and accordingly the board gave its go-ahead for a launch as soon as possible. Shortly afterwards, 19 September was set as launch date, with the futures contract to be based on Italian government bullet issues known as Buoni del Tesoro Poliennali [BTPs]. LIFFE also at this point expressed confidence that it would beat any rival Paris contract, in that some 40% of the cash market in BTPs (a total daily volume of about four trillion lire) was in London.

MATIF showed its hand on 2 July, announcing that it would launch its BTP future on 5 September, a fortnight ahead of LIFFE. At a news conference, Pfauwadel promised that once Italy had its own futures exchange in operation, then MATIF would 'repatriate' the BTP contract to it; and accordingly, he hoped that in the meantime support from the Italian authorities would give MATIF a competitive edge over LIFFE. On the same day LIFFE published the full specifications for its contract, to be based on a ItL200m Italian government bond with a maturity span of eight to ten and a half years and a 12% coupon, in contrast to the MATIF contract based on issues of six to 10-year Italian government bonds and carrying a 10% coupon. *IFR* gave two main reasons, in addition to the location of much of the cash market, why the odds favoured LIFFE despite its later launch (a lateness that was the cause of considerable anxiety at LIFFE): firstly, its contract was more straightforward and 'should appeal to the "innocents", looking for a simple, straight hedging tool'; and secondly, whereas MATIF was 'said to have done most of the work on its own and to have consulted very few market participants', LIFFE had 'apparently worked closely with members and BTP players to try to make the contract as good a fit as possible'. Over the next two months the main stress was on marketing and education, and MATIF committed the error of making its Italian presentations in French, whereas LIFFE did them in Italian – a significant difference not just for emotional reasons, but also because it was a very technical subject that was being explained. And in general, quite apart from the specific Italian value of the ECU futures exercise, LIFFE had the inestimable advantage of having learned from the Bund experience three years earlier, for in many ways this was the Bund revisited and fine-tuned.

MATIF, however, got off to a good start on 5 September, with over 7,000 contracts traded, and the first week averaged a daily volume of 8,211. Undoubtedly there was some concern at LIFFE, but in the event its BTP future got off to a flyer, with 15,136 lots traded in the first day, well above most forecasts. Over the next fortnight it was LIFFE that went decisively ahead. By 2 October (when it announced an option from the 24th on the BTP future) its daily volume was averaging 11,581 contracts, with open interest standing at 9,880 contracts; whereas the MATIF average daily volume (on a contract half the size) for September was 6,917 contracts, with an open interest of 7,893 contracts as of the 3rd. 'MATIF's contract is down and out,' one London trader told *Euroweek* in early October. 'We also trade on MATIF, so it doesn't matter much to us which succeeds, but the LIFFE contract was better specified and I think the general reputation of London as a market has made the difference.' The rest of October merely confirmed the outcome of the battle: on the 23rd LIFFE had a record day of trading in the BTP future, with 17,474 contracts traded, and open interest that day standing at 11,653; while by then MATIF's daily trading average for October had slipped to 1,405, with open interest virtually non-existent. By the end of the year LIFFE's BTP future had achieved a total volume of 483,477 lots – compared to MATIF's 148,491 – and most Paris traders seemed resigned to trading the contract on LIFFE, despite MATIF's reduction of initial deposits and commission fees. 'I'd like to think that I wouldn't chase a train that's already left the station,' one told *FOW*. 'MATIF has lost a monumental market.'

Meanwhile, the battle for the Bund had been hotting up nicely. In April 1991, following the previous month's trial run of the gentlemen's agreement, nine German banks publicly agreed to place bid and ask prices on the Bund future for at least 20 contracts throughout the trading day, though on the DTB itself some traders still felt that the domestic banks were not sufficiently committed to the exchange. George Austin, trading for BZW, told Reuters in May that many banks were worried that low liquidity would limit their room for manoeuvre. 'It is a real chicken and egg situation,' he added. 'So far as I can see, if the German banks really concentrated their business here for two weeks, it could wipe out a lot of the volume on LIFFE and lead people here.' Volumes did improve – in June, a daily average of 7,110 Bund future contracts – but well over four-fifths of market share still went to London. Moreover, noted Campbell in the *FT* on 17 July, 'on heavy trading days LIFFE tends to perform particularly well, and prices, even the German banks have to acknowledge, are generally dictated by London'.

In fact, heavy trading days had become rather less frequent during the summer than in the immediate past, reflecting the completion of German unification and low volatility in the cash markets, with the consequence that the battle for market share in the Bund future now assumed a new intensity, perhaps especially on the

Mario Cotto (right) launches the Italian Government Bond futures contract (BTP), 19 September 1991.

Wall Street Journal, 20 September 1991.

THE WALL STREET JOURNAL EUROPE FRIDAY - SATURDAY, SEPTEMBER 20 - 21 1991

Liffe's New Italian Bond Futures Contract Gets Off to a Solid Start, Outpacing Matif

By GLENN WHITNEY
Dow Jones Capital Markets Report

ZURICH – If the first day is any indication, the London International Financial Futures Exchange is giving the Paris-based Matif's Italian government bond futures contract more than a run for its money.

same cost. The Matif, however, is likely to attract some of the smaller participants in the market, dealers said.

Simon Prangell, a dealer at James Capel, said there was considerable "first-day speculation" at the Liffe, adding that volume is likely to be lower on Friday. He noted, however, that much of the volume

DTB's part. On 12 August it announced that for the rest of 1991 it was dropping its 51p fee for each transaction, 6p higher than LIFFE's charge, but Jenkins repudiated a price war: 'A better price is much more than the cost of clearing. When it matters LIFFE has the liquidity to keep spreads at the minimum.' The DTB's waiver became effective on the 16th, when it also launched an option contract on the Bund future. Three days later, on Monday the 19th, news came through that Gorbachev had apparently been overthrown in a coup, and LIFFE's Bund future, having recently been trading around 20,000 lots a day, turned over a hectic 123,011, while the DTB's volume doubled.

More significant, however, were developments in early November, when the DTB's volume in the Bund future jumped dramatically from some 9,000 on Monday the 4th to a record 44,314 lots on Wednesday the 6th, not far below LIFFE's 52,049 and indeed ahead for most of the day. Almost certainly the jump reflected a recent, well-publicised meeting, in which designated market-makers on the DTB contract discussed ambitious plans to commit themselves to trading at a minimum daily volume of contracts. Four banks – Deutsche, Dresdner, Commerzbank and J.P. Morgan – agreed to make such a commitment (going well beyond the April agreement), with other banks likely to join them shortly. 'We have never, and would not, institute any sort of guaranteed activity and indeed would probably be precluded from doing so under the Financial Services Act,' riposted Jenkins. Soon afterwards, as DTB volumes continued to flourish, an unnamed London source told *IFR* that the Frankfurt exchange was still insufficiently liquid: 'I've noticed that the DTB is supported on a rally, but bids disappear in a falling market. The price can drop ten ticks. If no one wants to make a price on LIFFE, someone will always come in only a tick or two lower.' And an equally anonymous Frankfurt source told the same publication that DTB would be hard pressed to beat LIFFE, because LIFFE's officials kept a close eye on DTB volumes and encouraged locals to trade in order to stake LIFFE volumes higher.

By the end of the month it was clear that the DTB had managed to increase significantly its market share, up from 10% to 20%, Barton told the board on 3 December:

> *In an effort to assess what was really happening on the DTB market, LIFFE had conducted a minute-by-minute analysis of activity on both LIFFE and DTB. This suggested that DTB were tracking LIFFE volume and that prices were led by LIFFE. The fact that open interest had not significantly increased suggested that some of this additional volume was accounted for by inter-market making transactions. ...*
>
> *LIFFE was planning to host a press day in the new year which would seek to educate the German press on the workings of both exchanges. To avoid possible future misconceptions it was noted that appropriate LIFFE press releases would*

be translated into German. It was agreed that in light of recent developments the exchange's 'Defend the Bund' Working Party should be re-constituted.

Barton perhaps underestimated the market share in the Bund future that the DTB now enjoyed. Its total volume for November was 489,200 lots, up 95% on October; while LIFFE's November volume was 904,872 lots, a 3% drop on October. The day after the board meeting, the DTB received an important symbolic shot in the arm when Dresdner Bank announced that it was ending its trading presence on the floor of LIFFE, an official saying that the decision reflected the DTB's increased activity, making it possible to transact there a large part of customer business as well as the bank's own business. The new-style gentlemen's agreement was by now fully operational, and it committed some fourteen of the leading German banks to trading an overall total of 20,000 Bund future contracts each day. The battle, in short, was still on, especially as the DTB in the course of 1991 had been adding to its range of products and generally doing well with them, achieving a total volume of 15.4 million contracts for the year.

By the end of 1991, then, the DTB was becoming an increasingly serious challenger to LIFFE, while MATIF, despite losing the crucial Italian battle, posted a total volume for the year of 36.9 million contracts, not far below LIFFE's almost 38.6 million (of which 10.1 million were in the Bund future, the exchange's first contract to hit ten million in a year). But who exactly was benefitting from this competition? In September, on the eve of LIFFE's launch of the BTP future, Richard Reinert, managing director of Refco Overseas, complained that 'as brokers to both markets we want more cohesion and mutual offset between exchanges' and that 'it's fundamentally flawed for two European exchanges to introduce the same contract'. A few days later the *Economist* took up the theme, contending that although competition between the different European exchanges spurred innovation, it came at a heavy cost: 'Rival listings divide liquidity: poor liquidity brings unpredictable prices and wide margins; both deter investors, so reducing liquidity further.' These were not arguments that Jenkins, speaking at about the same time at a forum organised by *Euromoney*, was much inclined to support:

I do not believe in competition for its own sake, but what do you have if you do not have competition? Some kind of cartel – 'you take that contract, we will take this one'? That is not right, as well as being contrary to European competition policy.

People might say that there is precious little liquidity in the ECU and that what there is has been split – and isn't that a damaging thing to do? I could not deny that. But by pioneering contracts we have contributed a lot to the establishment of derivatives. Before we started the bund contract, the people behind DTB were talking about just being an equities options exchange. The DTB – and now the Italian authorities – will be spurred to greater efforts.

As for wasting members' money – even on a complex product like the Italian bond futures contract, we would spend no more than £250,000 on a launch. More important, I admit, is what members have to spend in promoting products themselves. But if the board was doing something that the bulk of our members disagreed with, we would soon hear about it…

There was one other recurring motif in these years – namely, the entwined, often gruelling saga of the search for new premises and the merger with LTOM. By autumn 1988 the board was agreed that a move was essential and that the most preferable option was Billingsgate, though there were concerns that the floor space would be too large for LIFFE alone. Over the course of the winter, negotiations proved increasingly problematic and protracted, and in March 1989 the board noted with interest that the Stock Exchange had informally re-opened the possibility of LIFFE occupying part of its floor. By June it seemed that the Billingsgate site was no longer a realistic option, but as Jenkins put it to the board, 'the problem of going to the Stock Exchange was the need to ensure that there was a suitable arms-length relationship'. The Cannon Bridge development being under-taken by Speyhawk remained an option, but by September the Stock Exchange was the clear front runner.

In part, the background was that of amicable discussions having started in late 1988 between the two chairmen, Burton and Andrew Hugh Smith (who had succeeded Goodison), about the possibility of a renewed LIFFE/LTOM merger attempt. They had agreed in principle that it was essential 'for the future standing of the City of London' that merger talks recommenced 'at the earliest opportunity'. This time round there was no question of LIFFE coming under the larger umbrella of the Stock Exchange, especially as LTOM itself was now demanding virtual operational autonomy from the Stock Exchange. Some members of LTOM, moreover, increasingly saw a merger as the way to reverse the accelerating post-crash decline in its fortunes, while the Bank of England publicly favoured the development. In November 1989 Jenkins formally recommended to the board that relocating LIFFE's trading floor to the floor of the Stock Exchange 'was not only the most cost effective choice, but also provided a good location'. All sorts of possible snags were noted (including the levels of Stock Exchange development costs and service charges, the question of differences of view between LIFFE and LTOM, and the need to ensure that LIFFE 'retained adequate control over its market facilities'), but no one queried that LIFFE was heading for the Stock Exchange floor and merger with LTOM.

On 1 December, addressing a conference on the City's future, Burton explained the state of play:

Cannon Bridge, the proposed building above Cannon Street station, is not a feasible site for re-location. Costs would be substantially higher than the Stock Exchange, both in terms of one-off costs and operating costs. The date for occupation would probably be later than the Stock Exchange. The only practical course appears to be for LIFFE to move to the Stock Exchange and join with LTOM to build an integrated trading floor representing the full range of financial derivative products. This can be achieved with goodwill on both sides.

The implications for the City are enormous. To have two markets situated on one trading floor with the possibility of a third market [i.e. the International Petroleum Exchange] at some slightly later stage should help to underline the competitive advantage of the City in terms of financial products.

The concept of market integration is not, of itself, sufficient to enhance London's competitive edge. But it will be an important building block.

'LIFFE is so short of space at the Royal Exchange,' *FOW* remarked soon afterwards, 'it wants to move as soon as possible', adding perceptively that 'the urgency of its situation appears to have been the deciding factor which forced LIFFE's board members to abandon their political and emotional objections to moving into the Stock Exchange building'.

However, shortly before Christmas the Stock Exchange indicated that it would require an annual rent of around £3 million if LIFFE were to relocate to its market floor. This was roughly double the figure that the Stock Exchange had previously indicated and, the board was told by Foyle in January 1990, 'fundamentally changed the economics of the project', that indeed 'there appeared to be no scope for negotiations on this basis'. LIFFE accordingly made alternative proposals, and by March the Stock Exchange had agreed that the rent of the floor would be a peppercorn in return for LIFFE/LTOM financing the entire cost of the redevelopment work as well as paying a service charge and rates. 'However,' Jenkins told the board on the 12th, 'there would be difficulties in undertaking the development work with LTOM in situ and there was uncertainty as to what problems, and cost increases, might emerge as the work progressed'; and he added that 'the exchange had submitted an offer on the terms on which it was prepared to occupy Cannon Bridge', with the developer's reply now awaited. At the same meeting, 'concern' was expressed at the possibility of LIFFE 'forming links' with LTOM when that market was believed to be 'losing money'. The Stock Exchange floor with LTOM, Cannon Bridge with LTOM, Cannon Bridge without LTOM – those were now the three options.

At this point the decisive push towards merger came from the newly formed Derivative Users Group, some twenty major brokers on both LIFFE and LTOM who had a particular interest in financial derivatives, i.e. mainly stock index products and equity options. Meeting at James Capel House on 6 March, the brokers discussed why equity options in particular had failed to grow satisfactorily. Reasons cited included 'lack of real interest' on the part of member firms, the 'ambiguity' of the tax and regulatory situation, the 'conservative attitude of fund managers', the 'lack of support' from the Stock Exchange, and 'considerable adverse press coverage'. They also criticised LTOM for 'adopting too low a marketing profile', though it was recognised that its development had been 'severely hampered' by its links with the Stock Exchange, 'both in terms of management and financial resources'. As for a possible LIFFE/LTOM merger, the general view was that problems at the LTOM and Stock Exchange level were 'so deep-seated' that 'starting a new options market (albeit perhaps under a LIFFE umbrella) may be preferable to a merger'. Accordingly, the Group resolved 'that a derivatives exchange combining LIFFE products and LTOM products is formed, probably managed by LIFFE'. It was also agreed that the support of the Bank of England was to be sought for this purpose.

Later that month a meeting was held at the Bank, attended by the chairmen and chief executives of the Stock Exchange and LIFFE, at which it was agreed to set up a joint action group, to be chaired by the Bank's Pen Kent, that would recommend to the boards of both exchanges the best way to achieve integration. De Guingand, Stanislas Yassukovich, David Heron (of James Capel) and Ian Salter (of Société Générale) would represent the Stock Exchange, while Barkshire, Barton, Durlacher and David Wenman (of O'Connor Securities) would bat for LIFFE. The public announcement of a firm intention to merge was made on 3 April 1990, and press reaction ranged from mildly sardonic ('if peace and unity can span the Berlin Wall, they can cross from side to side of Threadneedle Street') to enthusiastic ('an idea whose time had come').

LTOM clearly had something to bring to the party, trading in the first five months of the year some 33,600 contracts daily even though (according to LIFFE's calculations anyway) it was losing money; but the overall politics of the situation were very different from 1987. 'The two exchanges had discussed merger in the past,' noted 'Lex', 'but LIFFE understandably balked at the prospect of falling into the stifling grip of LTOM's parent, the Stock Exchange'. And: 'Once LTOM had threatened to break away on its own, the SE was left with a back seat in any new structure. Although the two bodies could link up on the old SE floor, the move to wholly new premises is just as feasible.' While according to *IFR*, 'the Stock Exchange had agreed to relinquish LTOM, but it took the combined efforts of LTOM members, the Bank of England and LIFFE finally to wrest the options exchange away from what one LTOM member called "the dead hand of bureaucracy"'. Burton himself was keen to stress to the board on 9 April that 'contrary to reports in the press the initiative had not come from the Bank of England, but from pressure from LIFFE and also from the newly-formed London Derivatives Users Group'. At the same meeting, on the perennial question of location, Jenkins reported that it was becoming 'a particularly urgent decision', arguing that 'if it was concluded that Cannon Bridge was the best location it was important that a decision was made quickly to avoid costly construction re-work'. To which Burton added that Hugh Smith, although hoping that the Stock Exchange floor would be the preferred choice, had stated that the Stock Exchange 'would accept a decision by the two markets to establish the floor away from the Stock Exchange'.

Prior to the Action Group's report, the board reassured itself in May by coming up with a tenfold rationale for the creation of a single financial derivatives market in the UK under LIFFE management. Such a market would concentrate options resources and marketing; justify developing a retail base; concentrate resources on development of equity derivative products; maximise the return on systems investment; provide additional justification for a new floor; have the support of the authorities, thereby increasing the clout that LIFFE could bring to bear on government; simplify the regulatory regime for LIFFE members; diversify LIFFE's product line; reduce operating costs to joint members (estimated at a total saving of up to £200 million over a four-year period); and whilst being a draw on resources in the short term, could ultimately strengthen them if successful.

The Action Group itself reported on 29 June 1990, and put forward several of the same arguments to justify the creation of a merged exchange, to be called the London Derivatives Exchange [LDE]. Other recommendations included that it should broadly adopt the existing membership structure of LIFFE, that an issue of 'D' shares should be made to raise development capital of some £4–6 million for the new market, that its corporate governance should broadly follow the existing LIFFE model ('which blends widespread representation with flexibility'), that three-quarters of the initial board should come from LIFFE, that the LCH should provide the clearing and guarantee arrangements, and that the merger would be completed by the end of the year. The board accepted the report on the morning of 2 July, and later that day LIFFE and the Stock Exchange issued a joint press release explaining the structure and schedule of the merger. Jenkins was to be chief executive designate. 'It's gone LIFFE's way,' an LTOM member told *IFR*; 'they've got their chief executive and 75% of the merger.' It could hardly have been otherwise, granted the huge disparity in volumes, but Burton insisted to *FOW* that it would be 'a merger of equals – a coming together of like-minded people', adding that he hoped one or more of London's other futures exchanges might join LDE in due course.

One of the Action Group's main tasks was to decide where the new exchange should be located, and obviously LIFFE had a major input into its deliberations. The problem was too urgent to consider developing a greenfield site, and the main contenders remained the Stock Exchange and Cannon Bridge; but Billingsgate had unexpectedly re-emerged as a serious possibility, while there was also a new challenger from the Isle of Dogs. Jenkins recapped to the board on 2 July how the thinking had gone:

i) *The floor of the Stock Exchange*
- *it had a high capital cost and the necessary refurbishment would technically be difficult to achieve*
- *although it provided more floor space than the Royal Exchange it was not expandable*
- *it presented the problem of maintaining SEAQ and LTOM's operations during the refurbishment*
- *the building was 'tired' and it would be difficult to project an exciting new image*

ii) *Canary Wharf*
- *the main issue was one of risk; a move to Canary Wharf was not endorsed by members. (Approximately 80% of the members questioned thought that a move to this site would lead to an increase in their costs.)*
- *such a move would be 'pioneering' an untried location; the new exchange would be arriving as the first tenants with transport facilities still rudimentary*
- *there was the danger of isolation from the rest of the City*

iii) *Billingsgate*
- *this was an attractive proposition particularly financially*
- *the trading floor was 25,000 sq.ft.*
- *there would be major problems, however, in running the exchange because of its listed building status, which would be much more onerous than the Royal Exchange*
- *it was situated in an awkward location, it was difficult to get at, and access would need to be improved*
- *the air conditioning would need a major upgrade, this would be both costly and difficult in that particular building*
- *40% of the building is below ground level*
- *there was a real risk that it could become a white elephant*

iv) *Cannon Bridge*
- *floor area was expandable to a maximum of 35,000 sq.ft.*
- *it was an acceptable location. It is not as close to the Royal Exchange as the Stock Exchange but there are 180,000 sq.ft. of offices adjacent*
- *it is flexible and can, if necessary, be converted back to offices*

Jenkins then explained the financial aspect, where though Billingsgate perhaps had the edge, the decisive contrast was between the Stock Exchange's capital costs of £19 million and Cannon Bridge's £8.3 million, taking into account Speyhawk's contribution to the latter site. Accordingly, Cannon Bridge it was, with the fourth quarter of 1991 as the target to move the exchange to the River Building at the Cannon Bridge development, and LTOM to follow shortly afterwards. It was already known that Speyhawk was under financial pressure, following the collapse of the property boom of the late 1980s, and quite possibly it was felt that there might be some room for manoeuvre on the rent. The announcement was generally welcomed by the LIFFE community – so intolerably sardine-like had the Royal Exchange and the other premises become – but David Anderson of James Capel warned that if the future lay with screen trading it might prove to be 'a dangerous, hugely expensive move'.

In late October it was publicly conceded that the merger would not be completed even by January 1991. 'There were a lot more issues that we had to grapple with than we originally expected, which stemmed from two different organisations growing up separately,' explained Jenkins. At this stage there were two overriding problems. One, essentially technical and soluble, was the establishment of a joint clearing system, with LTOM members having to make the switch from their existing agency-based system to a principal-based system guaranteed by LCH, the latter system having implications for collateral that the LTOM constituency found hard to accept. The other problem, ultimately more serious because it went far beyond the technical, concerned stock borrowing. At the end of January 1991, following a leak, *The Times* explained something of what was at stake:

> *The dispute centres on the extent to which market-making members of LTOM will be able to continue borrowing equities when they join the proposed London Derivatives Exchange. Without the ability to borrow stock and go short in underlying equities, the ability of LTOM dealers to make markets in options would be badly hit since they would no longer be able to hedge their positions.*
>
> *LTOM is an offshoot of the Stock Exchange and it is this status that confers on members the right to borrow stock which is traditional, and vital, in making markets in the cash market in underlying equities. But the new LDE will be an independent body and unless the rules are changed will not inherit stock borrowing rights. To ensure these rights are carried over, delicate negotiations will have to take place…*

'The nub of the problem,' Jenkins elucidated further to the board on 5 February, 'was the existence of two categories of market maker on LTOM.'

On the one hand there were those, usually part of large integrated houses, who also made markets in the underlying equity market and had a built-in advantage with their privileged access to the underlying equity, especially in respect of stock borrowing privileges; on the other hand there were the so-called 'non-aligned' options market makers. 'It had been assumed that the existing stock borrowing privileges would be made available to LIFFE/LTOM,' Jenkins went on, but 'it had subsequently been recognised that this would be too restrictive and ran the risk that the non-aligned market makers may not subscribe for "D" shares.'

In the light of this serious problem, together with LTOM's increasingly disappointing general performance (volumes falling by 14.4% between the third and fourth quarters of 1990), Mather, Carew Hunt and de Guingand undertook a comprehensive review of LTOM's market structure, including why it was so seriously underperforming other equity options markets. In early March the completion date for the merger was put back until July 1991 at the earliest, but at least the 21-year lease with Speyhawk had at last been signed, with LIFFE's contractors to move on site on 11 March. Negotiating the lease had been largely the responsibility of Foyle in tandem with David Bell of Richard Saunders, and it contained various break clauses from 10 years onwards.

The review of the LTOM market was commissioned by the Corporate Merger Advisory Committee [CMAC] formed the previous year to make recommendations about the merger and comprising representatives of both LIFFE and LTOM. On 23 April, at a special board meeting, Mather gave a presentation, which demonstrated that LTOM was continuing to underperform badly and argued that its two primary needs were to encourage principal trading and to secure anonymity among participants. Accordingly, what was needed was to make stock borrowing available to all proprietary traders and to provide a fully automated trading environment for all individual stock options. At the same meeting, David Roden of BZW, chairman of the CMAC, 'explained that there was general agreement amongst LTOM participants that this diagnosis of the market was correct', though he added that 'the recommendation to move to a fully automated system was not fully endorsed by the LTOM board'. In the general discussion that ensued, 'it was questioned whether there could be a viable stock options market whilst the underlying market in equities was not transparent', i.e. that 'the current 90-minute reporting delay clearly prejudiced a fair market in options'. It was also 'questioned whether anonymity by itself would actually achieve the objectives', though 'it was recognised that it was important in the context of thinly traded options'. No hard decisions were taken, but Jenkins told the *FT* that, in the case of equity options, 'the only practical way we can see to achieve anonymity is through a fully automated trading system'.

LIFFE
CANNON BRIDGE
The London International Financial
Futures and Options Exchange

Over the next week or so it became clear that LTOM opinion was badly split. 'For the most part,' the *Economist* reported, 'the larger investment houses have been welcoming, saying that a screen-based system will provide more anonymity, encourage firm price quotations and offer more up-to-date price changes', whereas 'smaller firms are more wary' – 'they fear that the demise of pit trading will lead to job losses among floor brokers' and 'they are frightened by the cost of switching to sophisticated computer technology'. The article itself was somewhat mockingly titled 'A sort of merger, sometime'. It argued that the planned union was 'looking ever less like a merger and more like a rescue operation', noted that LTOM's daily trading volume was often dropping below the recently achieved break-even point of 30,000 contracts, and quoted one options trader who said that 'LTOM is quietly dying'. One way and another, the LDE was not looking like a marriage made in heaven.

Opposite: Cannon Bridge.

By mid-June 1991, moreover, it was clear that there was opposition to the screen-based plan for the equity options market from not only LTOM's independent options traders, but also LIFFE's locals, resistant to this potential erosion of the exchange's open outcry culture; and the boards agreed that the proposal would be deferred pending fuller consultation with members. During the next few weeks, as little or no visible progress was made over the merger as a whole, tempers started to become frayed, outside as well as inside LIFFE. Trying to achieve this merger was not quite like walking through spaghetti, but a note that Burton sent to Jenkins on 12 July (in the context of a recent, unacceptable LTOM business plan seemingly envisaging a major degree of LTOM autonomy within an enlarged market structure) evokes something of the rather testy mood that was starting to prevail:

You should be aware that at this morning's meeting, the Bank of England made it quite clear that there was no circumstance that they could envisage which would necessitate the LIFFE/LTOM merger being aborted. The Bank of England emphasised that both the LIFFE and LTOM Boards should be under no illusion that the support given by the government, Treasury, Bank of England and the Inland Revenue, plus from time to time other interested parties, is not given lightly. I was left in no doubt that the credibility of LIFFE and its management would be seriously questioned if the merger was aborted for whatever reason...

It is now becoming crucial that we achieve and maintain a tight grip on the progress towards the merger. It appears that the initiative has been lost in a number of areas, and this situation cannot be allowed to continue.

Burton also referred to 'the perception that you are seen by many as being strongly behind the move to automation which has a great deal to do with the difficulties we are now facing', and over the next phase it was the automation issue that dominated. On 25 July LTOM's 'Big Five' – BZW, County NatWest, Kleinwort Benson, Smith New Court and Warburgs – wrote to Burton, Geoffrey Chamberlain (LTOM's chairman) and Pen Kent (Bank of England) in order to express their 'deep concern' about what would happen to the trading of individual equity stocks following the merger:

> *We believe that the open-outcry system is eminently suitable for trading options on high volume contracts such as the FTSE index, but experience has led us to doubt its appropriateness when trading in less active option classes… We do not believe that the open-outcry system will be economically viable for integrated securities houses acting as options market makers and submit that the only possible solution to this problem is to develop a screen-based trading system in which the identity of the market participants is undisclosed… We therefore seek an assurance that the prospectus of LDE will include a commitment to transfer individual stock classes to a screen-based system at the earliest opportunity… Without such assurance, we do not believe that we will be able to present viable business plans to our respective Boards to maintain our current level of participation in these options classes.*

It was a clear, powerful blast against the apparent policy not to begin to move to a screen-based system for equity options trading until it had been seen whether volume (declining particularly steeply during the summer) picked up on the floor of the LDE.

At the next board meeting, on 6 August, 'there was general acceptance of the view that, while certain options may be successfully floor-traded there were doubts as to whether this would be the case for all equity options', and that 'therefore the exchange should develop (as soon as possible) a fully automated system'. Moreover, 'suggestions that the exchange should try to succeed without the commitment of the integrated houses, or should develop substitutes for equity options, such as futures on individual stocks, gained little support'. However, developing a fully automated system for equity options trading was likely to take up to a year and a half, and after the meeting Burton was careful to emphasise to the press that, although LIFFE was now committed to instigating the development of such a system, a final decision would not have to be taken for about a year, by when volume might have improved substantially, thereby justifying the continuation of floor trading. It was, in short, a compromise, driven by the worry that if LTOM split into two irreconcilable camps there would be nothing left to merge with.

Soon afterwards it was announced that LIFFE would be moving to Cannon Bridge on 16 December 1991, with the merger with LTOM to be consummated about a month later. That at last sounded like progress, but the mood was still

1 Juliette Proudlove	17 Phil Bruce	33 Stuart Sanders	49 Cliff Cochrane
2 Len Morris	18 Sam Mitchell	34 Mark Penny	50 Hugh Morgan
3 Tom Theys	19 Geoff Boardman	35 John Sussex	51 Alex Mainwaring
4 Steve Carr	20 Brian Muffet	36 Chris Wellman	52 Doug Fisher
5 Gordon Lawrence	21 Kevin Harding	37 Neil Hooper	53 John Young
6 Mark Stanton	22 Steve Westhorp	38 Alan Clayton	54 Neil Crammond
7 John Duchin	23 Nigel Ackerman	39 Steve Delaney	55 Tim Ockenden
8 Richard Stokes	24 Ian Morrell	40 John Chitty	56 Michael Partridge
9 Martin Taylor	25 Chris Henry	41 Ian Oliver	57 Nigel Andrew
10 Barry Heath	26 James Campbell-Gray	42 Frances Sheenan	58 Clive Roberts
11 Ken Herbert	27 Russell Geary	43 Alistair Neilson	59 Martin Parrott
12 David Morgan	28 Harry Watson	44 Alex Wilkinson	60 Lloyd Simmons
13 Gloria Hall	29 Craig Chapman	45 Nigel Bewick	61 Jonathan McGill
14 John Arnold	30 John Blade-Williamson	46 Paul Field	
15 Duncan McKinnon	31 David Kyte	47 Steve Rainbow	
16 Rowland Morris	32 David Letton	48 Phil Barnett	

uncomfortable. 'The compromise offered by the exchange – screen trading for less liquid option contracts, but only after a protracted period of systems development – is too weak,' asserted 'Lex' on 24 August. 'It should call the big houses' bluff, retain open outcry but install a central screen displaying anonymous orders for all to see. The big houses would still have free access to an efficient market, but the locals would have a crack at the business too.' At least the stamp duty and stock borrowing situation now seemed satisfactory, with Parliament having endorsed legislation which, following the implementation of intricately drafted regulations, would enable all members of the merged market to join the traditional Stock Exchange market makers in providing liquidity in the equity options market. Nevertheless, underlying doubts about the whole project persisted, not only on the part of the press, and were starting to be publicly voiced. 'The reasons given for the merger have always been perplexing,' Michael Stone, head of futures trading at Midland Montagu, told *Euroweek* in September. 'It seems to have been very much a government-driven initiative.' A dealer at one house that was active on both floors told the same magazine: 'The merger has never seemed wholly logical, because there is no synergy whatsoever between the client bases of the exchanges. LTOM is mainly institutional investors and equity traders; LIFFE is predominantly corporates, banks and bond traders. All LIFFE offers is an improvement over the dead hand of the Stock Exchange.'

Yet, perhaps if the name was got right, then everything else would follow. Over the past year there had been few *aficionados* of the Action Group's 'London Derivatives Exchange', but no one had managed to come up with anything better, perhaps because in their bones few LIFFE people could imagine that the now very well known LIFFE name could be dropped. Therefore, on 27 September, the board decided that the best policy would be to retain the LIFFE and LTOM names; to combine them into a new corporate logo; and to rename the exchange itself the London International Financial Futures and Options Exchange at the date of merger, while retaining the traditional pronunciation. That, at least, was settled, and it reflected more clearly than anything that it was not, and would not be, a union of equals.

On 28 October the long overdue merger prospectus was issued, inviting applications for £6 million worth of 'D' shares at £15,000 each. In his press briefing, Jenkins noted that in any computer-based trading system that might be developed, 'we

Ringing the Bell,
13 December 1991.
From left: Michael Jenkins,
Jack Wigglesworth, David
Burton, Brian Williamson,
John Barkshire.

Last flutter at the Royal
Exchange, 13 December
1991.

aim to ensure that every member of the market, whether a large securities house or a small independent local trader, will be able to use the computer system.' The offer closed on 21 November, with applications received for 307 'D' shares – well below the 400 shares on offer (of which 228 had been reserved for LTOM members), but comfortably above the 200 minimum that had been set. Unfortunately, it emerged over the next week or two that although sufficient market makers had put themselves forward to create a market in index options in the new exchange, not enough had committed themselves to making markets in the 67 equity options currently traded on LTOM. The offer of 'D' shares had been conditional upon LIFFE's board being satisfied about the adequacy of the market-making commitments. Accordingly, LIFFE announced on 11 December 1991 that the merger, due to take effect on 31 January 1992, would have to be delayed for at least two months. It was a thoroughly embarrassing situation, and over the next couple of days there was much press speculation that major LTOM players like Warburgs and Smith New Court were in effect applying pressure on LIFFE to speed up the introduction of screen-based trading for equity options. 'The problem,' wrote the *Evening Standard* on the 13th, 'revolves around the refusal of the big securities houses to operate under LIFFE's rules, fearing that the obligation to deal with all parties publicly would undermine their book positions.' And it claimed that Jenkins was 'touring the City in a last-ditch attempt to find market makers'. The 13th was a Friday, appropriately in one sense but perhaps not in another.

The sense in which it was not was that this invidious moment for Jenkins and his colleagues was also the final day of trading on the floor of the Royal Exchange. Barkshire rang the bell to close trading, a great deal of champagne was drunk, and it was clearly the end of an era in LIFFE's history. About to enter a new, physically much more spacious *milieu*, and on the verge of effectively taking over another London market, would LIFFE manage to retain the entrepreneurial, 'can do' culture that had characterised it for almost a decade? 'Fossilisation? Fear not!' Williamson had exclaimed in one of his last interviews as chairman. 'LIFFE has no desire to become an institution.' That, as much as anything else, was the challenge that lay ahead.

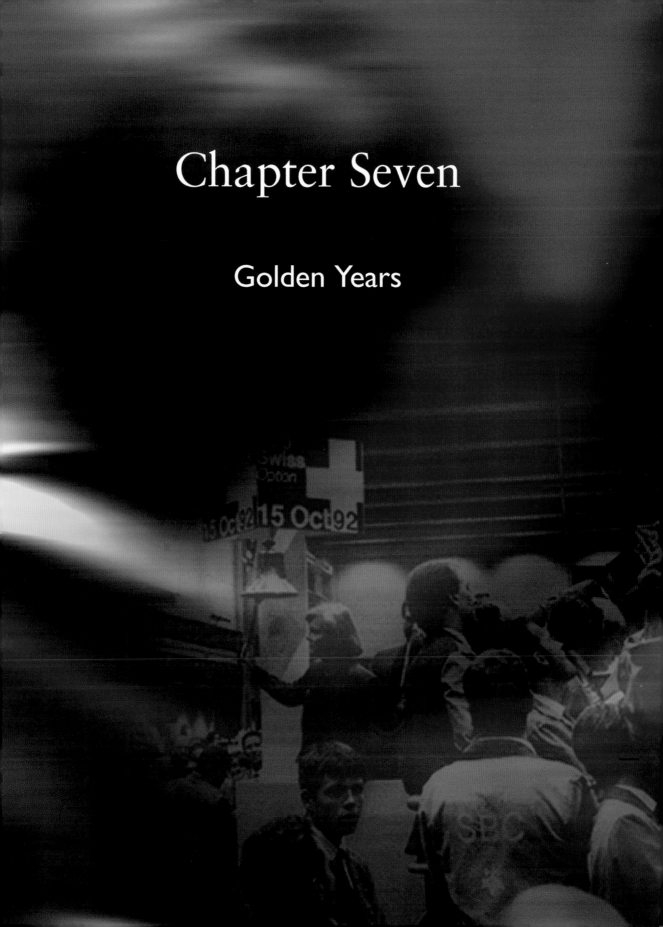

Chapter Seven

Golden Years

JUST BEFORE 7.30 am on a damp, dark, cold Monday morning – 16 December 1991 – and with London's transport system at a standstill because of terrorism, the Governor of the Bank of England, Robin Leigh-Pemberton, prepared to open LIFFE's new trading floor at Cannon Bridge. 'What recession?' one Bund futures trader shouted out as he prepared to speak, and for all the shortness of the speech (three minutes) and its praise of LIFFE's achievements, this rather patrician figure was not given the easiest of rides. He made the mistake of discussing London's need to become ECU centre of Europe, prompting a cry of 'Get on with it!'; and then, during the twenty seconds or so before 7.30 itself, there began the opening call as traders, according to their usual practice, yelled out prices to establish a trading range. Leigh-Pemberton hurriedly finished his speech before, typically good-natured, ringing the starting bell. Such a lack of decorum would have been unthinkable nine years earlier, when Leigh-Pemberton's predecessor initiated proceedings at the Royal Exchange, but that time there was not a Bund pit full of locals hungry for the action.

The new trading floor – like the old one, the responsibility of Steve Swain, who had succeeded Heymer in 1988 – covered some 25,000 square feet. It was

Robin Leigh-Pemberton
inaugurates trading at
Cannon Bridge,
16 December 1991.

two and a half times the area at the Royal Exchange, and there were 614 booths, 1,000 screens and 440 dealer board consoles. Whinney Mackay-Lewis were again the architects, and the whole thing cost some £31 million, with facilities designed to accommodate up to 3,000 traders and staff. 'LIFFE's new home has already been described as a mini Merc,' noted Emma Davey in *FOW* soon afterwards, in other words 'state of the art technology in a modern and bland environment'. Most people – traders and others – were pleased: there was a feeling that LIFFE had arrived, was now a 'real' exchange, allied to the luxury of having room to breathe, no longer needing (to put it at its most mundane) to queue for quarter of an hour to use one of the Royal Exchange's twelve lavatories. A few – a prescient few – wondered if the new floor was big enough.

Steve Swain.

Within a few weeks, certainly a few months, it was clear that the change of location had released an enormous volume of pent-up demand. Total volume in January 1992 was 5,309,277 contracts, a staggering 79% increase on the December 1991 figure and way ahead of the previous monthly record of 4.1 million contracts that had been set in November 1991. The trend continued, with volume for the first half of 1992 reaching over 32 million contracts, an increase of 73% over the same period in 1991. It was fairly obvious (if unprovable) that the failure to move earlier from the Royal Exchange had cost LIFFE a lot of volume. Moreover, in addition to space, the improved facilities now available made a significant contribution: the enhanced provision of booths allowed direct broking (i.e. not routed through members' offices) to take off, with big clients now having direct access to the point of execution; tiered booths lent themselves to better sight-lines and communication within the market; and bigger pits were more conducive to the trading process. In other words, this huge upsurge in volume, almost overnight after the move, was rather more complex than the 'M25 syndrome', though the analogy was striking. Within three years the trading floor was seriously full and the exchange was seriously starting to think about another move – the prospect of which would have amazed almost everyone who had watched the opening ceremony in December 1991 on that apparently cavernous floor.

The opening was the first of six major events in a hectic period between then and September 1992. The second took place on 11 February 1992, when the Queen visited LIFFE in its new home. She arrived at four o'clock, in time to watch the last few minutes of trading from the visitors' gallery. She then, according to *FOW*, 'unveiled the commemorative plaque in the trading hall in silence (save for the wolf whistles and cheering of the traders) and accepted her gift of a sterling silver trading badge, which was looked at with interest by Prince Philip'. There followed a tour of the trading floor, and among the carefully selected traders lined up to meet her was the inevitable David Morgan, suffering from a heavy cold. 'I hear you are very successful and have made a lot of money,' the Queen was quoted as saying to him. 'Ma'am, I lost money the first day I was on the floor, I've lost

The Queen at Cannon Bridge, 11 February 1992. Above: with cherubic traders. Opposite: with Chris Henry (Chairman of the Floor Committee).

money today, and now I've also lost my voice,' he replied. The other memorable moment came when she met a member of the board who, she quickly discovered, was American. 'Oh, and do you have exchanges like this in your country?' the Queen asked, to which he replied in the affirmative. The visit passed off very well, with the Queen overstaying her visit by three-quarters of an hour and confiding that she was sure that John Major would not mind having their weekly meeting delayed. The traders 'behaved absolutely stupendously' (in the words of a LIFFE official), and the only disappointment was the surprisingly small press coverage it received. It was also, of course, another sign of how far LIFFE had come in its brief history – no longer a semi-disreputable outsider, and in danger of turning into a pillar of the City.

The third event, altogether less glamorous and enjoyable, was the eventual completion of the merger with LTOM. By the second week of January market-makers had been found for each of LTOM's 67 individual stock options. Six firms were confirmed as market makers – J. G. Bolitho, City of London Options, Hills Independent Traders, James Capel, Kleinwort Benson and Swiss Bank Corporation – with four out of the 'Big Five' who had been so emphatically in favour of screen trading not making any such commitment to creating continuous bid/offer prices. Soon afterwards 307 'D' shares were provisionally allocated to applicants, both brokers and market makers, pending confirmation of the merger on 20 March,

with the first trading day to be 23 March. In the meantime, LTOM would physically move to Cannon Bridge on 3 February, and this it duly did, following a final day of trading on the Stock Exchange floor and in time for the Queen's visit.

Yet unbelievably, after having been so long in the making, the merger almost fell at the final fence. 'I am unhappy about the proposed management of the options market,' David Heron of James Capel had written to Burton on 8 January. 'I believe we need an externally appointed Managing Director of the equity options market accountable to a specialist options committee. Only 25–30% of "D" shares have been bought by people intending to trade stock options and it is important that this area has a proper voice which of course may not happen on the LIFFE Board.' Rightly or wrongly, LIFFE interpreted this demand as an attempt by LTOM to retain quasi-autonomy, as a market within the market. By mid-March, days before the merger was due to take effect, the matter remained unresolved, with Jenkins insisting that product development and marketing was the largest role that he could contemplate for a managing director for equity options, as opposed to the wish of James Capel and some of the other market makers for a managing director whose brief would cover *all* aspects of equity options. Such a role would, Jenkins wrote to David Wenman of SBC on the 19th, 'negate the objective of a fully integrated exchange and would be divisive'. In the end – though Jenkins in his desperation to get the thing through almost wobbled – the market makers backed down. The final decision had its drama. The LIFFE board meeting began at 9 am on the 20th, two hours before LCH was due to start transferring LTOM positions to LIFFE. The market makers met elsewhere, under the chairmanship of James Capel's Bernard Asher, to decide whether they would acquiesce in LIFFE's proposed management structure. They agreed, in writing, with 20 minutes to go. 'We have no wish to set terms and will certainly abide by Board decisions and support the Chief Executive,' two of them formally promised, though at the same time trusting that a business plan for the development of equity products would be in place by the end of May.

On Sunday the 22nd LTOM was formally sold to LIFFE – for the handsome price of £4 – and the next day the same trading and clearing systems were in operation for all. 'The merger has not been without its difficulties,' Jenkins admitted to the press. 'We've all been struggling to find a way forward: we're not sure if we've found it but we hope it will improve performance.' In all sorts of ways, many of them highly technical, it had been a phenomenally complicated and difficult process – eating up time, stalling progress on other fronts, souring relations between board and executive. In one sense it had been LIFFE doing its civic duty, in another it had been the City's revenge on LIFFE, the impudent upstart. And what was perhaps worst, few at LIFFE believed that it would result in the transforming of London's fortunes in the trading of equity options. The best foot would be put forward, but without joy in the heart or a song on the lips.

The LTOM merger.
Above: From left:
Pen Kent, David Parry,
Tony de Guingand.
Below: LIFFE's cheque.

Event number four, barely a fortnight later, was LIFFE's third general election. The early part of the campaign generated considerable volatility, and on 25 March the exchange announced that it would be opening the domestic contracts earlier than usual on 10 April, the morning after polling, because of demand from the marketplace. Indeed, there were some complaints that APT was not going to be made available through the night. The following week, reported *IFR*, 'the short sterling and long gilt contracts faced up to the possibility that Labour may win an outright majority', and it quoted one trader from a UK house: 'All of the economic fundamentals have gone entirely out of the window. It's being driven by the punters.' There was also high volume and volatility in the FTSE futures and options contracts, as (noted *IFR*) 'the March futures contract expired and hopes of a Conservative victory faded'. On Wednesday the 8th, the eve of polling, LIFFE took out a full-page advertisement in the *FT*: 'These are extremely testing times, even when you live with risk for a living. No election since the War has been harder fought or harder to call. Amid the frightening ups and downs, one name increasingly serves to steady nerves...' That name was not Ovaltine, and the advertisement claimed that 'in an uncertain world, LIFFE helps the international investor to control risk and manage exposure with a flexibility and efficiency that can't be matched anywhere'. In short: 'However difficult things get, LIFFE goes on.'

Election night was Basildon's night, and Robert Miller (not the financial futures specialist) described in the *Observer* the memorable morning that followed:

Market veteran Byron Baldwin, a director of BZW Futures, knew it would be a different kind of day from the start. 'By the time I arrived at 6.30 am most of the traders were already in to work. The atmosphere was quite incredible.'

When the bell signalled the start of trading at 7.15 am short sterling futures was the first open 'pit' into action. Two minutes later the sterling options pit fired up. To an outsider it looked like mayhem. In brightly coloured jackets, traders shout and gesticulate as they execute their clients' orders. Many of the yellow-jacketed runners, who carry orders from the side booths to the pit, joined LIFFE straight from school. Some are too young to vote.

By 7.18 above a chorus of 'Here we go, here we go...' from the Long Gilts pit waiting to start trading at 7.20, Roger Barton observed 'it's fast, very fast'. The prices board could only keep pace with the largest orders. 'It was bound to be this way because the election result was a surprise,' noted Barton. 'But the market's pricing well. You might have expected the bid-offer spread on contracts to have been much broader...'

The FTSE 100 Index pit opened at 7.25 am. Within 15 minutes around 2,000 contracts worth £55,000 per contract had been traded...

Over the day as a whole over 641,542 contracts changed hands, 60% higher than the previous record of 399,600 contracts set on 22 November 1991. The short sterling future was the most traded, with 139,046 lots, but all the sterling-based contracts were busy. 'This has been a very exciting day for the exchange,' reflected Jenkins, 'clearly demonstrating the efficiency of the facilities and systems that we now have at Cannon Bridge. Trading these sort of volumes would have been impossible at the Royal Exchange.' BZW's Baldwin was even more bucked: 'We've survived our baptism of fire. In spite of record volumes the market coped. We've proved we are a liquid exchange. It's been an amazing day.'

Five months later, on 16 September – Black Wednesday or White Wednesday according to taste – the Major government lost much of its authority, as Britain left the ERM and sterling was effectively devalued. The ignominious departure came after the market had closed, but base rates had already risen twice in a vain attempt to hold the line. The pace on LIFFE's floor was frantic – the sweaty atmosphere not helped by the air conditioning having been set for a cool autumnal day – and the post-election record was easily surpassed, as 886,110 lots changed

SOLD down the river

Their faces contorted with tension and their voices hoarse from screaming deals, traders at the London financial futures market h the floor running and didn't stop throughout the most hectic day they've ever known.

As deafening pandemonium broke out, a record 850,000 deals wer struck involving securities worth £243 BILLION.

THIS was Black wednesday madness yesterday as City "bookies" gambling on Britain's future went o an orgy of selling in an atmosphere of raw agression

Yesterday, with two interest rates announced in three hours and a devaluation on the way, there was only one message f sterling - sell, sell, sell.

hands. 'In historic session, London outtrades Chicago markets' was the *Chicago Tribune*'s headline, and indeed on that Wednesday, for the first time, both the CBOT and CME traded lower volumes. Almost a third of LIFFE's volume was accounted for by the short sterling future, with the Euromark future the second busiest contract. After it was all over, two exhausted traders talked to the *Daily Mirror*. 'I thought it was a hell of a day when the first rate rise came,' declared one. 'But when the second hit us, the place went mental. It's been selling all day. I've never seen anything like it.' 'Gazza' French said his bit over a pint of lager: 'Thank Christ that's over. I knew it was going to be a long day. But I never thought Lamont would freak like that.' And he added: 'The irony is that it's all been dead for us lately. No-one's wanted to have a punt and we've been scrambling about for the odd winner. Now, when it all turns to dust, we can make a bit of dosh.' A national humiliation hardly made City traders and speculators the flavour of the moment, but in practice the criticism was directed far less at LIFFE than at George Soros and the foreign exchange market in general. That was appropriate, granted the different nature of the products that LIFFE and the foreign exchange market were dealing in; and in what was increasingly a world of screen trading, it was becoming LIFFE's misfortune as well as blessing that it was so photogenic.

Opposite: Black Wednesday, 16 September 1992.

The final event in this quick-fire sequence came very soon afterwards – LIFFE's tenth anniversary, celebrated internationally with some 400 people attending dinners in Milan, Frankfurt, Paris and New York. In Britain the social climate had changed since 1987, and this time round the emphasis was on charity. Over £100,000 was raised, culminating in a huge charity ball held on Friday, 25 September in the grounds of the Honourable Artillery Company. Elaine Paige was the star turn of the cabaret during dinner; Richard Sandor won the car, but his wife persuaded him to give it back to auction on the basis that it would be good for Anglo-American relations; and over 2,000 guests danced until morning.

By this time there was a new chairman, Nick Durlacher. He had succeeded Burton in June, becoming the first chairman not to be one of the founding fathers. His background was City through and through, but he had already shown a marked capacity to move with the times and he would continue to do so. He also, unlike most sons of the City, had an economics degree, and in general an ability to grasp quickly the essence of an issue. From January 1993 Durlacher had a new chief executive working for him. Michael Jenkins, having turned sixty, had more than done his time, having made a contribution over 11½ years to the exchange's development that it would be difficult to overestimate. The feeling was that the new man should come from outside, and after a thorough search Daniel Hodson was appointed. An Oxford-educated Etonian, he was in his late forties and was

Ten charities get a lease of Liffe

TEN charities have received the keys to a brighter and more mobile future thanks to the London International Financial Futures Exchange and the Evening Standard. More than £100,000 was raised at a ball held to mark Liffe's 10th anniversary and other activities including an appeal on the exchange room floor raised enough to buy 10 Daf Leyland mini-buses and cover their running costs for a year.

LIFFE Locals raise money to launch British Brain & Spine Foundation

Traders raise £230,000 for charity

LIFFE donates money to the Royal Brompton Hospital

currently deputy chief executive and group finance director of the Nationwide Building Society. Importantly, his experience over the years had been treasury management, and having been one of the founder members of the Association of Corporate Treasurers he was now its president. Manifestly intelligent, and like his predecessor combining culture with commerce, he had the sophistication that would be needed to oversee an increasingly large, complex organisation.

Generals, however, need troops, and most of them were to be found on what was becoming an increasingly crowded trading floor, especially after the issue in April 1992 of 'E' shares, a rights issue aimed not at raising money but at creating more trading rights, to ensure that no contract failed to flourish because of insufficient traders. Accordingly, 466 'E' shares were issued, at only £2,000 each, and the trading permits linked to the shares were valid for all futures contracts except the Bund, Euromark, FTSE 100 Index, long gilt and short sterling. At the time of the move to Cannon Bridge the trading population was around 800, but by the end of 1992 it had almost doubled to 1,500, of whom some 350 were registered as locals. By September 1993 the local population was up to about 500, and in May 1994 a further rights issue was made, enabling a 25% increase in each category of trading permit except 'D' shares. That November, in the *FT*, Conner Middelmann looked at what it was like being one of LIFFE's infantry:

Opposite: Some of LIFFE's charity work.

Nick Durlacher.

Warning: derivatives trading can seriously damage your health. 'This is one of the toughest, most physically and mentally demanding professions in existence, apart from professional sports,' says the floor manager of a large member firm. 'The pressure you have to deal with on a daily basis can be unrelenting and absolutely merciless.'

For a start, there are the purely physical side-effects. 'If you're in this business long enough, you tend to go hoarse – as I have,' rasps one of LIFFE's old-timers. Foot problems also abound. 'When you're standing around all day, you tend to get swollen feet, callouses and lots of dead skin,' complains one trader. Orthopaedic shoes are hardly an option. 'If you appear in a pair of Scholls, you'll have the Shoe Committee on your back,' he laughs. The so-called Shoe Committee, a regular source of hilarity for LIFFE dealers, is a self-appointed 'watchdog' made up of floor traders who derive amusement from keeping 'unsuitable' footwear – such as Doc Martens, brown or suede shoes – off the floor.

The tight throng of human bodies in the pits also makes them perfect breeding ground for bacteria, which are transmitted through droplet infection as dealers shout out prices. 'If one person comes in with a cold, the next day half the pit will be sneezing and wheezing,' says a trader…

In an environment where tensions run high and fully grown men – for only 30 per cent of the floor population (including broking and administrative staff) are female – jostle for space in small pits, market participants can come to blows. 'There are many reasons for fisticuffs,' says a LIFFE dealer. For one, he says, 'working conditions are appalling – we're crowded into the pits like rats in a small cage and have to perform an exacting function where mistakes are not tolerated.'

Daniel Hodson.

What's more, many dealers trade their own money, and 'when they lose money, they can lose their temper,' he says. In volatile markets, these factors can create a highly charged atmosphere where people may be tempted to use physical violence – a temptation to which some occasionally yield.

However, the price of physical violence in the pits is high: a strict code of conduct is enforced by close supervision of the LIFFE trading floor, and offenders face harsh fines. LIFFE penalises offenders much more heavily than a court would do for the same offence, with fines for violent behaviour – which includes pushing and shoving – running as high as £5,000. The ultimate sanction for repeated misconduct is suspension from the trading floor. 'The exchange comes down very, very hard to ensure that business is not disrupted,' says a LIFFE spokeswoman.

The psychological impact of the stresses and strains of this job can be as serious as – if not more so than – the physical side-effects, and psychological burn-out can lead to a variety of stress-related illnesses. 'You are on edge all day, from the moment the pit opens until the moment it closes,' says Dorian Hart, floor manager for BZW Futures. 'Often your brain doesn't get any time to think; it's purely reactive,' he adds. 'This breeds a wide variety of stress-related afflictions, such as eczema, ulcers, nervous twitches, heart problems and alcohol abuse,' says a dealer.

Alas, many of the City's stress-sufferers do not actually acknowledge that they feel mentally or physically stretched. 'People who come to us will not necessarily present stress as their primary problem,' says Dr John Briffa, who runs Cannons' Health Enhancement Centre. 'Working in the City is inherently stressful, but a lot of people don't acknowledge that.' For one, he says, it's because 'everyone else is stressed, so they think it's the norm'. But even when they are aware of the stress burden, 'there's a fair degree of machismo in the City that doesn't allow them to admit that they can't cope'…

The potential financial rewards were of course handsome, but the article was an important reminder that the enormously high volumes that the exchange was now attaining were not achieved painlessly.

The figures for LIFFE's first three years at Cannon Bridge are eloquent enough. In 1992 a total of 71.97 million contracts, over 86% up on 1991; in 1993 a total of 101.87 million contracts, 42% up on 1992; and in 1994 a total of 153.03 million contracts, 50% up on 1993. Put another way, average daily volume in 1994 was 607,000 contracts – a volume which in 1982/3 it took LIFFE about half a year to achieve. ERM chaos, in 1993 as well as 1992, was of course an important factor behind these astounding volumes; while in early 1994 there were the consequences of the world's bond markets feeling the plates shift beneath them, as American interest rates rose for the first time in four years, and hedge funds in particular moved even more heavily into derivatives in order to unwind positions no longer making easy money. On 3 February that year the seven-figure barrier was broken for a single day's trading, over the rest of the month that barrier was crossed eight more times, and on 2 March a new daily record of 1.61 million contracts was established. 'This underscores LIFFE's continuing ability to provide a deeply liquid and efficient market for the management of risk, even at times of financial stress,' noted Durlacher with every justification. Indeed, for as many as twelve days in the first quarter of 1994, LIFFE traded a greater volume than any other derivatives exchange in the world. And though for the year as a whole it was still behind both the CBOT and CME (219.50 million and 205.18 million contracts respectively), the gap was closing fast. 'Perhaps much of this is to be expected because we are a Johnny-come-lately', in that 'the markets in North America are far more mature than we are,' Durlacher modestly told the *Chicago Tribune* in June that year; while the same paper commented that LIFFE's phenomenal rate of growth had 'set off alarm bells in executive suites at the CBOT, at the foot of LaSalle Street, and at the Merc, 30 S. Wacker Drive'. LIFFE, in short, was a contender, having moved from the European league to the world league.

LIFFE's core domestic contracts – long gilt and short sterling – continued during these years to perform always very respectably, occasionally sensationally, especially short sterling during sterling's travails during the autumn of 1992. For the long gilt contract, liquidity or otherwise in the cash market was as ever the crux, and near the end of 1994 the Bank of England at last announced its long-awaited plans for a repo market in British government bonds. Perhaps at last the gilt-edged market would become less idiosyncratic and more open to international investors.

Inevitably though, in terms of UK products, the main focus in the wake of the LTOM merger was on equity derivatives, above all LIFFE's own FTSE 100 future and the equity options that LTOM brought to the proceedings. Karin Forseke was recruited to head the equity products division from early 1993, while not long afterwards the 'LTOM' part vanished from the exchange's logo. Progress

Trading floor layout at
Cannon Bridge, December
1991.

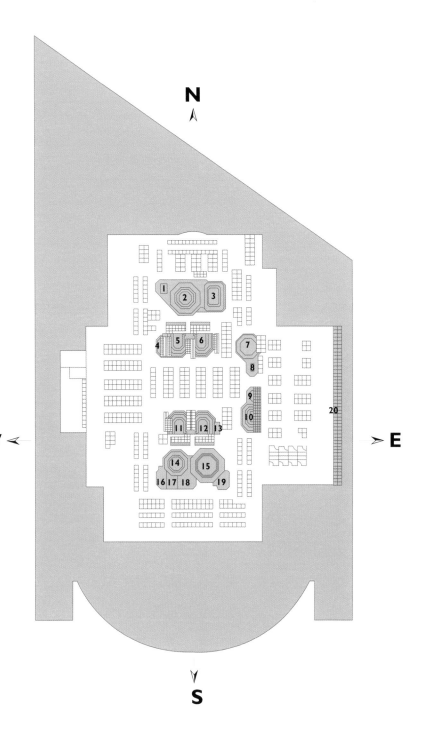

KEY

 1 Eurodollar
 2 Short Sterling
 3 Long Gilt
 4 Eurodollar Option
 5 Short Sterling Option
 6 Gilt Option
 7 FTSE Future
 8 Eurotrack Future
 9 Eurotrack Option
10 SEI and ESX FTSE
    Options
11 Euromark Option
12 Bund Option
13 BTP Option
14 Euromark
15 Bund
16 Euroswiss Franc
17 ECU Three Month
18 ECU Bond
19 BTP
20 Equity Options

614 booths

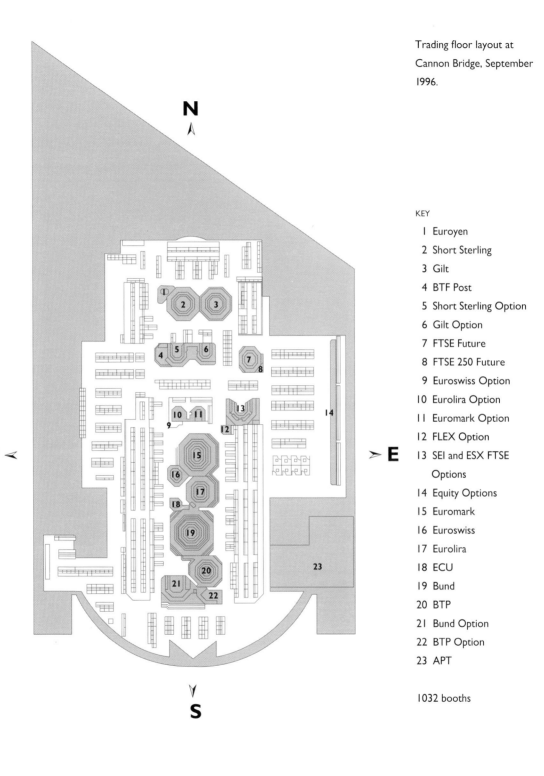

Trading floor layout at
Cannon Bridge, September
1996.

N

W   **E**

S

KEY

1 Euroyen
2 Short Sterling
3 Gilt
4 BTF Post
5 Short Sterling Option
6 Gilt Option
7 FTSE Future
8 FTSE 250 Future
9 Euroswiss Option
10 Eurolira Option
11 Euromark Option
12 FLEX Option
13 SEI and ESX FTSE
   Options
14 Equity Options
15 Euromark
16 Euroswiss
17 Eurolira
18 ECU
19 Bund
20 BTP
21 Bund Option
22 BTP Option
23 APT

1032 booths

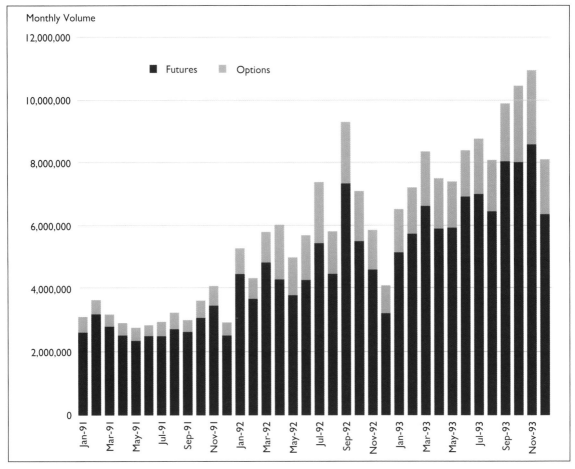

The growth of LIFFE business, 1991–93.

proved distinctly mixed. The success stories, relatively speaking, were the FTSE 100 future and option (the latter formerly traded on LTOM), which by the first quarter of 1994 were achieving between them an average daily volume of over 43,000 contracts. By then, not only had a recent Bank of England working paper by Gary Robinson found that futures trading, far from increasing stock market volatility, in fact significantly reduced it; but there was also trading on a new stock index. This was the FTSE Mid 250 future, launched by the England rugby captain Will Carling on 25 February 1994. The index was of medium-sized UK companies, and to LIFFE's displeasure the Stock Exchange had awarded a licence to trade a contract on its Mid-Cap 250 (introduced in October 1992) not only to it but to a rival London exchange, the London Securities and Derivatives Exchange (OMLX), an electronically trading subsidiary of Sweden's OM Group. OMLX launched three weeks earlier, but it was LIFFE who won the battle – 40,674 contracts during 1994, compared with OMLX's 19,070 – though the contract itself was at best a qualified flop, not helped by being launched at the peak of the market.

A far greater disappointment – to optimists, anyway – were individual equity options. In 1992 (from 23 March) they traded 3.53 million contracts, in 1993 4.76 million, and in 1994 4.30 million. Put another way, they contributed but a small part of the exchange's overall business, LIFFE's locals refused to get involved in what were only patchily liquid products, and most of the floor did not view equity options as integral to the market. All this was despite regular changes to the mix of equity options and a concerted campaign seeking to encourage more private investors to use traded options as part of their portfolios. 'Equity options have been slow to catch on in this country, due to misunderstanding and to a lack of the kind of promotion that they have received abroad,' Roger Barton explained to the *Sunday Times* in April 1993. The marketing drive that ensued was impressive, but it neither produced instant results nor could do anything about another abiding problem facing equity options – the lack of transparency in the cash market.

Will Carling launches the FTSE Mid 250 futures contract, 25 February 1994.

Inevitably this was a sensitive issue, and in 1994 there was considerable discussion at board level before LIFFE submitted in June its formal response to SIB's February discussion paper on 'Regulation of United Kingdom Equity Markets'. During that discussion, 'one view was expressed that major institutional investors wanted the present UK Equity market-making system in its existing form and did not therefore want to change the current structure'. Moreover, 'it was recognised that while LIFFE should be promoting an increase in liquidity and price transparency this should not be viewed as being to the detriment of the existing structure'. Overall, however, the strong opinion was (in the words of a press release paraphrasing LIFFE's submission) that the equity market had become 'one interdependent market', both cash *and* derivatives; that 'UK investors increasingly depend on both exchange-traded futures and options as risk management tools and see them as part of a multi-dimensional market'; that 'there must be a *controlled* move to greater, and eventually to full, price transparency in the cash market'; and that 'specifically, the current cash market (delayed) publication rules [90 minutes and in some cases up to 5 days] and lack of access to IDB [the Inter-Dealer Broker market, 'a secret screen-based auction market restricted to equity market makers'] and trade information are at the heart of UK price and volume transparency issues and are hampering the development of an efficient derivatives market in UK equities'. Altogether, LIFFE's submission was a significant contribution to what was evolving into a major, lengthy debate about procedures in the cash market – but for the moment, it did nothing to alter the miserable fact that the exchange continued to lie tenth in the world league table for equity options, with SOFFEX, OM [Stockholm Options Market], DTB and EOE all well ahead in the European time zone.

Nor was there excessive enthusiasm at large for LIFFE's non-UK, non-European contracts. The Japanese government bond future, relaunched in April 1991 and APT-traded only, 'has failed to excite London-based traders since its launch,' noted *FOW* in August 1992, 'despite frequent efforts by LIFFE to improve its fortunes.' However, 'most traders believe that it is beneficial for LIFFE to offer such a contract amongst its interest rate product range'. Matters improved in 1993, with total volume on the JGB future up to 421,454 lots (a 90% increase on 1992), and 1994 saw a further advance, to 610,925. These were hardly figures to keep the screens busy, but the dollar-denominated products – once so important to LIFFE – were a far sorrier tale. Even when flooding caused the CBOT to close briefly in April 1992, the expected volume failed to materialise in the T-bond pit; and in May 1993, having managed only 2 lots the previous month, the T-bond future did not trade at all. On 1 June, accordingly, both it and the option were delisted, victims of the increasing tendency in recent years of London-based firms to concentrate on European bond markets.

The Eurodollar future and option were also struggling, despite a change in settlement procedure from 1992 by which, at the wishes of the market, the quotes for the final settlement prices were taken from the British Bankers Association as opposed to from a sample of banks by the exchange itself, thereby making the procedure the same as that in the interest rate cash and forward markets. Mark Eynon, speaking to *FOW* that April, probably got it right about the Eurodollar: 'It is tightly priced to the cash market and does not get out of line. It is a very comfortable contract which is perfectly formed – it just has time-zone problems which can't be changed.' By the second half of 1994 the option was failing to trade, while the future was on a rapid downward spiral, from 6,912 lots in July to 1,673 in October to 586 in December. Towards the end of the year, following a survey of the more active Eurodollar market participants, Bruce told the board that the future 'was generally perceived of having very little chance of being a truly competitive product because of limited time zone advantage and the liquidity of competing products'. For the moment, however, both contracts stayed listed.

Europe more than ever was the prime battleground. In the course of 1992 three contracts were suspended, but two new ones launched. It had been clear by the end of 1991 that none of the Euro-indices was flourishing – a case, it was generally accepted by the industry, of liquidity being fatally split between exchanges – and LIFFE delisted on 17 June the Eurotrack futures and options contracts, the latter of which it had inherited from LTOM. A far more painful experience was the ECU bond future, which had started trading in March 1991. Against a background of volume flagging badly in comparison with MATIF's rival contract, LIFFE relaunched it in January with the backing of five dedicated market makers, as well as changing the contract design to include only sovereign debt and to allow greater flexibility in the selection of deliverable bonds. Having sunk to an embarrassing 5 lots for the whole of December, volume did somewhat pick up as a result, to several hundred a day, but one market maker told *IFR* that 'what is still missing is the commitment of the big cash market players'. Soon afterwards, in early February, Carrington informed the board that 'the relaunched contract was having difficulty becoming established', with LIFFE's market share in the contract being only 7–8% for January, adding that 'the fundamental problem was the lack of "paper" in the pit'. By March two of the five designated market makers had pulled out, and volume that month was only 1,514, compared with 148,720 lots traded in Paris. 'LIFFE was too late with its product,' one Paris trader told *Euromoney*. 'In derivatives nothing succeeds like success. By the time the LIFFE alternative came on line, the MATIF's had gained the liquidity which a contract needs to survive.' While in London an ECU bond trader at Bank of Tokyo Capital Markets argued that 'the market is not big enough to sustain two contracts' and that 'there just isn't the amount of deliverable bonds like in gilts or German bunds'.

Quite apart from being given such an obvious bloody nose by MATIF, it was not just another contract. 'If one believes that EMU is coming the exchange cannot just accept defeat,' Durlacher explained to *Euroweek* early in June. A fortnight later the board pondered the matter:

It was recognised that the only way of revitalising the ECU Bond contract was to get the support of additional market makers. In the absence of such support the future of this contract was questionable. However, the feeling was that if EMU were to go ahead the ECU Bond must represent a major contract opportunity and should therefore be kept constantly under review. The Exchange could not afford to accept that the battle for the ECU Bond contract had been finally lost. It was noted that LIFFE had nonetheless lost the 'image battle' for this contract...

In fact, June saw the last 10 trades in the contract ('Every time we see a trade, we go out and get drunk,' one London trader told *IFR* soon afterwards); by the autumn the prospect of European monetary union had sharply receded, in British eyes anyway, as the European exchange rate mechanism began to unravel; and on 5 November the exchange bowed to the inevitable by delisting the contract. Trading, however, continued in the three-month ECU future, albeit on a fairly modest scale. In fact, the ECU bond victory for MATIF was essentially symbolic, in that by the end of 1992 the Paris exchange remained essentially a one-product market, with the French treasury bond future (the *notionnel*) still almost all-dominant, being indeed at that time Europe's leading long-term interest rate contract. LIFFE, by contrast, not only had the breadth, but also the overall volume: in 1992 almost 72 million contracts traded, compared with MATIF's 55 million.

The first and more important of 1992's two new contracts was the three-month Eurolira future, launched on 12 May and aiming to cover the short end of the Italian market. There was some urgency, for as Carrington explained to the board in January, 'the Italians plan to have their own BTP contract [i.e. in Italian government bonds] by the summer, and their expected introduction of a Eurolira Contract shortly afterwards made it imperative that this launch was not delayed'. The bond future, initiated the previous September, was already well established (trading 142,000 contracts in January 1992), so it made sense in every way. The Eurolira started reasonably well, with a daily average of about 2,500 lots during its first week, but attention soon switched to the BTP future. On 3 June, following Denmark's rejection of the Maastricht treaty, nearly 68,000 lots were traded. Over the next few weeks volume remained high, and *IFR* noted at the start of September that the Italian government had 'provided plenty of incentive to use the future, with interest rate volatility, currency woes and political uncertainty occasionally driving traders into a frenzy'. LIFFE's strength in the contract provided a daunting challenge to Italy's new financial futures market, MIF, when it began trading on 11 September, two months behind schedule. 'With its range of government bond futures, LIFFE offers arbitrage opportunities unavailable on a domestic market featuring just one government's debt,' one Milan trader gloomily told the *FT*. In fact MIF got off to an excellent start, helped not only by the Italian financial crisis but by general volatility on the back of the French referendum on Maastricht, and for a time in

Carlo Gilardi launches the Three Month Eurolira futures contract, 12 May 1992.

October even ran neck and neck with LIFFE on the BTP future, before settling to about a 40% share.

Meanwhile, LIFFE had launched on 15 October its other new contract, an option on the three-month Euroswiss future. The announcement in July, *IFR* noted at the time, 'was received with apathy by the market, which said the contract may have difficulty attracting liquidity despite the success of the futures contract', the latter turning over almost 175,000 lots in June, well ahead of the rival SOFFEX contract. LIFFE's justification, however, was not only the growth in the futures contract but also the increasing volatility in the Swiss franc. Certainly there was no shortage of interest rate volatility by mid-October, and Rachel Lomax, Treasury deputy secretary in charge of financial institutions and markets, observed as she launched the contract that 'our problems have been your opportunity'. The option got off to quite a bright start before rather fading away in December, but the future finished the year in the knowledge (so to speak) that SOFFEX had delisted its rival. 'It has really been a question of liquidity,' one Swiss banker informed *IFR*. 'The spreads on LIFFE were always much tighter – and everyone wants a liquid market.'

Rachel Lomax launches the Three Month Euroswiss options contract, 15 October 1992.

According to a trader, the recent monetary turbulence had sealed the fate of the SOFFEX contract: 'When the currency is flying around, loyalty goes out the window. You go where you can get a good price.' Home to five other successful short-term interest rate futures, benefitting from London's position as the centre for Swiss franc forward swaps and options, supported by the three big Swiss banks – LIFFE had held all the advantages.

Much more critically, most of the high deutschmark cards also continued to belong to London, as became clear in the course of 1992. 'Although German banks had been told that they must put a certain level of business through the DTB,' Carrington told the board on 7 January, 'there was no evidence that LIFFE was losing business to the DTB'; and a month later she reported that LIFFE's market share during January in the Bund future had been 71%, with volume reaching a record 1.3 million lots. The Euromark future was also enjoying extremely healthy growth, trading 887,919 contracts. LIFFE's market share of the Bund future remained at 71% during February, and the following month Eynon (in his capacity as chief executive of the futures and options subsidiary of Warburgs) told *Banking Technology* that 'we will not shift our Bund futures business to the DTB', explaining that 'this has nothing to do with turnover figures or market liquidity, but with the flexibility of a trading system during times of high volatility'. He added that as soon as there was nervousness, then it was easier and quicker to change quotes on the floor in London than on the computer in Frankfurt. 'Our clients want to trade on that exchange where they can square positions quickest. The DTB is too complicated, especially during hectic and volatile periods.' Breuer, the DTB's chairman, naturally disagreed with that and other criticisms: 'People think there is more liquidity on LIFFE and that's wrong. They also think the spreads are better on LIFFE. But that's also wrong.' *Banking Technology* also quoted a senior DTB official, who stated that 'we are determined to overtake London this year' and predicted that volume in the Bund future would 'exceed the level recorded on LIFFE by the end of 1992 at the latest'.

Over the next few months the ratio stayed roughly constant, with LIFFE taking some 70% or just below of market share, and during the European political and monetary dramas of the summer LIFFE's Bund future featured in an enormous amount of spread trading, usually also involving the BTP future. Volume for the first eight months of the year was over 9 million contracts, a 130% increase on the same period in 1991. However, it was the Euromark future that really took the eye. Having limbered up on 16 July with a record 87,071 lots, as everyone that day waited for and then responded to a crucial Bundesbank announcement on rates, it then achieved monthly volumes from September to November of 1.79 million, 1.57 million and 1.42 million, in each month quite comfortably LIFFE's top contract. While as for the Bund, Jenkins spoke in November to *Securities & Investment Review* with the relaxed air of someone who felt he had won the battle: 'While some people find it convenient to use the DTB in Germany, particularly German banks, a lot of the more international players use LIFFE, and because there's good volume, because there's arbitrage between the two, there's liquidity on both markets.' It was probably at about this time that Jenkins was given a conducted tour of the Deutsche Bank's dealing room in Frankfurt. To his surprise, there was a commentary being broadcast from the LIFFE floor as to what was happening and who was doing what. When he queried this, he was told that it was the only way the traders got a real feel for the market and in particular what David Kyte was up to.

Indeed, Jenkins might have added to the press that the latest 1992 figures showed the DTB's market share of the Bund future on a downward trend: 27% in October and 25% in November, having been a little above 30% for the first nine months of the year. 'Clients are said to fear lack of liquidity in the DTB future,' noted *IFR* on 12 December. 'Locals enable the LIFFE Bund future to move in a one-tick range, while the DTB contract can jump three or four ticks at a time, according to one trader.' For 1992 as a whole, the DTB's Bund future posted a total of 5.32 million contracts, compared with LIFFE's 13.60 million, itself a 34% increase on 1991. In terms of overall volume, the DTB's 34.84 million contracts, though double the 1991 volume, was less than half that of LIFFE. Altogether, these were figures that LIFFE would happily have settled for as it took stock after the move to Cannon Bridge.

Still, even Don Bradman got the occasional duck, and LIFFE was about to score two in quick succession. The first was the futures contract in medium-term German government bonds ('Bobls'), launched on 21 January 1993 in direct competition against the DTB's very similar contract, that had been trading with increasing success since October 1991. There was strong support from members and clients for such a contract, and announcing it Durlacher noted that the contract placed LIFFE 'in the unique position of being able to provide products covering the whole deutschmark yield curve'. *IFR* recorded locals relishing its prospects in advance. 'The cash market is bigger than in the ten-year,' said one, 'and you could do butterflies between the two-year strips of the Euromark, the Bobl and the Bund futures.' Thirteen designated brokers (none of them German) were appointed; and in Durlacher's name the mandatory press invitations were sent out for the opening ceremony, due to be performed shortly after 7 am by Eddie George, who was himself on the verge of being appointed the Bank of England's next governor. Christopher Fildes replied in the columns of *The Spectator*: 'With his invitation comes a reply card asking me to say who I am and what I do. Against "Position" I have written: At that time of day, supine.'

The fairly widespread but not unanimous expectation in London was that, with Frankfurt trading only some 10,000 Bobl contracts daily, it would not take LIFFE long to establish an advantage. However, a market share of 42% on the first day was down to 29% a week later. LIFFE's daily average during February was 5,088 lots, less than a third of the DTB's 15,744, and a Frankfurt trader gave to *IFR* what was becoming a familiar explanation in these contests: 'It is purely a matter of liquidity. Traders will go where the natural market is, which for the Bobl futures is Germany.' Or as the DTB's Wilhelm Brandt defiantly put it to *FOW* soon afterwards: 'Why should investors automatically go to London just because LIFFE has launched its own Bobl? LIFFE is a good exchange but that is not a reason to leave.' Over the next six months LIFFE's market share remained thoroughly disappointing, fluctuating between 10 and 20%, and from the start of October a four-month fee holiday was introduced, LIFFE offering a free contract for each contract traded for own account in the Bobl. But at best this only stopped the erosion of market share, and by the end of the year it was pretty clear that the Bobl had gone. No doubt the almost inexorable 'first mover' advantage had applied; there was also a feeling on the floor that the sight-lines into the pit where the Bobl traded were inadequate; interest rates were relatively stable at the time of launch; and as Tracy Corrigan pointed out in the *FT* then, 'while LIFFE dominates bund future trading, cash market trading in shorter-term German debt is more concentrated in the domestic market, which could give the DTB a natural advantage'. Whatever the reasons, it was an unambiguous defeat – and eventually, in September 1994, the Bobl was delisted.

Bobby Charlton celebrates the FTSE 100 Tenth Anniversary with the traders, 3 May 1994.

The other flop was the futures contract in the almost equally delightfully named Bonos, in other words ten-year Spanish government bonds. It was a contract explicitly designed to compete head-on with an existing contract on Meff Renta Fija, the Spanish futures exchange based in Barcelona, and it should have been launched in late 1992. However, as Bruce explained to the board in October, 'recent ERM turmoil and the consequent imposition of peseta capital controls (although largely subsequently revoked) had led to a loss of support, at least in the short term, for such a contract'. By January 1993, following a delay, the climate was more favourable, with international investors' involvement in the cash market in Spanish bonds starting to pick up and the Spanish government increasing its borrowing requirement. Accordingly, LIFFE announced on 2 February that it was going ahead, immediately provoking an angry reaction from José-Luis Oller, MEFF's chief executive: 'We think it is the wrong policy for a market which is not very large. LIFFE is going to segment the market and split the liquidity.' And he added that 'we are convinced that LIFFE will not have the success they are expecting in capturing MEFF's international clients'. *Risk* could not resist the headline 'LIFFE miffs MEFF', while Barton attempted to defuse the situation by claiming that 'the launch will have a beneficial impact on the Spanish government bond cash market, broaden the holding of Spanish government bonds and will help the Spanish authorities'.

Entirely appropriately, it was Michael Portillo, Chief Secretary to the Treasury, who rang the bell on 10 March. Traders had cut the bell's cord in advance, but Portillo had been warned and, as a good politician, acted as if nothing had happened when the bell came off in his hand. MEFF was equally well prepared for the challenge, having reduced its trading and clearing fees drastically, and over the first fortnight LIFFE's volume ran at only about 1,000 lots daily, at best one-fifth of market share. On 29 March the London contract managed only 235 lots; and in mid-April, with LIFFE's daily volume still struggling at less than 1,000, compared to MEFF's 10,000, Richard Reinert of Refco told Reuters that 'institutional clients have preferred to use MEFF because of the better bid-ask rate, and greater liquidity has meant they have a better chance of getting larger volumes executed at a moment's notice'. In July only 17 lots were traded for the whole month, and though various remedies were considered – such as a fee holiday and a renewed commitment from market makers – the board decided early in August to suspend. Daily Bonos volume on MEFF by this time was some 23,000 lots, and Durlacher made a wry acknowledgement: 'When we launched the contract, we said we'd enhance the market. We didn't realise quite how successful we would be.' The experience had taught the valuable lesson that it was not easy to penetrate another country's government debt market if there was already an exchange in existence in that country; and pointed up what a huge stroke of fortune it had been to LIFFE that both Germany and Italy had been such sluggish starters in financial futures. Arguably an autumn 1992 start would have helped, so too might have a less sophisticated contract specification, but neither would have altered the fundamentals of the situation, granted that MEFF had been trading Bonos futures since April 1992.

On more familiar European terrain, LIFFE's products broadly maintained their ascendency during 1993/4. Italy's MIF achieved a roughly 30% share of the market in the 10-year BTP future, but never threatened overall repatriation of the contract; there was now no head-on product rivalry with MATIF; and the Bobl failure did no more than tarnish LIFFE's dominance of the market in German interest rate products. It was that latter area that remained the absolutely crucial one as far as LIFFE was concerned – in March 1993, for example, the Bund and Euromark futures accounted for approximately 3.6 million lots, out of a total exchange volume of 8.3 million. As between them, the Euromark made the running in the first half of 1993, but from August that year to November 1994 the Bund was ahead every month except May 1994. In 1993 the Euromark future traded 21.31 million contracts (75% up on 1992) to the Bund future's 20.44 million (up 50% on 1992); but in 1994 the Bund future was well ahead, with 37.33 million contracts to the Euromark future's 29.31 million.

In late 1993, with LIFFE still enjoying a comfortable 72% market share in the Bund future, the DTB announced that it would be initiating the following March a three-month future, known as the Fibor, to compete with LIFFE's Euromark future. 'The Euromark is a very, very liquid, fast-moving market,' one German trader told the *Wall Street Journal*. 'Frankfurt will have to build up big volume if it wants to develop the same liquidity.' And the head of money-market trading at one of the market makers lined up for the new contract complained that it 'should have been introduced 10 years ago, but there is something in our German mentality that is more concerned with market-using than market-making'. Soon after that move by the DTB took effect, LIFFE introduced serial options in the Bund option and Euromark option, on 10 May and 1 June respectively. The Bund option had always been the more major contributor of the two – for instance, a volume of 3.43 million lots in the first four months of 1994, making it the sixth most active contract in that period – and these serial options, allowing users to benefit from lower premiums, were broadly welcomed. The DTB's Fibor initiative, meanwhile, made little impact, with LIFFE by September having a 98% market share of Euromark contracts, while the Bund market share stayed remarkably stable at around 70%. Indeed, by year-end LIFFE had managed to get its market share of the Bund future up to some 75%. Moreover, for 1994 as a whole, LIFFE's 50% growth rate easily outstripped MATIF's 29% and the DTB's 18%. Clearly it would need something special to happen for the positions in the European league table to change.

LIFFE itself, however, remained healthily nervous about the future. This was particularly sensible in that, as it happened, the move to Cannon Bridge coincided with the flow of product development – successful product development anyway – starting to dry up. 'For some years contracts were developed in response to real demand,' Barton explained to *Risk* in January 1993. 'But we are now reaching the point in some countries where there is no more scope for the development of traditional futures and options. There is certainly less scope in London than there used to be. There are no more Bunds, Euromarks or BTPs round the corner.' And he added that 'in the US that point was reached earlier than in Europe', in that 'the really big contracts, such as the Eurodollar, S&P index and Treasury bond, were launched some time ago'. There was also the possible long-term threat of European monetary union to LIFFE's range of products, and in August 1993 the board accepted a recommendation by the strategy working party that 'the Exchange should diversify into products which would be unaffected or enhanced by EMU'.

In terms of new types of products, one possibility had already been considered and rejected. Barton told *Estates Times* in July 1992 that LIFFE was thinking about refloating the ill-fated property futures contracts launched the previous year by London FOX; but that October, writing in *FOW*, Robert Miller noted that 'having picked over the debris LIFFE has shown little interest even in developing the commercial property contract where genuine, albeit limited, trading interest was apparent before the FOX debacle'. He also made the general point, in relation to the expertise and training that would be required, that 'the marginal cost of a new exotic contract is far greater than that of a standard futures or options contract'.

There was, though, a more serious possibility of LIFFE moving into the area of reinsurance futures, with Miller being brought in as a consultant to investigate the question. This was an old idea in the industry, something that Richard Sandor had actively pushed in the early 1970s, and by mid-1992 the CBOT was making active preparations. As for LIFFE launching an insurance contract, Barton told *IFR* in June that 'we have found that there are a number of institutions looking to lay off risks (such as Lloyd's of London), but very few which are willing to take it on, particularly in these times. We believe that there is a product there, we just haven't found it yet.' That December, trading began on the CBOT in catastrophe contracts, but they fared poorly. Bruce the following March told the board that 'a reinsurance instrument would be difficult to design', granted that 'it would need to provide the reinsurance market with an effective catastrophe loss hedge and also, in order to attract non-risk averse capital from the financial markets, to be designed in a way in which sellers of such contracts could take on risk and be confident that the risk could be managed'. It was agreed that work should continue with reinsurance brokers 'in a co-operative project to develop further the loss index idea, specifically related to UK and continental European natural perils, and should progress the cause of London reinsurance derivatives in general'. In August the strategy overview specifically cited reinsurance as a likely area of diversification, but soon afterwards Barton insisted to *FOW* that LIFFE would never list a product which suffered the regulatory handicaps besetting the CBOT, with volume still low and most insurers legally unable to use futures to hedge risk. 'We would want to be reasonably certain that there were no cows on the line,' was how he put it.

A year later there was still no robust index in the UK against which to settle a possible catastrophe insurance contract; and although, as *FOW* noted in November 1994, 'there is plenty of interest from people to buy the contract, companies willing to write it would have to come forward'. Or in Durlacher's words, 'there needs to be a balanced marketplace and we can provide the medium'. Reinsurance, it had become obvious, offered no quick fix in terms of diversification. Yet the problem itself would not go away, as the financial futures industry – now two decades old – showed increasing signs of becoming mature.

GLOBEX, and LIFFE's relations generally with other exchanges, continued between 1992 and 1994 to occupy as much time as ever, possibly even more. Indeed, it sometimes seemed that the amount of talking was in inverse proportion to what was being achieved. 'Many good intentions have not delivered very many good results,' Durlacher remarked to *FOW* in July 1992, confessing to being 'a little bit cynical' about the whole area of co-operation and alliances. Nevertheless, in the course of his chairmanship, he came to accept as much as anyone that in the context of there being only a finite supply of products, a policy of splendid isolation was not really a feasible long-term approach.

In early April 1992, after some final glitches, Reuters at last announced that GLOBEX would begin trading on 25 June, during those hours when the floors of the Chicago exchanges were closed. So far MATIF was the only non-American exchange to have signed up. 'The restrictions in the GLOBEX agreement are still not acceptable to the LIFFE board,' David Burton told the *FT*; while soon afterwards *FOW* reported that 'most LIFFE brokers believe the exchange has too great an advantage in its spread of products' to need to fear GLOBEX in the short term. A week before the launch, the board discussed GLOBEX; and although the view was expressed that it was 'an attempt to lead the market in a direction that it would not naturally follow' – in other words, trading contracts outside their own time zones – there was a consensus that 'there could be some merit in putting forward fresh proposals covering the terms upon which the Exchange would be prepared to join GLOBEX'. In short, LIFFE's policy remained that of keeping its options open, especially now that the system was about to be launched. For the launch itself, the CME and the CBOT held back their most active products; and though Melamed hailed the debut as 'the dawn of a new era', CBOT's chairman, William O'Connor, frankly told his members that 'GLOBEX will become a tool that we will use to defend our market share'. Those heady, futuristic days of 1987 now seemed a long time ago, so chequered had GLOBEX's progress been in the interim five years, but at the Chicago launch there was only one movie that could provide the appropriate theme music for the occasion – *2001: A Space Odyssey*.

Of the 225 trading terminals for the GLOBEX system in operation on launch day, 45 were sited in London, and LIFFE continued to complain unavailingly that the system was anti-competitive because of Reuters' involvement on an exclusive basis. GLOBEX itself started smoothly but slowly, trading only 2,000 contracts in its first session. In a speech he gave at this time at a Euromoney conference in London, Burton astutely identified why GLOBEX was likely to pose only a muted threat:

There are many major global practitioners who believe that GLOBEX is a 'system too far'. A system of trading that is not demanded by the global market, that is out of touch with the real needs of the market, that seeks to impose or suggest needs that are simply not essential to the users of those markets. It is seen by many as a system designed to be the saviour of Chicago, to preserve Chicago's leadership.

Globalisation is happening in many markets and will continue to evolve, but it remains unproven that a global trading system is essential to support globalisation. The clear indication appears to be that business activity is becoming even more concentrated in the three time zones. In Europe for example there is very little demand for exchange trading hours to be extended. Dealers, traders, brokers, arbitragers and, more importantly, locals work extremely long hours and it is unlikely that they would be willing to actively support the concept of 24 hour trading. Passing the 'book' from time zone to time zone is simply a non-starter, totally unrealistic in today's markets.

Experience in London over the last few years indicates that cash market turnover in Japanese government bonds or Eurodollar products has declined, with the business moving back home where liquidity is much more secure. Similarly, there is very little evidence that demand exists in the United States or the Far East for LIFFE products outside the LIFFE trading day. U.S. involvement in LIFFE products takes place in London.

All major financial institutions are established, and therefore involved, in the three major time zones. Their policy towards so-called globalisation is clear: that the products of each time zone are, in the main, traded when the time zone is open for business. There will always be a degree of overlap between financial centres where arbitrage can be encouraged, but the global market is, in fact, clearly segmented and GLOBEX appears not to acknowledge this fact…

Seamless, non-segmented globalisation had, in other words, been a mid-1980s concept; but this was 1992. From LIFFE's specific point of view, moreover, there

Launch of GLOBEX,
25 June 1992. From left:
William O'Connor,
Leo Melamed, Gary Ginter,
Jack Sandner, Bill Brodsky,
Murray Finebaum, Rosalyn
Wilton, Thomas Donovan.

remained the basic truth of Jenkins' well-directed remarks on the day of the launch: 'GLOBEX is designed to attract business to Chicago. The people who run it, own it and control it, are the Merc and the Board of Trade. Any non-Chicago exchange is going to think seriously about that.'

LIFFE negotiated on a twin front during autumn 1992: with GLOBEX, seeking to establish exactly what terms were on offer; and with the CBOT, looking to establish a mutual offset arrangement for various products (including the Bund) and thereby detach the Board of Trade from its worryingly serious talks with the DTB along these lines. GLOBEX itself had been managing only modest volumes since its launch, but Durlacher emphasised to members that if LIFFE were to participate, its contracts would only be available on GLOBEX after APT as well as floor trading had closed for the day. The membership itself was surveyed in October by *FOW*, which found that only 41% favoured joining GLOBEX, the majority not believing that business conducted outside normal trading hours would justify the expense. Negotiations, anyway, were hardly easy, with Barton reporting to the board on 3 November that 'during recent meetings a divergence of opinions had emerged between the CBOT, CME, Reuters and the GLOBEX Corporation', and that LIFFE accordingly had written to those parties 'requesting them to come to a common position before taking discussions further'.

Negotiations over GLOBEX stuttered along through the winter; while in terms of a mutual offset linkage with the CBOT, at a board discussion in March

The Chancellor visits LIFFE, 7 June 1994. From left: Mike Stiller, Jack Wigglesworth, Kenneth Clarke, John Foyle, Nigel Ackerman.

1993 'the question was raised of whether the US T-Note was sufficiently attractive and whether the Exchange should not instead be devoting efforts towards inclusion of the T-Bond', to which the counter argument was made that 'the establishment of a fungible linkage would be of significant potential benefit to members and should envisage the possibility of subsequent widening to include T-Bonds and other products'. Over the next few weeks 35 members (including all firms represented by board members) were consulted about the possible LIFFE/CBOT link, and Durlacher told the board on 11 May that 'the conclusion of these consultations was that views were divided and there was no clear consensus either for or against a link'. There was, Durlacher elaborated, a threefold anxiety: that the prospective agreement was 'unbalanced', with LIFFE contributing more to it; that there was a 'risk of trading activity moving from London to Chicago particularly during overlap periods'; and that there might be a 'migration of clearing business from LIFFE members, as North American clients sought to have business cleared in the US'. The following month, in an entirely amicable spirit on the part of both exchanges, talks were suspended. 'We have been unable to construct linkage terms which provide sufficient mutual benefit to the members of both exchanges, and strike an acceptable balance in terms of products included, style of clearing and trading hours,' Durlacher told LIFFE's members. One day, some still fondly believed, a link with the CBOT would come off.

There were, from LIFFE's point of view, two other significant linkages in the air during the first half of 1993. One involved the Tokyo International Financial Futures Exchange [TIFFE], with whom LIFFE had been discussing since early 1992 the possibility of a joint venture in TIFFE's extremely successful three-month

Euroyen future. By October 1992 TIFFE had (Durlacher reported to the board) 'indicated that it would be pleased if an arrangement could be established whereby LIFFE traded its Euroyen contract, through a fungible link', but it was already proving a slow business putting such a link in place. The other putative link most certainly did not involve LIFFE. This was between DTB and MATIF, the two exchanges announcing in January 1993 their intention that DTB members would be able to trade MATIF's ECU contracts in return for MATIF members having access to the DTB's deutschmark interest rate contracts. There would also be joint arrangements for clearing, and 'Lex' saw it as a potential alliance that, not inconceivably, could 'mount a credible challenge to LIFFE'. There was still, however, an abundance of details to sort out, and Lisa Vaughan noted in the *Independent* that 'many exchange links have been tried in the past, and most either fizzled out or resulted in only modest cooperation'. MATIF itself was finally about to plug into GLOBEX, which it did in March, launching its first two contracts on the system and thereby replacing its previous reliance on telephones for after-hours trading. By June the French exchange was contributing some 80% of GLOBEX's volume (some 20,000 contracts daily), giving the potential to sell MATIF's products to American customers, and at the same time Pfauwadel told *IFR* that preparations for the DTB link were progressing smoothly. The interview was published on the day that the CBOT/LIFFE talks were suspended, and once again the spectre arose of London finding itself disadvantageously isolated.

In early August 1993, after it had become clear that MATIF refused to withdraw its pre-emptive right to list ECU products on the GLOBEX system and that the CBOT was equally not prepared to give up its right to start Bund trading on it, LIFFE suspended talks with GLOBEX. It was, thought *IFR*, 'a potentially lethal blow' to GLOBEX, which after thirteen months had just managed to trade its two millionth lot. There ensued, in the wake of Melamed's retirement as chairman of GLOBEX, a bitter public row between the CBOT and CME. The latter claimed that LIFFE had pulled out of the talks because of CBOT obstructionism, while the former insisted that quite apart from the question of the Bund there were many other critical issues that had remained unresolved, including LIFFE's insistence that it be allowed more authority in running GLOBEX's daily affairs and that if it chose to do so it could terminate its relationship with GLOBEX within a year of joining.

Yet within weeks, to the bemusement of observers, the situation changed again, when at Bürgenstock in September the CME made welcoming noises to LIFFE about resuming GLOBEX talks and the CBOT said that the Bund was back on the table. 'It would be important that there was a real commitment that we would have Bund exclusivity,' Barton told the press, while Hodson added that he wanted to see the Merc for its part put the Eurodollar on the table. There remained, though, a philosophical chasm. The CME's Jack Sandner (also the new chairman of GLOBEX) insisted that the concept of exclusivity was 'critical' to GLOBEX, and that to change that principle would turn the network into a trading facility with competing contracts – 'a vision,' noted *IFR*, 'Hodson said LIFFE was not averse to.' Put another way, the question was whether GLOBEX was essentially a protectionist or a free trade zone. LIFFE was prepared to consider the possibility of participating in the first, but would much have preferred the second.

Later that month Durlacher announced that LIFFE would be resuming negotiations with GLOBEX, after the board of the CBOT had voted to relinquish to LIFFE its exclusive right to list and trade Bund products on GLOBEX. Durlacher showed limited enthusiasm when he talked to the Chicago press in October: 'We are negotiating on the basis of this year's model. We want to know if next year's model is attractive. But we cannot overlook that there has been an enormous amount of water under the bridge.' As for GLOBEX in general: 'We think the 24-hour day may well arrive in our business lifetime. But when is certainly not clear and it's certainly a much slower burn than the founding fathers imagined. One of the things that went wrong is there was too much optimism about volume...' The reference to 'next year's model' was a reference to the April 1994 deadline, by which if GLOBEX had failed to reach a daily volume of 50,000 contracts then its partners could opt out of the agreement; and Durlacher noted that LIFFE during its earlier negotiations had not been familiar with that condition.

Also in Chicago, Barton emphasised to Sandner the difficulties that LIFFE would have in reopening discussions in a meaningful way until there was a ground swell of support for GLOBEX from amongst LIFFE's members. Soon afterwards, on 3 November, Sandner announced plans to restructure GLOBEX so that every exchange that joined it would have an equal voice in its management and the exclusive right to list its biggest financial instruments on the system. Barton called it 'an extremely welcome initiative'. It was hardly consistent, however, with the defence of Chicago, and over the winter it became increasingly clear that the CBOT wanted to leave GLOBEX, a decision confirmed in April 1994 when GLOBEX's agreement with Reuters was renewed without the Board of Trade.

A few weeks later, on 17 May, LIFFE formally – and at last, conclusively – said 'no' to GLOBEX. An important element in the board's decision was the fact that discussions with TIFFE on the proposed Euroyen linkage had progressed to the stage where it was appropriate to conclude a letter of intent between the two exchanges. Durlacher's public statement expanded on LIFFE's thinking:

Our decision was concerned with optimising the international distribution of LIFFE's products outside the European time zone. Our strategic priority is to develop bi-lateral linkages with exchanges outside our time zone, along the lines of our successful partnership with the Tokyo Stock Exchange for the Japanese

Government Bond contract, and our ongoing negotiations with the Tokyo International Financial Futures Exchange regarding a fungible link for the Euroyen contract. These arrangements will, where appropriate, be supported and complemented by the extension of trading hours, for LIFFE's European contracts, through the use of our well established automated trading system. They can also be supported by multi-exchange concepts like GLOBEX.

Regrettably, the terms on which our participation in GLOBEX were offered would have denied us further development of our preferred linkage strategy, and would have meant withdrawal from our TIFFE Euroyen discussions. In addition, we would have been precluded from extending APT beyond its current hours of use. These restrictive conditions were totally unacceptable to the LIFFE Board.

GLOBEX itself would continue, but dominated by after-hours trading in Paris and only the palest shadow of Melamed's 1987 vision. 'I have to say,' Hodson remarked in an interview in late 1993, 'that everybody that I have talked to associated with GLOBEX, including the existing partners and Reuters, believe that if they had their time again, things would probably be done differently.' There had indeed been a fair degree of human folly involved, but arguably the concept itself was fundamentally flawed. Apart from exceptional circumstances, futures traders trade in their regular working hours, when the cash markets in their own time zone are operating. There was a noble aspect to GLOBEX, as well as a less noble protectionist one, but the sci-fi vision fatally ignored the human factor. Melamed, however, had increasingly insisted that it would be decades, not years, before it became certain that the future of all markets lay in technology; and in those terms, only time could be the jury.

By spring 1994 little had been heard for some time about the putative MATIF/DTB link, but the DTB's Jörg Franke told *FOW* in April that the project was going according to plan, with the first trade from DTB terminals in Paris expected in the middle of the year. The DTB's Bund and Bobl contracts would be the first on the system, with MATIF products not going on screen until 1995. In the event, it was on 16 September 1994 that BZW Futures became the first institution to trade directly on the DTB in Frankfurt from its Paris offices – a 100-lot sell order in the Bobl. 'This is the first major step in the consolidation of pan-European exchange trading', said Graham Newall of BZW, though few expected LIFFE to be part of that consolidation. Over the next few months the DTB/MATIF link operated in only a fairly modest way, and Herklotz pointed out to the board shortly before Christmas that 'the critical time in respect of determining the success of the link will be when MATIF members decide on the products to be made available on the system'.

As for LIFFE's own links by the second half of 1994, there were three afoot in the more liberated, post-GLOBEX era. One of course was with TIFFE, still a possibility despite some opposition from TIFFE's members. The board noted this opposition in September, but was reassured by the fact that 'the Japanese authorities were keen to have a link in order to promote internationalisation of Japanese market practices'. And, despite a formal letter of intent remaining unsigned, the feeling by the end of the year was that there could still be a successful outcome over this Euroyen linkage. However, doubts over the Tokyo situation meant that LIFFE was by now pursuing a complementary Far Eastern linkage, namely with SIMEX over the distribution of Euromark futures in the Asian time zone. 'SIMEX is an important dollar/deutschmark trading centre,' Bruce told *F&O plus*, 'and where there is a forward market for the dollar, there is a natural role for the Euromark future.'

The third link that was by now on the cards was with the CBOT, fourth time around. The approach had come from the Board of Trade, within weeks of LIFFE's rejection of GLOBEX, and it initially concerned a possible linkage between LIFFE's APT system and the CBOT's own embryonic after-hours electronic system, Project A. A joint feasibility study was announced in July, and Hodson stated that 'this initiative clearly fits in with the Exchange's strategic objective to enhance the distribution of its products through bi-lateral linkages with exchanges outside our time zone and/or through the use of APT', adding that 'LIFFE and the CBOT have always enjoyed an amicable relationship'. Not long afterwards, at Bürgenstock in September 1994, Durlacher said that he hoped that such a link between the after-hours trading systems, enabling expanded mutual distribution, would be working by mid-1995. By November the terms of the possible link had notably broadened, into one envisaging open outcry mutual offset, with the CBOT proposing to permit LIFFE to trade CBOT products – including T-bonds – from 7.30 am until 1.00 pm London time in return for the CBOT trading LIFFE products – including the Bund and Euromark – from 4.00 pm until 8.00 pm London time, as well as from 11.20 pm to 2.05 am London time during the CBOT's evening session. That month the board noted that on the part of LIFFE's members 'whilst there was support to trade Treasury bonds in the London morning there was not broad-based support for an overlap with floor trading hours on LIFFE contracts'; nevertheless, 'by and large it was considered that this latest initiative represented the most promising start the Exchange had experienced to any linkage discussions it had held with the CBOT'.

All the time, the fundamental, underlying, sometimes hackneyed debate rumbled on: open outcry or screen trading? 'An efficient, liquid, transparent and well-regulated open-outcry market will always be the preferred method of trading by global practitioners,' wrote Burton at the time of GLOBEX's launch, 'provided of course that the range of products and the costs of trading those products encourage practitioners to trade on that particular exchange.

Competition between a screen and open outcry, for the more heavily traded products, can only have one outcome.' That was not, however, how it seemed to many at the time. 'GLOBEX – draw-down for pit?' was a fairly typical headline (in *Global Investor*), 'The future comes into focus on screen' (in the *FT*) was another; while in the immediate wake of GLOBEX's launch, *Time* declared that nothing was likely to slow 'the relentless race toward global electronic trading' and that 'the scenes of traders wildly waving pieces of paper from the floor pits will give way to those of traders around the world furiously typing orders into computers'. Even in October 1992, after GLOBEX's disappointing first few months, the *Economist* announced that 'The screen is the future, master', arguing that 'scores of adults bawling at each other' was 'hardly futuristic'. But writing that month in *FOW*, the seasoned observer Robert Miller counselled caution as far as LIFFE was concerned:

Will pit trading be a thing of the past by the year 2002? The best guess is that the current system of pit trading complemented by automation for trading outside ordinary hours will continue. If one were launching financial futures and options trading de novo, *no one would consider trading pits. But since LIFFE has a community of pit traders and a membership with much capital, human and material, tied up in open outcry any change to an automated system is highly unlikely.*

Over the next year or so there was no shortage of public defenders of the pit. Take just five examples. Mark Harding, financial markets specialist at Clifford Chance: 'I do not think anyone has found a computerised system which is user-friendly or simple enough to take the place of open outcry trading.' Professor Merton Miller, writing in the *Journal of Applied Corporate Finance*: 'The open outcry pits of the major futures exchanges are a remarkably cheap way of handling transactions in high volume at great speed and frequency in a setting of high price volatility.' Julian Rogers-Coltman of GNI: 'There is definitely an industry-wide preference for pit trading that is becoming increasingly apparent. All the big, international users are LIFFE members and unless the electronic system is considerably cheaper I don't see that they would move.' Alex Cooper, director of financial markets at Crédit Lyonnais Rouse: 'Nothing beats a centrally assembled marketplace, and nothing has convinced me that we will get the same liquidity on any of the systems that are around at the moment.' And David Kyte, by now running his own company of 60 traders: 'It's the perfect form of competition. Everyone, big and small, has the same opportunities to trade.'

In his *Securities & Investment Review* interview in November 1993, Hodson was typically measured, pointing out that the DTB, MIF and TIFFE were all successful futures exchanges that operated electronically and that therefore 'there is no general rule'; but at the same time he noted 'the particular advantages of transparency, of the liquidity afforded by the general participation in the pit scene and very specifically of the attraction which our markets have for locals where a significant amount of our business is performed by traders for their own account'. He went on: 'In many respects there are regulatory advantages through the open outcry system where the deals themselves can be seen to go through as they are done. You can see who is bidding, who is offering, and if there are any difficulties they can often be resolved on the spot by the pit observer.' And: 'In addition, a great many users like to be in touch with a physical market place, and to hear it in action, as they talk to their brokers on the floor.' The debate continued into 1994, though less high-profile as GLOBEX struggled and the DTB trailed behind LIFFE; and realistically, it was clear enough at this stage that LIFFE would stick to open outcry unless electronic trading was conclusively shown to be much cheaper and/or reasons of space meant that a decision could not be avoided about moving to a replacement trading floor.

This did not mean, contrary to some outside opinion, that LIFFE was being Luddite. 'Everything is there from telecommunications to on-site servicing and back-up systems,' Alex Cooper justifiably insisted to *FOW* in October 1993, not long after the exchange had invested £1.25 million in Sun hardware and software to upgrade and write new applications for its APT system. Or in terms of pit trading itself, take the key area of distributing data on the floor, as described in September 1993 by *FT Business Computing Brief*:

> *LIFFE uses the services of Micrognosis UK, the Japanese-owned dealing room systems developer and integrator, to provide systems integration and an architecture for data distribution which meets the key requirements of real-time, information democracy, flexibility and reliability. These requirements are achieved by a pragmatic approach which has resulted in an integrated hybrid system comprising hardware and software from a range of suppliers.*
>
> *Systems democracy applies strictly on the exchange floor both in terms of timely delivery of data and space allocation – the 411 trading booths and 221 administration booths used by the various member firms are each just 760 mm wide. There are preferred positions, and different members have different requirements for external data, so flexibility is essential. A major project to reconfigure the trading floor is now beginning less than 18 months after moving into the building.*
>
> *Democracy of information is ensured by using broadcast protocol to distribute data from internal and external sources to all booths at exactly the same instant. The application was tested by videoing users at far ends of the exchange as they called up and selected data from a page of information – the video frames were then counted to ensure delivery to test locations was at the same instant.*

Just over a year later, in November 1994, LIFFE unveiled at the FIA Expo '94 in Chicago a suite of new technology products aimed at enhancing international access. This was the mildly sinister-sounding trio of APT+, LOTS and EASy. APT+ was designed as a new options addition to APT, with full trading due to start by the end of the first quarter of 1995; LOTS was LIFFE Order Transit System, providing interactive electronic order management from members' floor operations to their back offices and, eventually, directly to clients; and EASy, the Exchange Access System, was a new telecommunications network, consisting entirely of fibre optic lines, that linked member sites with LIFFE's data centres. In sum, there was no let-up in the technological challenge and LIFFE's response to it.

By 1992 there were the clearest signs yet that institutional investors were no longer so frightened by derivatives. This even applied to those cautious fund managers in Edinburgh. 'If we make a strategic decision to sell the U.S. and buy Japan we either have to find the right dealer and the right stocks to buy and to sell at the right price – or we can implement the decision immediately through futures and unwind in to stocks at our leisure,' Robin Garrow, investment director at Scottish Widows, told Reuters in January. 'Futures facilitate investment decisions. So far we're building up our experience in the U.K. but one year from now we'd expect to be confident users.' That same month new guidelines – based on a LIFFE consultative document and endorsed by the National Association of Pension Funds – were published that not only provided UK pension fund managers with professionally agreed standards of performance measurement of derivatives for the first time, but also enabled trustees to assess more easily whether fund managers were using futures and options for investment or hedging purposes, or whether they were taking more speculative positions. Soon afterwards a KPMG survey revealed that 8 out of 10 of the UK's top pension fund management groups were using both futures and options in their funds, with the other two using either futures or options; though almost half said that considerable work still needed to be done in the area of improving fund managers' understanding of derivatives and how they could be used. It was also an indication of changing times when in March 1992 one of the City's more conservative investing institutions, Henderson Administration, took a 25 per cent stake in Sabre, one of the UK's leading managed futures fund management businesses.

Yet it remained, from LIFFE's point of view, a slow conversion. Later that year a survey by Phillips & Drew Fund Management revealed that less than a fifth of fund management firms used futures and options; and shortly before retiring as chief executive, Jenkins confessed in an interview that 'we are still really only scratching the surface in terms of potential users' of LIFFE's products, though he expected the use of derivatives to 'continue to grow throughout the 1990s'. It was a concern that his successor shared, Hodson telling *Securities & Investment Review* in November 1993 that, with fewer possibilities ahead in terms of developing new contracts, 'the challenge over the next few years on the interest rate side will be based less on product innovation and more on extending the user base'. Accordingly, in relation to all LIFFE's products, there would have to be an even greater emphasis than before on education and marketing.

Hodson was asked in the same interview if he was satisfied with the state of regulation in the derivative markets:

> *I don't think that one can be smug about the level of regulation on exchange-traded derivatives, but by and large the markets are well regulated. The risk management techniques in particular and the regulations applied by the exchanges themselves have worked well. So far as LIFFE is concerned, although we do have, as every exchange has, a certain number of disciplinary cases, you would expect that on an exchange which is turning over the best part of £100 billion a day. But, equally we do work extremely hard on improving the techniques which our market supervision people use and we are moving very fast into state-of-the-art market electronic surveillance which will again substantially enhance our ability to do that regulatory job.*
>
> *So, I can say hand on heart that this is a safe market on which to deal and certainly I believe that this is one of the attractions of dealing in London and dealing through LIFFE.*

There were few major disciplinary cases in the early years at Cannon Bridge. In July 1992 an options trader, Giles Robinson, was expelled, his offence being 'front-running' in long gilt options – in other words, taking a large order from a client but buying on own account before executing it, in the knowledge that the order will push the market up and thereby enable the trader to sell on own account at a profit. 'Mr Robinson's deals were picked up during routine market surveillance,' *The Times* reported. 'LIFFE's officials listen in on traders' telephones, check dealing slips and even video activity in the pits to ensure the market is running honestly.' In November 1993, following a lengthy investigation, four traders employed by BZW Futures were suspended from LIFFE, and BZW itself fined £67,500, after it had been found that the four had been using the firm's error account to execute trades to the disadvantage of clients. Inevitably, human ingenuity being what it is, even the most sophisticated surveillance technology could not catch everything. The general assumption, however, remained that LIFFE was essentially a clean market – not least, it was felt, because few traders would be stupid enough to jeopardise unnecessarily what was already a very good living without bending or breaking the rules.

But if LIFFE's own reputation was good, that of derivatives at large was about to be badly sullied. Already in 1992/3 both the New York Federal Reserve Board (in the person of its president Gerald Corrigan) and the Bundesbank had expressed serious concern that the rapid growth of derivatives posed a possible major threat to global financial stability. But it was in 1994 that the anxieties and criticisms were voiced loudly and insistently, against the background of a sequence of corporate disasters, mainly American, in the use of financial and other derivatives. 'Like alligators in a swamp, derivatives lurk in the global economy,' was how *Fortune* in March began an extremely prejudicial 9-page analysis of the disturbing phenomenon. John Plender, writing in the *FT* in May, sought to establish whether the fear that derivatives were a multi-billion accident waiting to happen was justified. 'Derivatives are a valuable addition to the financial armoury,' he concluded. 'The real problems, both for individual banks and the system, are about opacity, leverage and lack of managerial competence. Central bankers will have to be on their mettle if that potentially lethal combination is not to lead to trouble.' One of those central bankers was Brian Quinn of the Bank of England, and on 1 July he gave a speech at the Annual Managed Derivatives Industry Conference in New York that ended on a broadly sanguine note:

> *Progress is being made. The earliest apprehensions about derivatives have been replaced by a methodical analysis of the possible sources of difficulty. The facts are being collected to illuminate that analysis, and regulators and regulated seem generally at one on what needs to be done – although the detail will no doubt excite the usual passions on both sides. Central bankers are, as a whole, ready to take part in the exercise to trade off the costs and benefits of derivatives. With their interest in financial stability, that is both desirable and inevitable. We have a somewhat perplexed user group to persuade. There is therefore a joint interest, regulators and market participants, in finding a safe and profitable way ahead.*

Soon afterwards, Hodson argued publicly that amidst all the publicity there had been 'a failure to distinguish between exchange-traded contracts – the type found at LIFFE – and OTC products', pointing out that 'with the former, systemic risk is effectively eliminated', in that 'because a central clearing house stands between the major players in the market, a default by any single market player will have no impact on its counter parties'. Moreover, 'most derivatives exchanges have a system of variation margining to ensure the integrity of their contracts' – with at LIFFE all open futures positions being

Fortune, 7 March 1994.

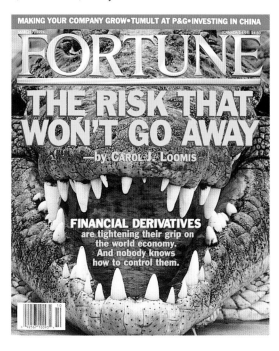

'"marked to market" on a daily basis', through which 'profits and losses resulting from price changes are paid to and collected from clearing members daily, while all clearing members deposit an "initial" margin for each open future position with the London Clearing House'. By contrast, 'such safeguards for the most part do not exist in the fast-growing OTC market, where most of the major losses in recent months have occurred'. It was, in other words, a problem of perception, and most professionals appreciated the difference between the two types of market, even if headline writers sometimes did not. No one imagined that the greatest yet explosion of interest in the D-word would take place because of the activities of a trader very much on an exchange floor.

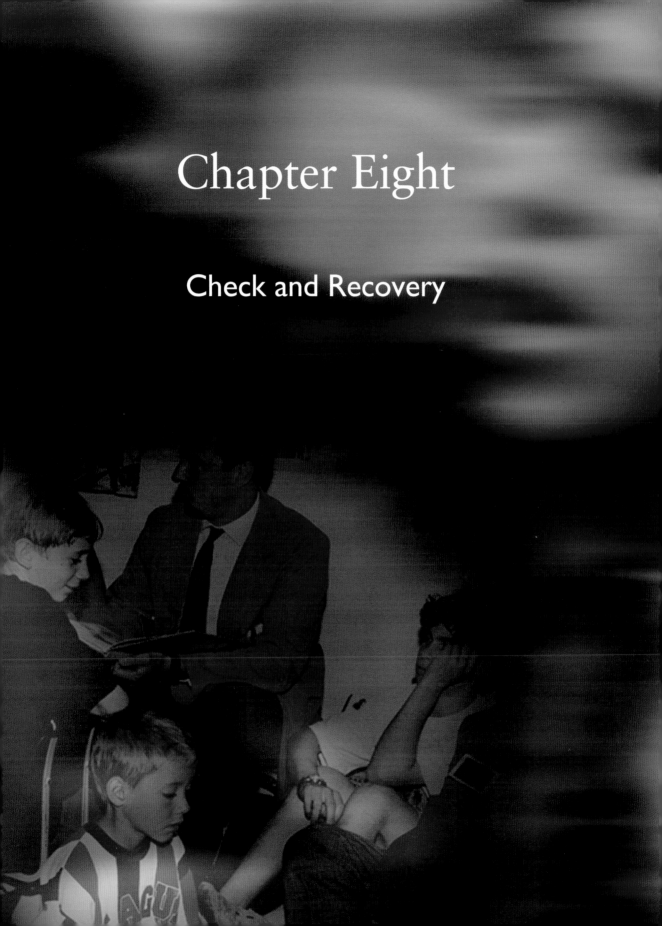

Chapter Eight

Check and Recovery

I N JANUARY 1993, on the grounds of inadequate return on overheads, Britain's oldest merchant bank decided to withdraw its broking presence from the floor of LIFFE. Barings did, however, retain an active presence on SIMEX; and two years later, over the last weekend of February 1995, the incredible story began to unfold of how a 'rogue trader' had brought down this venerable City institution. Soon the whole world was familiar with Nick Leeson and the fateful Error Account No. 88888. Over the ensuing difficult weeks, as the human drama began to fade and important questions started to be asked, LIFFE contended strongly that the fundamental fault lay neither with market structures nor with derivatives themselves, but with what had been palpably inadequate management controls. It was a view that professional opinion broadly accepted, but for all the

Independent,

27 February 1995.

THE INDEPENDENT

2,608 ·····   Monday 27 February 1995

Losses top £600m as collapse of 233-year-old institution rocks City and sends shock waves through world's financial markets

Bank fails to rescue Barings

BY JOHN EISENHAMMER
Financial Editor

The Bank of England's failure yesterday to put together a rescue package for Barings, the stricken merchant bank, sent shock waves through financial markets around the world this morning. The Tokyo stock market plunged in early trading today, just hours after the Bank of England abandoned frantic efforts to construct a lifeboat of financial support. A roll call of the City's most powerful financial institutions refused to sign what amounted to a blank cheque to keep Barings, one of the oldest and most distinguished of City names, alive.

The illustrious merchant bank's 233 years as one of the pillars of Britain's financial establishment were extinguished by the illegal dealings of a junior trader, understood to be Nick Leeson, 28, in the bank's Singapore office. His unauthorised speculation in high-risk derivative contracts, which had run out of control, engulfed the previ-

Leading article   14
Jeremy Warner   15
Reports   24,25

ously highly profitable Barings, in losses quantified yesterday to have already reached £600m.

Tokyo's Nikkei index of leading stocks plummeted more than 500 points to below the 17,000 barrier for the first time in over a year. Share prices on the London Stock Exchange were expected to be sent reeling, as analysts predicted a fall in the FTSE index of 100 points or more. The Bank of England, shocked by this first annihilation of a bank by derivatives trading, moved quickly to calm frayed nerves in the market, saying Barings was an isolated, tragic case brought about by one maverick individual. The pound touched a new low against the German mark in early Far East trading. This further pressure on sterling will add to the Government's difficulties this week as it faces a crucial Commons vote on Europe.

The Bank of E...

expose Barings to "unquantifiable further losses". The inability to set a limit on the losses inherent in such high-risk financial instruments was the main reason Barings was allowed to collapse into administration. The losses were expected to soar

East, and the full force of the markets turned on the derivatives contracts.

The elite of British banking, hurriedly assembled by Eddie George, the governor of the Bank of England, in a series of crisis meetings yesterday, had agreed to supply all the money

But the proposed lifeboat sank when it proved impossible to cap the potential liability.

Amid warnings that the Barings collapse would send alarm throughout the world's financial markets, and risked doing untold damage to Lond...

action. "The circumstances are unique to Barings, and should have no implications for other banks operating in London," it said in its statement. "The London market will open as normal. The Bank of England stands ready to provide liquidity to the...

Unable to continue trading, Barings applied last night for administration, in the same way the Bank of Credit and Commerce International was wound up. Ernst and Young, the accountancy firm, was appointed administrator for Barings is renowned for its

sets. The Bank said yesterday it had received strong interest, both from domestic institutions and powerful American, Swiss, German and Dutch banks, in parts of the Barings operation. Barings is renowned for its prowess in em...

a lucrative asset management operation with £30bn in funds, but most of this was thought not at risk because this operation is separate from Barings' securities dealings. Barings did, however, say any cash deposited with the bank, by corporate or individual clients, was at risk. Barings employs 4,000 people worldwide, of whom almost 2,000 work in London. The collapse of the bank also spells the demise of one of Britain's most active charities, which owns 100 per cent of the Baring bank holding company, last year spent £13.5m on charitable causes out of money from the bank's dividends.

Michael Marks, chairman of Smith New Court, the stockbroker, warned that the failure of Barings would damage the whole fabric of the City. "For the credit rating of the City, it will be disastrous should Barings be left to go to the wall," he said.

The illegal trades, which were essentially bets against the future performance of the Nikkei, Tokyo's index of leading shares, were made without the knowledge of senior Barings executives, the bank said yesterday. The whereabouts of Mr Leeson, believed to come from Watford, were unknown yesterday. Barings could not say how risky positions of this magnitude were built up, circumventing its normal controls. The bank suggested there could have been some collusion inside its Singapore office. Alastair Darling, Labour's spokesman on the City and financial services, said his party would today urge the Government to review the derivatives supervisory structure. "Even if this was a rogue trade, a rogue trader should never be in a position to ruin an entire bank," he said.

The intense debate about derivatives trading, fuelled at regular intervals by new scandals, the latest of which was the huge losses at Orange County in California, has led in recent years to a great deal being done to improve supervision and control. Central banks, among them the Bank of England, have taken a relatively relaxed view of deriv...

Eddie George, right, governor of the Bank of England, and Rupert Pennant-Rea, deputy governor, yesterday as the Bank made unsuccessful moves to save Barings   *Photograph: Philip Meech* amusement on LIFFE's floor about the social piquancy of the fall of Barings, there was no doubt that the episode did huge harm to the broader image of derivatives, an image that had already taken quite a pounding in the course of 1994. 'The general press have really had a go at the D-word, the work of the devil: derivatives,' Hodson would wryly remark, looking back in October 1995.

Eventually that storm would die down, and LIFFE had already done its best to abate it, including by participating fully in the Futures Industry Association Global Task Force set up by the industry to learn the lessons of the Barings case and produce recommendations. Writing in *World Statesman* (third quarter, 1995), Hodson saw what needed to be done as fourfold: to 'strengthen information-sharing arrangements between regulatory authorities and exchanges in different jurisdictions'; to 'disclose to all customers, the precise arrangements for protecting our clearing members and customer funds and for dealing with any insolvency in the system'; to 'lay out, for all to understand and see, the relative responsibility of customers themselves, brokers, exchanges and clearing houses'; and to 'understand, and where at all possible, harmonise, the effect of bankruptcy laws on exchanges in different jurisdictions'. There was, he added, 'some way to go in achieving all of these objectives', but he stressed that, like other exchanges, LIFFE was 'keen to learn the lessons of Barings and to ensure maximum customer protection'. He hardly needed to add that there could be no absolute protection against the catastrophic mixture of greed, stupidity and malice that had undone Barings.

It is almost impossible to gauge what degree of responsibility the Barings fiasco bore for LIFFE's falling volume in 1995. The run of monthly figures either side of the event (with equivalent figure for a year earlier) suggests the possibility of exaggerating its impact:

November 1994	11.41 million	(10.95 million)
December 1994	7.73 million	(8.12 million)
January 1995	11.26 million	(12.61 million)
February 1995	11.81 million	(17.83 million)
March 1995	14.16 million	(17.08 million)
April 1995	7.93 million	(12.24 million)
May 1995	12.11 million	(13.38 million)
June 1995	13.59 million	(14.06 million)

For the first half of 1995, LIFFE's total volume of 70.89 million lots represented an 18.73% fall on the same period in 1994. Soon afterwards, in one of his first interviews as the new chairman, Wigglesworth did not deny that the collapse of Barings had prompted derivatives users to examine how they managed operations, and that accordingly 'it wouldn't surprise me if there was an element of reduced trading activity while that took place'. It was not only LIFFE that

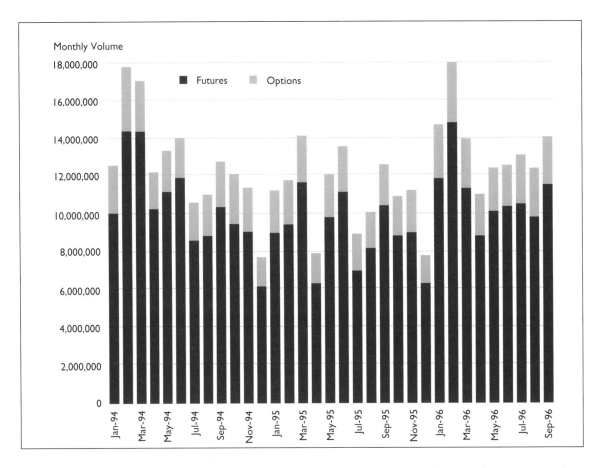

Monthly Volume

■ Futures   ▨ Options

The Leeson Effect: LIFFE business 1994–96.

suffered: the CME and the CBOT sustained 10% and 11.5% drops respectively in the first half of 1995, while MATIF slumped by as much as 35.7%. On the other hand, as many industry observers remarked, comparison with 1994 was arguably not realistic, granted the way in which that year's bond market volatility had massively inflated volumes. Either way, there was considerable nervousness in the industry by summer 1995. 'Trembling in the shakeout?' was *FOW*'s headline in June, and the accompanying article reported that on the floor of LIFFE there was a mood of retrenchment and foreboding. Suddenly, after 12 years of continuous and remarkable growth, there were no easy, automatic assumptions about the future.

By the end of 1995 there was still some anxiety, with a total volume for the year of 132.65 million contracts, representing a 13.32% drop on 1994. In the same period, volume had declined on the CBOT by 4%, on the CME by 11%, on MATIF by 24% and on the DTB by 2%. 'If Dante had been around to watch the downward spiral of last year's futures and options activity, he could have penned Inferno II by Christmas,' *FOW* proclaimed with some hyperbole in its global review of 1995.

Paradise, however, was just around the corner. In January 1996, against a background of volatility in US, German and UK interest rates as well as an increasing focus on the future of European monetary union, LIFFE enjoyed its busiest January ever – 14.74 million contracts – and on three days it traded a higher volume than any other derivatives exchange. But February was the month that really banished memories of 1995, with a volume of 18.04 million lots, a monthly record. Continuing uncertainty surrounding European interest rates, together with turbulence in the US bond market, provided a conducive climate; and on the 20th, as over 1.44 million contracts changed hands, LIFFE was busier than on any other day in its history, with the exception of 2 March 1994 (1.61 million). Indeed, for the month as a whole LIFFE's volume surpassed that of the Merc, prompting John Damgard, president of America's Futures Industry Association, to tell *Crain's Chicago Business* that 'LIFFE has been a great success story' and that 'we are in danger of allowing foreign exchanges to become more efficient than domestic exchanges'. While Hal Hansen of the Chicago-based brokers Cargill Investor Services added: 'There are some very clear efficiencies on LIFFE, particularly in the ability to clear on-line and handle business at a significantly lower cost than in the U.S.'

Volumes thereafter remained satisfactory, and by the end of September 1996 the total of 122.57 million contracts for the first nine months of the year was 19% up on the same period in 1995 and even just ahead of 1994. September itself – 14.09 million contracts, with an average daily volume of 677,257 – was LIFFE's best yet September, helped by not only Italian budgetary announcements but also an ever-sharper focus by the world's financial markets on the EMU question. On 30 September the volume for the day – a quiet day – was 445,037 contracts. Exactly fourteen years earlier it had been 4,265.

Equity products had long been the poor relation of the derivatives family, but LIFFE announced two important changes in the course of 1995. Only one, however, was quickly implemented, and this was the introduction in June of what were called 'Flex' options on the FTSE 100 Index, following the example of the Chicago Board Options Exchange and the London-based OMLX. LIFFE's new product allowed investors greater flexibility on both the expiry date and on the exercise price, and it aimed to offer a less risky, competitively priced rival to OTC products. This new contract was not greeted tumultuously – with a total volume of 60,699 by the end of 1995 – but did provide a service. The exchange's other equity announcement came in September. 'LIFFE bombshell on equity options' was the *Evening Standard*'s headline on the 5th, with a story revealing that – over three years after the LTOM merger – leading players in the traded options market were once again pressing hard for trading in individual equity options to go off the floor and on to electronic screens. 'In the two years since LIFFE set in motion an aggressive development plan,' the paper noted, 'equity options turnover has slumped by 18%', while that of the

FTSE 100 contracts had increased by 23% for the future and 58% for the option. A week later LIFFE confirmed that, following an eight-month feasibility study, it was indeed planning automated trading in UK equity options, with Wigglesworth saying that 'LIFFE's vision for the future is to have a fully integrated, order-driven automated market in which users are able to trade both cash and equity derivatives through a single screen'. No date, however, was set, and LIFFE stressed that automation alone would not solve the fundamental problem of lack of transparency in the cash market. In the event, a year later equity option trading was still being done on the floor, though the commitment to automation remained. There was, however, progress in the cash market, with the Stock Exchange being on the verge of unveiling a new system of automated order-driven trading for FTSE 100 stocks aimed at creating a more level playing field for all investors. Undeniably, with individual equity options managing an average daily volume of only 12,519 in September 1996, there remained ample scope for change and improvement.

The long gilt – on which short-dated serial options were introduced in February 1995 – remained active and, as during much of the 1990s, rather overlooked. In 1995 the future was the exchange's fourth most traded contract (13.79 million), a position it held in the first nine months of 1996. Volume for those nine months was only 2% up on the same period in 1995, hardly a striking endorsement of the new gilt repo market that had at last got going at the start of the year. As for the short sterling future, it was now established in third place overall, and though a long way behind the Bund and Euromark futures it still had some palmy days, most notably on 20 February 1996 when 268,612 short sterling contracts were traded, thereby beating its Black/White Wednesday record. There had been an expectation of future cuts in British interest rates, but disappointing remarks by Alan Greenspan reversed such predictions, to the benefit of the short sterling pit.

The Eurodollar contracts finally ceased trading, a cause of some poignancy for anyone with a sense of LIFFE's history. The option was suspended on 16 May 1995, the future on 18 March 1996. 'It is hard to believe,' one senior market practitioner told the *Evening Standard* after the decision was taken that LIFFE could no longer sustain a Eurodollar presence. 'These were among the first contracts traded on LIFFE.' However, Durlacher insisted to the press, 'LIFFE remains convinced of the strategic importance and potential of dollar contracts, as recognised in its strategic partnership with the Chicago Board of Trade'. If a dollar capability now depended on that partnership coming to fruition, there was at least no question of not having a yen capability. Volume in the JGB future improved in 1995, though still under a million contracts for the year, while after several years of patient negotiations with TIFFE the three-month Euroyen interest rate future at last came on stream in April 1996. It was an arrangement based on fungibility, with Euroyen contracts traded on LIFFE being transferred into TIFFE Euroyen contracts and subsequently cleared by TIFFE clearing members.

A key question, debated by the board in November 1995, was whether the contract would be traded on the floor at LIFFE or through APT, as the JGB future had been since 1991. That had been a clear nod towards LIFFE's Japanese members (about one-fifth of total membership), but this time it was felt that the largest participants in the contract would not be the Japanese members but more probably US and other international firms. Having heard that the Floor Committee strongly wanted floor-based trading, Wigglesworth threw open the debate, one with larger implications than just the Euroyen contract:

Strongly held views were expressed on both sides. These included, inter alia, being sensitive to the wishes of Japanese members; that the strategic issues should not be ignored, that is, if linkages are to continue they must be built on trust and respect and therefore the views of a significant portion of the market should not be ignored; the floor provided the best opportunities for a successful contract to be provided by the great majority of the LIFFE membership; floor trading would ensure a contribution from locals which would not be available if the contract were traded on APT; the contract could, if considered appropriate at some future time, move from the floor to APT whereas it could not move in the other direction; that APT represented only a contingency trading mechanism and that the exchange was not committed to the success of the system per se, but to the contracts traded on the exchange; that Japanese members would use the contract whether it was based on the floor or the APT screen. Furthermore, the views expressed by Japanese members were considered to be an indication of their preference rather than being an ultimatum; had it been the latter this would have been established at the beginning of discussions with TIFFE.

The matter was put to the vote, and by ten votes to five floor-based trading won the day.

Perhaps inevitably there was some disappointment in Tokyo about the decision, but on 11 April 1996 the contract was duly launched on LIFFE by the English rugby player Rory Underwood. The winger described the floor as 'the biggest scrum I have ever seen', while Wigglesworth proclaimed that 'this innovative and powerful link allows members and clients of both exchanges to have the benefit of trading into established liquidity'. Direct competition existed with the CME-SIMEX Euroyen link, established earlier in the year, and early signs were of a modest success, with 176,699 contracts traded by the end of September.

In the European arena, one significant element from LIFFE's point of view was the spluttering progress of the MATIF/DTB link. *World Equity* reported in January 1995 that 'resentment at the agreement is running high among MATIF members', in the context of MATIF having to choose two of its contracts to list on the DTB – contracts that would have to be taken off the floor and traded on the screen link.

Stalemate set in, and by spring 1996 – with barely a dozen MATIF members operating computer work stations in France trading DTB products – it was clear that the ambitious co-operative hopes of 1993 were not going to be realised, at least for the time being. On LIFFE itself, determined to keep its deutschmark products as competitive as possible, there was a noteworthy development in June 1995 with the introduction of basis trading in Bund futures. This was a facility that allowed the simultaneous purchase or sale of a bond in the cash market and offsetting purchase or sale in the futures market, and it drew inspiration from the CBOT, where basis trades were accounting for some 10% of activity in the T-bond contract. 'This is a mechanism to bring the cash and futures market closer together,' Bruce told the *FT*. 'It takes away unnecessary risk linked to the futures part of the transaction. The facility is intended to recognise that a user needs greater price certainty to exercise these basis trades.' The move proved a success, and by October over 2,500 contracts were trading daily through the Basis Trading Facility. This was not a new contract as such, but in September 1996 LIFFE announced that on 21 November it would be launching a one-month Euromark interest rate future. 'Leading market players judged,' reported *IFR* after the announcement, that 'it will make a positive contribution to the deutschmark cash and derivatives markets by extending yield curve hedging and arbitrage opportunities.'

In general, the Bund future and Euromark future remained largely unchallenged in their dominance, both in the exchange and in Europe. The Euromark contract had no rival, while LIFFE's market share in the Bund future held up very steadily at around 70% or just above and continued to appeal to a large international user base, in contrast to the essentially domestic support given to the DTB's Bund future. In September 1996, LIFFE's Bund future traded an average daily volume of 159,746 contracts, with the Euromark future managing 121,435. No other European contract came close, but the BTP future achieved a creditable 57,342 and lay in fifth place overall. It was followed, in terms of other European products with a reasonable volume, by the Eurolira future (34,164), the Bund option (29,556), the Euromark option (18,842), the Euroswiss future (13,082), the BTP option (11,979), and the Eurolira option (7,568), which last contract had been launched in May 1995 on the back of the reasonably prosperous future. Palpably, though, it was the mighty deutschmark that dominated, responsible for some 60% of LIFFE's volume.

By September 1996 three letters – potentially enticing, potentially frightening – pervaded all of LIFFE's thinking about its European and indeed sterling products: EMU. Back in September 1993, at the time of the virtual breakdown of the Exchange Rate Mechanism, Durlacher had been asked if he agreed that this 'relaxation' of the ERM represented good news for LIFFE. 'There was always an implied threat if EMU actually came about, because we thrive on trading interest rate futures on a diversity of European currency products,' he replied. 'If that

Rory Underwood launches the Three Month Euroyen futures contract, 11 April 1996.

diversity had disappeared then we would have simply lost our product base... The current moves certainly put that time horizon back and give us a continued opportunity to provide hedging opportunities for users across a wide range of currencies.' For some time thereafter the prospects of European monetary union this century seemed remote, but that started to change somewhat in 1995 and very definitely in 1996. The proposed start date remained January 1999; and early in 1996, soon after the Madrid Summit had decided that, from the start of EMU, participating central banks would intervene in the money market exclusively in the Euro and that new government debt would be issued in the Euro, an interview that Wigglesworth gave to *International Securities Regulation Report* caught the sense of the quickening pace as far as LIFFE was concerned:

> *LIFFE is crucially interested in the developments of the EMU. As you know, we're the most international exchange in the world by any standards. We have the most global membership of the exchanges. Also, in our products base, we're the only exchange which has anything like our range of different instruments of different currencies. So, anything which affects the European currencies, which most of our instruments are, of course, is very crucial. So it's important for us to see the way things are going so that we can end up after the event trading in whatever new currency instruments are available.*
>
> *The new 'Euro' presumably is intended to be a currency block against which we'll trade the yen and dollar products. But at the same time, we want to keep the residual instruments which would still exist, such as the bond products in the existing European currencies which, of course, can't be immediately merged into one. So we're very keen to make sure we get that one right because we recognise*

that it will be decisive in whether we remain the leading exchange in that sense. We have every reason to believe that we will because we think that whatever the new unit may be it will look like, feel like, smell like, taste like the deutschmark. We've got the majority of the trading in the DM product. We've got between 70 and 75% of the trading…

He added that 'politicians do drive these things forward', citing the example of German unification, when 'the politicians totally overrode the advice of the supposedly independent central bank'. In other words, EMU – in less than three years – was a very serious possibility.

It also had immediate practical implications, with the board having to decide by March 1996 what it should do about listing the March 1999 expiry month for the Euromark and short sterling futures contracts. The problem caused considerable agonising, but ultimately it decided that the only realistic policy was that from the March 1999 expiry onwards, these contracts would settle against a three-month Euro interest rate. This was on the assumption that the Euro had become the lawful currency of the relevant nation and that the exchange rate between the Euro and

The Times, 14 March 1996.

ECONOMIC VIEW   ANATOLE KALETSKY

EMU beginning to acquire an irresistible momentum

As 1999 nears, many more decisions will be made on living with a single currency

As John Major was publishing his Janus-faced White Paper on Europe on Tuesday, a more important European event, which could have a far greater bearing on Britain's future relationship with Europe, was going on at the other end of town.

The venue for this event was less familiar than the House of Commons: the London International Financial Futures Exchange. What was announced there was, at first sight, even more stupefyingly dull than the White Paper. The board of Liffe had decided on settlement procedures to cover short-sterling and Euromark futures contracts expiring in March 1999.

The question that confronted Liffe was one which has recently started to bother many European businessmen, rs and investors — wh that currency had been irreversibly fixed; if such was not the case, settlement would continue to be made against the national currency. The decision was announced on 12 March, and two days later, writing in *The Times*, Anatole Kaletsky argued that, although on the face of it an 'obscure technical decision', it was in fact the clearest sign yet that EMU was beginning to acquire an irresistible institutional momentum. From LIFFE's perspective it was a neat solution – 'the new contract provisions will provide clarity to the market and meet market needs, whether or not EMU starts on time and regardless of which country participates,' stated Hodson – but inevitably there could be no certain answer to the larger question of whether EMU, if it were to happen, would benefit or damage LIFFE, a question given an added twist by the probability of Britain staying out, at least in the first wave of monetary union. By definition no one knew, but LIFFE by September 1996 was making optimistic noises, its opinion based on two main planks: the exchange's deutschmark dominance, the currency likely to be the strongest element in the Euro; and secondly, the unrivalled (in relation to the rest of Europe) critical mass of skills and services centred in the City of London as a whole. Past experience indicated the high probability that the lion's share of derivatives trading in Euro-denominated products would go to only one European exchange. The battle for that share – in what would be one of the world's three great currencies – was likely to be brutal, possibly bloody. At this very early stage of the game, LIFFE was the one to beat.

Jack Wigglesworth had succeeded Durlacher as chairman in June 1995, the fourth and final member of the original working party to hold that position. A level-headed Yorkshireman but with a wide range of interests ('no mere lugubrious financial equivalent of Ray Illingworth', in the words of an *Evening Standard* profile), he had worked during a variegated City career for Phillips & Drew, Greenwells (where Gordon Pepper became his mentor), Lloyds Merchant Bank, Henderson Administration, J. P. Morgan Futures and Citifutures. He was proud of LIFFE's past, unsentimental about its future, and told a press conference that 'I want to keep the same lean and hungry approach that made LIFFE the success it is today'.

It was not an easy task. 'No longer the new kid' would be the title in March 1996 of an *FT* profile of the exchange, in which Wigglesworth himself was quoted as describing LIFFE as the 'fourth pillar' of the City, alongside the Bank of England, the Stock Exchange and Lloyd's. Another sign that LIFFE by now had an inherent credibility and no longer had to prove itself was that it was able to invite 'celebs' – as opposed to economic or political heavyweights – to open its new contracts. Indeed, the trappings of adulthood were becoming almost ubiquitous. Since September 1994 the exchange, in its pursuit of skilled staff, had been systematically recruiting and training graduates; the following February the new role of director of external affairs was created, with Richard Pratt being recruited from the Treasury to fill it; and in June, as Wigglesworth became chairman, LIFFE acquired its first two non-executive directors, in the persons of Lord Walker and George Cox. There was even inaugurated an annual LIFFE lecture, with the second speaker (in September 1996) being the leader of the Labour Party. 'Tony Blair's redefinition of socialism swept on yesterday,' the *Independent* reported, 'as he went to the heart of speculative capitalism in the City of London to embrace the profit motive.'

Jack Wigglesworth.

Predictably, as the fourth pillar grew, so there were grumbles, though they were few compared with the grumbles directed at the other three pillars. The board, some felt, had become too remote from the floor; others argued quite the reverse, that it listened too much to the locals and not enough to the big member firms. 'Lex' even contended in July 1996 that a member-run exchange had become an anachronism, and that what LIFFE needed to do was become a plc with a broader range of shareholders. 'On the contrary,' countered Wigglesworth in a letter to the *FT*, 'an exchange can only be successful if it serves the investing public. An exchange's member firms can only make profits if they meet those same needs. So giving control to members allows swift responsiveness to the needs of the market.' He added that LIFFE had 'experienced more than 40 per cent growth a year since 1982 to become the largest exchange of its kind outside Chicago – proof indeed that member-run exchanges can act commercially and exploit market opportunities'. Unlike the Stock Exchange, where traditionally the jobbers and then market makers had exercised an undue dominance, there was in LIFFE's membership no one excessively important interest group. As long as that remained the case, which by 1996 there were no signs of it not doing, then adherence to a member-run exchange still made sense.

One preoccupying question for the board – and an old favourite – was that of premises. Space had become a serious problem by 1994, with Hodson openly talking of the possibility of the market moving to Docklands, possibly but not necessarily Canary Wharf. The *Evening Standard*, though, quoted one opposed board member: 'Docklands is a dead-end place. You can't even get there on the train. LIFFE is a City institution and should remain so.' Soon afterwards the turn-down in trading volumes gave a breathing-space in making any fundamental decision, and as an interim step plans were made for the 26,000 sq ft trading floor at Cannon Bridge to be extended by a further 7,000 sq ft. Nevertheless, the annual report in May 1995 stated that not only was LIFFE pursuing a long-term strategy of finding a suitable site for purpose-built premises, but also that in the medium term it would be seeking 'to secure additional trading floor accommodation at another site allowing for trading activity to be split, if necessary, between the two sites'. Comfortingly, whatever the grumbles of some members about parsimonious rebates, there were resources available. 'When I became chairman,' noted Durlacher at this time, 'the exchange's reserves were severely depleted following the move to Cannon Bridge. But now, with cash reserves in excess of £100m, LIFFE can view the future with some confidence.' Even so, he also stressed that buying a brand new, purpose-built site would be 'imprudent', granted that 'we haven't got a secure enough base' to know the size and shape of the derivatives market in, say, five years time.

The Rt. Hon. Tony Blair MP gives the LIFFE City lecture, 16 September 1996.

That December, with volumes starting to recover, LIFFE and the Stock Exchange signed heads of agreement for LIFFE to lease the Stock Exchange's former trading floor and other office space. The lease would run for eight years from the latter half of 1996 and, providing emergency back-up as well as the possibility of split-floor trading, was consistent with LIFFE's medium-term premises strategy. 'It's a very important step, it recognises the growth in the exchange, how important we are now in the City of London, and we're quite excited at getting down and using it,' Hodson told BBC Radio 5, though adding that there were no firm plans to use the Stock Exchange floor, once it had been kitted out, unless trading volume warranted it. The ironies of the situation were, inevitably and unavoidably, writ somewhat large, though masked by the fact that relations between LIFFE and the Stock Exchange had become by the mid-1990s far better than ever before. Attention turned during 1996 to the long-term problem. 'We're looking at a number of sites around the London area for a single site for everything,' Wigglesworth told Reuters in January. 'We'll probably go for a sort of Chicago solution of having two floors, one above the other of about 50,000 square feet each. We're talking about 2000, 2001 when we might be doing that.' Over the ensuing months there was a fair amount of press speculation about where LIFFE might be moving for the new millennium, and an announcement was anticipated by the end of the year. The experience of finding a new home to replace the Royal Exchange perhaps counselled against undue holding of breath.

One did not have to be on the inside track to guess the two fundamental uncertainties surrounding the decision. What, if it happened, would be the impact of EMU? And in, say, 2000 would open outcry still be the preferred method of trading? On this latter question, the clear view of the exchange remained – though not without some critics – that pit trading had served LIFFE very well in the past and would continue to do so, certainly in the major, high-volume contracts. Speed of execution, enhancement of liquidity, sharpening of reactions and brain power – the familiar strong arguments continued to be made. Against them the main counter-argument – heard more during the check of 1995 than the recovery of 1996 – was that electronic systems of trading were more cost-efficient. As with the Chicago exchanges, the problem at LIFFE was how to separate out emotional attachment (or perhaps just familiarity) from rational justification; but by autumn 1996 it was becoming increasingly apparent in the industry as a whole that not only had the imminent death of open outcry been greatly exaggerated, but that (as *Futures* demonstrated in a two-part series) technology itself was helping to keep open outcry alive, for example by increasing the rapidity of orders to the floor. The answer, in other words, seemed to be a hybrid solution of technologically enhanced open outcry, with screen trading for after-hours and perhaps some of the less popular contracts. It was a hybrid that was fortified by the empirical evidence that many of the

The signing of the LIFFE-Stock Exchange lease: Jack Wigglesworth and John Kemp-Welch (Chairman of the Stock Exchange), 30 May 1996.

new, purely electronic derivatives exchanges had not particularly flourished in the course of the 1990s. *Au fond*, perhaps, it came down to one powerful gut feeling: if it ain't broke...

Technological enhancement continued to apply to all areas of LIFFE's activities – mainly successfully, but with one major embarrassment. In June 1995, for example, the LIFFE World Wide Web site was launched on the Internet, highly interactive and providing real-time access to the exchange; while soon afterwards LIFFE became the first derivatives exchange to publish its price histories on CD-ROM, containing every bid, ask and trade price going back to 1992 for each contract covered. Also in 1995 there was a significant upgrading on the surveillance front, with a £1.4 million investment in equipment that for the first time recorded video, sound and prices on a single tape. 'We synchronise video recordings – we can film the pits from several different angles and the booths also – with all the sound recordings we make of the 8,000 telephone lines going in and out of the exchange,' Wigglesworth explained in an interview. 'We then synchronise it all with the atomic clock... so we've got a pretty good audit trail.' There was also the automated order routing system, LOTS, seeking to connect sales desks, trading booths, admin booths and back office electronically. Six members participated in a dummy market in 1995, and Hodson told *Global Investment Technology* the following March that LOTS would be 'one of the ways in which we can enhance the productivity of the floor and cut down on the number of people who have to be on the floor of the exchange'.

The embarrassment was APT+. No one could accuse it of lack of ambition – aiming to be the only options system which allowed trading a multi-leg strategy simultaneously on the screen – but when it was launched live on the late afternoon of 25 January 1996, trading in Bund options, it had to be suspended after only eleven minutes, as the system began flooding traders' work stations with far more reference prices for bids and offers than they needed. Subsequently, the cause of the problem was discovered to be a program error in the reference price distribution mechanism, which had the effect that roughly a hundred times more prices were being transmitted than should have been. There followed a lengthy delay, while the whole system was retested; but notwithstanding this rare technological setback, LIFFE continued to express its confidence that APT+, though possibly in a more modest version, would ultimately add a significant, volume-enhancing dimension to options trading.

There was also an obstacle or two in the area of linkages, despite the buoyant headline – 'Links galore' – in *Futures* in June 1996 about the industry at large. The TIFFE linkage had, of course, been achieved by this time, over the Euroyen contract, but as far as LIFFE was concerned that and the TSE link in JGBs were the only actual links actually functioning. Talks with SIMEX meanwhile were continuing, over possible joint trading of LIFFE's Euromark futures contract. The key linkage – almost live, but not yet – was with the CBOT. In March 1995 the two exchanges signed the heads of what Durlacher called 'a comprehensive agreement' that it was hoped would be up and running within the year. As talks the previous year had indicated, the T-bond was still on the table, absolutely crucial from LIFFE's perspective; and Durlacher noted that the agreement marked, for the first time, 'a recognition that these are two equal exchanges talking, rather than a minnow and a shark'. It was an exciting prospect, with Foyle (by now deputy chief executive) telling Reuters that 'what will be possible here is that you can trade in London in the morning and close that position out on the Board of Trade during the afternoon or the next day'. The agreement was also an important affirmation that there would be no imminent move away from open outcry, with Foyle adding that 'once the Bund contract is established on the Board of Trade's floor we would expect to discontinue listing the Bund on APT in the evening'. Ironically, this round of talks had started with the mooting by CBOT of an electronic link, but as Hodson explained to *Futures Industry*, the two exchanges had 'quickly escalated to open outcry', on the assumption that 'it is easier to generate liquidity with an exchange that is quite alive and awake, than with a night trading desk'.

In June the CBOT's membership (now with a significantly greater overlap with LIFFE's than had been the case a decade earlier) overwhelmingly ratified the agreement, which in December 1995 was formally signed in Chicago. The T-bond

The signing of the LIFFE-CBOT link: Pat Arbor (Chairman of CBOT) and Jack Wigglesworth, 15 December 1995.

would trade open outcry on LIFFE's floor from 7.30 am to 1.00 pm London time, while the Bund would be traded on the CBOT first from 4.20 pm to 8.00 pm London time and then, in the middle of London's night, during the CBOT's evening trading session. Other contracts for fungible trading would be phased in subsequently. Wigglesworth hailed the agreement as an important milestone in LIFFE's history: 'This project will enable LIFFE's well-established German, Italian, and UK bond futures and options to be available for the first time throughout the American trading day, as well as diversifying our product range and consolidating our position as the international bond trading centre.'

In February 1996 a working date – 28 June – was set for going live, but by May it was clear that there was going to be a delay. Wigglesworth, in a letter to members, explained that though the systems and procedures were now in place for the inter-exchange clearing of contracts, nevertheless more testing, operational training and general preparation by members and their back office suppliers was still needed before actual trading could begin. 'Sources could not pinpoint the precise nature of the technical difficulties delaying the implementation of the plan,' noted *Securities Week* with a slightly suspicious tone, 'but indicated that they were not related to any lack of cooperation between the exchanges or their clearing houses.' Not long afterwards, on 8 July, a joint statement attributed the delay to the need to write or modify 'a vast number of clearing system programs to accommodate the trade mapping mechanism between the clearing houses'; and the same statement announced a firm start date for the open outcry linkage – 9 May 1997. 'It is unfortunate that it has been necessary to defer the commencement of this most important project,' Wigglesworth added, but 'it has simply taken longer than originally anticipated to develop precise systems' specifications to a level where the user interface to the system is sufficiently straightforward and causes minimum disruption of members' current business practices.' He remained thoroughly bullish – but history alone suggested a residue of doubt until this ambitious linkage finally went live. It was not that anyone doubted the strategy of links with markets in different time zones; it was just that they seemed so devilishly hard to pull off.

By September 1996 another end-game was apparently in process, again after more than a decade of discussions and false starts. This was the question of the ownership of the clearing house. From early 1993, after some very public problems over replacing LCH's expiring insurance policy by going into the syndicated loans market, it was clear that this time the clearing banks conclusively wanted to abandon the business. By autumn 1994 it seemed possible that LIFFE itself would assume a controlling interest; but the banks as ever found it difficult to make up their collective mind, the Bank of England became involved, the collapse of Barings simultaneously sharpened and clouded the debate, and at least one of LIFFE's clearing members stated publicly that there was something to be said after all for an independent clearing house. In July 1995 a Clearing Member Committee was set up, chaired by Jenkins.

Five months later the board debated the CMC's majority recommendation, which was that the London exchanges that used LCH should not have a shareholding in the re-structured clearing house, but that the issue of exchange shareholding should be finally resolved by reference to the boards of the relevant exchanges:

Strongly held arguments [recorded the minutes of LIFFE's board in December 1995] were put forward in favour and against the recommendations of the CMC. These included, inter alia, on the one hand that if LIFFE were to take a shareholding in the LCH it would put members' funds at risk; LIFFE's main objective should be viewed as maintaining and running a market and not the risk management of a Clearing House; the majority of LIFFE's members were possibly not in favour of the exchange having any shareholding in the re-structured Clearing House which they viewed should be owned by the clearing members. The contra views were also expressed strongly: that the LCH is a utility and as such it should be supported by as wide a shareholder base as possible, that is, an exchange shareholding would represent the interests of both clearing and non-clearing members of the exchange; LIFFE's representative(s) on the LCH Board would, in practice, be in a much weaker position if the exchange had no direct shareholding; since the interests of LIFFE and LCH were integrally linked together, it was considered highly appropriate for the exchange to have a shareholding; the LCH could lose part of its independence if it were to be owned by a sector of LIFFE's membership (i.e. only the clearing members).

By fourteen votes to five a clear preference was expressed for LIFFE acquiring a shareholding in the re-structured LCH.

By early 1996 it was apparent that the clearing banks wanted no stake at all (except as clearing members); that the divide would be 75% to the clearing members and 25% to the exchanges; and that a £150 million guarantee fund would be established to meet payments in the event of a clearing member defaulting, with £100 million top-up from insurance. In June the prospective arrangements were publicly announced: the six clearing banks to sell their share capital for an amount equal to LCH's last audited net assets, approximately £19.6 million (barely a third of what they had paid fourteen years earlier); LCH's 177 members to be asked to subscribe for £37.5 million in new shares; and the exchanges (including LIFFE) to subscribe the remaining £12.5 million, proportionate to their trading volumes. 'To place the clearing house in the hands of the people who use it' was, LCH's David Hardy told the *FT*, the best way forward. Jenkins, that *quondam* fierce critic of ICCH, would become the new chairman of LCH. LCH itself moved in September from Crutched Friars to Aldgate House, and by the end of the month it was clear that there would be easily enough take-up of shares by clearing members for the restructuring to go ahead.

After such a long period of ineffectual ownership, the justifiable hope was that the new set-up would encourage the clearing members to get more closely involved in the clearing process, while the exchanges brought a degree of discipline and, if need be, could take the larger view, including on behalf of the smaller and non-clearing members. As for the possibility that LIFFE itself might have run the clearing house, that moment had passed: quite apart from anything else, it would no longer have been an acceptable option to LIFFE's members, an increasing proportion of whom were members of other exchanges and naturally saw little economic attraction in having one clearing house per exchange. Whatever its virtues, it was a solution that had taken an inordinately long time to reach.

The London Commodity Exchange did not have a stake in the new LCH – for a very good reason. Jenkins had been chairman of LCE (returning to its old name following the London FOX scandal) since shortly before leaving LIFFE, and by 1994 he and his chief executive, Robin Woodhead, had done much to re-establish the exchange's profitability as well as reputation. By 1995, against the

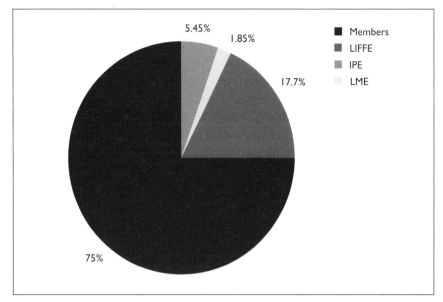

5.45%
1.85%
17.7%
75%

■ Members
■ LIFFE
■ IPE
□ LME

The new ownership of London Clearing House, October 1996.

background of increasing globalisation of commodity trading, LCE's leadership was actively seeking strategic alliances with other partners in order to secure a larger market for the exchange's products, generally regarded as mature. This was doing no more than following the trend in the futures industry at large, and Woodhead told *FOW* that 'in the past two years, the business has gone into new territory', and that 'global outreaching and global distribution is the way forward'. In July that year it emerged that the LCE was not only being courted by the Coffee, Sugar and Cocoa Exchange, its New York rival, but was itself in talks with both the International Petroleum Exchange (with which it already shared a trading floor) and LIFFE. 'We've already got a common clearing house, we've done some common marketing of products, and there's a very significant overlap in our membership,' Hodson told the *Wall Street Journal*. 'A closer relationship would be very natural evolution.'

The news that New York wanted to take over the LCE naturally led to a decision, and later that month LIFFE's board discussed the way ahead:

Two board members expressed considerable concern and reservations regarding any formal link being developed between LIFFE and the LCE. Their comments were primarily based upon the views that diversification into commodity markets would not be cost effective for LIFFE especially as the LCE represented a mature market which offered little potential for future growth, and that the work involved in developing any link would detract significantly from the Exchange's mainstream development priorities.

Nonetheless, the consensus amongst the remaining Board members was that, subject to conclusions of the fuller feasibility study, potentially it would be beneficial for LIFFE to develop a strategic partnership with the LCE. It was considered that the advantages of such a partnership would include product diversification, a further EMU defence for the Exchange, enhancing the position of the City vis-à-vis overseas competition, LIFFE possibly acting as the nucleus of a broader London exchange centre, and the resultant economies of scale that would accrue to both participating exchanges and members.

'I hope that a London solution can be found,' Wigglesworth told *FOW* after the meeting, noting that of the 44 LCE authorised floor members, 29 were also members of LIFFE or had parent companies who were members of LIFFE.

By mid-November, having received merger proposals from all three exchanges, the LCE announced that it had chosen LIFFE, which would pay £9.5 million, the sum equal to net asset value. Such a merger, Jenkins explained, 'offers a strong base from which to achieve our vision of a healthy international commodity market'. Hodson elaborated:

The London Commodity Exchange and LIFFE are the leading exchanges in their particular product lines in Europe. And we believe that by combining we have the potential to build a really strong and solid platform for the trading and development of agricultural and soft commodities in Europe. This is going to be extremely important in the coming years, particularly as reforms to the Common Agricultural Policy take place. And then again, on a more operating level we have a lot of common members. There are potential synergies in terms of cost, we have common clearing, we have common systems and so we believe that working together we can drive down members' costs and by pooling our resources bring more liquidity into the current LCE market.

LCE merger, 16 September 1996.
Right: Trading at Commodity Quay.

Opposite: Daniel Hodson, Robin Woodhead, Michael Cassidy (Chairman of the Policy and Resources Committee, Corporation of London), Jack Wigglesworth.

Some of the older commodity hands expressed fears that the LCE would be swallowed whole by a huge financial futures exchange – LCE's daily trading volume being worth less than 3% of LIFFE's – but reaction was broadly favourable, to some extent taking a cue from the Bank of England, which saw the merger as strengthening London's competitiveness as a derivatives centre.

In May 1996 the LCE's shareholders formally approved the merger, changing a provision in the articles that no one could hold over 10% of the shares and thereby clearing the way for LIFFE; and on 26 June the details were announced. 'It's genuinely a merger,' insisted Hodson in an interview. 'We're taking on all the LCE's staff; we're setting up a separate division and we hope to work very closely with them. It's not a question of their being absorbed into our exchange; it's really a question of partners working together.' The merger was to be completed by 16 September, and as was its custom – thanks in large part to Foyle's mastery of detail – LIFFE had achieved a complex scheme of corporate finance without recourse to specialist advisers from a merchant bank. The target was hit, and on the first day of trading in the new combined market Wigglesworth was able to claim that 'the merger of LIFFE and the LCE creates the only exchange in the world to offer trading in futures and options on financial, agricultural, soft commodity and equity index products, as well as options on individual equities'. For the time being commodity trading remained on the St Katherine's Dock trading floor, though with all

commodity futures and options – including cocoa, coffee, sugar, wheat, barley, potatoes and Baltic freight – being traded under LIFFE's administration and clearing arrangements.

The first day's trading went smoothly, though with overall volume a less than thrilling 6,828 lots. The traders donned coloured jackets and also received a badge proclaiming 'LIFFE gets physical'. It was a merger that could hardly have been imagined in, say, the mid-1980s. The financial and commodity cultures were then so very different, as indeed the regulatory experience in those years showed. In the intervening years, however, many of the traditional commodity firms had experienced lean times, with some (such as Woodhouse, Drake & Carey) even going out of business. Moreover, not only was commodity trading much more rigorously regulated by the 1990s, but some of the big commodity players were now the banks, seeking to play a bigger role in commodities than just trade finance, and financial service organisations generally. In one sense, of course, it was sad that a tradition of independent commodity trading in London was now being lost. Yet arguably, looked at in the long run, that distinctive world east of Gracechurch Street had only itself to blame: back in the 1970s the commodity markets had the opportunity – which they failed to identify, let alone take – to develop a financial futures market under their wing; that financial futures market instead developed autonomously; it grew like Topsy; and now, whatever its protestations, it was starting to take over the commodity markets. For the historian at least, if not all the participants, it was a satisfyingly shaped tale.

The heart of an exchange – a proper exchange – is its floor. When I first saw LIFFE's current floor, as I was starting work on this book, my almost immediate thought, once I had recovered my senses, was that it needed the pen of a Dickens to do it justice. A few months later, just before the fourteenth anniversary, BBC Radio 4 broadcast a talk not by Dickens, alas, but by the distinguished novelist and critic Michèle Roberts. The first of a series called 'The Writer's Day Out' – in which 'novelists leave the solitude of their desks for a day, venture somewhere new and record their impressions' – it was the most literary attempt yet to describe for the world outside the almost indescribable:

> *What the black and white pictures in newspapers don't warn the unsuspecting visitor about is the shrieking parrot-coloured costumes worn by the workers. I came to LIFFE, otherwise known as the London International Financial Futures and Options Exchange, expecting sober if not dreary business suits and found myself in the most surreal of carnivals. Nothing prepares you for this riot of clashing and uncoordinating rainbow hues. The entrance is all black and white marble, posh and expensive-looking and soulless. Designed to impress. Sitting, kicking my heels on an imitation leather sofa and waiting for the warder, sorry, the security guard to wave me through, I watched the parade of thin silk suits and shoulder pads as people hurried in and out looking very cool and important. I was puzzled by some louche types bustling past, clad in short dust-coats in banana yellow. I wondered if that was what the porters or the messengers had to wear. They did seem a bit skimpy, the kind of thing you see on schoolboys in old-fashioned films. Or perhaps they were actors in a film of an Oscar Wilde comedy being shot here. Characters with names like Archie or Ernest or Bunny in funny blazers just back from punting or a day out at Henley. No boaters though, no picnic hampers.*
> *No more time for speculation, however, for I was being allowed in, up in the lift to the second floor where I was greeted by the press officer. No chance of roaming about unnoticed. I was ushered into a small viewing gallery, one wall of*

which was a plate glass screen which could be slid back. To talk we kept the screen closed. When it was opened the roar from downstairs erupted into the tiny space we were standing in and boxed our ears. When you looked down on to the trading floor it's like seeing a mad modern ballet with an enormous chorus line weaving about, proud as peacocks, in a shrieking cacophony of circus colours. The men in suits had gone mad and ditched their black and grey for pink, red, orange, turquoise, lime green, powder blue, scarlet. It's like seeing a Jackson Pollock picture come to life. Here are all the hectic shades of Monet's late paintings, his Water Lilies suddenly flooding out of the frame and dancing frenetically back and forth. The frenzy of moneymaking here at LIFFE is articulated by the tango of primaries and pastels. Never in my wildest dreams did I imagine that men liked shrugging themselves into these little numbers, these short blazers in brilliant colours with logos on the back, so that it made them look like the playing-card jacks of hearts who've come alive in a version of Alice Through the Looking Glass, *screenplay by Fellini, choreography by Busby Berkeley.*

The press officer explained it all very patiently. With this hubbub and hullabaloo, you can't hear what people are saying too easily. In the braying frenzy the sort of gentlemanly introductions cherished by etiquette books are hard to make. Simpler to read your friend or foe by checking out his colour scheme. Rather perhaps like the way the Knights of the Round Table hacked it at tournaments. You read a man's identity off his brightly coloured trappings, his pennant, his shield, their heraldic devices. The jousting and jockeying, the boasting and prancing going on at LIFFE seemed straight out of Camelot. Any moment now Sir Gawain and the Green Knight would exchange a flourish of gloves and insults, lower their lances, charge each other and begin the battle skirmish, while up here in the glass tower we two ladies gazed down and waved the heroes on.

But I'm lying. There were some women down there, a few. I asked the press officer why the people in raucously coloured costumes were so overwhelmingly male. She thought a moment and replied, well, it's physically very demanding standing on your feet all day. Most women prefer the administrative roles so that they can sit down. So, the highly paid men in their loud jackets can all recognise each other at a glance. LIFFE's staff, for example, wear blue jackets with a red rim. The guys in yellow, such as those I'd noticed outside in the entrance hall, were trainees or admin staff or phone brokers. The few women I did spot were all in yellow, three of them parked into the electronic tickertape, perched on stools and busy with telephones. The boys in red were locals, that's to say freelancers rather than members. And all the trader members had their own gorgeous designs from some unsung couturier. Rose pink, lemon yellow, peach melba, they were wearing it.

The glass screen I gazed through was reminiscent of the transparent wall into a hospital nursery of premature babies and sporting toddlers. The games going on here might look infantile but are all very grown up and serious because they are

Overleaf: The heart of the exchange.

about making money, lots and lots of it. These red-faced chaps waving their hands in seemingly obscene gestures are engaged in trading, not practising their semaphore as you might have thought or doing chest-expanding exercises or waving jolly greetings back and forth. The scene settled down a little once it was all explained to me. But I don't pretend to understand what was really happening, since I loved the spectacle of dancing colours so much I just wanted to watch that and not have to translate it into stuff about interest rates. My resistance came, I know, from being an old leftie with old-fashioned notions about criticising the notion of the free market as the basis of moral values, believing in our being able to exercise some control over the greed of capitalists, not leaving the cost of money to bankers' whims and get-rich-quick schemes, etc, etc. This of course makes me the perfect person to visit LIFFE and listen carefully to the press officer's explanations and nod sagely and look as though I agree with the self-evident sense and wisdom of all the information she was so patiently and carefully imparting.

The bids come in by phone. Certainly, though you can't hear the phones, it's too noisy for that, you can see them ringing. Small coloured lights, green or orange or red, flash like the turning lamps on police cars above the traders' booths. The bigger the trader, the bigger his booth. It's obvious, isn't it? Idiot that I was, I hadn't understood why all the booths were not the same size. The order is then flashed into the pit and vocal trading, called open outcry, begins. Have you got that? Good. No, please don't ask me to explain. All I can do is tell you what it looked like when you stare down from above. The pits where the trading goes on are octagonal with steps polished bright as steel down into them. Screwed-up bits of paper float on the surfaces like white flowers. Young men clutching their pieces of paper, with bids scribbled to sell on one side and bids to buy on the other, stand round the pits and gesticulate at each other, very precisely, lifting their hands and putting them palm first against the air or flicking them outwards as though to wave off wasps, tapping their fingers against their foreheads and cheeks like Scouts rehearsing a secret language of signs.

What makes this speeded-up Noh theatre so utterly bizarre is that these frantic punches, stabs and summonses, this dumb show of the non-dumb, isn't about commodities at all, but about money, pure and simple, money which shows up as flickering, inscrutable, meaningless numbers on the screens and tickertapes and which changes its value at the twirl of a fingernail. Here capitalism's a carnival, a ball in fancy dress, a series of signs drawn in the air with the vanishing ink of gesture. It's nothing so banal as a £5 note. Money's a concept, a beat in time, an electronic pulse. It's hard to believe in all the deadly seriousness of this. I was amazed to learn that I'd been let in during the slackest period of the day. The market opens early, slows down for a lunch period starting at eleven, picks up speed again when America joins in in our early afternoon. What looked to me like frenetic activity was apparently a lull. When I peered closely I did notice people flicking darts, shadow boxing, flirting, skipping skittishly back and forth in front of each other like bored kids in the play ground waiting for the bell to ring. Above our heads, recording the doings of the prices of money, as people signalled its rise and fall, were banks of screens like those at airports indicating take off. Lift off at LIFFE, all done with a flick of a wrist, the stab of a button. Rejected, completed, outdated bids were represented by the screwed-up twists of paper littering the floor. How very odd, in this technological paradise they still use pad and pencil.

I'd been there an hour. The press officer had run out of information and my eyes were glazing over with the chat of statistics, equity-related derivative products, contract integrity and risk management services. It was time to go. I used a different exit route, a very long, deep, silvery escalator that floated down, down, down through a vast marble atrium. I felt like a rebel angel falling out of heaven. Paradise lost being this world where gods create money and profit and move in utterly mysterious ways. I read Das Kapital *when I was a young revolutionary, but there were jokes in Marx. There aren't at LIFFE. I couldn't help feeling it was all completely unreal. Yet those people help control our lives. It was the blaring, glaring, glorious colours of the men's jackets that remained with me. I hope that wearing such bright and bizarre gear consoles them for their stressed and hectic lives. I think we should urge royalty, and policemen too perhaps, to wear such outfits. Whoever thinks that modern men are doomed to sartorial dullness, grey and beige forever, should nip to Cannon Street and get a LIFFE…*

This is a vivid account of a very visual, intensely striking marketplace; yet precisely because it is so striking, LIFFE is a market that runs the constant danger of being trivialised, of being seen purely as theatre rather than as an exchange that has achieved astonishing success since its inception in 1982, that has provided major and increasing economic value, and that has been at the leading edge of the City of London's modern renaisssance. The founding fathers had a vision, and to a large extent that vision has been fulfilled. This book has attempted to tell an important as well as dramatic story.

It is perhaps appropriate to end with the words of another novelist – words peculiarly applicable to life at the Royal Exchange and Cannon Bridge in the late twentieth century. 'I have seen the West End, the parks, the fine squares, but I love the City far better,' reflected Charlotte Brontë's heroine in *Villette*. 'The City seems so much more in earnest. Its business, its rush, its roar, are such serious things, sights and sounds. The City is getting its living – the West End but enjoying its pleasure. At the West End you may be amused, but in the City you are deeply excited.'

Clive Furness

Nick Carew Hunt

Ivan Andrews

Karin Forseke

Helen Jenkins

Tony de Guingand

John Foyle

Phil Bruce

Review Group: LIFFE's senior management team, September 1996.

Simon Orebi Gann

Daniel Hodson

Ralf Herklotz

Juliette Proudlove

Richard Pratt

Appendices

Appendix 1

LIFFE Chairmen, Chief Executives and Deputy Chairmen
1981–1996

Chairmen

R.R.St.J. Barkshire	1981 – 1985
R.B. Williamson	1985 – 1988
A.D. Burton	1988 – 1992
N.J. Durlacher	1992 – 1995
J. Wigglesworth	1995 –

Chief Executives

M.N.H. Jenkins	1981 – 1992
D.H. Hodson	1993 –

Deputy Chairmen

H.R. Gamble	1981 – 1982
D.L. Burt	1982 – 1983
M.J. Mayo	1983 – 1985
A.D. Burton	1985 – 1988
N.J. Durlacher	1988 – 1992
C.J. Edwards	1988 – 1990
D. Heron	1992 – 1994
J. Wigglesworth	1992 – 1995
A.P. La Roche	1994 – 1995
M.J. Stiller	1995 – 1996
R.M. Eynon	1995 –
C.J. Hartley	1996 –

Appendix 2

LIFFE Board 1981–1996

R.R.St.J. Barkshire	16/10/81 – 30/05/91		A.J. Dickinson	14/05/87 – 31/05/90
D.L. Burt	16/10/81 – 30/03/83		S.S. Hanbury-Brown	14/05/87 – 21/05/92
A.D. Burton	16/10/81 – 26/05/94		M.J. Stiller	14/05/87 – 31/05/90
H.R. Gamble	16/10/81 – 30/03/83			
M.N.H. Jenkins	16/10/81 – 31/12/92		P.C. Barnett	12/05/88 – 30/05/91
M.J. Mayo	16/10/81 – 18/03/85			
R.B. Williamson	16/10/81 – 30/05/91		N.G. Ackerman	08/05/89 – 24/05/95
P.G.B. Wills	16/10/81 – 25/05/82		D.J. Keegan	08/05/89 – 21/09/93
			B.J. Lind	08/05/89 – 21/05/92
A.D. Buchanan	25/05/82 – 14/03/84		S.J. Sanders	08/05/89 – 21/05/92
C.J. Carter	25/05/82 – 18/03/85			
J.A. Cunningham	25/05/82 – 30/03/83		M.R. Bailey	31/05/90 – 23/05/96
J.B.R. Morris	25/05/82 – 14/03/84		C.H.F. Furse	31/05/90 –
S.E.J. Raven	25/05/82 – 14/03/84		D.M. Kyte	31/05/90 –
J. Wigglesworth	25/05/82 –		A.P. La Roche	31/05/90 – 23/05/96
C.S. McVeigh III	30/03/83 – 08/05/89		N.R.W. Harrison	30/05/91 – 26/05/94
E.R. Porter	30/03/83 – 06/11/90		M.J. Stiller	30/05/91 –
D.A. Whiting	30/03/83 – 18/03/86		E. Wright	30/05/91 –
			J. Young	30/05/91 –
P.C. Barnett	14/03/84 – 14/05/87			
J.A. Chitty	14/03/84 – 14/05/87		M.E. Aarons	13/04/92 – 24/05/95
N.J. Durlacher	14/03/84 – 23/05/96		J.J. Brown	13/04/92 – 20/05/93
C.J. Edwards	14/03/84 – 31/05/90		D.L.N. Heron	13/04/92 – 26/05/94
R.M. Eynon	14/03/84 –		S.G. Hills	13/04/92 – 20/05/93
C. Henry	14/03/84 – 24/05/95		G.A. Moller	13/04/92 – 19/03/96
A.P. La Roche	14/03/84 – 08/05/89		D.H. Wenman	13/04/92 – 24/05/95
C.J. Lucy	14/03/84 – 14/05/87		C.J. Hartley	21/05/92 –
R.J. Openshaw	14/03/84 – 08/05/89		S.M. Taylor	21/05/92 – 20/05/93
			V. Ward	21/05/92 – 24/05/95
A.J. Wadsworth	18/03/85 – 12/05/88			
R.S. Wilton	18/03/85 – 02/05/90		D.H. Hodson	01/01/93 –
			G.J. Anderson	20/05/93 –
R.J.G. Lowe	18/03/86 – 08/05/89			

A.T. Barrett	26/05/94 – 24/05/95	M.J. Callewaert	23/05/96 – 08/01/97
J.R. Waye	26/05/94 – 23/05/96	S. Gatterell	23/05/96 –
		D.J. Hands	23/05/96 –
J. Campbell-Gray	24/05/95 –	M.R.W. Stone	23/05/96 –
S.G. Hills	24/05/95 –	D.L. Stuart	23/05/96 –
S.H. Sparke	24/05/95 –	B.H. Graap	17/09/96 –
O.C. Wyer	24/05/95 –	M.W. Metcalfe	17/09/96 –
G.E. Cox	13/06/95 –	M. Overlander	17/09/96 –
Lord Walker	13/06/95 –	A. Ward	17/09/96 –

The London Financial Futures Working Party (comprising R.R.St.J. Barkshire [Chairman], A.D. Burton, N.B. Matthewson, M.J. Mayo, J.B.R. Morris, S.E.J. Raven, J.F. Tigar, J. Wigglesworth and R.B. Williamson) held its first meeting on 25 March 1980.

In March 1981 The Steering Committee was formed (comprising the members of the Working Party, excepting Matthewson, together with J.W. Beacham, A.J. Buchanan, The Hon L.H.L. Cohen, J. Cunningham, D.A. Dawkins, H.R. Gamble, J.H. Gunn, D.St.C. Harcourt [later replaced by D.L. Burt], G.W. Leahy, A.D. Orsich, R. Packshaw, P.G. Smith and P.G.B. Wills).

On 16 October 1981 the Exchange company, The London International Financial Futures Exchange Limited, was formed with a Board comprising seven of the Steering Committee and M.N.H. Jenkins (Chief Executive) as shown above. The Steering Committee continued as an advisory committee to the Board until the first General Meeting of members on 25 May 1982, at which the initial directors retired and a Board of directors was elected by the members.

John Foyle was Company Secretary from October 1981 until September 1989 and Ian Nash has served as Company Secretary since then.

Appendix 3

Dates of Inception and Suspension of Contracts

Date of Inception	Date of Suspension	Futures
30 Sept 82	18 Mar 96	Three Month Eurodollar
30 Sept 82	17 Dec 90	British Pound
14 Oct 82	18 Jun 90	Deutschmark
4 Nov 82		Three Month Sterling
18 Nov 82		Long Gilt
30 Nov 82	12 Apr 90	Swiss Franc
1 Dec 82	12 Apr 90	Japanese Yen
3 May 84		FTSE 100
21 Jun 84	1 Jun 93	US T-Bond
10 Sept 85	17 Jan 90	Short Gilt
30 Jan 86	12 Apr 90	Dollar/Mark
13 July 87		Japanese Government Bond
7 Jan 88	17 Jan 90	Medium Gilt
29 Sept 88		German Government Bond (Bund)
20 Apr 89		Three Month Euromark
26 Oct 89		Three Month ECU
7 Feb 91		Three Month Euroswiss
6 Mar 91	5 Nov 92	ECU Bond
3 Apr 91		New Japanese Government Bond (JGB)
26 Jun 91	17 Jun 92	Eurotrack
19 Sept 91		Italian Government Bond (BTP)
12 May 92		Three Month Eurolira
21 Jan 93	7 Sept 94	Medium Term German Govt Bond (Bobl)
10 Mar 93	9 Sept 93	Spanish Government Bond (Bonos)
25 Feb 94		FTSE Mid 250
11 Apr 96		Three Month Euroyen

Date of Inception	Date of Suspension	Options
27 Jun 85	16 May 95	Three Month Eurodollar
27 Jun 85	14 Sept 90	British Pound
30 Jan 86	12 Apr 90	Dollar/Mark
13 Mar 86	1 Jun 93	US T-Bond
13 Mar 86		Long Gilt
30 Sept 86	22 Mar 89	FTSE 100
5 Nov 87		Three Month Sterling
20 Apr 89		German Government Bond (Bund)
1 Mar 90		Three Month Euromark
24 Oct 91		Italian Government Bond (BTP)
15 Oct 92		Three Month Euroswiss
10 May 94		Serial Options on Bund
1 Jun 94		Serial Options on Euromark
14 Feb 95		Serial Options on Long Gilt
16 May 95		Three Month Eurolira

On Monday 23 March 1992 LIFFE merged with LTOM (London Traded Options Market). From this date LIFFE started trading equity options, index options and Eurotrack options.

Appendix 4

Annual Volumes of LIFFE Products 1982 – 1996

	1982	1983	1984	1985	1986	1987
Total Exchange	241,881	1,367,763	2,582,407	3,548,184	6,973,675	13,558,257
Short-term interest rate products						
Futures						
Three Month Sterling	41,812	200,569	341,213	493,322	959,089	1,497,070
Three Month Euromark						
One Month Euromark						
Three Month Eurolira						
Three Month Euroswiss						
Three Month ECU						
Three Month Euroyen						
Options						
Three Month Sterling						14,749
Three Month Euromark						
Three Month Euroswiss						
Three Month Eurolira						
Long-term bond products						
Futures						
Long Gilt	28,387	527,737	775,702	688,049	2,618,303	6,976,982
German Government Bond (Bund)						
Italian Government Bond (BTP)						
Japanese Government Bond (JGB)						134,154
Options						
Long Gilt					278,818	1,034,463
German Government Bond (Bund)						
Italian Government Bond (BTP)						
Equity products						
Futures						
FTSE 100 Index Future			73,500	88,735	122,410	460,173
FTSE Mid 250 Index Future						
Options						
FTSE 100 Index Options (SEI)						
FTSE 100 Index Options (ESX)						
FTSE 100 Index FLEX Options						
Equity Options (individual)						
Delisted contracts						
Futures						
British Pound	42,134	121,698	146,306	116,966	41,700	12,566
Deutschmark	7,064	25,841	28,417	20,415	17,110	8,193
Dollar/Mark					532	116
ECU Bond						
Eurotrack						
Medium Gilt						
Short Gilt				43,473	61,373	235
Swiss Franc	1,124	12,309	12,656	6,689	5,858	5,162
US T-Bond			169,282	627,091	1,546,304	1,549,662
Yen	526	19,013	11,774	9,829	7,779	5,837
Bobl						
Bonos						
Eurodollar	120,834	460,596	1,023,557	1,282,652	1,106,623	1,735,207
Options						
Dollar/Mark					8,546	2,689
FTSE					2,849	9,053
British Pound				139,648	105,192	15,549
US T-Bond					52,483	54,415
Eurodollar				31,315	38,706	41,982

1988	1989	1990	1991	1992	1993	1994	1995	1996
15,550,170	23,811,008	34,025,662	38,583,877	71,997,018	101,875,805	153,034,471	132,654,219	167,940,452
3,538,203	7,110,024	8,346,539	8,064,449	11,296,327	12,135,981	16,603,152	15,314,576	15,793,775
	951,245	2,659,026	4,783,649	12,173,431	21,318,942	29,312,222	25,737,379	36,231,178
								48,644
				375,514	1,479,012	3,456,437	4,005,125	6,936,873
			547,883	1,970,438	1,846,376	1,698,736	1,749,774	3,229,058
	15,884	64,134,	114,810	316,781	720,788	622,457	693,526	602,518
								242,413
444,929	826,479	1,353,366	1,594,268	2,648,009	2,666,711	4,057,878	3,348,945	2,213,494
		246,481	514,075	1,964,405	2,906,476	2,943,936	3,427,376	4,888,942
				17,412	32,163	19,245	33,781	45,568
							100,129	953,558
5,587,199	4,062,467	5,665,734	5,639,081	8,804,639	11,808,998	19,048,097	13,796,555	15,408,010
315,224	5,328,570	9,520,794	10,112,305	13,604,523	20,440,442	37,335,437	32,231,210	39,801,928
			483,447	3,773,105	6,344,233	11,823,741	9,612,899	12,603,754
121,735	117,177	46,092	106,081	221,370	421,454	610,925	845,329	816,059
1,141,203	714,642	769,043	843,561	1,812,576	2,059,142	2,357,348	1,756,533	1,361,344
	464,321	1,758,114	2,452,554	2,749,670	4,416,480	8,574,137	6,988,655	8,462,806
			16,496	395,354	602,096	1,030,672	1,130,762	2,456,177
466,162	1,028,055	1,444,261	1,727,382	2,618,629	3,119,971	4,227,490	3,373,259	3,627,044
						40,764	35,068	34,068
				2,182,696	2,647,304	3,640,668	2,915,214	3,764,079
				388,937	792,156	1,145,988	1,518,872	2,974,876
							60,699	65,701
				3,553,030	4,767,093	4,308,050	3,975,831	4,298,010
7,352	4,611	143						
4,092	2,192	12						
40	73							
			54,233	7,434				
			2,721	81				
54,108	2,628							
2,650	2,579							
2,042,503	966,905	756,301	462,703	272,077	4,660			
2,509	2,014	10						
					1,049,640	73,043		
					28,318			
1,648,813	2,056,802	1,247,949	993,753	709,305	244,728	91,738	2,720	
1,706	136							
1,435								
9,728	1,061	269						
84,388	72,484	83,010	39,798	68,369	2,626			
76,191	80,659	64,384	30,628	72,906	20,015	12,400		2

Appendix 5

Annual Average Daily Volume of the Big Five Futures Markets 1990–1996

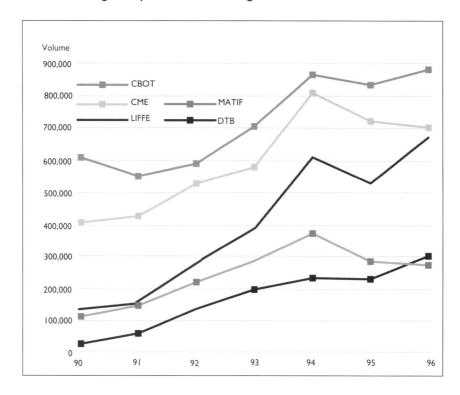

Acknowledgements

T HE MAIN SOURCE for this book has, obviously, been LIFFE's own records. These have been supplemented by the papers of the first three chairmen, as well as records at the Bank of England and the Stock Exchange relating to the exchange's pre-history and early history.

Contemporary history always involves a strong element of oral history, and I was able to interview – mainly in person, but sometimes by telephone – over 70 people. There were a few whom I was unable to interview, for one reason or another, but not many. I have also made use of interviews given to the National Life Story Collection.

The press is a key source, and I have plundered it ruthlessly – both the specialist press (notably *Futures & Options World* and *International Financing Review*) and the nationals. Some excellent journalists have written about the financial futures industry, and I am very grateful to them.

Not surprisingly, there is only a modest shelf of books relevant to LIFFE's history. The following, however, are helpful:

Caryl Churchill, *Serious Money*, London 1987

David Courtney, *From Forum to Futures: 2000 Years of Britain's Commodity Markets*, London 1991

William Cronon, *Nature's Metropolis: Chicago and the Great West*, New York 1991

Leo Melamed, *Leo Melamed on the Markets: Twenty Years of Financial History as Seen by the Man Who Revolutionized the Markets*, New York 1993

Leo Melamed with Bob Tamarkin, *Escape to the Futures*, New York 1996

Bob Tamarkin, *The Merc: The Emergence of a Global Financial Powerhouse*, New York 1993.

I am grateful to the Bank of England for allowing me to consult and reproduce material relevant to the pre-history and early history of LIFFE; to the Chairman of the London Stock Exchange for similarly allowing me to see and use Council records of the late 1970s and early 1980s; to the National Life Story Collection, at the British Library National Sound Archive, for permission to quote from the interview with John Barkshire in the 'City Lives' collection (ref: C409); and to Michèle Roberts and the BBC for allowing me to quote from her September 1996 Radio 4 talk on LIFFE.

The following kindly provided me with oral and/or written reminiscences and other material: Nigel Ackerman; Kim Albright; Gary Anderson; Nigel Andrew; Pat Arbor; Marc Bailey; John Barkshire; Phil Barnett; Roger Barton; Neil Blurton; Bill Brodsky; Phil Bruce; David Burton; Nick Carew Hunt; Mary Lou Carrington; William Charles; Polly Costley-White; Chris Cotton; Russell Dalton; Douglas Dawkins; Alan Dickinson; John Duchin; Patricia Duncan; Nick Durlacher; Ted Ersser; Mark Eynon; Tommy Fellowes; Christopher Fildes; John Foyle; Clara Furse; Tony de Guingand; Gordon Gemmill; Sir Nicholas Goodison; John Harding; Mark Harding; David Hardy; Chris Henry; Ralf Herklotz; Ken Heymer; Brian Hilton; Daniel Hodson; Michael Jenkins; James Johnston; Peter Jones; Pen Kent; David Kyte; Richard Lambert; Tony LaPorta; Roy Leighton; Ian McGaw; Charles McVeigh; Peter Mather; Neil Matthewson; Leo Melamed; Robert Miller; Christopher Morgan; David Morgan; Ian Nash; Peter Ottino; Robin Packshaw; Jacques Pézier; Gérard Pfauwadel; Tony Pike; Juliette Proudlove; Stephen Raven; Gerry Rodgers; Jack Sandner; Richard Sandor; Christopher Sharples; Trevor Slade; Mark Stanton; Mike Stiller; Ginger Szala; Victoria Ward; Derek Whiting; Jack Wigglesworth; Brian Williamson; Peter Wills; Rosalyn Wilton; Brian Winterflood. None of the above will agree with every word that I have written, and quite a few may disagree with quite a lot. The book, however, would not have been possible without them.

At LIFFE itself, the three people most closely involved with my work have been Jack Wigglesworth, Richard Pratt and Samantha Honeywood, and I owe a particular debt to them. In addition, I am grateful to Nicola Handley, Sophie Jackson, Carolyn Ladd, Jane Mould and Isabella Robins for their help; and I would also like to thank Caroline Denton and her colleagues in the Press Office. Finally, on the design side, the book owes an enormous amount to the work of Mary Luckhurst and her colleagues in the Design team.

Outside LIFFE, I have various other 'thank yous' to make. John and Bernadette Grimmett introduced me to Mary Lou Carrington in December 1995 and thereby unwittingly paved the way to my authorship of this history. Henry Gillett, Archivist at the Bank of England, went out of his way to enable me to look at records at the Bank. Amanda Howard typed up my dictated tapes – challenging in all sorts of ways – with astonishing speed and accuracy. David Blomfield has been a sympathetic and very careful copy editor. Stephanie Zarach and her colleagues at Book Production Consultants have again demonstrated their expertise in the never entirely unproblematic field of corporate histories. And, last but not least, Lucy and the children – Laurie, George and Michael – have been the most supportive of families, and I owe them more than I can express.

Picture Acknowledgements

The author and publishers are grateful to the following for permission to reproduce photographs and illustrations:

pp.ii, 40, 196 The Governor and Company of the Bank of England; p.3 Chicago Board of Trade; p.4 Guildhall Library, Corporation of London; p.6 Chicago Mercantile Exchange; p.7 Leo Melamed; p.10 Richard Sandor; pp.12, 72 *Investors Chronicle*; p.14 Reuters; pp.23, 43, 62-63, 64, 65, 80, 81, 82, 261 Tom Hustler; pp.24, 196 Kim Albright; pp.34, 48, 51, 88, 114, 130, 133, 176, 184, 199, 217, 220, 227, 258 *Financial Times*; p.45 *Accountancy Age*; pp.52, 73 *Financial Weekly*; pp.61, 135, 139 Sound Stills Limited; p.68 Terry Quirk; pp.74, 88, 300 *The Times*; p.84 *Evening Standard*; p.88 *Economist*; p.88 *Financial Futures*; p.93 *Harper's and Queen*; p.95 *Mail on Sunday*; pp.112, 123, 173 Telegraph Group Limited; pp.118, 119, 120, 148, 202, 224, 230, 243, 244, 247, 249, 252, 253, 254, 255, 256, 267, 270, 273, 280, 302 Thistle Photography; pp.120, 227 *Futures and Options World*; p.159 *Daily Mail*; pp.163, 292 *Independent*; p.167 *Wall Street Journal*; p.172 Royal Court Theatre; pp.227, 233 *Wall Street Journal Europe*; pp.233, 271 Paul Mellor Photography; p.258 Mirror Syndication International; p.279 Bob Tamarkin/HarperCollins; p.289 *Fortune*; p.299 John Manning; p.304 The London Stock Exchange; p.306 Randy Tunnell Photography; pp.310, 311 Paul Hackett; pp.314-315 Judah Passow; dust jacket (back flap), pp.318-319 David Kampfner.

All other pictures were provided by LIFFE.

They would also like to thank Michèle Roberts and Aitken & Stone Ltd. for their kind permission to reproduce an extract from 'The Writer's Day Out', which appears on pp.312-317.

Every effort has been made to obtain permission for the reproduction of illustrations and photographs in this book; apologies are offered to anyone whom it has not been possible to contact.

Index